Construction Law

BRIAN M. SAMUELS,
P.ENG., M.B.A., LL.B.

Attorney-at-Law (Colorado),
Barrister and Solicitor (British Columbia)

Prentice Hall
Englewood Cliffs, New Jersey   Columbus, Ohio

Library of Congress Cataloging-in-Publication Data
Samuels, Brian M.
    Construction law/Brian M. Samuels
        p. cm.
    Includes index.
    ISBN 0-13-325192-6
        1. Construction contracts—United States. 2. Construction industry—Law and legisla-
tion—United States. 3. Construction contracts—Canada. 4. Construction industry—Law and
legislation—Canada. I. Title.
    KF902.S26 1996
    343.73'07869—dc20
    [347.3037869]   94-44263
                                                                                       CIP

Cover photo: Courtesy of Henning J. Wulff and PCL Constructors Pacific Inc.
Editor: Ed Francis
Production Editor: Stephen C. Robb
Design Coordinator: Jill E. Bonar
Text Designer: Mia Saunders
Cover Designer: Thomas Mack
Production Manager: Patricia A. Tonneman
Electronic Text Management: Marilyn Wilson Phelps, Matthew Williams, Karen L. Bretz,
    Tracey Ward
Marketing Manager: Debbie Yarnell

This book was set in Dutch 801 and Swiss 721 by Prentice Hall and was printed and bound by
R. R. Donnelley & Sons Company. The cover was printed by Phoenix Color Corp.

Printed in the United States of America

10 9 8 7 6 5 4 3 2 1

ISBN: 0-13-325192-6

Prentice-Hall International (UK) Limited,London
Prentice-Hall of Australia Pty. Limited, Sydney
Prentice-Hall Canada Inc., Toronto
Prentice-Hall Hispanoamericana, S.A., Mexico
Prentice-Hall of India Private Limited, New Delhi
Prentice-Hall of Japan, Inc., Tokyo
Pearson Education Asia Pte. Ltd., Singapore
Editora Prentice-Hall do Brasil, Ltda., Rio de Janeiro

To my parents

Preface

During my legal career, I have been involved in many construction disputes as counsel to contractors, designers, and owners. Many of the disputes were preventable; almost all of them were costly and disruptive to the litigants, notwithstanding favorable results.

It is essential in today's construction industry for all participants to have an understanding of the basic principles of law in areas that affect the construction process, such as contracts, negligence, insurance, bonds, liens, and delays. For that reason, many colleges and universities offer courses in their engineering and architecture departments in construction law, and in some institutions it is a required course. Technical colleges offer similar courses in their building technology programs. This book is intended to be used by students in such courses, as well as by practicing construction professionals.

The purpose of the book is twofold; first, to educate the reader as to the concepts and rules that make up the law in a number of subject areas in which construction claims and disputes are prevalent; and second, to provide practical advice that, if followed, should allow the reader to avoid legal disputes in many situations and to increase the likelihood of success where such disputes are unavoidable.

It is not intended that the reader will become an expert in construction law. Rather, through understanding basic legal principles and being able to recognize certain legal issues, the reader should know when to obtain legal advice and how to avoid prejudicing his or her legal position. Some of the issues are presented through examples (which are taken primarily from actual cases) that illustrate the principles involved. I have purposely avoided including numerous or lengthy cases or case extracts.

Many construction professionals are required at some point to retain legal counsel. This book is intended to make the reader a more sophisticated consumer of legal services and more able to obtain appropriate advice.

Each of the subject areas could easily be a book in itself. Numerous texts are already written on all of them. To reduce a subject such as contracts, for example, to a single chapter requires that much must be omitted and simplified.

I have also written this book from a sense of need; I have been unable to find a suitable construction law text for the courses that I have taught and continue to teach. Construction law covers a broad range of subject areas, some of which (such as insurance and delay claims) are either omitted or given little attention in other texts.

The law is not static, nor is it uniform from one jurisdiction to another. However, the basic principles are generally well established and consistent, not only between the states but also between the United States and Canada. Where significant differences exist, I have put the U.S. position in the body of the text and the Canadian law in footnotes.

Finally, in writing this book, I have tried to remember what it was like as a young engineer in the construction industry. Issues arose that did not lend themselves to simple analysis, such as the dual role of the design consultant and conflicting pressures exerted by various parties. This is the book that I wish I had at that stage in my career.

Acknowledgments

During my career as a professional engineer and lawyer, I have had the privilege of working with some excellent and dedicated individuals, including project managers, tradesmen, superintendents, engineers, architects, and lawyers. I have learned from all of them, and some of their practical knowledge and experience is contained in this book. I thank them all, though it is impossible to name them all.

While researching and writing this book, I received encouragement and helpful criticism from Professor Alan Russell, without which this book would be diminished in quality. I would also like to thank my editor, Ed Francis, for his assistance and guidance throughout the process.

The first draft of the manuscript was reviewed by one of the most knowledgeable construction lawyers I have ever worked with, Byrum C. Lee, Jr. Many of his suggestions have been incorporated into the final version.

Finally, I would like to thank my wife Lacey for her encouragement and enthusiasm and for affording me the opportunity to work on this project.

Table of Contents

Chapter 1   Introduction

1.1   Claims and Disputes 1
1.2   The Legal Process 2
1.3   Construction Law Subject Areas and Principles 4

Chapter 2   Contracts

2.1   Overview 7
2.2   Types of Construction Agreements 9
       Fixed Price Contracts   9
       Cost-Plus Contracts   9
       Unit Price Contracts   10
       Choosing the Form of Contract   11

2.3   Contract Formation: Offer and Acceptance 12

2.4   Consideration 13

2.5   Voiding a Contract 16
Mistake   17
Misrepresentation   17
Duress   18
Unconscionability   18
Frustration and Impossibility   19

2.6   Damages 19

2.7   Termination 21

2.8   Quasi-Contract 22

Chapter 3   Selected Construction Contract Issues

3.1   Introduction 25

3.2   Structuring the Team 26
Design/Build Contracts   26
Multiple Prime Contractors   27
Multiple Prime Consultants   28

3.3   Agency and Authority 28

3.4   Indemnities 31

3.5   Change Orders 35
Extras for Design Negligence   36
Impact Costs   37
Timing and Pricing of Changes and Performance Under Protest   37

Chapter 4   Negligence

4.1   Overview 41

4.2   Duty of Care 42
Directions Courts Have Taken on Duty of Care Issues   43
Establishing a Duty of Care Defense   47

4.3   Breach of Duty 48
Experts and Specialists   50
Compliance with Codes and Standards   50
Avoiding Claims Based on Breach of Duty   52

4.4   Proximate Cause 53
4.5   Loss Caused by the Breach 53
4.6   Deep Pockets in Negligence Case 54

Chapter 5   Risk, Responsibility, and Dispute Avoidance

5.1   Introduction 57
5.2   Common Law Presumptions 58
5.3   Shifting Risk 59
5.4   Disputes Caused by Client Dissatisfaction 60
5.5   Project Documents 62
5.6   Disclaimers 63

Chapter 6   Bidding

6.1   Introduction 65
6.2   The Bidding Process 66
6.3   Bid Shopping 69
6.4   Mistakes 70
6.5   Bid Depositories 72

Chapter 7   Insurance

7.1   Overview 75
7.2   Operating Without Insurance 77
7.3   The Duty to Defend 78
7.4   Subrogation 78
7.5   Insurable Interest 79
7.6   Claims-Made and Occurrence Policies 80
7.7   Limitation Periods 81
7.8   Material Nondisclosure and Prejudice to Third Parties 82

7.9   Cooperation and Conflict Between Insurer and Insured 83
7.10 Builders' Risk Policies 84

Chapter 8   Bonds

8.1   Overview 89
8.2   Indemnities and Other Surety Recourses 91
8.3   Bid Bonds 91
8.4   Performance Bonds 93
8.5   Defenses Under a Performance Bond 95
8.6   Payment Bonds 96

Chapter 9   Mechanics' Liens

9.1   The Purpose of Lien Legislation 99
9.2   Making and Proving a Lien Claim 101
9.3   Who May Claim a Lien 102
9.4   Lien Security 104
9.5   Trust Provisions 105
9.6   Holdback 107
9.7   Risk to the Contractor and Owner 108

Chapter 10   Delay Claims

10.1 Introduction 111
10.2 Critical Path Delays 112
10.3 Compensable, Excusable, and Contractor-Caused Delays 114
10.4 Concurrent Delays 115
10.5 No Damage for Delay Clauses 115
10.6 Proving a Delay Claim 116
      Heads of Damages   117
      Required Documentation   119
      Total Cost and Measured Mile Approaches   120

Chapter 11   Conflicts of Interest and Ethical Considerations

11.1 Overview 123
11.2 The Duty to the Public 124
11.3 The Client's Interest 126
11.4 The Employer's Interest 127
11.5 The Duty to the Profession 128
11.6 The Dual Role of the A/E as Owner's Agent and Impartial Arbiter 129

Chapter 12   Labor Law

12.1 Overview 133
12.2 Establishing Union Representation 135
Definition of Employee   135
Employer Resistance to Union Representation   137
12.3 Craft Unions and Jurisdictional Disputes 138
12.4 Union Security and Right-to-Work 139
12.5 Work Stoppages 140
12.6 Secondary Activity 141
12.7 Successor Employers and Single Employers 141
12.8 Enforcement of Collective Agreements 142
12.9 Employment Law 143

Chapter 13   Dispute Resolution

13.1 Introduction 145
13.2 Litigation 146
The Pleadings   146
Counterclaims and Third-Party Claims   147
The Discovery Process   148
Trials   150
Summary   150
13.3 Arbitration 150
13.4 Negotiation 153

13.5 Mediation 154

13.6 Other Dispute Resolution Methods 155

APPENDICES

Appendix A   AIA Document A201-1987: General Conditions
of the Contract for Construction   157

Appendix B   AIA Document B141-1987: Standard Form
of Agreement Between Owner and Architect   188

Appendix C   AIA Document A310-1970: Bid Bond   195

Appendix D   AIA Document A311-1970: Performance Bond
and Labor and Material Payment Bond   197

Appendix E   CCDC 2—1994: Stipulated Price Contract   203

Appendix F   CCDC 3—1986: Cost Plus Contract   241

Appendix G   CCDC 220—1979: Bid Bond   271

Appendix H   CCDC 221—1979: Performance Bond   273

Appendix I   CCDC 222—1979: Labour and Material
Payment Bond   275

Glossary   279

Index   285

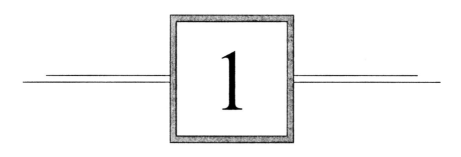

Introduction

1.1 CLAIMS AND DISPUTES

Construction claims and disputes are a fact of life on large projects and are not uncommon on small ones. They include claims for delay, negligence, breach of contract, refusal to pay, and other causes of action. Disputes and claims are costly to resolve, not only in terms of the amounts paid in settlement but also in terms of legal and expert fees, preparation time for employees, and the effects of uncertainty and contingent liability on the ability to carry on business.

Many parties are involved in the construction process: the owner; architect; engineers, including structural, mechanical, electrical, and geotechnical; the contractor; subcontractors; suppliers; individual workers; estimators; construction managers; and others. When disputes develop, many if not all of these parties become involved. Thus, one of the characteristics of construction litigation is the large number of parties. Another is the large number of documents generated during the project. The combination of numerous parties and documents renders litigation of these cases very expensive and time consuming. In some instances, the costs of litigation can exceed the amount of money in dispute.

1

Despite the variety and complexity of construction claims and disputes, the majority are resolved according to only a handful of legal principles. These are the principles embodied in the law of contract and negligence. Cases involving delay, for example, are usually framed in terms of both breach of contract and negligence. A good understanding of these basic principles assists not only in analyzing and resolving disputes but in avoiding them in the first place. One of the purposes of this text is to provide the reader with a sufficient grasp of legal principles to avoid some of the common pitfalls that lead to claims and disputes in the construction industry.

In certain circumstances, claims and disputes may be unavoidable. An owner may become insolvent, for example, and be unable to pay the contractor. Or an accident may cause serious injury or property damage. In such instances, parties must be aware of the steps that must be taken, often quickly, in order to preserve legal rights. For instance, an unpaid subcontractor may need to file a lien or assert a claim against a labor and material payment bond, and these steps must be done in accordance with the applicable mechanics' lien legislation and in accordance with the terms of the bond, respectively. If the claimant is unaware that these remedies exist or that limitation periods and procedural requirements must be met, serious prejudice to the claimant's rights can occur. In the event of an accident, where insurance coverage may exist, the insured party must comply with requirements of the insurance contract or risk losing coverage. One of the objectives of this text is to assist the reader in recognizing when to seek legal advice in order to avoid such consequences.

Allocation of risk is a common theme throughout this text. The construction business is risky. The risks of accident, failure, financial loss, and unforeseen results are ever present. Participants in the process will try to minimize their risks in various ways:

- Contracts may be designed to allocate risks between the parties to the contract.
- Insurance is used to shift risk to a third party, the insurer.
- Bonds are used to protect parties against risks of nonperformance and nonpayment.
- Waivers of lien and statutory declarations are demanded in order to reduce the risks associated with liens.
- Disclaimers are included in the review stamp used by architects and engineers on shop drawings in an attempt to reduce risk.

All the principles discussed and explained in this text should be considered in the context of the risks that are present, which parties are at risk, and how those risks are allocated.

1.2   THE LEGAL PROCESS

Law is an imprecise and somewhat unpredictable field. It is disconcerting to construction professionals who present a legal problem to an attorney, only to be advised, for example, that there is a 60 percent likelihood of a favorable result, and the amount of recovery could range from $50,000 to $150,000.

One reason for this lack of predictability and precision is that the law is not static. It changes from time to time and from place to place. What is considered to be settled law today may not be the rule tomorrow. Unlike the laws of nature, man-made laws can be rewritten by legislatures and reinterpreted by courts.

The principles of construction law in the United States and Canada are very similar. The laws in both countries originate from English common law. However, because every state and every province has its own legislature and court system, variations exist from one state to another and from one province to another, as well as from one country to another. For the most part, these variations are minor. Throughout this text, where such variations exist, they are identified and explained.

Laws are created in several ways. The federal and state (or provincial) governments enact statutes[1] that regulate some of the areas of construction law, such as joint and several liability in negligence, mechanics' lien rights, formalities of contracts[2], and workers' compensation requirements. These laws are then interpreted by judges. In theory, judges do not make laws, they only interpret them. In practice, however, the act of interpretation unavoidably results in the creation of new laws.

Large bodies of law are not statute based. Neither created by legislatures nor the result of interpretation of statutes, they are created by judges based on principles of law and equity established and modified over hundreds of years, tracing their roots to England. These judicial precedents have gradually created the **common law** of both the United States and Canada. Almost all jurisdictions in the United States and Canada are common law jurisdictions.[3]

Legislation frequently empowers certain agencies to create regulations that may be considered law. For example, a state board of registration for engineers may enact bylaws, a breach of which can give rise to liability for damages as well as other consequences.

Custom and usage in the industry may also have the same practical effect as law. If the custom is so widespread as to be considered an industry standard, failure to act in accordance with that standard may also create grounds for liability. Many of these standards have been codified.

---

1. **Statute law** must be compatible with the applicable constitution in order to be enforceable.

2. In many jurisdictions, there are statutes that require certain types of contracts to be in writing. Construction contracts generally do *not* have to be in writing, whereas surety contracts must be.

3. In some jurisdictions, all law is statute based. These are called civil law jurisdictions. Quebec is one example of a civil law jurisdiction. Louisiana is another.

1.3   CONSTRUCTION LAW SUBJECT AREAS AND PRINCIPLES

As stated, most claims and disputes arising out of construction projects involve principles of contract law and negligence. An understanding of the basic principles in these two areas is a prerequisite to the study of other areas of construction law, such as delay claims, bonds, and insurance.

Contracts are voluntary agreements between two or more parties that set out the rights, responsibilities, and liabilities of the parties to the contract. Although construction contracts are usually in writing, oral contracts are legally enforceable, except for certain special types of contracts. They take many forms; fixed price, unit price, cost plus, guaranteed maximum price, and turnkey contracts are some of the variations familiar to contractors. Standard forms of agreements published by organizations such as the American Institute of Architects and the Canadian Construction Association are widely used in the industry. Some of them are included in the appendices. Many of the clauses in these standard forms are explained throughout this text, as they apply to various subject areas. By way of example, delay clauses are discussed in the chapter on delay claims (Chapter 10), and insurance clauses are discussed in the chapter on insurance (Chapter 7).

The fundamental principles of contract law are concerned with enforceability. Concepts such as offer and acceptance and consideration are used to determine whether a binding agreement exists and, if so, what the terms of that agreement are. Even if a binding and enforceable agreement exists, subsequent events may cause the agreement to become voidable. Chapter 2 explains these basic concepts of contract law.

Construction contracts follow the same rules of law as other commercial agreements. However, provisions are found in construction contracts, such as change order clauses, that are less frequent in other contracts. There are also contract issues that, if not unique, are at least commonly identifiable with the construction process, such as the agency relationship between the designer and owner. Some of these common provisions and issues are discussed in Chapter 3.

Negligence is but one aspect of the law of torts. Torts are acts committed by one party in violation of the rights of another that are considered sufficiently reprehensible as to give rise to liability. Although intentional torts such as fraud, fraudulent misrepresentation, and trespass do occur, intentional torts, with the exception of trespass, are seldom involved in construction disputes. Negligence constitutes the vast majority of tort claims.

A negligence claim is customarily asserted by a party who has been injured, either financially or physically, by the act (or omission) of another party with whom the first party has no contract. However, it is not uncommon for negligence claims to be made between parties who have a contractual relationship. Such parties may rely on both breach of contract and negligence theories. The contract may provide remedies superior to those available under the law of negligence.

To prove a negligence claim, it is necessary to show that the defendant could reasonably foresee, at the time the allegedly negligent act was committed, that the plaintiff would suffer an injury or loss as a result. It is also necessary to show that the defendant did not meet the standard of care that should be expected of someone in his or her position. And finally, it is necessary to show that the failure to meet that standard of care was the legal cause of the loss suffered by the plaintiff. All these elements of negligence are explained in Chapter 4.

Much of the remainder of the text deals with subject areas in which various problems in the construction industry have arisen, including bidding, mechanics' liens, bonds, and insurance. Bidding, for example, is the traditional method of contract formation on the construction side (although other traditional methods are customary on the design side). The bidding process creates its own unique problems. Mechanics' liens are unique to the construction industry, and the principles of law governing mechanics' lien statutes must be understood in order to avoid some of the common pitfalls associated with lien claims. Bonds and insurance are required on many large projects, and parties must be aware of circumstances that can cause a surety or insurer to deny coverage.

Chapter 11 is concerned with conflicts of interest and ethical issues that engineers and architects often face. Although the chapter may be of some use to contractors, it is intended primarily for design professionals.

In contrast to Chapter 11, Chapter 12 is directed primarily at contractors. The chapter contains a survey of labor law principles and a brief introduction to employment law. To a labor lawyer, the field of labor law is not a subset of construction law; rather, it is a field unto itself. Interpretation of labor legislation and negotiation of collective agreements requires specialized training and experience. Yet the fields of construction law and labor law are related to some degree if only because the construction industry creates problems that are unique to labor relations. Common site (or common situs, as it is sometimes referred to) picketing and pre-hire agreements are two such problems. Contractors who are unaware of basic labor law principles may find that they have unknowingly committed an unfair labor practice, the consequences of which can be very costly.

One recurring theme in this book is dispute avoidance through understanding of legal principles and recognition of common fact patterns. Despite best efforts, however, disputes cannot always be avoided, and they must be resolved. Chapter 13 is concerned with dispute resolution. Established methods of dispute resolution are explained and compared.

It has been said that ignorance of the law is no excuse.[4] The time is passed when an architect, engineer, or contractor could rely on technical competence in his or her field and ignore the law. For participants in the construction industry, the likelihood of being involved in a lawsuit, whether as plaintiff or defendant, is much greater now than in the recent past, and the cost of prosecuting, defending, and settling claims cannot be ignored. Similarly, the cost of avoiding disputes and claims, because it is so much less, should not be ignored.

---

4.   It has also been said that the statement does not apply to trial court judges, who have court of appeal judges to correct their errors for them.

Many areas of law that surface from time to time in construction cases are not covered in this text. Trespass claims, for instance, are occasionally made against contractors, owners, and consultants. Product liability claims are frequently made against material suppliers. Many subtopics of law in contracts, negligence, and other areas have been intentionally omitted. Many of these topics are of only marginal relevance to the construction professional unless a claim happens to be made specifically related to that topic. Many excellent references are available covering each of the subjects in this text, and the reader is encouraged to consult a specialized text should the need arise.

Basic understanding of the legal principles explained in the following chapters will not make the reader an expert in construction law. But it will sensitize the reader to many fact patterns and situations in which legal advice is needed and to the steps that must be taken in those circumstances in order to preserve legal rights and avoid problems.

This text is not intended as a substitute for legal advice. Legal problems are fact specific, meaning that a slight change in the facts can often lead to a different conclusion. Furthermore, the law differs from one jurisdiction to another and changes over time. A nonlawyer should obtain specific advice for specific legal problems and should not attempt to act as his or her own counsel.

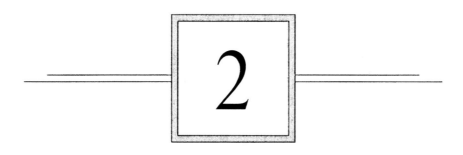

Contracts

2.1 OVERVIEW

A **contract** is a voluntary agreement between two or more parties. Contracts can take many forms; they may be written, they may be oral, they may be partly written and partly oral. They may contain terms that have never been expressly discussed between the parties but that are taken for granted (known as "implied terms"). They may be enforceable by a court, or they may be unenforceable because of defects in their form or content. Although the law requires certain contracts to be in writing in order to be enforceable (such as contracts relating to purchase and sale of land), contracts for construction or design services need not be.

The purpose of a contract is to set out the rights, responsibilities, and liabilities of the parties. At least that is the purpose most often described by professors of contract law. But the purpose of a contract can be described from a different perspective; it is to allocate risk between the parties. Contracts can be enforced by the parties to the contract.[1] They may also be enforced by par-

---

1.   A party to the contract is said to be *privy* to the contract. The parties to the contract are in **privity**.

7

ties who are not privy to the contract but for whose benefit the contract was intended.[2]

Contract disputes occur on many construction projects. Many are resolved amicably. The ones that cannot be so resolved are turned over to an impartial tribunal, such as a judge, jury, or arbitrator for resolution. These disputes often occur as a result of an event that causes financial loss to one of the parties, such as an accident, a downturn in the real estate market, or deficiencies in the construction. Sometimes the dispute is precipitated not by an event but by the realization by one of the parties that the deal they agreed to may not turn out as planned.

When a contract dispute is turned over to a court, one of the functions of the court is to determine whether the complaint is really a risk that one of the parties assumed at the outset. If it is, the party who assumed the risk should bear the loss. If the cost of materials increases after the contract has been entered into, for example, and it is a fixed price contract, the contractor has accepted that risk. If it is a cost-plus contract, the owner has accepted it.

In this chapter, the basic principles of contract law are explained. Most of the rules relate to enforceability; the issue is whether a court will enforce the contract (or a portion of it) in the event of a dispute. Some agreements are unenforceable due to a flaw inherent in the contract or in its formation, and some become unenforceable because of events that occur subsequent to the creation of the contract.

Two principles that determine whether an enforceable contract exists to begin with are contract formation (**offer and acceptance**) and consideration. If there has been a valid offer and acceptance, and the contract contains mutual consideration, the contract will likely be enforceable. Both of these concepts are fully explained later. Other requirements for an enforceable contract, such as the legal capacity of the parties to contract and the necessity for a lawful purpose of the contract, are seldom relevant in construction disputes.

Contracts may become voidable because of subsequent events, such as coercion, frustration, impossibility, or the discovery of a mistake. Other grounds for avoiding a contract (for example, misrepresentation or unconscionability) have been included in the same section of this chapter even though the flaw in those contracts must have existed when the contracts were formed. This is true of contracts voidable due to mistake as well. They are discussed together because they are generally raised as defenses to claims that arise during or following performance of a contract.

The triggering event for the majority of contract disputes is the failure by one party to perform his or her obligations. This is called breach of contract. Breaches and remedies for breach of contract, the most common of which is the payment of money (damages) by the party in breach, are discussed in this chapter. One remedy

---

2.   In Canada, intended third-party beneficiaries *cannot* enforce the contract, except in rare circumstances. Until recently, they could not enforce them at all, but the case of *London Drugs Ltd.* v. *Kuehne & Nagle Int'l Ltd.*, [1992] 3 S.C.R. 299 now allows employees to rely on exclusion clauses entered into by their employer.

that may be available if the contract is determined to be inapplicable to the circum-stances is *quasi-contract*, which is also covered in this chapter.

2.2 TYPES OF CONSTRUCTION AGREEMENTS

There is no limit to the different types of contracts that can be made. However, a few basic categories of construction contracts have been developed and are avail-able in standard form.[3] Contracts between the owner and the contractor are fre-quently divided into three categories: fixed price, cost-plus, and unit price. Each of these categories has several variations, usually determined by the type of fee the contractor is to be paid.

Fixed Price Contracts

A **fixed price** contract means that the contractor is to receive a lump sum amount, which compensates the contractor for the cost of performing the work, including labor, materials, and equipment, as well as overhead and profit. Such contracts are also referred to as stipulated price contracts or lump sum contracts. Under these contracts, the owner usually has no right to direct the contractor in the means and methods of construction and has no right to inquire about the actual cost of per-forming the work. The contractor will be entitled to keep any additional profit earned as a result of cost-saving measures but will also be responsible for overruns, subject, of course, to complying with the terms of the contract and provided no changes have been necessitated by the owner.

Cost-Plus Contracts

A cost-plus agreement usually requires that the contractor be compensated by the owner for the actual costs of construction, plus a fee that may be fixed or may vary with the cost of construction. In such agreements, it is imperative that the "costs of construction" be accurately defined.[4] This has been the source of many disputes, particularly regarding overhead items.

Cost-plus agreements may provide the contractor an opportunity to use transfer pricing as a means of increasing profits. For example, the contractor requires a pro-ject office and decides to rent a trailer for twelve months. Rather than rent from an

---

3. The American Institute of Architects publishes a variety of standard form agreements, as does the Canadian Construction Association. The AIA documents can be obtained by writing to the American Institute of Architects at 1735 New York Ave., N.W., Washington, DC 20006. The CCA documents are available by writing to the Canadian Construction Document Committee, 85 Albert St., Ottawa, Ontario, Canada K1P 6A4.

4. The CCDC 3 cost-plus agreement, Article A-9, contains such a definition. See Appendix F.

outside source, the contractor may purchase the trailer for its own account, then rent the trailer to the project. After twelve months, the owner has effectively paid for most of the purchase price but is left with nothing, whereas the contractor is left with the trailer. Such results occur when the owner fails to exercise control over costs or has not provided a contractual means of control. For these reasons, cost-plus contracts should generally allow meaningful involvement by the owner in the details of construction, including means and methods.

A contractor operating under a cost-plus contract with a fixed fee has no incentive, other than the prospect of repeat business and a sense of ethics, to save money for the owner. The profit remains fixed. A fee based on a percentage of the costs of construction provides the wrong incentive; the contractor may attempt to increase the cost in order to increase the fee. For these reasons, various incentive formulae have been devised. One such formula is known as a **target price** contract, which provides that the fee is fixed as long as the cost of construction exceeds a certain figure (the target), but savings below the target will be shared between the owner and the contractor, with the savings formula determined in advance, such as $50/50$ or $60/40$. Some target price contracts also require the contractor to absorb all costs of construction above the target. These target price contracts are hybrids of the fixed price and cost-plus agreements, and are commonly known as **guaranteed maximum** price (GMP) contracts. They give the owner the primary advantage of a fixed price contract, which is a guarantee that the total price will not exceed the agreed amount. They have the attributes of cost-plus contracts in that they allow the owner to audit the contractor's costs if the contractor claims any portion of the cost savings.

A cost-plus agreement does not necessarily entitle the contractor to be reimbursed the cost of correcting work that was negligently performed. Even though those costs are incurred in completing the construction, it is an implied term of every construction contract (unless there is an express term to the contrary) that the contractor will perform competently.

Unit Price Contracts

Unit price contracts require that the owner pay a stipulated amount for each unit or quantity of work performed, such as $100 per cubic yard of concrete in place. These contracts are common on roadbuilding, earthmoving, and pipeline projects. In theory, such contracts could be used for almost any component of construction, such as square footage of drywall or lineal footage of conduit installed; however, such usage is rare.

Although unit price contracts do not guarantee the final cost, they may be advantageous for different reasons. Where the quantity of work may vary, requiring a contractor to bid on a lump sum basis often results in a contingency within the price to protect against the risk of a quantity different from that estimated. Thus, under a fixed price contract, the owner ends up paying a premium.

The requirement that the owner pay the agreed price per unit is not absolute. Many unit price contracts contain a provision that adjusts the compensation per unit if the total quantity varies from the estimate by more than a given percentage. The logic behind this adjustment is that the job becomes materially different than anticipated when quantities vary widely. The contractor's mobilization costs may remain unchanged, and a significantly smaller quantity may result in the contractor having fewer "units" in which to recover the mobilization. On the other hand, a large increase in quantity, though reducing per unit overhead, may also mean that part of the job must be performed in inclement weather or result in other increased costs. If no formula is included in the contract, a significant change in quantities is likely to result in a claim based on "changed conditions."

Choosing the Form of Contract

Years of legal analysis and substantial experience have gone into drafting and fine-tuning the standard forms of contract that are commercially available. Nonetheless, they are not perfect for every project or every party. For that reason, many contracts are custom-made to suit individuals and projects. In many cases, standard form contracts can be used with minor modification. There is no need to reinvent the wheel with respect to many of the more common provisions that appear in most standard forms.

When standard form agreements require modification, such changes should be accomplished by an attorney. Some of the provisions have been litigated and their meanings determined by courts; changing a word may well alter the intent of the provision. Additionally, many of the agreements contain interlocking provisions and internal cross-references, such that deletion of one paragraph may affect provisions elsewhere in the agreement or within related agreements.[5]

Two schools of thought exist regarding objectivity and bias in standard form agreements. Owners have been heard to complain that these agreements are drafted by contractors' groups or consultants' groups and are biased in favor of such groups. Similar complaints have been voiced by contractors and consultants. Yet the contracts are widely used, indicating that the perception of bias is not widespread. Some parties, primarily owners, have had contracts drafted that are tailored to their particular needs, and these tend to be extremely one-sided. This is particularly true where the owner has greater bargaining power than the contractor or consultant and is in a position to say "take it or leave it." Many attorneys believe that it is their duty to draft every provision such that it favors their client, resulting in a contract that is very onerous for the other party. Others recognize that a contract that is too

---

5. For example, the AIA General Conditions (Document A201-1987) in the General Information states that it "is frequently adopted by reference into a variety of other agreements, including the Owner-Architect agreements and the Contractor-Subcontractor agreements, in order to establish a common basis for the primary and secondary relationships on the typical construction project."

one-sided will increase costs and ultimately cause disputes that, even if resolved favorably to the client, nonetheless result in a higher overall cost than that of creating a fair and balanced contract.

In simpler and less litigious times, written agreements were far less common. Even today where, based on past dealings, there is a level of trust between the parties, a formal contract may not be used. Multimillion-dollar deals as well as numerous small projects have been done on a handshake. However, one advantage of a written agreement is that it forces the parties to address potential risks before they arise, make conscious decisions regarding who should bear those risks, and provide a written record of those risk allocations.

Where no written agreement is used, and a dispute develops, a court may imply terms into the oral agreement that appear consistent with the intention of the parties. Even though the parties may not have addressed such issues, courts will usually imply terms consistent with industry custom and practice. If a particular standard form is widely used in the jurisdiction, the court may simply adopt all the terms of the standard form as the contract between the parties. In effect, failure to enter into a written agreement may result in a standard form agreement by default, except for those terms that are inconsistent with any terms agreed to orally.

2.3   CONTRACT FORMATION: OFFER AND ACCEPTANCE

In the construction industry, many contracts are formed as a result of the bidding process. The law relating to bidding and the bid process itself are sufficiently complex that it is discussed in a separate chapter. The following discussion of contract formation is limited to circumstances that do *not* involve competitive bidding.

To form a contract, there must be an offer capable of being accepted, and there must be an acceptance. Disputes have arisen regarding whether a statement constitutes an offer, that is, whether it is capable of acceptance. If it is too vague, it is not capable of acceptance. If too many essential terms are not defined during a proposal, such as the price, the time for performance, and the scope of the project, it will probably not qualify as an offer. A solicitation for offers is called an invitation, and it does not qualify as an offer.[6]

Many contracts are formed through negotiations. Offers and counteroffers are sent back and forth, until one of the counteroffers is accepted. An important rule of contract formation is that if an offer is rejected, it cannot later be accepted unless it is revived by the offeror. A counteroffer has the same effect as a rejection, in that it

6.   On this point, Canadian and U.S. law have taken divergent paths. In Canada, an invitation for bids is legally an offer, whereas in the United States it is not. That is the source of the difference between U.S. and Canadian law in this area.

terminates the offer. Either party can walk away from negotiations with impunity if no contract has been formed.

The general rule is that an offer can be revoked at any time before it has been accepted. For the revocation to be effective, it must have been received by the offeree (the person to whom the offer was made).[7] If an offer does not state the duration that it remains open for acceptance, it is assumed to be open for a "reasonable" time, which means a period that is commercially reasonable under the circumstances.

There is an exception to the general rule that is particularly important in the construction context. An offer (which may be in the form of a bid) may be irrevocable for a period if certain conditions are met. Owners who solicit bids require time to evaluate them and may insist that they be irrevocable for a period of 30 or 60 days. Similarly, general contractors rely on subcontractor prices in order to put a bid together and demand that the subcontract prices be irrevocable for a similar period. For an offer to be irrevocable, there must be an *enforceable* promise not to revoke.[8] This is sometimes called an **option contract;** the offeree is given the option to accept, which must be exercised during the option period. What makes the promise enforceable is "consideration," the subject of the following section.

2.4   CONSIDERATION

Consideration is an old legal concept. It means something of value, however small, given or promised by each party to the contract.[9] The primary consideration given by the owner in a construction contract is the promise to pay the contract price. The primary consideration given by the contractor is the promise to perform the construction. It is not necessary that the consideration given by each party be of equal value. One party may benefit more than the other. Courts do not usually consider who got the better deal unless it is so one-sided as to be unconscionable. As long as a bargain was struck, courts will generally try to enforce it. A promise without consideration is a gift, and courts will not enforce a promise to give a gift.

Consideration may be a promise by one party to give up a legal right rather than a promise to pay money. For example, a contractor may agree to give up its right to

---

7.   This is the same rule as for rejections of offers; in order to be effective, it must be communicated to the offeror.

8.   Another way to enforce an irrevocable offer is to prove that the promisee relied on it and has suffered a detriment as a result. This is known as **promissory estoppel**. For example, a general contractor who relies on a subcontractor's price would be able to force the subcontractor to hold that price open. Otherwise, the general contractor would be stuck with that price component in his or her bid, without anyone to do the work at that price.

9.   One definition is "either some right, interest, profit, or benefit accruing to the one party, or some forbearance, detriment, loss, or responsibility, given, suffered, or undertaken by the other." *Currie v. Misa* (1875), L.R. 10 Ex. 153, at 162.

sue the owner for delay in exchange for the owner granting an extension of time to complete the contract. That is an enforceable agreement.

Construction contracts may be amended during performance because of changed circumstances. Each amendment must be supported by consideration. If not, it is unenforceable. Such problems arise on construction projects where one party demands changes to the contract in midstream. In one case, the contractor was required to deliver and install the windows by a certain date, and as the date approached, refused to perform on time unless the owner agreed to increase the contract price. The owner reluctantly agreed in order to avoid a delay to the final completion date. After the contract was completed, the owner refused to pay the additional money, arguing that there was no consideration.[10]

The court agreed that the window contractor was already under an obligation to perform the work by a given date and thus did not offer anything new or relinquish any rights in exchange for the promise by the owner for more money. The contractor's duty to perform was a "pre-existing duty," or "past consideration." Had the contractor promised to accelerate the schedule by one week in exchange for the price increase, the amendment to the contract would not have failed for lack of consideration.

Historically, seals have been used as a substitute for consideration. In other words, one party could make a promise in writing that was not supported by consideration, put the document under seal, and thereby make it enforceable. A seal is no longer a valid substitute for consideration in most states in the United States.[11] To be truly irrevocable, offers must either be supported by consideration or cause detrimental reliance.[12]

CASE STUDY
Smith v. Dawson (1923), 53 O.L.R. 615 (Ont. C.A.)

The following judgment is an appeal from a County Court judgment in favor of the plaintiffs (the contractors). The plaintiffs built a house for the defendant for a fixed price. When the house was close to completion, it was severely damaged by fire. The defendant was insured, the plaintiffs were not. After the fire, an agreement was reached whereby the plaintiffs would complete construction in consideration for the additional payment of the insurance proceeds.

---

10. *Modular Windows of Canada* v. *Command Construction* (1984), 11 C.L.R. 131 (Ont. H.C.).

11. It is still recognized in Canada.

12. See footnote 8, *supra*.

Riddell, J.: The situation then seems quite clear—the plaintiffs, learning that the defendant had received some insurance money on the house, objected to go on without some kind of assurance that they were to get the insurance money—the defendant demurred, as she had lost considerably by the destruction of her furniture, but finally said, "All right, go ahead and do the work." If this constitutes a contract at all, it was that she would give them the insurance money she had received, if they would go ahead and do the work they were already under a legal obligation to do.

In some of the United States a doctrine has been laid down that (at least in building contracts) the contractor has the option either to complete his contract or to abandon it and pay damages. These Courts have accordingly held that the abandonment by the contractor of his option to abandon is sufficient consideration for a promise to pay an extra amount.

The Courts of Illinois, Indiana, and Massachusetts seem to have adopted this rule: 9 Corpus Juris, p. 720 "Building and Construction Contracts," sec. 53; 13 Corpus Juris, p. 354.

But such a course is to allow a contractor to take advantage of his own wrong, and other Courts reprobate it: 9 Corpus Juris, p. 720; 13 Corpus Juris, p. 354 sec. 210, and cases cited in notes.

This is not and never was the law in Ontario, and is not and never was the law in England.

It has long been text-book law that "not the promise or the actual performance of something which the promisee is legally bound to perform" is a consideration for a promise: Halsbury's Laws of England, vol. 7, p. 385, para. 798; "the performance of an existing contract by one of the parties is no consideration for a new promise by the other party:" Leake on Contracts, 7th ed., p. 455 and cases cited.

I am of the opinion that the promise (if there was one) to pay for the work to be done was not binding for want of consideration, and would allow the appeal . . .

Middleton, J.: Unless the legal situation is kept clearly in mind, the case seems to present some aspect of hardship.

The plaintiffs undertook to build the house for the contract price and to hand it over complete to the defendant. In the absence of any provision to the contrary in the contract, the destruction of the building by fire would not afford any excuse for non-performance of the contract.

When the work was going on, the material and labour which went into the building became the defendant's property subject to any lien in the plaintiff's favour; so she had an insurable interest in the property, and she effected an insurance for her own protection.

The builders had an insurable interest, not only because of their lien, but also because the destruction of the property by fire would injure them, as under the building contract they would be bound to replace. They did not insure, preferring to carry the risk themselves. There was no obligation on the part of the owner to insure for the benefit of the contractors, and the contractors have no equitable or other claim on the money received by the owner as a result of her prudence and expenditure.

As I understand the evidence, there was no more than a demand by the owner upon the contractor to complete his contract. If there was more, it did not amount to a new contract, as there was no consideration.

In its essence the defence is an attempt to shift the loss resulting from the fire—legally a loss falling on the contractors—to the shoulders of the owner, who, fortunately for her, is not liable . . .

Questions

1. According to the contractor, what was his consideration for the additional payment?
2. If this case had been tried in Illinois, instead of Ontario, would the result have been different? Explain.
3. What is meant by "abandonment by the contractor of his option to abandon"?
4. Would the result have been different if the contractor had abandoned the contract, been sued by the owner, and then entered into a settlement with the owner whereby the contractor was to receive the insurance proceeds? Should the result depend on whether there is an actual abandonment?

Analysis

1. The contractor's argument was that he had given up something of value, namely, his right to abandon the project. In other words, he argued that his forbearance in not exercising that option was consideration for the increased payment. It is questionable whether the contractor had a "right" to abandon although he certainly had an option to abandon and suffer the consequences, which would include damages for breach.
2. Yes. According to this court, the courts in Illinois and some other states agree that agreement not to exercise the option to abandon is sufficient consideration.
3. That is the description of the "consideration" that the contractor relied upon to support his claim.
4. A different result is likely. Once actual abandonment has occurred, the owner must sue the contractor to recover damages. There is a dispute between the parties at that point, and a settlement agreement to resolve a bona fide dispute is usually enforceable. It is the policy of the courts in most jurisdictions to enforce settlement agreements, regardless of who had the stronger case.

2.5   VOIDING A CONTRACT

When projects run into trouble, and in some cases before performance begins, one party may realize that the contract entered into is not in his or her best interest.

Courts will void a contract only in rare circumstances. Such circumstances include mistake, misrepresentation, duress, unconscionability, frustration and impossibility.

Mistake

Not every mistake will make a contract voidable. First, the mistake must be significant, not trivial.[13] Second, the mistake must have existed at the time the agreement was made; a mistake made after the agreement was entered into will not do. And third, the mistake must have been either a "mutual mistake," which is a mistake made by both parties, or else it must be a mistake made by one party of which the other party was aware or should reasonably have been aware.

A number of disputes have arisen where mistakes have been made in a bid. If the mistake is not caught until after the contract has been executed, the contractor will have to show that the mistake was obvious on the face of the bid.[14] Consider the case of an owner who receives six bids, five of which are within 10 percent of each other, with the sixth being approximately 50 percent lower. That should at least raise a doubt in the owner's mind about the existence of an error.

There are no hard and fast rules on the percentage difference that qualifies as an obvious error. In some trades, such as steel erection, it may be customary to receive bids that are very close together. It may depend on how active the market is at any given time. In other trades, such as painting, a 25 percent variation may not be unusual.

Mistakes are often caught after the bid has been submitted but before a contract has been entered into. If the bid is irrevocable, or if there is a bid bond, the contractor may be required to enter into the contract or forfeit the bond penalty unless the error in the bid is obvious to the owner.

Misrepresentation

An innocent or negligent misrepresentation is a statement made by one party to another that is false or misleading but involves no intent to deceive or mislead. For a fraudulent misrepresentation to occur, the party making the statement must be aware that the statement is false. In both cases, a party who has entered into a contract in reliance on the statement may be able to avoid the contract, but it may be more difficult to do if there was no fraudulent intent.

Allegations of fraudulent misrepresentation have been made in the context of subsurface conditions. It is common to see a clause in many construction agreements that requires the contractor to make a complete investigation of the site prior

---

13. In legal terminology, it must be "material."

14. This has been referred to as the **sore thumb rule.**

to submitting the bid in order to be satisfied with respect to site conditions.[15] It is equally common for owners to commission a geotechnical investigation that is made available to bidders, together with a disclaimer that the owner makes no representations regarding the accuracy of the investigation or the nature of subsurface conditions. In some cases, the bid documents require the contractor to conduct its own soils investigation. Given the realities of putting a bid together, the constraints of time and cost often make it unreasonable to expect any contractor to undertake an independent study.

As long as the contract provides for an increase in price due to unforeseen subsurface conditions, the appropriate remedy is to authorize an extra to the contract.[16] Difficulty arises if the contract contains no such mechanism and the owner had knowledge that calls into question the bid assumptions. In many jurisdictions, the owner has a positive obligation to make available to bidders all relevant information, where such information is not reasonably available to bidders, and failure to do so is actionable.

Duress

Construction cases in which allegations of **duress** have been made usually involve modifications to the contract made during performance. A good example is the *Modular Windows* case, where a demand was put on the owner to amend the agreement or else face a long delay.[17] For duress to exist, the party claiming duress must prove that it did not have any meaningful choice. There is a fine distinction between legitimate business pressure and illegitimate pressure that amounts to duress. Courts will examine whether practical remedies were available such as hiring a replacement contractor and suing the party who made the threat and whether the demand for new terms was justified.[18]

Unconscionability

Courts will not void a contract or portion of a contract simply because it favors one party over another. In order for **unconscionability** to exist, there must have been an

---

15. AIA Document A201-1987, clause 1.2.2 states: "Execution of the Contract by the Contractor is a representation that the Contractor has visited the site, become familiar with local conditions under which the Work is to be performed and correlated personal observations with requirements of the Contract Documents."

16. The CCDC 2 Agreement GC 6.4, and AIA Document A201-1987 clause 4.3.6, contemplate such an increase.

17. Footnote 10, *supra*.

18. Other factors are relevant as well, such as the availability of legal advice and whether the "innocent" party took prompt action to avoid the contract after the pressure ceased. For a good discussion of the law of duress, see the case of *Pao On* v. *Lau Yui* [1980] A.C. 614, 3 All E.R. 65 (P.C.).

extreme inequality of bargaining power at the time the contract was formed. It is extremely rare for construction contracts to be held unconscionable.

A clause or contract that is particularly harsh toward one party may be some evidence of an inequality of bargaining power. A court faced with such a clause can deal with it in one of two ways; it can refuse to enforce it, or it can interpret the clause as generously as possible so as to avoid an unfair result. An example is the "no damages for delay" clause, which some owners try to insert into construction agreements. These clauses are an attempt to preclude the contractor from suing the owner for any delay. Courts are reluctant to find such clauses unenforceable but will more often construe them against the owner.

Frustration and Impossibility

When an event occurs that was not foreseen at the time the contract was entered into, and that event makes the performance of the contract either impossible or of no value, a party may have the contract rescinded. For example, if the land on which the construction is to take place is expropriated prior to performance, the owner could rescind. It is essential that the risk of the event is *not* a risk that was allocated to one of the parties; otherwise, the doctrines of **frustration** and **impossibility** would not apply.

Most standard form contracts contemplate almost any risk that could materialize. Typical contracts contain **force majeure** clauses, which provide for an extension to the contract time because of a force majeure event.[19] Force majeure events used to be referred to as "acts of God" but now often include such events as labor disputes, fires, delays by common carriers, and unavoidable casualties. It would be difficult to prove frustration or impossibility under such contracts.

2.6   DAMAGES

When a breach of contract occurs, the innocent party may have a choice of remedies. A court may order one party to pay money to the other (known as **damages**); it may order one party to perform specific acts (known as **specific performance**); it may make an order prohibiting a party from doing something (known as an **injunction**); or it may make a declaratory order that simply gives the court's opinion without requiring anyone to do anything. Specific performance is rarely ordered for construction, engineering, and architecture contracts.

---

19.   AIA Document A201-1987 clause 8.3.1; CCDC 2 clause GC 6.5.3. The AIA clause does not specifically address the issue of compensation and lumps together delays caused by the owner with delays that are beyond the control of both the owner and contractor. The CCDC clause deals only with delays caused by neither party. Delays for which the owner is responsible are covered under GC 6.5.1 and 6.5.2.

By far the most common remedy is damages. The amount awarded is supposed to put the innocent party in the same position as if no breach had occurred. For a contractor whose contract has been wrongfully terminated, the damages would include anticipated profit. For an owner whose opening date has been delayed, the damages may be lost rents.

Recovery of damages is subject to three limitations. The first is **mitigation.** The plaintiff must take reasonable steps to reduce or mitigate the loss. For example, if an owner suffers a delay caused by the contractor, and as a result, sale of the building falls through, the owner must try to sell the building to another and recover from the contractor only the difference in sale price and other additional costs incurred.[20]

The second limitation is that the damages cannot be too speculative. A party claiming loss of anticipated profits must be able to prove with a reasonable degree of certainty that a profit would have been earned and how much it would have been.

The third limitation is **remoteness.** If the loss was not reasonably foreseeable at the time the contract was made, it is considered too remote. It is reasonably foreseeable that delay to a completion date might cause the owner to lose revenue, but it may not be reasonably foreseeable that such a delay would put the owner into bankruptcy. For this reason, serious consequences of a possible breach that are not ordinarily foreseeable should be brought to the attention of the other contracting party before the contract is entered into. The contractor, for example, might advise the owner that another project is scheduled to begin immediately after the scheduled completion date and that any delay caused by the owner would mean that equipment such as cranes and hoists would be needed. Failure to advise the other party of unusual risks might preclude recovery of damages for those risks on grounds of remoteness.

In industrial construction contracts, such as repair to refineries and mills, it is common for the contractor and engineer to insist on a **consequential damages** clause. Consequential damages has different meanings in different contracts and contexts, but it is generally understood to mean indirect losses, such as loss of business. A contractor doing repair work on an oil refinery, for example, might have a contract worth $1 million, with anticipated profits of 5 percent, or $50,000. The refinery must be shut down for the repairs, and every day of shutdown costs the refinery owner $500,000 in lost profit. Assume that the shutdown period is one week. If the contractor were to delay startup by one day, it would expose him or her to liability equal to ten times the expected profit. Clearly the risk is not worth the expected profit, and the risk of delay is great because the shutdown period has little or no float due to the cost of downtime.

To avoid this risk, engineers and contractors generally require owners to accept this risk by agreeing to a provision in the contract that excludes damages for consequential loss. Courts will carefully interpret such clauses, and if any ambiguity exists,

---

20. If the new sale price is higher, there is no loss suffered, except perhaps for the financing charges for the period of delay.

it will be resolved against the party who is trying to claim the benefit of the clause. For that reason, these clauses should be drafted by an attorney.

Consequential damages clauses are less common in building construction or design contracts. Instead, liquidated damages clauses are used.[21] **Liquidated damages** means that the loss is estimated before the contract is signed and before any breach has occurred. The parties agree beforehand that if a certain type of breach occurs (typically a delay), damages will be fixed at a certain amount, such as $1,000 per day. If the liquidated damages are set unreasonably high in order to terrorize a party into performing, it will be considered a penalty and may not be enforceable.

2.7   TERMINATION

Contracts must eventually come to an end. This can occur in a number of ways. The most common is by performance. After each party has performed all of his or her obligations under the contract, and after all warranty periods have expired, the contract comes to an end.

Other events may cause a contract to terminate. As discussed earlier, there may be an event that frustrates the contract or makes it impossible to perform. Or the parties may agree to terminate the agreement before it has been completely performed. The agreement to terminate would set out the terms of termination, including final payments, if any, by one party to another.

In some cases, one party may terminate the contract without the consent of the other. This unilateral termination either will be provoked by a breach of contract or will itself be a breach of contract.

Breaches of contract can be divided into two groups: fundamental breaches and less serious breaches. A fundamental breach is one that goes to the root of the contract, one that deprives the innocent party substantially of the benefit of the contract. For instance, the benefit of the contract to the contractor is to get paid and to have the opportunity to earn a profit. Failure by the owner to pay may be considered a fundamental breach. If one party commits a fundamental breach, the other party has two options: continue to perform and sue for damages or declare the contract to be at an end and sue for damages.

A less serious breach does not entitle the innocent party to treat the contract as ended. The only remedy is to sue for damages. It is sometimes a matter of judgment whether a particular breach amounts to a fundamental breach. If the innocent party treats it as a fundamental breach and terminates the contract, but in fact it is less serious, the innocent party will have itself committed a fundamental breach and will be liable for damages. For that reason, terminating a contract unilaterally is a very

---

21. A liquidated damages provision may be used in conjunction with a consequential damages provision.

serious step with potentially disastrous consequences and should never be done without careful deliberation and legal advice.

Repudiation of a contract is where one party either by words or by conduct lets the other party know that it does not intend to perform its obligations. Repudiation without justification is a fundamental breach.

Anticipatory breach is one in which no breach has yet occurred, other than conveying the intention to breach. Most jurisdictions require that in order for an anticipatory breach to exist, it must be clear and unequivocal. For example, a contractor who is falling behind schedule has not committed an anticipatory breach unless it is absolutely impossible for the contractor to make up the lost ground. An anticipatory breach may also be anticipatory repudiation if the breach is fundamental.

Most contracts contain termination provisions. These clauses list the acts by either party that entitle the other party to terminate the contract.[22] Most provisions require that the party about to terminate give notice and allow the party in breach to remedy the breach promptly. It is imperative that the terminating party strictly comply with all limitation periods and notice requirements, or else the termination might be considered wrongful, and the terminating party will be in breach.

2.8   QUASI-CONTRACT

As the result of fundamentally changed conditions, mutual mistake, or abandonment of the contract by one party, the contract may become inapplicable as a basis for determining compensation for the contractor. Yet the owner has received the benefit of the contractor's work and should pay something for it. The principle of **quantum meruit** is used to compensate the contractor. The phrase simply means the amount it is worth. The contractor is paid the reasonable value of the work, including a reasonable profit. Quantum meruit is not, strictly speaking, a form of contract and is therefore referred to as **quasi-contract.** For quantum meruit to apply, there must be no contract in place that applies to the work.

The most frequent application of this principle to construction contracts is with respect to changes in the work. If the change is one that is covered by the change order provisions of the contract, quantum meruit will not apply. But if the changes are such that they fundamentally alter the nature of the contract, quantum meruit may be the best way to deal with compensation.

Most construction agreements contain provisions for valuing changes. They frequently require the owner and contractor to agree on a price before the change is approved. But the reality of building construction is that many changes are required on an expedited basis, and the paperwork containing the owner's signature may follow the event by weeks or even months. Therefore, most standard form agreements

---

22. AIA Document A201-1987 clause 14.1 contains provision for termination by the contractor, and clause 14.2 is termination by the owner for cause. The CCDC 2 provisions are in clause GC 7.1 and 7.2.

provide that if there is no agreement, the owner may order that the contractor proceed with the change and will be paid on a cost-plus basis.[23] In essence, even though the contract may be for a fixed price, the change is performed as though it were under a cost-plus agreement. This is the same result in most cases as if the change were being paid for on a quantum meruit basis.

Another variety of changes is known as **constructive changes:** changes necessitated by the owner with a refusal by the owner to acknowledge that any change has occurred. For example, the owner might wrongfully refuse access to a portion of the site, requiring the contractor to employ more expensive methods of hoisting material. If the owner refuses to acknowledge the change, it will be considered a constructive change, and the owner will be required to pay for it on a quantum meruit basis.

2.9   PROBLEMS

1. An engineer has not been paid the last installment for his consulting work on Project A. The owner says, "If you agree to give up your claim for the remaining fees, I will consider using you as the consultant for Project B. The engineer agrees. Project B is ultimately awarded to another engineer. Is the agreement to forego the fees enforceable? Explain.

2. A contractor has entered into a cost-plus agreement with an owner. While performing the work, the contractor's level of efficiency is lower than expected. The owner refuses to pay the full amount of the contractor's costs. What legal issues are involved? What other facts are needed in order to resolve the dispute?

3. A contractor meets a prospective client at a party. The client says, "I'm looking for someone to build a 50,000 square foot warehouse for me, with cast-in-place concrete walls, on my property on the north side of the city." The contractor replies, "I can build those for $50 per square foot." The client sends a fixed price contract to the contractor, in the amount of $2.5 million. The contractor refuses to sign it. Is there an enforceable agreement? Explain.

4. An owner has failed to make a progress payment when it is due. The contractor delivers a letter that states, "Unless we receive payment by tomorrow noon, we will consider your failure to pay a fundamental breach and the contract at an end." The owner replies, "We will pay you tomorrow at 4:00 p.m. We hope that is acceptable." The contractor replies that it is unacceptable. At 4:00 p.m., the owner presents payment, but the contractor has abandoned the site and sues for fundamental breach. Discuss the legal issues and who should prevail in the lawsuit.

---

23.   AIA Document A201, clause 7.3.6, and CCDC 2 clauses GC 6.1, 6.2, and 6.3.

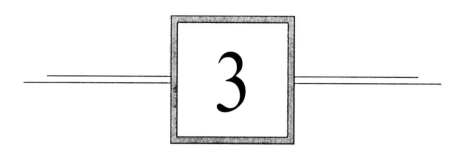

Selected Construction Contract Issues

3.1 INTRODUCTION

Contract issues are at the heart of many construction disputes. Certain issues occur relatively rarely, such as the capacity of the parties to contract or the impossibility of performance. Other issues recur frequently. These frequent issues are the subject matter of this chapter. The four issues discussed are the structuring of contractual relationships among all participants, agency, indemnities, and change orders.

The contractual interrelationship, or privity, between the parties to a construction project will often determine what remedies are available as well as allocation of responsibility and liability. Privity of contract can be maintained between an owner and all the trade contractors if the owner is willing to contract directly with each of them. The price for doing so may well be acceptance by the owner of the responsibility to coordinate the trades. The organization of contractual relationships among members of the design and construction team is often an issue in disputes involving allocation of coordination responsibility although it affects other matters as well.

Agency becomes an issue in many cases where both architect (or engineer) error and construction error are alleged. That is because the contractor will try to prove that the A/E was acting as the owner's agent, and therefore, any error committed by the A/E should be imputed to the owner. Such a finding, in some jurisdictions, can result in an owner losing the right to sue in negligence.[1] An understanding of agency and the limits of agency is essential for any architect or engineer who acts as a consultant on a construction project.

Indemnity provisions are frequently used to determine the intent of the parties to a contract in allocation of risk. Although these provisions are often the most important in a dispute, they receive little attention during negotiations. Indemnity provisions should always be drafted or reviewed by an attorney before they are agreed to.

Change order provisions are used to amend the contract when additions or deletions to the work are required. Disputes often arise when the need for a change is too urgent to allow the procedure set out in the contract for documenting changes to be followed. A further source of frequent difficulty is claims by contractors for impact costs after changes have been approved.

3.2   STRUCTURING THE TEAM

Most building construction projects are set up with two distinct teams: the design team and the construction team. The design team is usually headed by the architect as prime consultant, together with the various engineering consultants. For industrial projects, the prime consultant is more likely one of the engineers. The construction team is often headed by a general contractor, who in turn subcontracts much of the work to specialty subcontractors. But these arrangements are not cast in stone. In fact, the current trend is toward arrangements customized to fit each project. The organization of the team can take different forms, and the form may have a significant effect on the liabilities and responsibilities of the parties.

Design/Build Contracts

Under a **design/build** contract, the owner retains a single party to perform both design and construction services. There is one great advantage to the owner: If anything goes wrong, the contractor cannot point to any other party as being at fault.

One difficulty associated with design/build contracts is that the owner must determine in advance the design parameters. The contractor must be given guidelines; otherwise, the owner might end up with a finished product that does not meet its needs. This is done by specifying the performance criteria. For example, an owner who wants a power generating station built would specify the required output, the environmental constraints, efficiency requirements, and other operating parame-

---

1.   In jurisdictions that have not enacted a "comparative negligence" statute, the common law rule is that a plaintiff who is contributorily negligent cannot recover anything. For further discussion, see footnote 13.

ters. It is not uncommon for the owner to have a conceptual design prepared, on which the design/build contractors will bid.

Design/build contracts are most appropriate in industries where the contractors have the design expertise. For example, in pulp mills, boiler design is done by the boiler contractor. In building construction, the detailed design of elevator systems is often done by the elevator subcontractor.

Multiple Prime Contractors

Every construction project requires coordination of the subtrades. Someone must perform that function, whether it is the owner, a general contractor, or a construction manager. When a general contractor is hired, that contractor gets paid a fee in order to assume that coordination responsibility and to accept liability for any failure to coordinate.

For various reasons, owners may prefer to hire all the trade contractors directly and not hire a general contractor. Each of the trade contractors is then considered a prime contractor because each has contracted directly with the owner. Because there is privity between the owner and each contractor, the owner can sue the trade contractor for breach of contract, and vice versa.[2] This arrangement will save the owner the fee charged by the general contractor. The owner must then perform the coordination function or else hire a construction manager.

Unless the owner has the in-house expertise needed to manage a construction project, a construction manager is a necessity. Standard form agreements for construction managers include provisions relating to review of design, scheduling, coordination, safety, cost analysis, construction feasibility, and claims evaluation.[3]

It is easy for disputes to develop in the absence of a general contractor, and the risk to the owner is greatly increased. If one trade contractor is delayed by another, liability will likely end up back with the owner for failure to coordinate. Similarly, if someone is injured on the site, the responsibility for safety may fall on the owner if that responsibility has not been delegated to a general contractor or construction manager.[4]

There is one further reason that construction managers are sometimes preferred to general contractors. A general contractor is often in an adversarial relationship

---

2.   Under a single general contractor arrangement, the owner could sue a subcontractor for breach of contract because the owner is an intended third-party beneficiary of the contract between the subcontractor and the general contractor, but the subcontractor could not sue the owner for breach. In Canada, under a single general contractor arrangement, neither the owner nor the subcontractor could sue each other for breach of contract. The right to sue under the contract may be significant since the contract may allow remedies different from the law of negligence, and different limitation periods may apply.

3.   Several forms are available, including those published by the AIA, the CCA, the Associated General Contractors, and the General Services Administration.

4.   For a good analysis of the liability of construction managers, see *Construction Litigation* (published by the Practicing Law Institute) by Cushman, chapter 7.

with the owner to some degree because the contractor must look out for his or her own interest. The construction manager, on the other hand, is required to act in the owner's best interest.

Using a multiple prime arrangement affects more than the ability of the parties to sue in contract. It may also have an effect on the mechanics' lien rights of the parties. Although mechanics' lien statutes vary from one jurisdiction to another, some jurisdictions limit a lien claimant's holdback rights to a percentage of the dollar value of the contract between the owner and the prime contractor under whose contract the work is being performed. Using multiple prime contractors under such a scheme would reduce the holdback available to any one claimant. In some jurisdictions, the limitation period for filing a mechanics' lien claim is triggered by substantial completion of the contract between the owner and the prime contractor. Multiple prime contracts would create a multitude of limitation periods.

Multiple Prime Consultants

When hiring consultants, the owner may choose to retain one designer with responsibility for all aspects of the design or, instead, choose to contract directly with each consultant. Similar considerations apply as with contractors. For example, a subconsultant has no privity of contract with the owner and, therefore, cannot sue the owner to recover his or her fee.

Even under a multiple prime consultant arrangement, there is still a need for coordination between design disciplines. The owner should ensure that at least one of the consultants is charged with the responsibility of coordinating all the design work; otherwise, discrepancies in the drawings may cause the contractor to claim for cost increases that the owner may not be able to recover from anyone.

Other functions are typically performed by a prime consultant, such as evaluation of progress claims and extras, and site inspection. It is essential that the owner designate at least one of the consultants to fulfil the traditional role of prime consultant, even if contracting directly with all consultants.

3.3   AGENCY AND AUTHORITY

An agent is a person who is authorized to enter into a contract on behalf of another party. The **agency** relationship is essential to virtually all construction projects. A poor understanding of the mechanics of agency or the scope of authority has been the source of many construction disputes.

There are three parties to an agency relationship: the principal, the agent, and the third party. Typically, the owner is the principal, the architect or engineer is the agent, and the contractor is the third party.

The principal can give the agent authority in one of two ways: express authority or apparent authority. Express authority (sometimes called actual authority) is created by a contract, which may or may not be in writing, between the principal and the agent. For example, the agreement for design services between the owner and architect should define the limits of the architect's authority to bind the owner. The AIA agreement provides that the architect:

> ... may authorize minor changes in the Work not involving an adjustment in the Contract Sum or an extension of Contract Time which are not inconsistent with the intent of the Contract Documents.[5]

Any change authorized by the architect that fits within the express authority will be binding on the owner, even if the owner does not like the change.

Apparent authority (sometimes called ostensible authority or implied authority) is created by representations made by the principal to the third party. This will create an **implied agency** relationship. The contract between the owner and the contractor will almost always contain such representations. The CCDC 2 contract makes the following representation:

> The Consultant will have authority to act on behalf of the Owner only to the extent provided in the Contract Documents, unless otherwise modified by written agreement.[6]

Even in the absence of any agreement between the owner and architect, the representation by the owner to the contractor will create an apparent authority in the architect. In fact, implied authority may be created simply by appointment of the architect or by other conduct of the owner. If the owner knows that the architect is exceeding his or her authority, but does nothing to correct the situation, that may expand the apparent authority.

As illustrated by the extract from the CCDC 2 document, not all grants of authority are absolute. An agent may be authorized to do certain acts or to enter into only one transaction on behalf of the principal, or monetary limits may be placed on the agent's authority, such as the right to approve change orders with a value of less than $10,000. The principal must make these limits known to the third party; otherwise, the principal will be bound if the agent exceeds the limits of actual authority but is within the apparent authority.

An agent owes a duty to act in the principal's interest.[7] But not every act performed by an architect or engineer on a job site is done as the owner's agent. The consultant must act impartially in some cases, such as in approving payments, issuing the certificate of substantial completion, and evaluating claims. The consultant must always be aware of whether the act being performed requires **impartiality** or fidelity to the owner.

---

5.   AIA Document B141, clause 2.6.13.

6.   CCDC 2, clause GC 2.1.1.

7.   This is called a fiduciary relationship.

CASE STUDY

Massachusetts Bonding and Insurance Co. v. Lentz, 9 P.2d 408 (Ariz. S.C. 1932).

A contractor entered into a written agreement to construct a building according to plans and specifications prepared by the architect, Nolan. It was expressly stipulated that the owner should not be liable for any extras or additions to the contract unless pursuant to a written order signed by the owner or a written order from the architect stating that the owner has authorized the change. The architect orally approved some changes, which were performed by the contractor.

The contractor, seeking to recover for these extras, argued that the architect was acting as agent for the owner, and therefore the owner was bound by the requests for extras made by the architect. The court made the following ruling:

> The fallacy of the appellant's position is in regard to the authority of the architect to bind the owner. It contends, and truly, that under the provisions of the contract the architect was the agent of the owner, but it overlooks and disregards the fact that such agency was not an unlimited one, but one which was specifically limited, so far at least as changes in the contract were concerned, by the provisions that such changes be in writing, either signed by the owner or by the architect, and in the latter case the order must specify that the owner had authorized the change. The contractor . . . knew of the limitation of the agency, and it was incumbent on the appellant to prove that the appellee had waived that provision of the contract and authorized the architect to make oral changes therein.
>
> We hold, therefore, that so far as changes in the contract made . . . without the consent of the owner are involved, they constitute, not a change in the contract, but a breach thereof by the contractor for which the owner, if damaged, may recover.

Questions

1. Would the result have been different if the architect had signed the change orders and stated that the owner had authorized them, even if the owner did not authorize them?
2. Assuming the facts in question 1, would the owner have had any recourse? Explain.
3. Does the contractor have any recourse against the architect?
4. How would the contractor prove that the owner had waived the provision of the contract?

Analysis

1. The result would have been different. Even though there would be no actual authority, there would be apparent or implied authority, which the contractor would have relied on in performing the changes.

2. The owner could sue the architect for breach of contract, assuming that the contract between the owner (principal) and architect (agent) did not authorize such conduct.

3. Perhaps. The contractor could claim against the architect for "breach of warranty of authority" on the theory that the architect represented himself as having authority when in fact he did not.

4. He could show that the course of conduct between the parties was such that the provision was never enforced.

3.4 INDEMNITIES

Many construction contracts contain an indemnity provision. A contractual indemnity is a means of allocating risk. When one party (the indemnitor) indemnifies another (the indemnitee) against a specified risk, it means that if that risk materializes, the indemnitor will bear the loss. The CCDC 2 contract contains the following indemnity clause:

> The Contractor shall indemnify and hold harmless the Owner and the Consultant, their agents and employees from and against claims, demands, losses, costs, damages, actions, suits or proceedings (hereinafter called "claims"), by third parties that arise out of, or are attributable to, the Contractor's performance of the Contract, provided such claims are:
>
> 1. attributable to bodily injury, sickness, disease, or death, or to injury to or destruction of tangible property, and
> 2. caused by negligent acts or omissions of the Contractor or anyone for whose acts the Contractor may be liable, and
> 3. made in writing within a period of six years from the date of Substantial Performance . . . or within such shorter period as may be prescribed by any limitation statute of the province.[8]

The effect of this provision is to make the contractor liable for any loss that the owner may suffer as a result of a claim by another party that is attributable to the contractor's negligence (or the negligence of a party for whose acts the contractor is liable) that results in property damage or personal injury.

In the absence of an indemnity clause, the contractor is still liable to the owner for the contractor's own negligence. The contractor is also liable to third parties (including the owner) at common law, without such a provision, for the negligence

---

8. Clause GC 12.1.1.

of its employees because of the doctrine of **vicarious liability**.[9] However, in the absence of such a provision, a contractor would not normally be liable for the negligence of an independent contractor such as a subcontractor. The CCDC 2 indemnity provision could expose the contractor to liability for such negligence.[10] The AIA indemnity provision expressly includes subcontractors' acts.[11]

Many indemnity provisions include attorneys fees as one of the losses indemnified. This would mean that the owner would be reimbursed for the reasonable defense costs associated with such a claim.

In the CCDC 2 indemnity provision, the contractor indemnifies the owner for the contractor's negligence. The contractor is essentially saying, "I'll pay you if I am negligent and it causes you loss." Some indemnity provisions make the indemnitor liable for the negligence of the indemnitee. This would be like the contractor saying, "I'll pay you if *you* are negligent and suffer loss." In essence, it makes the indemnitor an insurer. Some courts have had difficulty with such provisions because they may seem unfair at first glance, and because they may promote a disregard for safety, but a properly drafted indemnity is likely to be viewed as an allocation of risk and as such is likely to be enforced.

The indemnity clauses in many standard form contracts do not expressly exclude liability for design errors.[12] If the owner is sued for a loss caused by a combination of both design and construction error, an indemnity that is not limited to contractor negligence will expand the liability of the contractor. Many jurisdictions have adopted comparative negligence statutes that have the effect of reducing the liability of each party to the percentage of fault attributable to them, but a wide indemnity such as the CCDC 2 provision could negate that effect.[13] These provisions are critically important in determining liability and should be examined carefully during negotiations.

---

9. Vicarious liability, also called *respondeat superior*, is a rule of law that makes one party liable for the acts of another. For example, an employer is vicariously liable for the negligence of his or her employees, and a partner is vicariously liable for some of the acts of his or her partners.

10. Although an argument could be made that the wording "for whose acts he may be liable" does not create any new liability.

11. AIA Document A201-1987 clause 3.18.1.

12. The CCDC 2 does not contain an express exclusion. The AIA A201 indemnity, on the other hand, is "only to the extent caused" by contractor (or subcontractor) error.

13. The common law rule, in the absence of a comparative negligence statute, is that if two parties contribute to the same loss, both parties are jointly and severally liable for the full amount. If the plaintiff was also contributorily negligent, the defendants are not liable. Comparative negligence allows a negligent plaintiff to recover but reduces the amount according to the plaintiff's percentage of fault. Fault as between the defendants is also apportioned, thereby allowing each defendant to ultimately pay only that percentage attributed to him or her (assuming none of the defendants is impecunious). Some jurisdictions have adopted comparative negligence statutes that eliminate joint and several liability entirely.

The indemnity provision does not limit the liability of the indemnitor. It creates liability where none may have existed, but it does not take away liability that is otherwise existing. The owner, for example, is given an indemnity with respect to claims by third parties. But if the contractor is negligent and causes the owner loss, even if no one sues the owner, the contractor would be liable. Many standard form contracts contain language that states this principle.[14]

CASE STUDY
Jacobsen Construction Company v. Blaine Construction Co., Inc., 863 P.2d 1329 (Utah App. 1993).

The following is an extract from the case report:

On March 31, 1986, Jacobsen Construction Co. (JCC), a general contractor, entered into a construction contract under which Blaine was to provide all concrete work necessary for the construction of the University Park Hotel, owned by University Inn Associates (UIA). The contract also contained an indemnification provision under which Blaine agreed to indemnify JCC and UIA from enumerated items of property damage and personal injury unless the harm was caused by their "active negligence." On September 25, 1986, one of Blaine's employees, Modesto Ruybal, suffered bodily injury when he fell through a hole in the concrete floor that Blaine had constructed. Mr. Ruybal fell through the hole while he and another workman were carrying a sheet of plywood.

On August 17, 1989, Mr. Ruybal filed suit against JCC and UIA, alleging that both JCC and UIA failed to provide a hazard-free work environment, and thus were liable for his injuries. Subsequently, JCC and UIA filed a third party complaint against Blaine seeking indemnification under the contract.

Blaine argues that the indemnification provision in the contract is void because it contravenes public policy. We agree. Utah Code Ann. ss. 13-8-1 (1992) provides in pertinent part:

A covenant, promise, agreement or understanding in, or in connection with or collateral to, a contract or agreement relative to the construction, alteration or repair or maintenance of a building . . . purporting to indemnify the promisee against liability for damages arising out of bodily injury to persons or damage to property caused by or resulting from the *sole negligence* of the

---

14. The CCDC 2 provision is GC 1.3.1, which states that "Except as expressly provided in the Contract Documents, the duties and obligations imposed by the Contract Documents and the rights and remedies available thereunder shall be in addition to and not a limitation of any duties, obligations, rights and remedies otherwise imposed or available by law."

promisee, his agents or employees, or indemnitee, is against public policy and is void and unenforceable (emphasis added).

In other words, an indemnity agreement in the construction industry violates public policy if it requires indemnification of the indemnitee for its sole negligence.

The indemnity agreement between Blaine and JCC provides that if an injury is the result of "active negligence on the part of the owner or contractor . . . and is not caused or contributed to by an omission to perform some duty also imposed on subcontractor . . . such indemnity shall not apply to such party guilty of such active negligence."

Thus, if JCC or UIA were solely and *actively* negligent, they would not be indemnified by Blaine. However, if JCC or UIA were solely and *passively* negligent, Blaine would be required to indemnify them. Because the indemnity agreement mandates that Blaine indemnify JCC and UIA in the event they are solely and passively negligent, the agreement violates public policy as expressed in the Utah Code. Accordingly, we vacate the grant of summary judgment and remand the case for trial.

Questions

1. Assume that the injuries were caused by a combination of Blaine's and JCC's negligence. Would the indemnity apply in the absence of the Utah statute? Explain.

2. Assume the facts given in question 1. Is it fair to make the indemnity agreement unenforceable because of the possibility that there might be sole and passive negligence at some other time? Could the court have said that the agreement is enforceable *except* where there is sole and passive negligence?

3. How could the contract have been drafted so as to be enforceable?

Analysis

1. In the absence of the statute, the indemnity would seem to apply. To answer definitively, one would need to review the complete indemnity clause. The exclusion becomes effective (according to its own terms) if there is no negligence on the part of Blaine, but as long as Blaine is at fault, it probably cannot invoke the exclusion.

2. Fair or not, the court has taken the approach that as long as there is any chance that a situation can arise that brings the clause in conflict with the statute, the clause must be held void. It is the duty of the party drafting the contract to anticipate such possibilities.

3. It could have expressly excluded any indemnity where there was sole negligence, active or passive, on the part of the JCC or UIA.

CASE STUDY

Goldman v. Ecco-Phoenix Electric Corp., 396 P.2d 377 (Cal. S.C. 1964).

The prime contractor, Goldman (operating under the name Clovis Construction Co.) agreed, as one of the terms of its contract with the owner, to indemnify the owner for damage caused as a result of the construction. The subcontract (as most subcontracts do) incorporated by reference the terms of the prime contract into the subcontract. Clovis argued that the subcontractor therefore assumed this indemnity obligation. The court held:

> We conclude only that an indemnification agreement calling for financial protection against one's own negligence cannot rest upon language so loose and obscure as that of the instant contract.... The provision would only apply if the injury resulted solely from Ecco's negligence.

Questions

1. Why was the court reluctant to find that the indemnity applied to these facts?

2. How could the indemnity have been drafted so as to be enforceable?

Analysis

1. It was included in the subcontract by reference only, rather than directly, which cast some doubt on whether the subcontractor knew it was taking on that risk.

2. If the provision explicitly stated that the subcontractor agreed to indemnify the general contractor for its own negligence, and was receiving consideration for accepting that risk, it would have a greater likelihood of being upheld.

3.5   CHANGE ORDERS

Construction agreements almost always contain a provision for changes to the scope of work.[15] In this respect, they differ from many other commercial agreements. It is not uncommon to have hundreds of change orders issued during a large and com-

---

15. Changes that result in an increase in the contract price are called "extras."

plex project, and even on small and simple jobs, one can anticipate that some changes will be made.

Changes to scope of work can be caused by a variety of reasons: The owner may want an enhancement or change in design; unforeseen conditions may become apparent that necessitate additional work; one of the parties may suggest cost-saving measures; design error may necessitate changes; or the municipal authorities may demand changes to suit their interpretation of the building code. The cause of the change will determine who is responsible for paying for it.

The owner will, of course, be responsible for requested enhancements and requested changes to design. In addition, the owner is generally responsible for changes caused by hidden conditions. It does not matter that the condition was unforeseen; what is relevant is whether the condition was reasonably foreseeable. This class of extras is most prevalent on renovation projects because the existing structures are often not accurately documented by drawings, and detailed investigation may not be possible until demolition is performed. Extras due to unforeseeable conditions are also common in the context of claims for subsurface soils conditions, and some contracts contain express provisions for such claims.[16]

Extras for Design Negligence

It is not unusual for the designer to have a different interpretation of the relevant code than the officials who must enforce it. Failure by the designer to anticipate the official interpretation is not necessarily negligence. If the designer's interpretation was reasonable, and reasonable inquiries were made, that should exclude liability for negligence. Whether or not the designer is responsible, the contractor will generally be entitled to an extra for the increase in cost. Liability of the designer is relevant only to the issue of whether the owner can recover the extra from the designer.

It is understood by most participants in the industry that no design is perfect and that a small level of changes due to design error should be expected. For this and other reasons, owners often carry a contingency in the budget to cover change orders. Contingencies usually range from 5 to 10 percent of the contract amount, but may be more than 10 percent or less than 5 percent depending on the complexity, size, and duration of the job. In theory, the owner is entitled to recover from the designer the extra costs due to design negligence, but in practice, if the cost is within the acceptable and expected range, the owner will not generally attempt to recover from the designer. No hard and fast rule exists on what range is acceptable.

---

16.   The AIA Document A201 clause 4.3.6 requires that the unknown condition "differ materially" from those indicated in the contract. CCDC 2 clause GC 6.4.1 authorizes extra payment if conditions differ materially from those indicated in the contract or if "physical conditions of a nature . . . differ materially from those ordinarily found to exist and generally recognized as inherent in construction activities of the character provided for in the Contract Documents."

Impact Costs

When an owner approves a change for a quoted price, it is usually with the expectation that the price includes all costs associated with the change. If the contractor were to come back at a later date and say, "By the way, about that price of $10,000 I quoted you for change order number 25, I didn't include some of the costs, and the total is now $100,000. And that work is now complete, so pay up," the owner could justifiably say, "If I had known that the change would cost $100,000, I would not have approved it."

The change order clauses in most standard form agreements provide, as one method of valuation, that the contractor and owner may agree on a fixed price for the change. The purpose is to provide some certainty to the owner, who must ultimately decide whether the change should proceed.

Yet many contractors submit their change order quotations with the following qualification (or words to this effect):

> The price quoted does not include any allowance for delay or impact associated with this change. The Contractor expressly reserves the right to claim at a later date for all costs associated with delay and impact resulting from this change.

If the owner accepts the quotation subject to this qualification, the contractor would not be barred from making such a claim at a later date. The owner would not obtain any certainty from the price because the impact claim could be substantial.

For this reason, owners often include language in the request for quotation, which requires the contractor to include in the price all costs associated with the change, including impact costs, and identify *before the change is approved* how much of a delay is being claimed.

One reason owners and contractors take these positions is the cumulative impact of many changes. One small change may be unlikely to cause a significant delay. But 100 small changes could amount to 10 percent of the contract price and delay completion by a month. Contractors therefore seek to protect themselves from this impact by reserving the right to claim for it at a later date.

One method of compensating the contractor for impact while providing the owner certainty in pricing is to force the contractor to make all claims for incremental delay at the time the change is being quoted. For example, a small change such as adding some finishes might add a half day to the schedule. If the change does not affect any critical path items, no delay or impact would be approved. The contractor would be forced to evaluate the financial effect of a half-day delay and include that component in the quotation.

Timing and Pricing of Changes and Performance Under Protest

Standard form contracts may require the contractor to obtain approval for the change before proceeding with the work, or else proceed at risk. The AIA form states that the contractor "shall proceed promptly, unless otherwise provided in the change order."[17] The CCDC 2 contract states that "The Contractor shall not perform a change in the Work without a Change Order or a Change Directive."[18] Because of the wording in the AIA document, owners using that document will often issue a request for a price from the contractor before formally issuing or approving the change order.

Documentation of change orders frequently cannot keep up with construction activity. Contractors are under pressure to perform work that has been requested by the owner, with the promise that the documentation will follow. Disputes develop when the documentation does not follow, and there is disagreement over what was said or promised.

Almost all construction contracts contain a provision allowing the owner or architect to order that work proceed in the absence of a change order, with the cost and schedule issues to be resolved later.[19] These provisions are necessary in two situations: where no agreement is reached on price and where there is fundamental disagreement on whether the work is truly a change or is part of the original scope of work.

There have been cases involving contractors who performed work as directed by the owner or consultant and have been denied the right to compensation on the basis that the act of performance was deemed to be an admission that the work was part of the contractor's responsibility. In other words, the contractor is directed to perform work that the contractor believes is an extra, but that the owner contends is part of the contractor's original responsibility. In the absence of a contract provision that allows the issue to be resolved later, the contractor is faced with a very difficult choice: Either refuse to perform the work or perform it. If the contractor refuses to perform and turns out to be wrong (that is, it is part of the contractor's work), the contractor will be in breach of contract, and the owner may be entitled to terminate the contract or sue the contractor for damages. If the contractor does perform, he or she may be denied compensation even if it is a legitimate extra.[20]

Some jurisdictions[21] have enacted legislation to address this harsh result and allow the contractor to perform under protest. As long as a formal protest is issued in a timely manner, that preserves the contractor's right to prove that the work is extra to the contract. To ensure that the contractor is given this basic right, the contract should contain such a provision as well. It is essential that the contractor com-

---

17. AIA Document A201-1987 clause 7.1.3.

18. Clause GC 6.1.2. A change directive is an order to proceed with the work where the Owner and Contractor cannot agree on the price or method of pricing the change.

19. CCDC 2 clause 6.3 and AIA Document A201-1987 clause 7.3 allow the owner to issue a "construction change directive" in the absence of total agreement on the terms of a change order.

20. That is what happened to the contractor in the case of *Peter Kiewit Sons' Co. of Canada Ltd.* v. *Eakins Construction Ltd.*, [1960] S.C.R. 361.

21. For example, British Columbia, *The Law and Equity Act*, RSBC 1979, c. 224, s. 58 as amended.

ply with all formal requirements for protest, including notice requirements (typically, protest in writing, delivered to all parties), limitation periods, and any other statutory and contractual requirements.

CASE STUDY
Julian v. Keefer, 382 S.W. 2d 723 (Miss. C.A. 1964).

The plaintiff, a contractor, sued the defendant owner to recover payment for work performed on the theory of quantum meruit. The contractor alleged that as a result of changes ordered and performed without written authorization, the contract had been abandoned and therefore the owners should pay the entire cost of construction on what would amount to a cost-plus basis. The court disagreed:

> Seeking to avoid the binding effect of the building contract, plaintiffs charge that they were misled by defendants' conduct into an honest belief that defendants intended and consented to an abandonment of the contract.... We find no persuasive significance in the foregoing. The contract specifically provides that "the owner may order changes in the work, the contract sum being adjusted accordingly." ... And, although the contract further provides that "such orders and adjustments be in writing," we believe that the course of action practised by the parties indicates a mutual waiver of that requirement. It is the established rule that the habitual acceptance of extra work done on oral orders in connection with a contract, and payment therefore, amount to a waiver of a contract clause providing that no claims for extra work or materials shall be allowed unless same be done or finished in pursuance of an order in writing.

Questions

1. Would the result be different if the changes performed by the contractor had never been paid for by the owner?
2. The court was agreeable to award the contractor compensation for all changes ordered whether or not they were in writing. Is this not the same as a quantum meruit ruling that the contractor was seeking?

Analysis

1. Likely so. For there to be a mutual waiver, some conduct by the owner must be different from the terms of the written agreement.
2. It is not. A finding that the contract had been abandoned and compensation on a quantum meruit basis would apply to the original fixed price portion of the contract, whereas the court's ruling applies only to extras.

3.6 PROBLEMS

1. A contractor is asked by the architect to add some concrete foundation walls, at substantial cost. The work is urgent and must be performed before a price can be agreed on. Following performance, the contractor submits a price, containing impact costs. The architect rejects the price but is prepared to agree if the impact costs are deleted. The architect threatens to delay the approval process unless the contractor agrees. Reluctantly, the contractor agrees. After the project is complete, the contractor claims for those impact costs. Discuss the legal issues raised.

2. The agreement between an owner and contractor states that the engineer can approve change orders with a value of less than $10,000. The owner instructs the engineer not to approve changes with value greater than $5,000. The engineer approves a change, without the owner's permission, with a value of $8,000. The owner is informed after the fact and refuses to pay for the change. Is the owner bound by the change order? Why or why not?

3. A contractor indemnifies an owner "for any and all losses, including pure economic loss, attributable in whole or in part to the negligence of the contractor." The contract is subject to the law in a jurisdiction that has not abolished joint and several liability. Because of a combination of design error and construction error, the owner suffers a $100,000 loss. The architect is 50 percent at fault. What is the maximum possible liability of the contractor? Why?

4. An owner developing a warehouse project in the United States hires a general contractor, who in turn subcontracts the concrete work to a subcontractor. The general contractor fails to pay the subcontractor. The work performed by the subcontractor is deficient. Can the subcontractor sue the owner, and can the owner sue the subcontractor, for breach of contract? Explain.

Negligence

4.1 OVERVIEW

Although claims against participants in the design and construction process may assert a variety of theories, most will include both breach of contract and negligence, and virtually all will include claims based on negligence. Accordingly, an understanding of the principles of **negligence** is essential.

The law of negligence in its modern form was born in the late 1920s and early 1930s.[1] Since then, the law of negligence has evolved considerably. Yet the basic elements of negligence are consistent from one jurisdiction to another. To succeed in a negligence claim, the plaintiff must prove:

1. That the defendant owed the plaintiff a "duty of care"
2. That the defendant breached that duty

---

1. The ground-breaking case in the United States was *Palsgraf* v. *Long Island Railroad Co.*, 248 N.Y. 339, 162 N.E. 99 (1928). In Canada, it began with the English case of *Donoghue* v. *Stevenson,* [1932] A.C. 562 (H.L.).

3. That the plaintiff suffered loss or damage

4. That the breach was the proximate cause of the plaintiff's loss

These elements also form the basis for important defenses against negligence claims. A defendant need prove only that any one of the elements does not exist, and the claim must fail. If there was no duty of care owed, or if there was no breach, or no damage suffered, or no causation, there can be no recovery.

The elements of negligence—duty of care, breach, damage, and causation—are defined and discussed in detail in this chapter. Of these elements, duty of care is the least settled area of the law. Several examples such as the duty owed to subsequent purchasers and the duty with respect to pure economic loss are examined. Breach is a legal concept that involves the establishment of a standard of care. The discussion of the standard applicable to architects, engineers, and contractors focuses on problems that have given rise to litigation and avoidance of those problems. Causation and damage (or the lack thereof) are often raised as defenses in construction negligence cases, and it is in that context that those two elements are discussed. Finally, this chapter includes a brief explanation of joint and several liability and the role it can play in creating a "deep pockets" judgment against a defendant in a construction negligence case.

The basic principle on which negligence law is based in both the United States and Canada is reasonable foreseeability. The law does not demand perfection. Instead, it sets standards of reasonableness, a term that may seem vague and subjective, but that has been defined by many courts over many years. The mere fact that an error or failure has occurred is not sufficient, in most cases, to prove negligence.

Claims in negligence against construction professionals can be particularly distressing, not just because of the financial implications, but because they impugn the professionalism and competence of the defendant. The long-term consequences of a successful claim of negligence on the reputation of a designer or contractor can, in extreme cases, put the defendant out of business. For all these reasons, such claims are frequently defended vigorously.

4.2   DUTY OF CARE

The early cases established that a duty of care must be owed before a negligence claim can succeed. Duty of care is a concept based on foreseeability. If the defendant could reasonably foresee, at the time he or she committed the negligent act, that the plaintiff might suffer loss or damage, then a duty of care is owed to the plaintiff. For example, an engineer designing a building should reasonably foresee that if the design is performed negligently, a tenant might be injured in the event of a collapse. Therefore, any occupant injured in such a collapse would be owed a duty of care by the engineer. On the other hand, if the building is used by an occupant for a purpose that could not reasonably have been anticipated, such as storage of explosives, and such use destroys the structure, no duty of care would be owed.

Many courts have been afraid that allowing one party to sue another, despite the lack of a contractual relationship between them, might open up the floodgates to excessive litigation. Some might argue that the floodgates are indeed open in the United States. Various cases have caused courts to try to close the floodgates, to a degree, by using duty of care. In the construction context, some of the instances in which duty of care has been applied defensively include questions regarding:

1. Whether an engineer owes a duty to an owner, assuming there is no privity between the engineer and owner

2. Whether an architect owes a duty to a contractor to point out construction errors and whether a duty is owed for errors in the plans and specifications

3. Whether the designer owes a duty of care to construction workers with respect to safety issues

4. Whether a contractor owes a duty to subsequent purchasers for construction defects, particularly where the contractor has provided a narrow warranty to the original purchaser

5. Whether a duty of care is owed for pure economic loss, where no physical damage or injury has occurred

The possibilities are endless. The issues described here have not all been decided consistently from one jurisdiction to another. Duty of care is more easily established if there is a pre-existing relationship between the plaintiff and defendant. If the parties have contracted together, it is extremely likely that a duty of care will be established, absent any contractual language to the contrary.

Directions Courts Have Taken on Duty of Care Issues

Duty of the A/E to the Owner

It is now generally accepted that both architects and consulting engineers owe a duty of care to protect owners despite the lack of contractual privity between them. In the case of *District of Surrey* v. *Carroll Hatch and Associates*, the engineer in question notified the architect of his concerns since his contract was with the architect. He failed to tell the owner and was found liable.[2] The same conclusion has been reached by U.S. courts.[3] Thus liability may exist with or without the existence of a contractual relationship.

Duty of the A/E to the Contractor

A more interesting question is whether the designer who prepares plans and specifications for bid owes a duty of care to the successful bidder for losses caused by

---

2. (1979) 101 D.L.R. (3d) 218 (B.C.C.A.).

3. In the United States, intended third-party beneficiaries of a contract can also sue to enforce that contract. The owner is an intended third-party beneficiary of the contract between the prime consultant and the subconsultant. Therefore, the owner could sue the subconsultant in both contract and negligence. This third-party beneficiary rule is not the law in Canada.

errors in those plans and specifications. The Supreme Court of Canada recently considered the issue in the case of *Edgeworth Construction Ltd.* v. *N.D. Lea & Assoc. Ltd.*[4] and concluded that a duty of care was owed. This conclusion was based in part on the fact that the bidding period is too short to allow bidders to conduct a thorough review of the accuracy of the engineering work and that duplication of the work would be costly. This result is consistent with the approach taken in the United States.[5]

The floodgates have opened wide on this issue in California, where a designer was held liable to the contractor for failing to supervise the contractor.[6] This result has been criticized since it allows the contractor to escape responsibility for its own negligence and breach of contract, and to place that responsibility on the architect.[7]

Duty of the A/E to Workers and Other Third Parties

Industry custom and practice dictates that contractors rather than design professionals are responsible for means, methods, and techniques of construction, absent contractual language to the contrary. The standard form of agreement between architect and client published by the AIA is consistent with this approach.[8] However, if the designer accepts responsibility for supervising the construction, a duty of care may be owed to workers for safety hazards.[9] This is one area of the law that contains divergent case authority. In some jurisdictions, lawsuits by injured workers against their employer are barred by virtue of the applicable workers' compensation legislation. Some workers' compensation legislation bars lawsuits against *anyone* registered as an employer under the statute, and the designer may be registered in some circumstances.[10]

Claims by third parties who are not part of the construction process (that is, excluding contractors, subcontractors, suppliers, workers, owners, and consultants)

---

4. [1993] 3 S.C.R. 206.

5. *C.H. Leavell & Company* v. *Glantz Contracting Corp. of Louisiana, Inc.*, 322 F. Supp. 779 (E.D. La. 1971).

6. *U.S.* v. *Rogers and Rogers*, 161 F. Supp. 132 (S.D. Cal. 1958).

7. See *Architects and Engineers* by Acret (McGraw-Hill, 1984, 2 ed.), p. 47, as well as *Architect-Engineer Liability Under Colorado Law* by Byrum C. Lee Jr. (The Cambridge Institute, 1987), pp. 39–40.

8. AIA Document B141-1987, s. 2.6.5.

9. In the case of *Hortman* v. *Becker Const. Co.*, 92 Wis. 2d 210, 284 N.W. 2d 621 (1979), no duty was owed because of the wording of the contract although the court looked to the contract to determine the extent of the architect's control.

10. For example, in British Columbia, the *Workers Compensation Act*, RSBC 1979, c. 437, s. 10 states that "The provisions of this Part are in lieu of any right and rights of action, statutory or otherwise, founded on a breach of duty of care or any other cause of action, whether that duty or cause of action is imposed by or arises by reason of law or contract, express or implied, to which a worker, dependant or member of the family of the worker is or may be entitled against the employer of the worker, or against any employer within the scope of this Part, or against any worker, in respect of any personal injury, disablement or death arising out of and in the course of employment and no action in respect of it lies."

for physical loss or injury can be made against owners, occupiers, designers, and builders, as long as reasonable foreseeability can be established. Such claims are subject to the same definition of duty that applies to claims by workers against architects.

Duty to Subsequent Purchasers

Courts do not determine whether a duty of care exists strictly on the basis of legal analysis. Policy considerations are a factor as well. Consider the problem of the contractor or developer who is aware of latent defects in a recently completed project. A **latent defect** is one that is not discoverable through reasonable inspection. The contractor or developer discloses all these defects to the purchaser, who demands (and receives) a substantial reduction in the purchase price on account of the defects. The purchaser then resells the property to a subsequent purchaser without disclosing the defects despite the legal obligation to do so. The subsequent purchaser eventually discovers the defects, cannot locate the original purchaser, and sues the contractor in negligence.

Strict legal analysis might dictate that a duty of care is owed because the contractor could reasonably foresee, at the time the negligent construction was performed, that a subsequent purchaser might suffer loss. But fairness might dictate the opposite result. This example is given to illustrate the point that some legal problems, such as duty of care, may not be susceptible to rigid analysis and can give rise to opposite conclusions by different courts.[11]

CASE STUDY
Wright v. Creative Corp., 498 P.2d 1179 (Colo. C.A. 1972).

The plaintiff was a subsequent purchaser of a home built by the defendant. Wright's son was injured by running into a plate glass sliding door, and Wright alleged that tempered glass should have been installed and that failure to do so amounted to negligence. Wright also sued for breach of an implied warranty on the theory that such a warranty should apply not only to the original purchaser, but to subsequent purchasers as well.

Wright succeeded on the negligence claim and failed on the warranty claim. Following are extracts from the reasons of the court:

---

11. For example, see *Robert E. Owen & Assoc.* v. *Gyongyosi,* 433 So. 2d 1023 (Fla. App. 4 Dist. 1983), and *Howe* v. *Bishop,* 446 So. 2d 11 (Ala. 1984). In Canada, it has recently been established by the Supreme Court of Canada that subsequent purchasers can recover against designers and contractors for physical damage as well as pure economic loss, except where such loss is with respect to shoddy workmanship that creates no danger. See *Winnipeg Condominium Corporation No. 36 v. Bird Construction Co. Ltd.* (not yet reported).

The Colorado Supreme Court has held that, in matters of negligence, liability attaches to a wrongdoer, not because of a breach of a contractual relationship, but because of a breach of duty which results in an injury to others. . . .

The court then reviewed the *MacPherson* doctrine, which says that after work has been completed and accepted by the owner, the contractor will not be liable to third parties injured as a consequence of the construction even though manufacturers of chattels (movable property) would be liable.

Aside from the technical requirement of privity, the reason given for such a rule is that there would be endless liability for the contractor or builder if liability did not cease with acceptance of his work. It is argued that the nature of most structures on real estate is so complicated that defects would be attributed to the contractor which were actually the result of the owner's negligence or of other extraneous factors such as the weather.

This reasoning is not persuasive, and we can see no purpose in distinguishing between chattels and structures on real property when applying the *MacPherson* view of tort duty.

Questions

1. What was the court's concern in the *MacPherson* case? How could the courts or the legislature deal with those concerns without providing a complete immunity to contractors after acceptance by the owner?
2. What would be the advantage of suing for breach of warranty?
3. Conceptually, is there any reason the principles of negligence should not apply to a claim by a subsequent purchaser against the original builder?

Analysis

1. The court's concern was that the floodgates would be open and unending litigation would result. Some legislatures have in fact dealt with the problem by creating limitation periods, known as statutes of repose, that start to run on substantial completion.
2. Under some theories of breach of warranty, strict liability is imposed. This means, in the case in product liability cases in the United States, that negligence need not be proved in order to succeed. Further, there may be different limitation periods that apply or different categories of damages that can be claimed.
3. There is no reason, other than the floodgates argument, that duty of care, breach of standard, causation, and resultant loss cannot be applied to these facts.

Duty with Respect to Pure Economic Loss

What courts refer to as pure economic loss is loss suffered by a party in the absence of any physical loss or injury. For example, an engineer may issue instructions to stop work on the site, which causes the contractor delay with its accompanying financial implications. There is no bar to such a claim for breach of contract, but courts in some states will not allow such a claim in negligence.[12]

The trend in Canada is the same as it is in the United States: Claims for pure economic loss are allowed in a wider class of cases than in the past. The *Edgeworth* case[13] is an example of such a claim, and similar examples can be found that do not involve designers.[14]

There is a category of negligence known as negligent misrepresentation. A person who negligently provides erroneous information to another in the performance of his or her profession will be liable if the recipient of the information suffers loss as a result of reasonably relying on that information. One major difference between misrepresentation and ordinary negligence is that reliance is a necessary element. These cases typically involve pure economic loss.

Some claims against designers for pure economic loss are made by contractors whose work or reputations have been commented on with disfavor by the designer to the owner. In such instances, the designer may assert the defense of qualified privilege. This defense allows the designer to provide advice to the owner when requested, as long as the designer honestly believes the advice to be true and the advice is given without malice.

There have been claims brought by contractors against engineers and architects based on negligently prepared bid documents, framed in negligent misrepresentation. Some have succeeded, and others have failed.[15] This area of the law is not yet settled.

Establishing a Duty of Care Defense

It is not possible for any party in the construction process to eliminate entirely the risk of a negligence claim. Most of the preventive steps available relate to prevent-

---

12.   For a listing of those states that permit an action for pure economic loss based on negligence, see *Architects and Engineers,* by Acret, 3d ed., p. 218. But a note of caution: The law is not static, and the list of states may have changed since its publication.

13.   See footnote 4, *supra.*

14.   A leading case on economic loss, recently decided by the Supreme Court of Canada, is *C.N.R.* v. *Norsk Pacific Steamship Co.*, [1992] 1 S.C.R. 1021.

15.   In the case of *Texas Tunneling Co.* v. *City of Chatttanooga,* 329 F. 2d 402 (6th Cir 1964), the claim failed. In *Craig* v. *Everett M. Brooks Co.*, 222 NE 2d 752 (S.C. Mass. 1967), the claim succeeded. One difference between the two cases is that in the latter, the plaintiff's identity was known to the defendant.

ing a breach from occurring. Preventing a duty from existing is more difficult although not always impossible.

By the use of contractual limitation clauses and exclusionary language, contractors and design professionals can eliminate or restrict certain duties owed to the party with whom they have contracted. The AIA contract for design services makes it clear that the architect has no duty to the client to supervise construction. Similarly, there is nothing to prevent the contractor from negotiating a provision into the construction contract excluding responsibility for the adequacy of the design.

It is less obvious, but no less true, that limitation or exclusion of duties and responsibilities based on a contract with one party (the owner, for example) can influence whether certain duties are owed to third parties who are not privy to the contract. As stated earlier, the limitation of the architect's duties regarding contractors' means and methods of construction can prevent a court from finding that such a duty is owed by the architect to workers on the site. The reverse is equally true: Inclusion of such a duty may influence a court to hold that a similar duty is owed to others.

Therefore, care must be taken during the contract negotiation and drafting stage by each party to reduce or exclude risks and responsibilities that properly belong to others. A well-drafted contract may assist in establishing a duty of care defense.

4.3   BREACH OF DUTY

Breach of duty is another way of saying that the *standard* of care was not met. Participants in the construction process are expected to use the same level of skill, care, and diligence as do other competent members of their profession. The rule quoted here is equally applicable to all common law jurisdictions, including Canada and the United States, and applies equally to engineers and contractors (even though it is stated in reference to architects):

> An architect undertaking any work in the way of his profession accepts the ordinary liabilities of any man who follows a skilled calling. He is bound to exercise due care, skill and diligence. He is not required to have an extraordinary degree of skill or the highest professional attainments. But he must bring to the task he undertakes the competence and skill that is usual among architects practicing their profession. And he must use due care. If he fails in these matters and the person who employed him thereby suffers damage, he is liable to that person. This liability can be said to arise either from a breach of his contract or in tort.[16]

The mere fact that an error has been made is not sufficient to establish negligence. However, in most cases, if that error is of such a kind that reasonable skill, care, or diligence would have prevented it, liability is likely.

---

16.   *Voli* v. *Inglewood*, [1963] A.L.R. 657 (Austr. H.C.).

This standard is established in each case by the use of expert evidence. Each party to the lawsuit customarily calls an expert witness, who is a practitioner of the same profession as the defendant, who will provide evidence that the conduct of the defendant was (or was not) consistent with what is expected in the profession and therefore met (or did not meet) the standard of care and skill.

The relevant standard is the one that was in place at the time the alleged negligence occurred, not at the time of trial. Changes and improvements in the state of the art may have occurred during the intervening period, and it would be unfair to require designers and contractors to predict these future improvements.

There comes a point where it is impossible to say what is generally accepted among the profession and what is the general practice of years past. Not everyone adopts new methods on the same date. There is a transition period in some cases during which there may be two or more schools of thought, each using a different design method or construction technique. In an English medical malpractice case, the court expressed this principle, which applies equally to construction professionals:

> [A doctor] is not guilty of negligence if he has acted in accordance with a practice accepted as proper by a responsible body of medical men. . . . Putting it the other way round, a doctor is not negligent, if he is acting in accordance with such a practice, merely because there is a body of opinion who takes a contrary view. At the same time, that does not mean a medical man can obstinately and pig-headedly carry on with some old technique if it has been proved to be contrary to what is really substantially the whole of informed medical opinion.[17]

The standard of care may vary from one jurisdiction to another. For example, A/Es are frequently asked to provide cost estimates. There is no obligation to provide a perfect estimate, but a reasonable level of accuracy is required. In one state, a 10 percent variation may be acceptable[18], and in another the standard may be 15 percent.

In rare cases, a court may reject entirely the expert evidence regarding standard of care. If the entire profession adheres to a standard of practice that is careless or unsafe, the court may exercise its own judgment. In the *T. J. Hooper* case, a well-known American judge, Judge Learned Hand, stated:

> Indeed in most cases reasonable prudence is in fact common prudence; but strictly it is never its measure; a whole calling may have unduly lagged in the adoption of new and available devices. It may never set its own tests, however persuasive be its usages.[19]

---

17. *Bolam* v. *Friern Hospital Mgmt. Committee*, [1957] 2 All E.R. 118 at 122 (Q.B.).

18. See *Kellogg* v. *Pizza Oven, Inc.*, 157 Colo. 295, 402 P 2d 633 (1965), where 10 percent was considered acceptable.

19. 60 F 2d 737.

Experts and Specialists

If an A/E holds himself or herself out as an expert or specialist, a higher standard will be applied. The general rule regarding standard of care for specialists is the same as for an "average" engineer, architect, or contractor, except that the "profession" is defined differently. The profession for a specialist is other specialists. It is therefore no defense for a specialist engineer to claim that the design was as good as one should expect from an average engineer.

What constitutes a specialist? In law, anyone who represents himself or herself to the public as a specialist or expert, even if he or she does not possess special expertise, will be held to the higher standard.

Compliance with Codes and Standards

Unless adopted by reference into legislation, a code is a recommendation only, and compliance with it is not mandatory. However, for practical purposes *in the event of a failure*, the code becomes a minimum mandatory standard. In other words, an engineer has the right to exercise independent judgment and may even go back to first principles. But if a problem occurs and the engineer is called on the carpet to justify the design, there will be a presumption against the engineer that would be very difficult to overcome in most cases. Even though violation of the standard is not conclusive evidence of negligence, it can be persuasive evidence. A statement of this principle is found in the New Zealand case of *Bevan Investments Ltd.* v. *Blackhall and Struthers (No. 2):*

> ... bearing in mind the function of codes, a design which departs substantially from them is *prima facie* a faulty design, unless it can be demonstrated that it conforms to accepted engineering practice by rational analysis.[20]

That is half the equation. The more difficult question is whether one can be held liable if there has been full compliance with the code. The simple answer is that such a situation is highly unlikely in most cases although it is possible. There are four sets of circumstances where such liability can be found.

The first is where the engineer has actual knowledge that the code requirements are inadequate. Suppose that the code gives a range of values for a particular design parameter, such as the density of material to be stored. Assume that the code does not recommend material testing and contains no recommendation that test values be preferred to the range given in the code. Assume further that the material to be stored has been tested, and its density falls outside the range given in the code. The engineer is not entitled to ignore the test results if they would govern the design.

---

20. [1973] 2 NZLR 45 at 66.

Second, an engineer may be held liable where he or she reasonably should have been aware that the code is inadequate. For example, it may become common knowledge—as a result of a failure, study, or theoretical research—that changes to the code are required. The revisions to the code may not have kept up with knowledge in the industry for a variety of reasons. It may be that the code revisions are being drafted following a major study. The design engineer has some obligation to keep up with developments in the field, in particular with respect to areas in which that engineer is a specialist.

Third, in rare cases, the courts have held that an industry cannot be permitted to set its own standard where that standard is careless.[21] Examples of courts finding that adherence to the applicable standard may be insufficient defense to a claim in negligence can be found in some of the automobile design and manufacture cases.

Finally, where the design is leading edge or unique, a different standard may apply. If a designer or contractor seeks to use a new approach that deviates from common practice, what effect will that have on potential liability? This question is relevant at only two stages in the process: at the time of contracting and in the event of a failure or problem.

When negotiating with a client, if one is contemplating using such a new approach, it will most likely be because of anticipated cost savings. In such a case, it is essential to fully inform the client of any risks associated with the method, such as the effect it might have on use or maintenance costs, or on safety factors, and let the client make an informed decision. The decision by the client to take the risk, in the hope of achieving savings, may afford the designer or contractor a defense against the client although it may be no defense against a third party who did not accept the risk.

In the event of a failure, a court will impose a very high standard on the designer or contractor, particularly if a tried and true method is known and available or if the risks were not fully canvassed with the client.

Many construction failures occur because of a coincidence of factors. Design error, construction error, poor inspection, and unforeseen use, or some combination of these factors, may play a role in eating away the intended safety factor until failure occurs.

The initial choice of safety factor is usually made by the engineer. A minimum standard may be mandated by law, or recommended by code, but it is the design engineer who determines through the design process whether that safety factor will be exceeded, reduced, or met precisely. In a disciplinary hearing following a roof collapse, the panel had the following comments:

> Codes of practice set forth minimum standards to which there should be adherence. The engineer cannot deviate from the requirements of the Code without adequate grounds to do so. If the Code is in any way ambiguous and requires interpretation, the

---

21. See footnote 19, *supra*.

engineer must ensure that the interpretation is based upon sound engineering principles and is consistent with the intent of the Code.[22]

Codes of ethics for engineers in both the United States and Canada dictate that public safety is paramount.[23] This obligation to public safety is used to establish the duty of care owed by the engineer to members of the public in negligence cases. Although contractors may not be bound by a formal code of ethics, there is no doubt that the same duty is owed by contractors.

Avoiding Claims Based on Breach of Duty

No one sets out to do negligent work. The vast majority of breaches of standard of care fall into two categories: incompetence (lack of skill) and lack of care.

Education *per se* does not make an engineer, architect, or contractor competent. Experience and training are equally important. In some jurisdictions, once an engineer has qualified for a professional license, there is nothing except the code of ethics to prevent that engineer from doing work in another field of engineering for which he or she has no training or experience.

Cases involving lack of skill are relatively rare compared to those involving lack of care. That is because most professionals have the integrity to avoid doing work they are unqualified to do. Yet engineers, architects, and contractors get into trouble when they take on work for the first time in a new field. No law requires anyone to do the same type of work forever. In some cases, the desire to move into a new area is motivated by financial necessity. Any venture into a new field should be preceded by additional training, and ideally, the first project in the new area should be done in partnership with or under the guidance of an experienced practitioner in the area.

Certain branches of architecture, engineering, and construction can be learned through written materials alone. Other areas cannot. For example, design of silos and bunkers in the United States is governed by the ACI 313[24] code. Although this code is not law, it is adopted by enough silo designers that deviation from it would be a *prima facie* breach of standard. Yet the code does not follow a cookbook format. It is a guide for those who are already familiar with silo design principles. A structural engineer who ventures for the first time into silo design armed only with the code is a lawsuit waiting to happen.

---

22. Association of Professional Engineers of British Columbia Inquiry Re: Harrison, Tacy, London, and Man (Aug. 1989).

23. The ASCE Code of Ethics states that "Engineers shall hold paramount the safety, health and welfare of the public in the performance of their professional duties." Similar wording has been used by Canadian engineering associations.

24. The American Concrete Institute Recommended Practice for Design and Construction of Concrete Bins, Silos, and Bunkers for Storing Granular Materials (ACI 313-77).

Claims caused by lack of care can and do happen to experienced professionals. But just as lack of skill is preventable through additional training and association with others, lack of care is equally preventable.

One proven method of reducing claims due to lack of care is to establish procedures that require a certain level of care. Checklists should be created that set out procedures, and those checklists should then be followed. Calculations should be checked by someone other than the person who did them, if possible. Peer review has been tried with success in many situations, and the cost of such review is more than offset by the savings in claim reductions. Professional associations and liability insurers are good sources of advice on peer review and other claims reduction programs, and in fact, some associations require members to institute programs after a claim or claims have been made.

A third method of reducing the likelihood of such claims is to ensure that the contract governing performance of the work, whether for design or building, does not set an unreasonable standard of care or create a guarantee of results.

4.4   PROXIMATE CAUSE

For an event or act to be considered legal cause of a loss, it must satisfy the "but for" test: But for the act, the result would not have occurred. After the test is met, the cause is analyzed to determine whether it is proximate. The term *proximate* has been used by many courts to distinguish between causes that play a significant part in producing the result and those that are too remote.

Consider the example of a contractor who leaves a trench excavated and installs barricades around it. A municipal crew removes the barricades and fails to replace them. A motorist then drives into the trench, causing injury and loss. It is true that "but for" the contractor's act of performing the excavation, the injury and loss would not have occurred. But clearly the act was not a proximate cause of the loss.

Lack of causation can be an effective defense in negligent misrepresentation claims. That is because the reliance requirement of a misrepresentation claim can be seen as an aspect of causation. If there is no reliance, it means that the claimant would have followed the same course of action whether or not the advice was given, and therefore the "but for" test is not satisfied.[25]

4.5   LOSS CAUSED BY THE BREACH

Although a negligent act or omission may be proved, it is possible that no loss or damage was occasioned by it. In many cases, that is precisely what happens. If there is no causal connection between the loss and the negligent act, the claim will fail.

---

25. This defense was asserted by the consulting engineers in the case of *Driver v. William Willett (Contractors) Ltd.* [1969] 1 All E.R. 665.

To illustrate, suppose that an architect designs a building with two levels of exposed parking and ten floors of enclosed offices above. The architect fails to appreciate that the lowest office floor will need insulation because it is exposed to the elements below. Immediately prior to constructing the floor in question, the contractor points out the error. It is corrected by adding insulation and heating elements in the floor, at a cost of $50,000. The client is upset at the additional cost. But is any loss suffered? The way to address the issue is to ask whether the cost would have been incurred in any event, whether or not the negligence had occurred. If the architect had recognized the need during the conceptual design phase, and the contractor had increased its bid by $50,000, the client would have suffered no loss. If, on the other hand, a less expensive solution had been designed at an earlier point, the loss would be equal to the difference between $50,000 and the cost of the less expensive solution.

The most serious losses occur when work that has already been performed has to be torn apart and redone. In such a case, all the cost involved will be claimable as flowing from the breach.

4.6   DEEP POCKETS IN NEGLIGENCE CASES

Most construction cases involving negligence usually have several defendants. The architect, consulting engineers, contractor, and subcontractors are typically sued when things go wrong. There is always enough blame to spread around, but not always enough money.

Many jurisdictions still retain the principle of joint and several liability in negligence. **Joint and several liability** means that each defendant whose fault has contributed to the loss is individually liable up to the full amount of the loss. If the loss is $100,000 and two defendants are jointly and severally liable, the plaintiff can choose to collect the full amount from one of the defendants, leaving that defendant to recover (if possible) a portion from the co-defendant. If one of the defendants is impecunious, the defendant with deep pockets will bear the entire loss. Deep pockets in many cases is synonymous with insurance coverage.

Joint and several liability may be excluded by contract, but if there is no contractual privity between the plaintiff and the defendants, it may be difficult to avoid the unfair result of a joint and several judgment. A contractor does not usually investigate the financial resources of the design team, and the designers may not have the right to reject a low bidder on the basis of financial resources. However, it is quite simple to avoid joint and several liability for negligence claims brought by parties with whom there is contractual privity.

Many claims against designers and contractors are brought by the client, the project owner. The contract between the owner and the contractor can be negotiated to include a provision that prevents the owner from asserting a claim against the contractor on account of designer error. Similarly, the designer can request a provision excluding claims based on contractor error. It is essential that any such exclusion or limitation clause be drafted by an attorney, in order to ensure its enforceability, because courts have been known to strike down exclusionary clauses that are unreasonable in scope.

4.7   PROBLEMS

1. An architect negotiates a term into her contract with the owner that states: "The architect shall not be liable to third parties for damage caused by error in design." An error in the architect's design causes a parapet to collapse, injuring a pedestrian. The pedestrian sues the architect in negligence. Is the architect liable? Explain.

2. The architect for a building project has entered into an AIA Document B141-1987 with the owner. While conducting one of the periodic inspections, the architect advises the contractor to change the falsework and shoring below some formwork for an impending concrete pour. The contractor complies, and an accident occurs. An injured worker sues the architect and contractor. The architect argues that the contractor is responsible for means and methods of construction. Who should prevail? Why?

3. A professional engineer contractually responsible for structural design of a building hires an engineer in training (EIT) to do the calculations for a column. The engineer checks the calculations but fails to catch an error. A collapse results. Ignore any issues of contractual liability. Is the engineer liable in negligence? Is the E.I.T. liable in negligence? Draft an argument to be used in each of their defenses (without case citations—just basic principles).

4. An architect has prepared plans for a new office tower. The municipal building authority approves the plans subject to changes in the emergency egress and fire suppression systems. The changes will cost $30,000. The owner is upset and inquires why these changes are necessary, and the architect responds that the municipal authorities have recently changed their requirements. What defenses would be available to the architect if sued in negligence?

5. An engineer designing the boiler for an industrial installation determines that a particular design complies with all applicable codes and standards, but barely. The contractor, who is very knowledgeable, suggests to the engineer minor enhancements that would increase the safety factor by a significant margin at modest cost. The engineer declines to act on the suggestion. The boiler fails, and the owner sues the engineer. What defenses, if any, are available to the engineer? What are the weaknesses in those defenses?

Risk, Responsibility, and Dispute Avoidance

5.1 INTRODUCTION

The principles of contract law go only so far in guiding the parties to the contract or guiding a court as to how a contract should be interpreted. Ultimately, the purpose of a contract is to allocate risk and responsibility between the parties: risk of loss in the event of failure, risk associated with unforeseen events (such as rejection of plans by a municipal authority), responsibility for making decisions, and responsibility for ensuring certain results. Designers, contractors, and owners can reduce or eliminate certain types of risk both at the contract negotiation phase and during the performance of agreements simply by recognizing the potential risks and responsibilities and by taking a few simple steps to either knowingly accept them or shift them to other parties.

Responsibility will sometimes be allocated between parties even if the parties fail to address those issues in their contract. The law will make presumptions and imply terms into the contract. Some of the presumptions more commonly made in construction contracts are examined in this chapter.

Risks that properly belong to one party may be inadvertently accepted by the other. These risks are easily avoided as long as they are recognized. In this chapter, methods of avoiding those risks are discussed.

Risk of conflict is greatly increased where the client of a contractor or designer is dissatisfied. Client dissatisfaction is often unrelated to the quality of construction or design, but rather is a function of poor communication. Methods of avoiding these conflicts are suggested.

Finally, this chapter discusses risk allocation through the use of specifications and disclaimers. Designers are frequently required to draft specifications and can use them to allocate risks that were not specifically addressed in the contract.

5.2   COMMON LAW PRESUMPTIONS

Construction participants, with the exception of individual homeowners, are generally viewed by the law as relatively sophisticated parties. In other words, the law will usually presume that the terms of the contract were fairly negotiated, and if the party did not object to a term of the contract, he or she will be bound by that term.[1] An argument that the contract would have been awarded to someone else if the term had not been agreed to is of little avail. Rarely will a court be persuaded by an argument of duress or adhesion. Freedom of contract and the ability to walk away from unacceptable terms is presumed. The answer is to live with the onerous term, or let someone else live with it.

The law also presumes that if a risk is identified in the contract, the parties addressed their minds to that issue, and the law is reluctant to substitute its own allocation of risk for the parties' choice. For example, the doctrines of frustration and impossibility, as discussed in Chapter 2, refer to circumstances that would render the performance of a contract either physically impossible or to no purpose. If the risk has been addressed in the contract, a court will generally let the contract determine the outcome.

A popular misconception by the consumers of architectural and engineering services is that the designer guarantees the result of his or her work. In fact, the law makes no such presumption. What the law provides, in the absence of contractual language to the contrary, is that the designer will act with the level of competence and care that would be expected of the average practitioner in that field.[2] For that reason, designers should be extremely careful to avoid any contractual language that places them in the position of guarantor or surety. It is rare to find perfection

---

1. Individual homeowners will usually be bound by the specific terms of contracts to which they have agreed. However, it may be easier for them to argue that they have never been involved in a construction project before, and therefore, they had no knowledge of custom and practice in the industry and should thus not be bound by implied terms that would apply to regular industry participants.

2. Of course, different standards apply to those who hold themselves out as experts or to those who guarantee results, as discussed in Chapter 4.

in the design of any complex project; that is one reason owners put contingencies in their budgets. If the designer represents to the owner, either in the contract or by letter, or even verbally, that the desired result will be obtained, the defense of reasonable care may be eroded.

The law does not necessarily presume that contractors guarantee that their work will provide the results desired by the owner, but it will imply certain warranties. The law (in most jurisdictions) will imply in a contract for construction of a residence that the final product will be fit for human habitation. It will also imply certain minimum standards of quality and workmanship in the materials and labor.

If the contractor is aware—or reasonably should have been aware—of a defect in design, there is an implied obligation to bring that defect to the owner's attention. The law does not often imply any warranty of the design, by the contractor, into the construction contract unless the plans and specifications would indicate to an average contractor that the design would not work.

The presumptions regarding the contractor's responsibility may be modified by terms of the contract. For example, the CCDC 2 contract states:

> The Contractor shall review the Contract documents and shall promptly report to the Consultant any error, inconsistency or omission the Contractor may discover. Such review by the Contractor shall be to the best of his knowledge, information and belief and in making such review the Contractor does not assume any responsibility to the Owner or Consultant for the accuracy of the review. The Contractor shall not be liable for damage or costs resulting from such errors, inconsistencies or omissions in the Contract Documents which the Contractor did not discover. If the Contractor does discover any error, inconsistency or omission in the Contract Documents the Contractor shall not proceed with the work affected until the Contractor has received corrected or missing information from the Consultant.[3]

A similar clause is found in the AIA standard form.[4] The clauses modify common law presumptions with respect to errors that a reasonably competent contractor would normally be expected to discover. Under the contract, the contractor is not liable, whereas at common law, liability may exist.

5.3   SHIFTING RISK

By virtue of training, designers are constantly aware of the duty to protect the owner's interest. But looking after the owner's interest does not mean in every case that the designer's own interest must be ignored. The owner's interest may be paramount to the personal interest of the designer, but the two are not always in conflict, and in many cases the two will coincide. Yet many designers will accept risk

---

3.   Clause GC 3.4.1.

4.   AIA Document A201-1987, clause 3.2.1.

that should properly belong to the owner in the mistaken belief that it is somehow improper to leave that risk with the owner.

For example, assume a mechanical engineer is hired to design the HVAC for an office building. The engineer in sizing a piece of machinery, such as a chiller, determines that there is one unit that would be marginally adequate but might fail in the event of high demand. A larger unit would certainly be adequate but would cost substantially more. The engineer might reason, "I know this job is on a tight budget, and every request for upgrade has been rejected. The owner would never agree to the increase in cost." If the engineer simply specifies the less expensive unit, and it proves inadequate, liability is likely. Similarly, if the engineer specified the more expensive unit, the owner might complain (once it became apparent) that the increased cost was unnecessary.

The solution is to write to the owner explaining the problem, and setting out the possible consequences and likely costs, thereby allowing the owner to make an informed decision. At least the owner is then unable to argue that he or she would have been more than willing to accept the increase in cost in order to avoid the risk.

5.4   DISPUTES CAUSED BY CLIENT DISSATISFACTION

Client dissatisfaction is one of the prime causes of litigation. The dissatisfaction may be justified, or it may be only a matter of perception. Justified dissatisfaction will result in the owner winning the case, and perceived dissatisfaction may have the opposite result. In either case, all parties will incur the cost and aggravation of a legal battle.

Much of the following discussion is focused on disputes between the designer and the owner. However, the principles apply equally to disputes between the owner and contractor.

In some cases, disputes can be avoided simply by advising the owner of the choices available, outlining the advantages and disadvantages of each choice and allowing the owner to make an informed decision. The HVAC example is a good illustration. However, owner choice is not a necessary ingredient. Even where there is no practical choice, keeping the owner apprised of the likely results can avoid disputes as well.

To illustrate, suppose the owner, who is constructing a parking garage, advises its structural engineer that the cast-in-place concrete slabs are to be flat, with no ponding of water. The engineer knows that over time the slab will develop creep deflection, and unless camber is designed and built in to the structure, a flat slab today will mean ponding in the future. Furthermore, there will be short-term deflection caused by removal of the formwork so that measurements taken before stripping the forms will differ from those taken afterward. The amount of deflection will be even greater when live load is imposed, making the timing of measurement critical. The only way to avoid these deflections is to grossly overdesign the structure. (Even then, the deflections cannot be avoided completely; they can only be reduced to a negligible level.)

In these circumstances, measurement of the flatness of the slab after pouring of concrete might lead the owner to be dissatisfied. The problem can be avoided by informing the owner beforehand what to expect. That way, ponding of water before the forms have been stripped will not be cause for complaint.

It is highly unlikely that the owner would ever choose to grossly overdesign the structure to avoid ponding. Clearly, there is no meaningful choice for the owner. But it is extremely likely that the owner—without having been informed of the explanation of camber and deflection—on finding water puddles after the first rain, would consider suing the engineer for providing a design that did not accomplish the requested result.

It is always advantageous to offer explanations before rather than after a result has been obtained. Explanations after the fact are often seen as self-serving and are less reliable in a court of law. Statements made after a dispute has developed, and especially after litigation has commenced, are not given the same weight as those statements made before litigation was contemplated.

In some cases, the owner will try to pressure the designer into making a design choice that should properly be made by the owner. As in the case of the chiller described earlier, the owner might simply say, "Do whatever you consider appropriate." If possible, the designer should avoid being drawn into making the choice. But if that is not possible, it would be prudent to inform the owner (by letter) what choice will be made, for what reason, with what possible consequences, and at what cost, and to advise the owner that if he or she is not happy with that choice, immediate notification should be provided so that the decision can be reconsidered.

A common theme in defense litigation is that a large number of claims against architects and engineers are precipitated by claims for unpaid fees. The typical scenario involves a request at the end of the job by the designer for the last installment of the fee, and a response by the owner to waive or reduce the fee because the job ended up overrunning the budget due to alleged errors and omissions by the designers. The designer refuses to give up a portion of the fee because he or she believes the fee is already too small and there were no errors of any significance. A claim is filed for the fee, and the owner counterclaims for the losses caused by the alleged negligence. It is not uncommon for the counterclaim to be many times greater than the claim for fees.

This raises the question of how these counterclaims can be avoided. Some designers have suggested requiring the owner to pay the fee, or a portion thereof, as a retainer, as some attorneys require. This is simply impractical in many cases since owners are often unwilling to agree to such an arrangement. But more important, it would not remedy the problem. The requests by owners that fees should be reduced stems from a more fundamental problem: a poor understanding, at the start of design, of what will be required and how much it will cost.

Examples include designer involvement in changes and inspection of building projects. The owner may expect that once the detailed design phase is complete, involvement by the designer should be minimal. The reality on construction projects is that changes are often required in the field for a variety of reasons, including contractor error, owner and tenant requests, unforeseen conditions, and designer error. The designer may have contracted for one or two visits per week, either as part of the fee or on an hourly basis. Or the contract may specify that design changes due to owner requests are not included in the basic fee. After being billed for extra services, the owner may be upset. Even sophisticated owners have been known to balk at such requests.

One of the causes of this lack of understanding is that retainer agreements may be poorly drafted and do not clearly specify the scope of the designer's services. There is a distinction, for example, between supervision and inspection, which many designers take pains to ensure is documented.[5] An architect who is responsible for supervision will want to be on site every day. Inspection, on the other hand, connotes a lesser degree of involvement. Although the architect may appreciate the distinction, the owner may not.

Good communication is a key ingredient to a successful business relationship. It cannot be overemphasized how important it is to maintain a good relationship with the client, and doing so is the least expensive and most cost-effective way to avoid claims. Attention to simple matters, such as returning telephone calls, can mean the difference between a client who is prepared to forgive small design errors and one who is looking for any excuse to sue.

5.5   PROJECT DOCUMENTS

There are typically at least five parts to a construction contract:

1. The written agreement, signed by the parties
2. The standard form general conditions
3. Special or supplementary conditions peculiar to the project
4. The technical specifications
5. The drawings

Allocation of risk and responsibility as between the owner and contractor is largely determined by the contract, and the designer will play a role in making that allocation through the drafting of the drawings and specifications. Likewise, the designer will influence certain risks and responsibilities as between the owner and designer (by virtue of those same documents).

Hundreds of years ago, when the common law of England was in its infancy, construction was performed by "master builders" who were responsible for much of the

---

5. AIA Document B141 clause 2.6.5 describes the extent of the architect's visits as "intervals appropriate to the stage of construction . . . " and explicitly states that continuous on-site inspection is not required.

detailed design work in putting a project together. In other words, the owner relied more on the contractor for the design function than is the case today. As the professions of architecture and engineering developed, owners and developers have come to rely on design professionals for the complete design.

There is still a residual design responsibility in the contractor in some cases. In recent years, designers have tried to shift responsibility for certain aspects of the design to the contractor through the use of certain types of specifications.

The term of art for these specifications is **performance specification**. Until performance specifications became popular, the designer would specify the details of the system in question as well as the manufacturer of all components. A performance specification, on the other hand, requires the contractor to achieve a *result* but does not tell the contractor how to achieve it.

For example, elevator subcontracts are commonly bid based on a performance specification. The designer does not design the length of elevator rail, or its gauge, or the motors needed to operate it. The suppliers have their own engineers on staff, who have greater design expertise. The designer will instead specify the number of elevator cars required, the number of floors, the speed required, perhaps the passenger capacity, and other operating parameters. Some designers may simply call for a recognized manufacturer's system "or equivalent."

This approach can be used for almost any building system. The mechanical engineer can design in detail the entire heating system or can specify performance parameters, such as the number of BTUs to be produced. The electrical engineer may leave the layout of conduit to the contractor and simply locate the outlets and fixtures.

The disadvantage in using a performance specification approach is that the designer loses some control over the design process. Trying to regain that control through the shop drawing review process can be costly because the contractor will argue that any interference resulting in increased cost justifies increased compensation, which in turn can precipitate a claim against the designer by the owner. Performance specifications offer greater opportunity for the contractor to influence the final product, perhaps in ways that were unanticipated but still comply with the intent of the specification.

On the other hand, a contractor who bids on a performance specification warrants that the system will meet the parameters specified. The designer has therefore shifted some of the risk, namely, the possibility that the system will not function as intended.

5.6   DISCLAIMERS

As discussed previously, it is common to find clauses in contracts that attempt to preclude or limit the liability of one of the parties.[6] These clauses, known as excul-

---

6. For example, see Chapter 4, section 4.2.

patory clauses,[7] address consequential damages, negligence, "no damage for delay," and a host of other issues.

Disclaimers are not always contained in contracts. They may be posted in conspicuous places[8] or contained in letters. Depending on the type of disclaimer, in order to be effective, it may be necessary to bring it to the attention of the party against whom it is intended.

Disclaimers may be conveyed by placing a note or paragraph in the drawings or specifications. For example, architects and engineers frequently place a stamp on shop drawings they have reviewed, advising the contractor that the designer's review is only for general conformity with the intent of the design and is not a detailed review. Invitations for bid frequently disclaim the accuracy of soils information and require the contractor to make an independent investigation.

Disclaimers that are inconsistent with the contract entered into by the party attempting to benefit from the disclaimer are often invalid. For that reason, it is advisable to obtain legal advice when attempting to incorporate a disclaimer into drawings or specifications. Furthermore, disclaimers that are unreasonable in scope, such as attempts to preclude claims for fundamental breach of contract or gross negligence, run the risk of being found unenforceable by courts. However, if carefully drafted, exculpatory clause can be a very effective method of shifting risk.

5.7   PROBLEMS

1. A contractor and owner have entered into a standard form AIA A201 contract. The architect drafts the specifications, which contains the following clause: "The contractor agrees to check the design of the roofing system and inform the architect and owner of any errors." The contractor was aware of the clause before bidding on the project. An error in the roofing system (designed by the architect) is not detected by the contractor, and the owner sues the contractor and architect. Who is responsible? Why?

2. An elevator specification requires the contractor to deliver a system based on operating parameters only. While the building core is being constructed, the engineer tells the contractor that the shaft walls are not sufficiently plumb to comply with the specifications and that remedial work will be needed before the elevator rails can be installed. The contractor disagrees but performs the remedial work. If the contractor makes a claim for extra work and interference, what legal and factual issues will be involved?

---

7. They are also known as exclusion or limitation clauses, and are commonly referred to as disclaimers.

8. In some jurisdictions, a party can limit its liability to lien claimants by posting a particular type of notice.

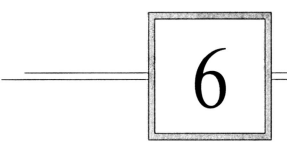

Bidding

6.1 INTRODUCTION

For those who witness the bidding process for the first time, the frantic activity and secrecy at the closing of a bid must seem surprising and unnecessary. Surely there must be a more orderly and civilized way of choosing a contractor and its subcontractors for a building project. Yet to those involved in the process, the reasons for such behavior are self-evident. In this chapter, a description of the bidding process is given, along with an explanation of some of the practices that are now generally accepted as custom in the industry.

Most disputes involving the bidding process arise either because of an attempt to bid shop by the owner or general contractor or because of a mistake contained in a bid. In this chapter, bid shopping is examined in the context of the legal remedies available to the author of the bid. The law relating to mistakes is reviewed as well, with respect to the right of the bidder to withdraw a bid and whether the recipient of a bid is entitled to enforce a bid bond if the bid contains a mistake. Bid depositories have been developed in order to deal with some of the problems inherent in the bidding process, including bid shopping. Depositories are discussed at the end of this chapter.

6.2   THE BIDDING PROCESS

Contract formation (offer and acceptance) in the construction industry is usually accomplished through the **bidding process**.[1] The process involves a number of stages:

1. Preparation of the bid documents
2. Solicitation or invitation of bids
3. Pricing by the contractors
4. Submission of bids
5. Evaluation by the owner
6. Award of the contract

The law relating to bidding recognizes various rights, obligations, and liabilities at each of the stages in the process. There have been lawsuits brought by unsuccessful bidders, by successful bidders who have made mistakes in their bids, by subcontractors and suppliers whose pricing information has been used by general contractors to bid shop, by general contractors against subcontractors who have withdrawn their prices after those prices were incorporated into general contractors' bids, and by owners and general contractors against each other seeking to keep a bid deposit or bid bond.

The first stage is preparation of the bid documents. These documents typically include the drawings, specifications, general conditions, special or supplementary conditions, instructions to bidders, and the invitation to bidders. Most, if not all, of these documents will be prepared by the design team. On larger and more complex projects, the instructions and invitation to bidders may be prepared by an attorney, and the attorney may review the nontechnical aspects of the specifications and general conditions.

In the private sector, almost all invitations to bidders contain a statement that the lowest or any bid may not be accepted and that the owner reserves the right to accept or reject any bid in its sole discretion. These statements are similar to disclaimers in that they are designed to protect the owner against liability for improper rejection of a bid. Public bodies (such as municipalities) may be required by statute or charter to follow certain rules in the evaluation and acceptance of bids, which usually requires that the lowest conforming bid from a qualified contractor be accepted. The statement that the lowest bid may not necessarily be accepted cannot always be taken at face value because the owner's discretion to

---

1.   In Canada, it is also referred to as the tendering process. The legal case reports index bidding cases under "tendering."

reject a low bid may be limited by statute (in the case of public bodies), by regulation (if the bids are submitted through a bid depository), or by common law in some jurisdictions.

A bid may be invited in one of three ways: by invitation only to a select group of prequalified contractors, by open invitation, or through a bid depository. The method used may have an impact on the rights of the parties, particularly if there are allegations of bid shopping.

The drafting of the invitation may be very important in determining the terms of the agreement between the owner and the successful bidder. The invitation will usually require the bidders to conduct an independent site investigation and may require detailed site surveys and soils investigations to be performed as well. The invitation is one of the tools available to owners to allocate various construction risks to the contractor. It should be drafted with care and with the benefit of legal advice.

The invitation may also affect the right of the owner to reject bids and to determine the ground rules for acceptance. In jurisdictions that limit the owner's rights of acceptance and rejection, the invitation is the owner's opportunity to set out the factors to be used for acceptance and rejection.[2]

After invitations are made, contractors must prepare their prices. The time between the invitation and the closing of the bid period is often very short, and contractors must work quickly to estimate all the labor, material and equipment. Very few general contractors have the expertise to perform all the work with their own forces, and out of necessity they rely on subcontractors not only to perform the work but also to price it. Similarly, the subcontractors often must obtain prices from suppliers and subsubcontractors before submitting their prices to the general contractors.

To avoid having their prices shopped around, contractors, subcontractors, and suppliers submit their prices as late as practicable. This results in many subtrade prices being delivered to the general contractor on the same day (or, in extreme circumstances, in the last hour) that bids are due. The general contractor often cannot investigate or evaluate subtrade prices before deciding whether to use those prices. If a very low price is received from an electrical subcontractor, for example, with whom the general contractor has never dealt, the general contractor is faced with a difficult choice: Use the price and face the risks that the subcontractor is unreliable

---

2. In the United States, private owners who reserve themselves the discretion to accept or reject bids as they see fit are generally free to do so (except in a bid depository situation). In Canada, the rights of private owners are more restricted, particularly in some provinces. In British Columbia, for example, the statement that "the lowest bid may not be accepted" does not allow the owner to bid shop or to reject a bid for a purpose inconsistent with custom in the industry. See *Chinook Aggregates Ltd.* v. *Abbottsford* (1989), 40 B.C.L.R. (2d) 345 (B.C.C.A.).

and the price contains an error, or don't use the price, in which case a competitor will use it and be awarded the contract.

Submission of the bid usually requires the contractor to comply with instructions on timing, form, and content. If the bid is late, the owner may be required to reject it, and even if the owner is not required to do so, rejection is likely. Requirements as to form and content usually mean that the bid cannot contain substantial exclusions or qualifications. The bidder may specify in the bid, for example, that the price is based on acceptance by the owner of certain conditions that are inconsistent with the invitation, such as an extension to the schedule. The owner may be prevented from accepting a nonconforming bid by statute (for public bodies) or by regulation (for members of a bid depository).[3]

Evaluation of bids by the owner is usually done with the assistance of the prime consultant or construction manager. The owner will consider whether the lowest conforming bid is within the construction budget and will evaluate cost-saving alternatives proposed by the bidders. A low base bid may not be low once an alternative is accepted. Another factor considered during the evaluation phase is the reputation of the low bidder and its ability to perform the work. Private owners frequently begin negotiations with bidders during the evaluation phase.

The consultant or construction manager may recommend that a particular bidder be rejected, based either on the reputation of the bidder or on past dealings. Rejected bidders have sued consultants for giving such advice, basing the action in defamation. However, as long as the recommendation is made in good faith and without malice, the consultant or construction manager is protected by the defense of qualified privilege.

The award of the contract constitutes the acceptance of an offer and thus crystallizes contractual rights between the owner and the successful bidder. It may also crystallize rights, obligations, and liabilities of other parties, including sureties.[4] Subcontractors and suppliers whose prices have been used will also be affected by the award of the main contract in that those prices will be irrevocable due to reliance on them by the general contractor. In fact, the subcontractor and supplier prices may become irrevocable when the general contractor submits its bid, if that bid is irrevocable,[5] based on the doctrine of promissory **estoppel**,[6] which means that the subcon-

---

3. In jurisdictions that restrict a private owner's right to reject a bid, the owner can retain its discretion to either accept or reject a nonconforming bid by including language in the invitation that informs bidders that technical nonconformance *may* be considered grounds for rejection.

4. For a discussion of the surety's position on acceptance of a bid, see section 8.3, "Bid Bonds."

5. The existence of an obvious and material error in either the subcontractor's or general contractor's bid will prevent it from being accepted and therefore prevent the crystallization of those rights and liabilities.

6. For an explanation of promissory estoppel, see Chapter 2, footnote 8.

tractor will be bound to hold its price open to the general contractor, but the general contractor will not be bound to use it.[7]

6.3   BID SHOPPING

Bid shopping is understood to mean the practice by an owner or contractor of using a price submitted by one party to obtain a lower price from another party. It may not create a legal cause of action but is widely considered unethical.[8] Bid shopping may occur by a general contractor either prior to submission of its bid or afterward. Courts have struggled with the issue but have had difficulty fitting it into traditional legal frameworks, with the result that in many jurisdictions there is no remedy for a party whose price has been shopped.

The first legal theory to be tested in this respect was breach of contract. In the United States, the courts have held that submission of a price by a subcontractor and use of that price by a general contractor does not create a contract.[9] Promissory estoppel will protect the general contractor but not the subcontractor because of the lack of detrimental reliance by the subcontractor. Some disgruntled subcontractors have tried to use the theory of **unjust enrichment** but to no avail.[10] Theoretically, it is possible to base such an action on the tort of deceit, but it would be necessary to prove that the general contractor actively solicited a price from the subcontractor with no intent to consider that subcontractor.[11] There are practical difficulties associated with proving such a case.

Although many courts have been unable to provide a remedy to the victims of bid shopping, the practice is considered sufficiently unethical that a general contractor who has attempted to bid shop will jeopardize its right to hold that subcontractor to its price.[12]

---

7.   In British Columbia, there is case law that provides a general contractor who has used the price of a subcontractor and nominated that subcontractor in its bid is contractually bound to use that subcontractor if the bid is accepted by the owner. *Westgate Mechanical Contractors Ltd.* v. *PCL Constr. Ltd.* (1989), 33 C.L.R. 265 (B.C.C.A.), affirming (1987), 25 C.L.R. 96 (B.C.S.C.). In the United States, and in other provinces of Canada, the nomination of the subcontractor has been held to be immaterial. *Merrit-Chapman & Scott Corp.* v. *Gunderson Bros. Engineering Corp.* 305 F. 2d 659 (9th Cir. 1962).

8.   In Canada, it can create a cause of action for breach of contract.

9.   *James Baird & Co.* v. *Gimbel Brothers, Inc.* 64 F. 2d 344 (2d Cir. 1933).

10.   For example, see *Ron Brown Ltd.* v. *Johanson and JCL Ventures Ltd.* (unreported), B.C.S.C., Vernon registry No. 337/87, Aug. 10, 1990.

11.   In other words, the general contractor is using the subcontractor to provide free estimating services in order to verify the accuracy of the price submitted by another subcontractor that the general contractor always intended to use.

12.   For an excellent discussion of the case law on bid shopping, bid chopping, and bid chiselling, see *Construction Bidding Problem: Is There a Solution Fair to Both the General Contractor and Subcontractor?* by Richard Oertli, [1975] St. Louis U. L. J. 552.

Public owners are often precluded from bid shopping by statute, which usually requires that the contract be awarded to the lowest qualified bidder. The primary purpose of these statutes is to ensure the prudent use of public funds and to prevent public servants from abusing their position, but a secondary effect of the legislation is to preclude bid shopping by public owners.

6.4   MISTAKES

A mistake must be both obvious and material in order for it to render a bid incapable of being accepted, even if the bid is irrevocable. Of course, if the matter relates to a risk that has been knowingly accepted by the contractor, and the "error" is a matter of judgment by the contractor, it may not be considered an error.

For a bid to be irrevocable, it must be supported by consideration.[13] If the bid is irrevocable, and the contractor catches an error before the bid has been accepted, revocation by the contractor will result in forfeiture of any bid bond or bid deposit unless the error is obvious and material.[14] Even if the bid is not expressly irrevocable, some jurisdictions use the firm bid rule.[15] However, if the owner accepts the bid prior to notification of error or withdrawal, the contractor must prove obvious and material error in order to avoid the formation of a contract with the owner.

If the bid is withdrawn prior to acceptance by the owner, assuming the bid is revocable, the owner will usually enter into a contract with the next lowest qualified bidder. In such circumstances, has the owner suffered any loss? Legally, the answer is no, as long as the correction of the mistake would cause the bid not to be low.[16] It is recommended by some bodies that the owner return the bid deposit or bond and allow the bid to be withdrawn if the contractor can prove the error is genuine.[17]

---

13.   In Canada, use of a seal will substitute for consideration.

14.   In Canada, the leading case on this point is *R. in Right of Ontario* v. *Ron Engineering & Construction (Eastern) Ltd.*, [1981] 1 S.C.R. 111, 119 D.L.R. (3d) 267.

15.   The **firm bid rule** states that a bid on public work remains irrevocable until the owner has had a reasonable opportunity to evaluate it. The bid may still be revocable if it contains a mistake.

16.   It would therefore seem unfair to penalize the contractor who made the mistake and caught it before acceptance. For that reason, the *Ron Engineering* case (footnote 14, *supra*) has been criticized.

17.   The CCDC Document 23 "A Guide to Calling Bids and Awarding Contracts" recommends that no penalty should be assessed in the case of serious and demonstrable error. The AIA approach is similar. The Public Construction Council of British Columbia, in its September 1989 publication entitled *Procedures and Guidelines Recommended for Use on Publicly Funded Construction Projects*, states that irrevocable tenders " . . . should be used only when there is good reason for doing so. In normal circumstances a bidder should be allowed to withdraw his bid at any time before it is accepted. If a tender is to be irrevocable, the fact must be clearly stated on the Form of Tender. Legally, it must be supported by consideration or the tender must be sealed."

CASE STUDY

Peerless Casualty Co. v. Housing Authority of the City of Hazelhurst, 228 F. 2d 376 (5th Cir. 1955).

The contractor Ivey submitted a bid in the amount of $463,733. It was in response to an invitation for bids that contained the following requirements:

1. A certified check or bank draft . . . or a satisfactory bid bond executed by the bidder and acceptable sureties in an amount equal to 5 percent of the bid shall be submitted with each bid.

2. No bid shall be withdrawn for a period of thirty days subsequent to the opening of bids without the written consent of Hazelhurst.

Ivey's bid was low and was accompanied by a bid bond. On the day following opening of bids, Ivey discovered an error (which was not obvious), advised the owner in writing of the error, and withdrew its bid. The owner had not yet accepted the bid but had adopted a motion to accept the bid "subject to approval of the Public Housing Administration." The owner called on the bond and contracted with the next lowest bidder. Following is an extract from the court's reasons:

> It is an elementary rule of the common law of contracts that an offer may be withdrawn at any time before it is accepted. Unless the acceptance is unconditional and without variance from the offer it is of no legal effect as an acceptance and operates as a rejection and counteroffer. The condition, annexed by the Authority to its attempted acceptance, that it was subject to the approval of the Public Housing Administration, was not one that changed the terms of the offer but merely deferred the time when the acceptance should take effect.
>
> There was not here any valuable consideration to Ivey, the bidder and principal on the bond. So . . . we can see no liability on the bond against the principal Ivey and absent any liability of the principal there is not, as we have noted, any liability of the surety.
>
> Our reversal of the trial court is made without reluctance because of our feeling that an affirmation would result in an unjust enrichment of the Appellee Housing Authority. The withdrawal of the bid before acceptance and the letting of the contract to the bidder who, but for the Ivey bid, was the low bidder, resulted in no injury to the Authority.

Questions

1. The bond was sealed by the surety, and the owner argued that the seal operates as consideration. Assuming that is so, why is the surety not bound by the bond?

2. How can an owner avoid the result obtained by the owner in this case?

3. Why did the court conclude that there was no harm to the owner?

4. Would the result have been different in Canada?

Analysis

1. A contract of suretyship is a secondary obligation. For the surety to be liable, there must be primary liability of the principal (the bidder).

2. The owner could pay each bidder a nominal sum (say, $1.00) in consideration for making the bids irrevocable for a fixed period. This is known as an option contract.

3. If Ivey had discovered its mistake prior to submitting its bid, the owner would have been in exactly the same position: The next bid would have been low.

4. Yes. That is because the bid would not be characterized as an offer, but rather as an acceptance, thereby creating a contract and making the bid irrevocable for a period of thirty days.

6.5   BID DEPOSITORIES

A **bid depository** is an organization used by owners, contractors, and suppliers that is designed to facilitate bidding according to specified rules. Typically, one must be a member of the depository to use it. Members of the depository must agree to abide by its rules or else risk losing membership privileges, which includes the right to bid on projects that are handled by the depository.

Plans, specifications, and other bid documents are deposited in the bid depository for bidders to review, and bids must be submitted through the depository. For contractors who do not want to pay for a set of plans and specifications for the purpose of bidding, the depository allows members to use the plan room to perform take-offs.

The bid depository regulations are created to ensure an orderly and ethical bidding procedure. The inadequacies of the common law in dealing with unethical bidding practices have created a demand by participants in the industry for a less chaotic and more predictable system, and bid depositories are the result.

The frantic compilation of subcontractor prices by general contractors at the eleventh hour (in the open bidding process) has led most depositories to include a requirement that subcontractors' bids be deposited at least a minimum period (one day, perhaps) prior to the deadline for submission of general contractors' bids.

Virtually all depositories prohibit bid shopping. This can be done in a number of ways. For example, subcontractors are given the opportunity to bid only to those general contractors with whom they are willing to work. This is done by placing a sealed envelope in the contractor's mailbox. The contractor then has the choice of taking the envelopes of those subcontractors with whom the general contractor is willing to work. Some bid depositories insist that the general contractor use the lowest conforming bid from the envelopes accepted and contract with that subcontractor if the contractor's bid is accepted. Failure to do so may result in a claim for breach of contract on the theory that the members have contracted with each other to abide by the rules of the depository.

Some contractors consider using their own forces for a particular subtrade but would use a subcontractor if a low enough price were available. To deal with that situation, the bid depository may require the contractor to submit a subtrade price *to itself* in a sealed envelope and treat it the same as other bids. Only if it is low would the contractor be entitled to use its own forces for that work.

6.6   PROBLEMS

1. A subcontractor makes an error in a price submitted to a general contractor, who uses it in his bid. The general contractor's bid is not irrevocable. The subcontractor catches the error before the general contractor's bid is accepted. Can the subcontractor be forced to enter into a contract? Explain.

2. Assume the same situation as in problem 1, except that the general contractor's bid has been accepted. Does that make any difference? Why or why not?

3. An architect is assisting the owner in evaluating bids. The low bid is from a contractor who successfully sued the architect on another project for interference. The architect is reluctant to work with this contractor again and recommends to the owner that the second lowest bidder be selected because the lowest bidder "has a propensity to litigate." The owner rejects the low bidder based on the architect's statement. Discuss the legal issues created by the making of the statement.

7

Insurance

7.1 OVERVIEW

Insurance policies are contracts of indemnity and as such are governed by principles of contract law. They are, however, a special form of contract and are thus interpreted according to a specialized body of case law, developed originally to protect insurers and more recently to protect the rights of policy holders as well.

The basic principles of contract law, including offer and acceptance, consideration, and mistake, still apply. Other principles of contract law that apply specifically to insurance contracts are discussed in this chapter. Understanding the laws and principles that govern insurance contracts allows greater control over the process of negotiating the terms of policies and helps avoid costly mistakes that can prejudice the rights of the insured and result in loss of coverage.

In this chapter, basic principles of insurance and characteristics of insurance contracts, such as the duty of the insurer to defend a claim, subrogation, and insurable interest are explained. The duty to defend is distinct from the duty to indemnify and may exist even where there is no duty to indemnify. Subrogation is an inherent right of the insurer, which allows it to recover losses from third parties. Insurable interest is the legal principle that is used to determine whether the insured has a right to obtain property insurance coverage.

Loss of coverage is a serious problem because of its financial implications, and it can occur for a variety of reasons. These reasons are canvassed in this chapter and include gaps in coverage related to the coverage period, expiry of a limitation period, material nondisclosure, and failure to cooperate.

Every policy of insurance must have a coverage period. This period will determine whether the policy is a "claims-made" or an occurrence policy. A claims-made policy covers claims that are made during the policy period. Occurrence policies cover claims in which the insured event occurred during the policy period. Limitation periods are contractual or statutory requirements for a notice of claim to be made or legal action to be commenced within a certain period.

Material nondisclosure refers to the duty of the insured to provide all relevant information to the insurer when purchasing the policy. Failure to disclose can relieve the insurer of its obligation to indemnify. The duty to cooperate deals with the conduct of the insured *after* a claim has been made.

Finally, this chapter contains a discussion of builders' risk policies. These policies are a special form of property insurance common to the construction industry. A body of case law has developed dealing with exclusion clauses typical to these policies, and the principles underlying these cases are explained.

Every policy of insurance must state the perils covered, which are the *events* that trigger the obligation of the insurer to indemnify, defend, or both. For property insurance, the events include loss of or damage to the insured property that occurs as a result of insured risks. For liability insurance, the event is typically a claim by a third party.

Construction insurance policies generally fall into two categories: liability insurance and property insurance. Liability coverage protects the insured against claims made by third parties, such as a claim against a design engineer for errors and omissions. Property insurance, on the other hand, protects the insured against loss or damage to property in which the insured has an interest as a result of certain causes such as fire or theft. A claim by a third party against the insured is not a prerequisite for property insurance although it is for liability coverage. On the other hand, insurable interest is a prerequisite for property insurance.

Most construction contracts require the contractor and the owner to obtain various policies of insurance. The AIA general conditions stipulate that the contractor must have liability coverage for, among other things, claims under workers' compensation and disability benefit Acts, claims for injury or death to employees and others, claims for property damage (not including the property that comprises the work being performed), and claims arising out of negligence of the contractor, its employees, and subcontractors.[1] A policy that covers claims by others for bodily injury and property damage is commonly referred to as a **comprehensive general**

---

1.   AIA Document A201-1987, s.11.1.1.

liability (CGL) policy. The owner is required to purchase property insurance in an all-risk form, which covers the interests of the owner and all contractors on the site.[2]

Other standard form contracts require the parties to obtain further coverage.[3] Some agreements call for boiler insurance, which typically covers damage to property and other losses caused as a result of explosions of pressure vessels; marine and transportation insurance, which covers shipments to and from the job site; delayed opening and business interruption insurance, which protects against loss of rents or profits.[4] Many of these perils are specifically excluded from typical builders' risk and liability policies. It is essential to review all insurance policies with a knowledgeable broker or agent in order to determine if there are any gaps in coverage.

7.2 OPERATING WITHOUT INSURANCE

The basic purpose of insurance is to spread risk and to shift risk. Few engineers, architects, or contractors—with the exception of some very large and well-established firms—can afford to "self-insure," that is, absorb the full amount of any potential loss. Through the mechanism of insurance, the risk of loss is spread over many individuals, some of whom will profit by insurance (because of claims against them) and others who will realize no benefit from their premiums except for peace of mind.

By operating without insurance, or "going bare," one takes the risk of being wiped out financially as the result of a large claim. Because of the market supply and demand for insurance, there have been periods when coverage has been either prohibitively expensive or impossible to obtain, forcing individuals to go bare. Some individuals and corporations have gone bare on the assumption that lack of insurance makes them less desirable targets and therefore less likely to be sued or pursued. There is some truth to that assumption, but it is a great risk for anyone with assets they wish to preserve.

It is certainly *not* recommended that anyone with anything to lose operate without insurance. Even the most competent professionals get sued though sometimes for no valid reason. The cost of defending a frivolous claim can be enormous. In the United States, it is difficult to recover attorney's fees except in truly frivolous cases, whereas in Canada the successful litigant usually recovers only a portion of legal costs (generally less than 50 percent). One great advantage to carrying insurance is that the insurer must defend the suit in most cases although the insured may be required to expend the deductible first, depending on the wording of the policy.

---

2. AIA Document A201-1987, s. 11.3.

3. For example, see CCDC 2 contract GC 11.1.

4. For a more detailed discussion of these forms of insurance, see *Construction Bonds and Insurance* (6th ed.) published by Jardine Rolfe Limited.

It is not uncommon for professionals to try to make themselves "judgment-proof," which involves taking steps to put assets beyond the reach of creditors, such as putting assets in one's spouse's name or removing assets from a corporation. Although there are perfectly legal means of protecting and transferring assets, there are also risks and ethical considerations associated with these methods. For example, transferring assets to a spouse in anticipation of litigation will, in some jurisdictions, be regarded as a fraudulent transfer and will be reversed by a court in order to satisfy the creditor. Another method used to try to protect assets is to incorporate and keep a minimal level of capitalization in the company. This may be ineffective for two reasons. First, courts can "pierce the corporate veil" in order to find the shareholders liable if the corporate shell is used for an improper purpose though this is rarely done. Second, and more important, an individual can be sued in his or her personal capacity for negligence even though he or she was working as an employee or officer of a corporation at the time.

7.3   THE DUTY TO DEFEND

Most liability policies create two duties in the insurer: the duty to indemnify and the duty to defend. Sometimes the duty to defend is of more value, particularly where the claim is not likely to succeed. The insurer is obliged to appoint an attorney, who will defend the insured at the expense of the insurer (subject in some cases to the deductible being exhausted first).

If the claim only alleges conduct that is outside the scope of the policy, such as fraud, there may be neither a duty to defend nor to indemnify. For this reason, an experienced plaintiff's attorney will usually try to frame the complaint in such a manner that at least a portion of it falls within the four corners of a typical policy. However, in some cases, even though there is no duty to indemnify, there may still be a duty to defend.[5]

7.4   SUBROGATION

Subrogation means that the insurer is entitled to the rights of its insured as against third parties. In other words, the insurer is entitled to assume the legal position of the insured in order to recover from some other party the amount it has paid out on a claim. For example, suppose that the architect of record for a commercial building retains a specification writer to draft the specifications. The waterproofing section is inadequate, and the owner is forced to tear up the material already installed and redo it, at great expense. The architect is sued, the insurer defends, and judgment is awarded against the architect, which the insurer pays. The insurer then has the right

---

5. *U.S. v. U.S. Fidelity and Guarantee Co.*, 601 F. 2d 1136 (10th Cir 1979).

to sue (subrogate against) the specification writer, just as the architect could have if he or she were not insured.

For the insurer to make use of its subrogation rights, the insured must have legal rights that are capable of being assumed and enforced by the insurer. The insured party must take care not to relinquish or impair its rights against the party who was responsible for the loss. Occasionally, a waiver of subrogation clause is included within a design or construction contract and operates to contractually preclude a subrogation claim. Architects, engineers, and contractors must exercise care with respect to such clauses since the unauthorized waiver of the insurer's subrogation rights may allow the insurer to escape its indemnity obligation.

Parties to the construction process have attempted various methods of preventing subrogated claims against each other. One method, as just described, is by using a waiver of subrogation clause. Predictably, insurers take a dim view of their insureds giving away rights of subrogation, and depending on the wording of the insurance contract, most courts have agreed that doing so may cause sufficient prejudice to the insurer so as to relieve it of the obligation to indemnify. In order to avoid this problem, the AIA has included a clause in its standard form agreement that requires the insured, in essence, to obtain the consent of the insurer to such a waiver by requiring that the policies include an endorsement to that effect.[6]

A simpler method is to have all the project participants named as insureds in the same policy. Such insurance, commonly referred to as a project policy, though valuable, may not be available on all projects, particularly small dollar value projects. It is a basic rule of insurance law that subrogation cannot be obtained against an insured. This principle was tested in a case where the insurer tried to make a subrogated claim against an insured subcontractor. The court refused to allow the claim.[7]

7.5   INSURABLE INTEREST

For a person or corporation to be entitled to recover insurance proceeds following a loss, that person or corporation must have an insurable interest in the insured property. Insurable interest is a somewhat loosely defined concept, but in essence, it means that the insured party benefits from the existence, or would be prejudiced by the loss, of the insured property.

Insurable interest can become an issue when a party does not own the property involved but is simply performing a limited amount of work on it. A subcontractor would have an insurable interest in the entire value of a project even though the subcontract value is only a small fraction of the total. This was the issue in the *Commonwealth* case:

---

6.   AIA Document A201, clause 11.3.7, states, " . . . The policies shall provide such waivers of subrogation by endorsement or otherwise."

7.   *Commonwealth Construction Co. Ltd.* v. *Imperial Oil Ltd.* (1977), 69 D.L.R. (3d) 558 (S.C.C.).

On any construction site, and especially when the building being erected is a complex chemical plant, there is ever present the possibility of damage by one tradesman to the property of another and to the construction as a whole. Should this possibility become reality, the question of negligence in the absence of complete property coverage would have to be debated in Court. By recognizing in all tradesmen an insurable interest based on that very real possibility, which itself has its source in the contractual arrangements opening the doors of the job site to the tradesmen, the Courts would apply to the construction field the principle expressed so long ago in the area of bailment. Thus all the parties whose joint efforts have one common goal, e.g. the completion of the construction, would be spared the necessity of fighting between themselves should an accident occur involving the possible responsibility of one of them.[8]

The issue of insurable interest is also recognized in the AIA standard form general conditions, which require that the owner purchase and maintain property insurance until "no person or entity other than the owner has an insurable interest in the property. . . . "[9] In any situation where one party is procuring insurance on behalf of others, if the AIA document is not being used, it is recommended that a similar clause be included in the agreement.

7.6 CLAIMS-MADE AND OCCURRENCE POLICIES

A **claims-made policy** is one in which coverage exists only for claims that are made while the policy is in force. An **occurrence policy** covers claims for which the occurrence (often an act of negligence) took place while the policy was in force without regard to whether or not the policy remains in force when the suit is filed. The distinction is important for determining whether a claim is covered. Most A/E liability policies are of the claims-made type.

It is essential to be aware of the type of policy when changing coverage; otherwise, a gap in coverage may be created. This can occur when an architect or engineer retires or changes insurers. The prudent way to deal with this situation is to maintain coverage after retirement. Such "run-off" coverage can usually be obtained at rates substantially less than those charged during periods of active practice. If, for example, all the insured's projects are in a jurisdiction with a six-year limitation period, coverage should be maintained for at least that period.

Another way in which a gap may be created is if an architect or engineer was employed by a company that goes through a corporate change, which causes the named insured (the company) to change. The former employee may have been insured under a policy that covered present and past employees but is no longer a past employee of the new company.

---

8.   Footnote 7, *supra*, pp. 562–563.

9.   AIA Document A201-1987, clause 11.3.1.

When changing insurers, one has an obligation to notify the prospective insurer of all potential claims as well as actual claims. Failure to do so will likely result in a lack of coverage for such claims. There may be some reluctance to disclose a possible claim that looks as if it will disappear, but if there is any doubt, it should be disclosed. If both the new and old policies are of the claims-made type, and a claim is made after the new policy has come into force, which the insured was aware of, the old policy will no longer cover it if the original insurer was not notified of the claim.

Some policies are considered to be a hybrid of the occurrence and claims-made types. The policy period clause in these hybrid policies requires that the occurrence (for example, a negligent act) must have taken place during the policy period, *and* the claim must be made either during the policy period or during a specified period following. The descriptions of the policy period may be subject to varying interpretations by different courts. For that reason, the prudent course of action is to report any potential claim as soon as the insured has notice of it.

7.7   LIMITATION PERIODS

Many states in the United States have **limitation periods** beyond which claims against a designer or contractor on a construction project are barred. A common period is six years from substantial completion (with some extensions if the claim is discovered during the sixth year). In most provinces of Canada, the clock does not begin to run until the defect should reasonably have been discovered, which in theory means that a party can be sued for negligence twenty or thirty years after project completion. If a designer has retired, and has canceled insurance coverage, a claims-made policy that was in force prior to retirement will be useless against a claim made after retirement even though the policy was in force at the time of the design.

State legislatures have not been consistent in their drafting of limitation period statutes, and courts have not been consistent in their interpretations. Some states[10] have adopted what is known as the discovery rule, meaning that the clock does not begin to run until the plaintiff should reasonably have been aware of the defect.[11] Legislators and courts have struggled to achieve a balance between the rights of plaintiffs and defendants. If the cause of action begins to run upon completion of the building, the defect may not appear until after the limitation period has expired, and accordingly, the plaintiff will have lost the right to sue even before any damage became apparent. On the other hand, it appears inequitable to hold designers and builders liable indefinitely when they may have retired and ceased to carry insurance.

---

10. As well as most provinces in Canada.

11. Strictly speaking, it is not always discovery of the defect that triggers the limitation period. The legal test is that the plaintiff should reasonably have been aware that a cause of action existed. This often coincides with the discovery of the defect, but in some cases it may depend on other factors, such as the extent of damage apparent.

The balance achieved in some states is to enact a Statute of Repose, or a "long stop" limitation period. Not all states have used the same period, and some states have chosen not to adopt such an approach at all.[12]

Limitation periods can cause difficulties for defendants as well. It is not unusual in construction cases for defendants to make third-party claims against each other and against others. For example, when an owner sues its prime consultant (often the architect), that consultant may allege that some of the complaints relate to work performed by subconsultants such as the mechanical, electrical, or structural engineers. If the claim is against the prime contractor, it may result in third-party claims against various subcontractors. Alternatively, the contractor may allege that the defects complained of by the owner were the result of faulty design and name the designers as third parties. Limitation periods typically also apply to such third-party claims although the period may not necessarily be the same.

From a practical perspective, an architect, engineer, or contractor who has been given notice of a claim, or who is aware that a claim is possibly brewing, should take the following steps immediately:

1. Determine as precisely as possible the nature of the complaint.
2. Determine what other parties may have been involved and have potential liability.
3. Obtain legal advice with respect to defending the claim, filing third-party complaints and notifying insurers.

Failure to file the third-party complaint in a timely manner may result in the defendant being liable but losing the right to obtain contribution or indemnity from the party who really caused the problem.

Limitation periods exist not only for the commencement of a lawsuit, but for filing the proof of loss or notification to the insurer. The time limit for notifying the insurer of a claim may depend on the terms of the policy as well as the statute governing insurance claims. If there is any doubt about when these steps must be taken, legal advice should be obtained. Failure to comply with limitation periods can result in complete loss of coverage.

7.8   MATERIAL NONDISCLOSURE AND PREJUDICE TO THIRD PARTIES

Material nondisclosure refers to the failure by an insured party to disclose all relevant information when purchasing an insurance policy. One might ask why it is nec-

---

12. For a list of states that have adopted Statutes of Repose, see *Architect and Engineers* by Acret (McGraw-Hill, 3d ed.), pp. 368–369.

essary to protect insurers. The reasons that were present in the eighteenth century are still relevant more than two hundred years later. By the very nature of an insurance contract, the insurer is at a disadvantage when it comes to access to information. The insured must therefore disclose all material facts that might affect the insurer's decision to provide coverage.

Insurance contracts have been described as "contracts of utmost good faith." An insurer is entitled to be informed of any and all facts that could influence its decision to provide coverage or the amount of the premium to be charged. Even if the nondisclosure is unrelated to the loss, coverage may still be denied. To illustrate, suppose that an engineering firm applies for errors and omissions insurance, and it fails to disclose that one of its employees had a negligence claim against him in the past year. A policy is issued, and then a claim is made against the firm based on alleged negligence of a different employee. The insurer can argue that if full disclosure had been made, a higher premium would have been charged or coverage would have been denied.

In the design and construction process, one party frequently relies on another party to procure insurance coverage. For example, the owner of a project may purchase a project policy that covers all participants, including the design team and all contractors. In that case, failure to disclose a material fact by the owner could void the policy, resulting in a denial of coverage. Whenever one party relies on another to arrange for insurance, such risks are present.

Prejudice to the rights of others can also occur if the party procuring the insurance simply fails to pay the premium when it becomes due. All the insured parties would like to be notified of such circumstances in order to determine whether to pay the premium themselves, obtain separate coverage, or let the policy lapse. It is prudent to require the party obtaining the insurance to notify all the insured parties of any material change in coverage. Some jurisdictions require the insurer to make such notification.

7.9   COOPERATION AND CONFLICT BETWEEN INSURER AND INSURED

It is a term of virtually all policies of insurance that the insured has an obligation to cooperate with the insurer in the defense of a claim. Cooperation can take many forms; it may mean supplying documents in the possession of the insured, testifying at deposition and trial, and providing pretrial assistance to the defense attorney. It certainly means not doing anything to prejudice the result, such as admitting liability or giving a release. Although cooperation may be costly, in terms of lost time and expense, failure to cooperate can result in a denial of coverage and, therefore, be even more costly.

In the defense of a claim, the interests of the insurer and insured may be identical. Both want to see the claim defeated. But situations may arise where the interests of the insurer and insured diverge. These situations include denial of coverage by the insurer; claims that allege conduct that may be outside the scope of coverage such as fraud; desire by the insured to defend in the face of a reasonable offer to settle; claims that exceed the limits of coverage; and offers to settle that require compromise of a counterclaim such as a claim by a designer for fees.

Where no conflict of interest exists, only one attorney is appointed, who will represent the interests of both the insurer and insured. However, where there is a conflict or potential conflict, it is imperative that the insured retain separate counsel to look after only the insured's interest. In some jurisdictions, in certain conflict situations, the insurer may be required to pay not only the fees of the attorney it selects, but also the fees of the attorney selected by the insured.

Claims that exceed the policy limits can expose the insured to personal liability. This puts the insurer in a difficult position where liability is doubtful, but the potential damages are large. For example, an architect who carries $1 million in coverage for errors and omissions may be sued for $2 million. The claim has a poor chance of success, and the plaintiff offers to settle for the policy limits of $1 million. The insured would be well advised to put the insurer on notice that the insured would like to have the claim settled within the limits. If the insurer then decides to defend rather than settle, the insurer would be exposed to a claim for bad faith for refusing to settle. It is common to see such letters sent by the insured's attorney to the insurer's attorney in such claims.

The circumstances in which the potential for conflict of interest is present is not limited to those outlined here. To recognize the need for independent counsel, the insured should understand that the insurer's goal is to resolve the claim for as little cost as possible. If the insured has any other objective, such as preservation of reputation or recovery of fees, separate counsel should be considered. And if any issue is raised that could lead to denial of coverage, independent advice is a necessity.

7.10   BUILDERS' RISK POLICIES

Most of the discussion thus far has focused on liability policies. **Builders' risk** (also known as **all-risk**) policies are property insurance. They are designed to cover all perils except those specifically excluded, whereas the more common forms of property insurance will cover only those perils specifically enumerated. A description of these policies and their purpose is found in the *Commonwealth* case:

> In England, it is usually called a "Contractors' all risks insurance" and in the United States it is referred to as "Builders' risk policy." Whatever its label, its function is to provide to the owner the promise that the contractors will have the funds to rebuild in case of loss and to the contractors the protection against the crippling cost of starting afresh in such an event, the whole without resort to litigation in case of negligence by anyone connected with the construction, a risk accepted by the insurers at the outset. This purpose recognizes the importance of keeping to a minimum the difficulties that are bound

to be created by the large number of participants in a major construction project, the complexity of which needs no demonstration.[13]

A note of caution: The reference to insurers accepting the risk of negligence by anyone connected with the construction should not be taken at face value. Some all-risk policies exclude certain acts of negligence, and most exclude faulty design. Each policy must be examined based on its particular wording.

The exclusions are particularly relevant to the designers since virtually all builders' risk policies exclude losses due to faulty design, materials, and workmanship. This exclusion is akin to the "inherent vice" exclusion typically found in marine insurance contracts and is based on the theory that insurance companies are in the business of insuring risks, not sure things.[14] If there is an inherent defect or fault due to design error, for example, the structure is bound to experience failure sooner or later, which puts the risk in the category of a sure thing.

Contractors are likewise affected by the "faulty design" exclusion in that courts have struggled to define the meaning of the exclusion. Contractors have argued that construction methods are not included within the meaning of design, and insurers have argued that they are included.[15] In a case involving a wall that was blown down by high winds, because of inadequate bracing, the court held that design is wider in scope than the design of the finished product and is wide enough to encompass methods of construction.[16] In a similar case, also involving the collapse of a wall because of high winds, the court came to the opposite conclusion.[17]

U.S. courts tend to construe the exclusion clauses more narrowly against the insurer. The examples involving collapsed walls both appear to involve contractor–employee negligence. Cases in the United States have held that employee negligence is not an excluded peril unless it is specifically enumerated as such. In the *Barre* case, ten wooden arches were blown down by strong winds, where the contractor had used two guy cables instead of the six called for on the erection

---

13. Footnote 7, *supra*, at p. 566.

14. In the case of *MacLab Enterprises Ltd. et al.* v. *Commonwealth Insurance Co. et al.*, (1983), 2 C.C.L.I. 267 (Alta. Q.B.), the exclusion clause read: "mechanical breakdown or derangement, latent defect, faulty material, faulty workmanship, inherent vice, gradual deterioration or wear and tear."

15. These two competing interpretations were discussed by the court in the case of *Pentagon Construction (1969) Co. Ltd.* v. *U.S. Fidelity and Guarantee Co.*, [1977] 4 W.W.R. 351 (B.C.C.A.).

16. *Simcoe and Erie General Insurance Co.* v. *Willowbrook Homes (1964) Ltd.*, [1980] I.L.R. 1-1236 (Alta. C.A.).

17. *Todd's Men and Boys' Wear Ltd.* v. *Diamond Masonry (Calgary) Ltd. et al.* (1985), 12 C.C.L.I. 301 (Alta. Q.B.). The court distinguished the *Willowbrook Homes* case on the basis that there was a clear element of design involved in *Willowbrook* from the outset, whereas there was no such element in *Todd's* case. But this rewards the contractor who makes no effort to calculate a safety factor over the contractor who makes imperfect calculations.

plans, and the cables were of inferior tensile strength. The court held that this was neither faulty design nor faulty workmanship.[18] Of course, there is always a case in which the opposite result can be found.[19]

In interpreting exclusion clauses, courts have also considered whether negligence must be present in order for there to be faulty design, workmanship, or materials. Some courts have held that a design may be faulty even though no one was deemed negligent. In one well-known case, a bridge was washed out by unforeseeably high flood waters. The court held:

> But a man may use skill and care, he may do all that in the circumstances could reasonably be expected of him, and yet produce something which is faulty because it will not answer the purpose for which it was intended.[20]

This reasoning has been followed in other cases as well. With all due respect to the learned judges in those cases, the reasoning ignores the fact that no design is intended to withstand any and all perils. If legislation requires that designs be adequate to withstand winds, floods, or earthquakes up to a specified return period, that reflects a policy choice by the government, which should not be translated into a "fault" in the design, thereby depriving an insured party of coverage.

Even where a loss is excluded under the "faulty design, materials, and workmanship" exclusion, portions of the claim may be in fact covered. That is because the exclusion clauses typically contain an exception, which provides for coverage to *other* property that may be damaged. For example, if two towers are being constructed side by side, and one of them is underdesigned and as a result collapses into the second tower, damage to the second tower may be covered even if damage to the first is not.

Other perils are typically excluded from all-risk policies, such as fraud by employees and loss of revenue due to delay. If a loss occurs and there is a question about whether coverage exists, legal advice is recommended. Even if the insurer denies coverage, that may not be the last word on the matter, as shown by the many cases litigated over the interpretation of policies. Courts may disagree with the interpretation given by the insurer. This applies not simply to all-risk policies, but to all policies of insurance.

---

18. *City of Barre* v. *New Hampshire Insurance Co.*, 396 A. 2d 121 (1978 Vermont S.C.).

19. *U.S. Industries, Inc. et al.* v. *Aetna Casualty & Surety Co. et al.*, 690 F. 2d 459 (5th Cir. 1982). In that case, the loss involved a steel cylindrical tower 240 feet high and 15 feet in diameter, which became deformed during the construction process as a result of a heat treatment operation that deteriorated the metal. The *Barre* case was distinguished on the basis that there were no defects in the wooden arches in *Barre*, whereas in this case, the construction procedure caused faults in the tower itself.

20. *The Queensland Gov't Railways and Electric Power Transmission Property Ltd.* v. *Manufacturers' Mutual Insurance Ltd.* (1969), 1 Lloyd's Law Reports 219, 118 C.L.R. 314 (H.C. Australia).

7.11 PROBLEMS

1. A contractor procures a policy of property insurance covering the equipment of his competitor. A loss occurs. Can the insurer deny coverage? If so, on what grounds?

2. A claim is made against a structural engineer in negligence. The engineer has an errors and omissions policy in place. Part of the engineer's work involving mathematical modeling was subcontracted to an independent consultant. The negligence was in fact caused by an error of the subconsultant. The engineer discusses the matter with the subconsultant, who has few assets and no insurance, and the engineer agrees to release the subconsultant from liability in exchange for $10,000. The engineer then reports the claim to the insurer. May the insurer deny coverage? Explain.

3. A contractor is constructing the concrete core of a high-rise tower. A blockout is left at each floor to allow conduit to pass through. Electrical conduit is run in an enclosed duct. Because of design error, a fire erupts in the conduit, damaging not only the conduit and wiring, but also the finishes in the room that the conduit passes through. The policy in place is a builders' risk policy. Discuss the coverage issues.

4. An individual purchases property insurance covering the perils of fire and theft. A theft occurs, and the insurer denies coverage, arguing that the insured failed to disclose the fact that he was a foreigner (a resident alien), not a citizen, and that the insurer would not have accepted the risk of insuring an alien. Was this nondisclosure material? Why or why not? (Note: The facts for this problem were taken from the case of *Horne* v. *Poland*, [1922] 2 K.B. 364. The result in that case would be different today.)

5. A wall under construction collapses because of an error in design, destroying not only the wall itself, but an electrical switchgear on the ground and a sports car parked next to the job site. The contractor and owner have used a standard form AIA contract and have procured the required insurance. Are the losses (the wall, the switchgear, the car) covered? Which policies cover what losses?

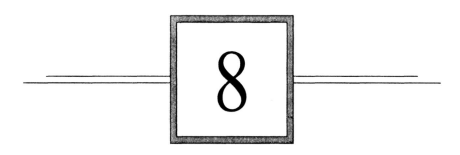

Bonds

8.1 OVERVIEW

Three types of bonds are normally used on construction projects: bid bonds, performance bonds, and payment bonds. **Bonds** are a special form of contract known as contracts of suretyship. Like contracts of indemnity, they are interpreted according to the rules of contract law but are subject as well to additional rules (as are insurance contracts), such as the right of subrogation. In this chapter, each of the three types of bonds is discussed and explained.

The role of the bonding company (or surety) is to guarantee the performance of one party, usually the contractor. The purpose of the bond is to provide some comfort and protection to another party, usually the owner, because of the risks inherent in the contracting business.[1] If the contractor fails to perform, the owner can look to the surety instead of suing the contractor (who may not have the money to

---

1. It is possible for the surety to guarantee performance of a different party's obligations. For example, a subcontractor's performance may be guaranteed to the general contractor. Unless noted otherwise, the contractor/owner example will be used in the remainder of the chapter.

satisfy a court judgment). In some ways, the surety appears to be in the role of an insurer. However, there are important distinctions between an insurer and a surety, and a bond is not insurance.

A surety agreement involves three parties: the principal, the surety, and the obligee.[2] In the context of a bid bond and performance bond, the principal is the contractor, and the obligee is the owner.[3]

Two separate agreements (which contain separate obligations) are at work. The primary obligation is between the principal and the obligee, and exists separately from any surety contract. The contractor enters into a contract with the owner, and that contract contains various obligations owed by the contractor to the owner, such as performing the construction in a timely manner. Obligations such as those are referred to as the primary obligations. The second set of obligations is created by a contract between the principal and the surety.[4] The contractor pays the surety a premium, just as a premium would be paid to an insurer, in consideration for the surety accepting the obligation to guarantee the performance by the contractor.

The premium paid by the contractor will vary, depending on the financial resources of the contractor, its bonding capacity, billing level, asset base, and other factors. For an established contractor with a solid financial base, the premium may be less than 1 percent of the contract value, depending on market conditions. But this premium is not the only consideration given by the contractor to the surety. Indemnities are given as well.

Typically, the surety will require the contractor *and its major shareholders* to indemnify the surety against any loss. In fact, the indemnity given by the principal is one of the things that distinguishes a suretyship contract from an insurance contract. The indemnities given to the surety are discussed later, as are the acts of the surety that can negate the indemnities.

It is not only the indemnitors who may be released from their obligations; the surety may also be released because of certain acts by the obligee (owner) that cause prejudice to the surety or because of other circumstances. These are known as defenses of the surety and are discussed in this chapter as well.

---

2. The principal is also referred to as the obligor because the principal owes the primary obligation to the obligee.

3. In theory, even though the owner is named as obligee in the bond, the owner does not negotiate the terms of the bond or pay the premium and therefore may be considered an intended third-party beneficiary to the contract rather than a party to it. The difference is immaterial because an intended third-party beneficiary (in the United States) can enforce the contract. Some authors (Cushman, *Construction Litigation*, p. 390) consider the owner to be a third-party beneficiary, whereas others (Jardine Rolfe Ltd., *Construction Bonds and Insurance*, 6th ed., p. 16) call construction bonds "three party agreements."

4. A surety's obligations are considered secondary obligations because they depend on the existence of a primary obligation owed by the principal.

One of the requirements of a contract of suretyship that differs from contracts in general is that they must be in writing to be enforceable. Standard forms have been developed that are widely used in the industry.[5]

8.2   INDEMNITIES AND OTHER SURETY RECOURSES

After the surety pays out money to satisfy its obligations under a bond, it is subrogated to the rights of the owner. The surety is entitled to assume the rights of the owner in order to sue the contractor to recover the monies paid out. This right of subrogation exists at common law as one of the characteristics of a suretyship agreement.

In addition to the right of subrogation, sureties often demand indemnities from the contractor and its shareholders. The indemnity from the contractor fulfills the same function as the right of subrogation: It allows the surety to recover its losses from the contractor.

But the indemnity from the contractor and the right of subrogation may be useless remedies, particularly where the contractor has become insolvent during performance of the contract. Absent any other form of security, the shareholders of the contractor might be willing to let the company go out of business in the face of a serious problem rather than put more money into the company and see the problem through to its resolution. It is for this reason that sureties often demand indemnities from the shareholders as well. The managers of the company are forced to treat each and every claim by an owner as though it were made against the individuals behind the company and not against an empty corporate shell. Once the shareholders become indemnitors, they are personally liable for the losses incurred by the surety.

8.3   BID BONDS

Invitations for bid often require that the bid be accompanied by a **bid bond** in the amount 5 or 10 percent of the amount of the bid. Failure to include a bid bond with the submission will usually result in the bid being rejected out of hand. For that reason, the contractor must enter into an agreement with a surety to provide the bid bond.

---

5. In the United States, see the AIA Documents A310 (bid bond) and A311 (performance bond and labor and material payment bond). In Canada, the Canadian Construction Document Committee publishes similar documents that are widely used. The Bid Bond is CCDC 220, the Performance Bond is CCDC 221, and the Labour and Material Payment Bond is CCDC 222.

What obligation of the contractor does the surety guarantee under a bid bond? The contractor is obligated to enter into a contract with the owner if the bid is accepted or else pay the owner the difference between the amount of the contractor's bid and the amount of the bid accepted by the owner, up to a maximum of the value of the bond.[6]

In the absence of such a bond, a contractor who withdraws an irrevocable bid could be liable for the difference between its bid and the next lowest, even if that amount exceeded 10 percent of the bid amount. The existence of a bid bond may limit the contractor's liability. In fact, the CCDC bond contains the statement that "The principal and the Surety shall not be liable for a greater sum than the specified penalty of this Bond." By requiring the contractor to submit a standard form bid bond, the owner may have limited the damages available from the contractor to the amount of the bond.

By contrast, the AIA Document A310 contains no such express limitation. However, even though there is no express limitation, it is arguable that the owner's request for a bid bond is akin to a liquidated damages provision and that by implication the contractor's liability is limited to the surety's under the bond.

The surety can never be in a worse position than the contractor in its relationship to the owner. In other words, the obligations of the surety to the owner depend on the obligations of the contractor to the owner. Therefore, any defense that the contractor has against a claim by the owner is available to the surety as well. Whenever a claim is made against a surety on a bid bond, the surety will first look to the defenses of the contractor.

One defense on a bid bond relates to revocability of the bid. If the bid is revocable, and the contractor revokes before it is accepted, that is a complete defense. Of course, revocability may depend on a number of factors, such as whether the bid was stated as being acceptable for a specified period, whether any consideration was paid to keep the bid open, whether there was detrimental reliance, and the custom and practice in the industry.[7]

Another defense available to the contractor and surety is the existence of an obvious mistake in the bid. If it should have been obvious to the owner that the bid contains a material error, the owner is not entitled to "snap it up."

Other defenses may be contained in the bond itself. For example, the CCDC bid bond provides that any suit under the bond must be made within six months from the date of the bond. A suit by the owner against the contractor brought on a basis other than the bond, such as breach of a promise not to revoke, would not be sub-

---

6. The owner cannot simply accept any bid. It must mitigate its loss. This usually means taking the next lowest bid from a qualified contractor. The AIA Document A310 is explicit in that the owner must "in good faith contract" with another bidder or risk its claim against the surety. The CCDC bid bond does not contain a "good faith" requirement explicitly, but the obligation to mitigate is implied into every contract.

7. Bid revocation is discussed in greater detail in Chapter 6.

ject to the limitation period. This is an example of the surety being in a stronger position than the contractor.

The owner may choose to sue either the contractor or the surety or both. Because the surety is more likely to have the resources to pay the damages, the surety is the primary target even though it has the secondary obligation.

A contractor that becomes aware that it has made a mistake in its bid, or that it must revoke its bid for some other reason, should obtain legal advice immediately. Failure to take appropriate action immediately could result in the bid being accepted and the bond forfeited, the cost of which will ultimately fall on the contractor. A contractor should never treat a claim against a bid bond lightly. The surety will pursue all its indemnitors, including shareholders, to recover monies paid out under a bid bond.

8.4   PERFORMANCE BONDS

Under a **performance bond,** the surety guarantees the obligation of the contractor to perform its contract with the owner. Performance bonds, like bid bonds, can have any face value, but are usually written in an amount equal to fifty percent of the contract value. The contract between the owner and contractor is incorporated by reference into the bond.

On large contracts, the prime contractor will often require the major subcontractors to provide performance bonds. For all intents and purposes in the following discussion, if the subcontractor provides the bond, the prime contractor would be in the position of the owner (i.e. the obligee) and the subcontractor would be the principal.

The bond does not come into play until the owner notifies the surety that the contractor has defaulted on its obligations. It is a condition precedent to any obligation on the part of the surety that the contractor be in default.[8]

Once the surety has been put on notice that its principal is in default, it generally has six options:

1. It may remedy the default, which means getting the contractor to perform its obligations or correcting the default itself.

2. It may complete the contract itself in accordance with its terms and conditions.

3. It may solicit bids for completion of the work, and pay the owner the difference between the accepted bid and the remainder owing to the principal under the original contract, up to the face value of the bond.

---

8. Both the AIA and CCDC performance bonds contain the following language: "Whenever [the contractor] shall be, and declared by [the owner] to be in default under the Contract, [the owner] having performed [the owner's] obligations thereunder, the Surety may promptly remedy the default, or shall promptly . . . "

4. It may pay the owner the amount of the bond.

5. It may assert a defense and refuse to do anything.

6. If there is a genuine dispute between the owner and the contractor, it may take a "wait and see" approach to determine whether the contractor was in default.

When the surety has been notified of a serious default, it should obtain legal advice immediately. The surety should conduct as thorough an investigation as possible in the time available, and if possible make a decision as to the appropriate course of action. Each one has advantages and pitfalls.

If the cost of completing the contract bears some relation to the amount owing to the contractor, it makes sense for the surety to solicit bids for completion. The cost to the surety should be relatively small. If the cost to complete is well in excess of the amount owing, it may be the result of overpayment by the owner to the contractor, which could provide a defense to the surety. The owner will typically have relied upon its architect or engineer to certify progress payments to the contractor, and if those certifications were done negligently, resulting in overpayment to the contractor, the surety or the owner may sue the consultant to recover the overpayment.

Often the choice is between soliciting bids or having the surety complete the work (either with its own forces or by delegating the work to another contractor). If time is of the essence, the surety may elect to complete the work. The danger in this option is that there is no financial limit to the surety's obligations. The option of soliciting bids is expressly limited to the face value of the bond, whereas completing the work puts the surety in the position of the contractor, complete with warranty obligations. These risks must be considered by a surety which is contemplating taking over the completion of a contract.

There is also great risk in the final option, which is to wait and see. Some sureties take the position that they cannot act as the arbiters of disputes between the owner and contractor, and if there is a genuine dispute, they must wait for it to be resolved. In such circumstances, the surety is caught between a rock and a hard place.

Suppose the surety were to decide that the contractor is in default, as the owner has claimed, and pays money to complete the contract. The contractor then sues the owner, and proves that in fact the owner was in default rather than the contractor. The surety would then be unable to collect on its indemnity from the contractor. The surety would be considered a "volunteer" at law, and would have prejudiced its rights under the indemnity.[9]

The other possibility is that the surety decides to wait and see, in order to avoid becoming a volunteer. If it turns out that the contractor was in default, the surety may be liable for more than the face value of the bond, because its failure to respond in a timely manner has aggravated the damages suffered by the owner. The

---

9. At law, a volunteer is someone who pays money to another without any legal obligation to do so.

law is not clear on whether the surety would be liable for more than the value of the bond, but the risk is present.[10]

The same risk is present for the surety if it raises a defense and refuses to step in and complete the work. The failure to act may be considered wrongful, with the same risks as waiting for a resolution.

8.5   DEFENSES UNDER A PERFORMANCE BOND

As with bid bonds, the surety is entitled to raise against the owner any defenses available to the contractor, as well as any other defenses available under the bond. As stated above, it is a condition precedent to any claim by the owner that the owner must have performed all of its obligations under the contract. For example, if the owner has not paid the contractor as required, the contractor's refusal to perform further may be justified. Notification by the owner to the surety of default in these circumstances would result in the surety raising the owner's default as a defense.

When sureties agree to provide a bond, it is an assumption of risk. The risk is based on the terms of the contract between the contractor and owner as well as the financial strength of the contractor. If the owner does anything to significantly change the risk, unless the change is contemplated in the bond, that may discharge the surety's obligations.

At common law, a material change in the contract time could be considered a material change in risk. A minor change would not have any effect on the surety's obligations. However, the AIA Document A311 provides that "The Surety hereby waives notice of any alteration or extension of time made by the Owner." Therefore under this document, an extension would not discharge the surety.[11]

A material change in the amount of work, type of work, or schedule of payment for work could materially affect the risk and prejudice the surety. It is generally understood that changes will be made and change orders issued on a project, and changes which fall within the type generally contemplated will not materially alter the risk. However, an excessive number of changes or changes which are excessive in size could do so. A prudent owner, when considering a significant change to the project, should contact the surety and obtain prior approval.

Substantial overpayment to the contractor, as discussed above, also prejudices the surety to the extent of the overpayment, thereby providing a defense.

The bond might contain time limitation defenses as well. The AIA Document A310 states that any suit under the bond must be made before two years from the

---

10.   Some courts have held the surety liable for failure to act, with damages in excess of the face value of the bond. For example, see *Continental Realty Corp.* v. *Andrew J. Crevolin Co.* 380 F. Supp. 246 (S. D. W. Va. 1974).

11.   No such waiver is found in the CCDC performance bond.

date on which final payment under the bond is due. The CCDC performance bond contains exactly the same requirement.

8.6   PAYMENT BONDS

A **payment bond** is meant to guarantee the performance of a payment obligation. The contractor has an obligation to pay all of its subcontractors, suppliers and workers. Failure by the contractor to meet these obligations can result in liens being filed and prejudice to the owner. Similarly, the subcontractor has these same obligations. Failure by the subcontractor can result in prejudice to the general contractor. Owners and general contractors may require labor and material payment bonds in order to protect against liens by unpaid subcontractors, suppliers, and those working under them.

Payment bonds are typically required in two situations; the owner requires one from the contractor, and the contractor requires one from its major subcontractors. In rare situations, where the financial stability or solvency of the owner is in question, the contractor may require one from the owner.

A labor and material payment bond (also referred to as an **L & M bond**) is structured somewhat differently than a performance bond. The owner is the obligee, but only as trustee for "claimants" as they are defined under the bond.[12] A claimant is anyone who has a direct contract with the contractor or one of its subcontractors.[13] If a claimant has not been paid the money owed for work done on the contract, it may make a claim under the bond.

The surety is entitled to any defenses available to the contractor. If the claimant is not in fact owed the amount it has claimed, due to deficiencies or other set-offs, the surety is entitled to raise such defenses against the claimant.

The surety's obligation is limited to the amount of the bond. Most labor and material payment bonds state that the face value of the bond is to be reduced by any amounts paid by the surety in respect of mechanics' liens filed against the property.

Finally, the surety will be entitled to raise as a defense any limitation period contained in the bond which has not been complied with. These limitation periods vary from one bond to another, and claimants should be extremely careful as to the timing of their claims.

There is a relatively new form of payment bond in use in the construction industry. It is called a lien bond. A lien bond requires the surety to pay a lien claimant if

---

12.   A trustee is someone who is required by law to act on behalf of and in the best interests of the beneficiary of the trust. The claimants are the beneficiaries. The AIA Document A311 does not use the term *trust*, but describes the obligee as "the Owner, for the use and benefit of claimants." These words create a trustee–beneficiary relationship. The CCDC Document 222 expressly refers to the owner as a trustee for the claimants.

13.   That is, under the AIA Document A311. The CCDC bond defines claimants as those having a direct contract with the contractor. In other words, the AIA form allows one more "level" of claimants.

the lien is found to be valid. The bond is used in substitution of the land as security for the lien, so that the lien may be removed from title to the land.[14] The lien bond is not put in place until the lien has been filed, unlike a labor and material payment bond which is put in place at the beginning of the contract.

8.7   PROBLEMS

1. A surety has provided a performance bond to the owner, guaranteeing performance of the contractor. The contractor has been paid $400,000 on a $1,000,000 contract, but has completed 50% of the work, and is in default. Bids are solicited and the lowest acceptable bid is $550,000 to complete. How much money will the indemnitors have to reimburse the surety?

2. A surety has provided a labor and material payment bond. A subcontractor makes a claim against that bond in the amount of $10,000. The general contractor advises the surety that the subcontractor is only owed $5,000. What should the surety do? Explain.

3. An owner receives irrevocable bids, and each bid is accompanied by a bid bond in amounts equal to 10% of the bids. The lowest bid is for $90,000, and is accepted. The contractor refuses to enter into a contract, for no excusable reason. The next lowest bid is for $95,000. However, that bidder also refuses to enter into a contract. The third bid is for $100,000, and is accepted, and a contract is signed. What is the liability of the surety for the lowest bidder? Why? What is the liability of the surety for the second lowest?

4. Assume that one of the obligations of the contractor under its contract with the owner is to promptly pay all of its subcontractors, suppliers and workers. Does a labor and material payment bond do anything in addition to a performance bond in these circumstances?

---

14.   For further explanation of liens and lien bonds, see Chapter 9 and, in particular, footnote 9.

9

Mechanics' Liens

9.1 THE PURPOSE OF LIEN LEGISLATION

Every jurisdiction in the United States and Canada has a mechanics' lien statute.[1] They vary in content from one jurisdiction to another but are similar in many respects. Their purpose is twofold: to provide security of payment for the suppliers of labor and materials[2] on construction projects and to facilitate credit in the construction industry.

On almost every construction project, money flows from the lender to the owner, through the general contractor to the workers, suppliers, and subcontractors. Typically, each month a progress draw is requested by the general contractor, approved (in whole or in part) by the consultant, and paid by the owner. Monies will not be released by the lender or owner without evidence that work has been performed or materials have been delivered with value equal to the amount of money claimed.

---

1. In most jurisdictions, they are called mechanics' liens although in some, they are referred to as builders' liens or construction liens.

2. Some statutes include lessors of equipment.

This means that workers, contractors, and material suppliers must do their work and supply materials before they get paid.

That payment follows performance is not in itself unusual or peculiar to the construction industry. Many businesses provide goods on credit. Large purchases such as houses and automobiles are made with little or no money paid in advance. What distinguishes the construction industry from others is that the security for payment used in other industries does not work in construction. If the vendor of a car or house remains unpaid, the car or house can be repossessed. Conditional sales agreements, mortgages, and chattel mortgages are commonly used to create security and rights of repossession. But if a drywall or painting subcontractor remains unpaid, for example, repossession is not a practicable solution.

Without some form of security, many contractors and other participants would be unwilling to supply labor and material without getting paid in advance. Requiring payment in advance would be unacceptable to most lenders and owners. It is therefore in the interest of everyone—lenders, owners, contractors, and all who work under them—to have in place a mechanism such as a mechanics' lien statute to facilitate credit and secure payment.

Lien statues use various methods to secure payment. The primary method is the lien itself. A **lien** is a claim against property[3] and is required to be registered in the appropriate land registry against title to the property. The effect is to make the property difficult to sell or borrow against until the lien is removed, giving the owner incentive to deal with the claim.[4] Ultimately, the lien claimant may force the property to be sold to satisfy the lien. A second method is the creation of a trust, which requires that monies paid to the general contractor be used to pay those working under the contractor. A third method is the use of holdback. Each of these is discussed in more detail in this chapter.

A mechanics' lien is not the only remedy available to an unpaid party. The unpaid party also has a claim for breach of contract against the party who retained him or her.[5] The subcontractor can sue the general contractor in contract, the supplier can sue the subcontractor, the laborer can sue the employer. Unfortunately, a claim in contract is a hollow remedy against a party who has no assets or who has absconded. What lien legislation does is create a cause of action against the owner's property even though the lien claimant may not be in privity with the owner. This is based on the theory that the owner's property value has increased because of the labor or material of the claimant.

---

3.   In some jurisdictions, the lien is described as a claim against the *interest* of the owner in the property. In those jurisdictions, if the "owner" has a leasehold interest or something less than a full ownership interest, the lien would attach only against that interest.

4.   That is because a purchaser would be unwilling to purchase subject to a lien, and a bank would be unwilling to finance the purchase.

5.   There may be other remedies as well, such as unjust enrichment.

In some jurisdictions, the lien legislation (or some portion of it) does not apply to government projects.[6] There may be separate legislation dealing with such projects. Because of the short limitation periods found in lien statutes, if there is any question regarding the applicability of legislation to the project in question, the claimant should obtain immediate legal advice. In the event the lien is barred because of lapse of time, the action for breach of contract may remain viable since the limitation period for such actions is typically much longer.

Mechanics' lien statutes typically contain procedural and substantive requirements with respect to notice and filing requirements, limitation periods, and categories of claimants. In this chapter, these requirements are reviewed. These statutes also typically contain three separate components that provide security or a remedy to the claimant: the lien itself, the trust provision, and the holdback. The lien is a charge against title to the property, which can inhibit transfer of the property or secure payment for the lien claimant when the property is sold. The trust provision creates an obligation in the contractor to use contract funds to pay those subcontractors, workers, and suppliers under the contractor. The holdback is a method of keeping some of the contract price out of the hands of the contractor until the project is complete in order to determine whether other parties have been paid. Each of these components is explained in this chapter. Finally, practical advice is given to minimize the risks associated with liens.

9.2   MAKING AND PROVING A LIEN CLAIM

After a supplier of labor or material has performed, and has not been paid, a claim of lien must be filed. This is usually done by filing one or more documents with the land registry office. Some statutes require a "Notice of Intent" and a "Mechanics' Lien Statement," whereas others require an "Affidavit of Claim." The form and content of this preliminary notice is set out in the statute in each jurisdiction. The legislation will also contain time limitations and procedural requirements. The limitation periods may limit the amount of time between the last day of work performed by the claimant and the day of filing, or the amount of time between notice to the owner and filing, for example. Further requirements usually exist regarding what registry must be used and notarization of documents. Failure to comply with procedural and substantive requirements can result in the claimant losing his or her lien rights. For that reason, it is prudent to obtain legal advice at this point in the process.

The claim of lien is only that—a claim. It is not conclusive of the amount ultimately owed to the claimant. The claimant must commence legal action to prove

---

6. It may not be possible to file a lien against title on a public project, and for that reason, some mechanics' lien statutes exempt public projects from the statute. But some courts have held that the trust provisions of the statute still apply to public projects.

the claim.[7] It will usually be necessary for the claimant to prove that the work was performed or material supplied to this particular project, that payment was demanded but not made, and that the claimant complied with all the requirements of the mechanics' lien statute. It is frequently necessary to commence the action within a specified period (six months or one year) after the notice was filed or the work performed. The defendants may raise defenses, such as deficiencies in the work, set-offs, the fact that payment was made, limitation defense, and other defenses available under the legislation.

It may be necessary for the plaintiff to file a *lis pendens* after the lawsuit has been started. A lis pendens is a document that states that a dispute has been commenced. The lis pendens is usually filed in the land registry to give notice to prospective purchasers and lenders that the property is the subject of a lawsuit.

Once the claim has been proven, it must be enforced. If security has been put up in lieu of the property, enforcement is relatively simple. Otherwise, the claimant (who is now a judgment creditor) can either wait for the property to be sold or commence proceedings to have the property sold. It is relatively rare for property to be sold in order to satisfy a lien creditor.

As with any lawsuit, the plaintiff and defendants should not proceed without legal advice. Even though the claim may be small, the area of mechanics' liens is sufficiently complex that unrepresented parties frequently lose because of technical and procedural difficulties.

9.3 WHO MAY CLAIM A LIEN

The issue of who is entitled to claim a lien has been litigated in many states and provinces, with differing results. Some jurisdictions require that the claimant have either physically worked on the site or provided materials to the site. Under those requirements, an architect who has furnished plans to the owner would not be entitled to the benefit of the lien legislation, but an architect who supervised work on the site would be. There are always gray areas, such as truck drivers who remove earth from a site without driving onto the site itself.

Other jurisdictions allow architects and engineers to claim liens even if they never set foot on site on the basis that their work was done at the request of the owner and increases the value of the land.

Claimants typically include workers, contractors, subcontractors, and material suppliers. It is not necessary that the claimant be in privity with the owner or general contractor. Two or more tiers of contracts may be interposed between the claimant and the owner.

---

7. In some states, the action is called a foreclosure action. Some refer to it as an action to "perfect" the lien.

Material suppliers often have difficulty proving their claims because it is necessary to prove that the material was delivered to the site. Material suppliers frequently supply to several job sites for the same contractor and are unable to say what material went to what site. For example, a lumber supplier may prepare a load of lumber for its client, the general contractor, who picks it up and makes the rounds from one site to another. The supplier has no way of knowing how much was delivered to each site. Without being able to prove delivery, the supplier will be unable to prove a lien. To prevent this problem, the supplier must designate each order for a particular job site and keep accurate records of deliveries.

CASE STUDY
Henges Co. v. Smith 409 S.W. 2d 489 (Miss. C.A. 1966).

A firm of architects claimed a lien for unpaid fees. The work performed by the architects consisted of plan preparation, cost estimating, and putting the project out for bid. The issue was whether an architect is entitled to the benefit of the lien statute:

> For generations it has been the rule in the courts of Missouri that the mechanics' lien statute is to be liberally construed in order to effectuate the beneficent purposes for which the statute was adopted. . . .
> Appellants maintain that, even if no lien is allowable for their services in drawings plans and specifications, a lien does lie for supervision of construction. . . .

The court, after reviewing the contract and finding no distinction in the fee structure between design and supervision, stated:

> What results is a contract in which no specific amount or percentage of a promised total fee is designated as compensation for appellants' services in supervision. Under these circumstances there is no contractual basis for the imposition of a lien for supervision alone.

Questions

1. Why should it make a difference whether the services were for design or for supervision?
2. If an architect is entitled to a fee for design, should an accountant be entitled to a lien for preparing financial statements to obtain project financing?

Analysis

1. Many lien statutes require that the claimant perform work on the site or deliver materials to the site. An architect who performs supervision is anal-

ogous to a site superintendent or foreman who does not perform any physical labor but is more directly connected to the physical construction.

2. Conceptually, once the courts allow anyone who has contributed to the project such that the value of the land has increased to claim a lien, the class could be expanded beyond designers to include accountants and others. For this reason, courts have looked for a more direct physical connection, such as attending on site to perform services.

9.4   LIEN SECURITY

Once a lien is registered, it serves as notice to the public that the property is subject to the lien. Anyone who purchases or lends money against the property with notice of the lien (that is, after it has been registered) does so subject to the lien claimant's interest. If the property is sold, for example, the lien claimant must be paid out of the proceeds in accordance with the lien's priority.[8]

The order of priority between the mortgage lender and lien claimants also varies from one jurisdiction to another. Some states have adopted the "obligatory advances" doctrine, which means that if the lender is contractually required to advance the amount of the mortgage, it will rank in priority ahead of lien claims filed afterward.[9] In other jurisdictions, the construction lender will rank ahead of lien claimants only to the extent of funds advanced before the lien was filed. That means that funds advanced after a lien was filed will rank below the lien. In those jurisdictions, before the lender releases funds each month to pay the progress draw, it will conduct a search of the title to the property in order to confirm that no liens have been filed. If a lien has been filed, the lender will refuse to advance funds until the lien is removed.

Because a lien can inhibit the release of funds in some jurisdictions, it can be a powerful tool for enforcing payment. Once it becomes apparent to the contractor and others that no payment is forthcoming, construction activity can quickly grind to a halt, and other liens can quickly be filed. To avoid that possibility, lien statutes

---

8.   Priority depends on the timing of registration of the lien and other charges against title to the property, such as mortgages, easements, and judgments. In some jurisdictions, the lien, once registered, "relates back" to the last date work was performed. Each jurisdiction has its own statute governing how priorities are determined. The importance of priority is that it determines the order in which parties get paid out of the proceeds of sale of the property. If there is not enough value in the property to pay all the registered charges against title, those at the bottom of the priority list may remain unpaid.

9.   Assuming, of course, that the mortgage was registered in advance of the lien.

often allow the owner or contractor to remove the lien by providing alternative security for the claim.[10] This allows the flow of funds to continue.

9.5   TRUST PROVISIONS

A **trust** is a legal mechanism for separating the legal interest in property from the equitable interest.[11] In practical terms, it means that while one party (the trustee) has legal ownership and perhaps possession of the property for the time being, the trustee must use the property for the use and benefit of another party (the beneficiary).

Some mechanics' lien statutes create a trust in the funds paid by the owner to the general contractor. As soon as the funds are paid to the contractor, they are impressed with a trust. The contractor is a trustee, and those workers, subcontractors, and suppliers below the contractor are the beneficiaries. The terms of the trust require that the contractor pay all the beneficiaries before using any of the funds for any other purpose. The same trust is created as soon as the contractor pays a subcontractor: The subcontractor must pay its workers and suppliers first.

To illustrate, suppose the general contractor receives $100,000 as a progress payment, of which $90,000 is owed to subcontractors and laborers. If the contractor were to use $15,000 of the payment to pay down a bank loan or buy equipment, and had insufficient funds from its own resources make up the $5,000 difference, it would constitute a breach of trust.

One of the consequences of a breach of trust is that it may give rise to criminal charges. In some jurisdictions, the statutes contain penalties of fines and imprisonment for breach of trust, and in others, the violation may be prosecuted as criminal theft. Furthermore, directors and officers of the contractor may be personally liable and face criminal sanctions under some statutes, and anyone who knowingly participates in a breach of trust may be prosecuted.

Breaches of trust sometimes occur because the contractor is experiencing cash flow problems on one job and uses funds from another project honestly intending to make up the shortfall. It is a dangerous practice and is easily avoided simply by maintaining separate bank accounts for each project and refusing to co-mingle funds. The temptation may be great if the money is sitting there in another account or if a new lucrative contract has just been awarded. But the consequences are so severe that it is simply not worth the risk.

---

10.   The land and building under construction then cease to be security for the lien, and instead, the lien is secured by another form of security. For example, the owner can provide cash, a letter of credit, or a lien bond equal to the amount of the lien claim. This alternative security is then held in trust until the lien claim is resolved or abandoned. If the claim is proved, the claimant is paid out of the cash, letter of credit, or bond. If the claim is defeated or abandoned, the security is returned to the owner.

11.   The property need not be land. For the purposes of mechanics' lien legislation, the property is money.

CASE STUDY
Mackenzie Redi-Mix Co. Ltd. v. Miller Contracting Ltd. (1987), 20 B.C.L.R. 283 (B.C.C.A.).

The owner of the bridge project in question was the Ministry of Transportation and Highways (a government body similar to the state departments of transportation in the United States). Miller Contracting Ltd. was the general contractor, and Procon Builders Ltd. was the concrete placing subcontractor. Procon purchased its concrete from the plaintiff Mackenzie.

Miller paid Procon less than the full subcontract price. In fact, if Procon had completed its work, there would have been $46,000 more to be paid by Miller to Procon. However, Procon failed to complete, and Miller hired a replacement subcontractor to complete the Procon contract. Procon had not paid Mackenzie for concrete delivered while Procon was still on the job and owed Mackenzie approximately $109,000. Miller was able to show that it paid the replacement subcontractor an amount exceeding $46,000 to complete the Procon subcontract.

Mackenzie's argument at trial (and on this appeal) was that as a trust beneficiary, Mackenzie was entitled to be paid before Miller used any of its contract funds to pay itself. The effect of such a finding would be, if it were accepted, to make Miller a guarantor of its subcontractors' financial obligations to those working under the subcontractor. The courts in at least one other province (and some states) have held for plaintiffs in the position of Mackenzie. The British Columbia Court of Appeal did not agree:

> If a contractor who has paid a subcontractor in full may also be liable for that subcontractor's debts to materialmen, he will be unwilling to pay the subcontractor without assurances that those below in the construction chain have already been paid. The subcontractor will have to pay those materialmen before receiving contract moneys from the contractor, but from what funds is the subcontractor to make such a payment? The logical flow of money is from the contractor to the subcontractor and then to the materialmen. This payment flow will be hindered if each trustee must ensure that all those below have been paid before he pays those with whom he contracts.
>
> There is another problem if the appellants' interpretation is adopted. None of the contractors or subcontractors could appropriate any of the money to expenses or overhead, nor take any of the proceeds of the project as profits, until the whole job was complete and everyone fully paid. I think it rather unlikely that the legislature intended such an interpretation. . . .
>
> In my view, the answer to the question raised by this appeal must be that a head contractor who has paid to a subcontractor the amount properly payable to that subcontractor has discharged his trust obligation with respect to those who would have had a claim against the funds before they were paid to the subcontractor. In this case, Miller held money in trust for Procon and those below, including Mackenzie. When Miller paid all that was payable to Procon and Procon's replace-

ment, it discharged its trust obligation to Procon and those further down that line, including Mackenzie.

Questions

1. Would Mackenzie have had a lien remedy as well as a trust remedy?

2. If the answer to question 1 were yes, why would that not force the general contractor to assure itself that those "down the chain" had been paid before advancing funds?

3. If the answer to question 1 were yes, under what circumstances would Procon want to pursue the trust remedy as well as the lien remedy?

4. Is there a cause of action against Procon? If so, why would it be necessary to pursue Miller and the owner?

Analysis

1. Normally, yes. However, in the jurisdiction in question (as in many others), there is no lien remedy against government land. Were this a private owner on privately owned land, there would probably have been a lien claim.

2. Where there is a lien remedy, the general contractor would be prudent to make inquiries and obtain assurances before funds were advanced. Failure to do so could cause the general contractor to bear the loss.

3. The lien remedy in British Columbia limits the lien to 10 percent of the contract price (that is, 10 percent of the contract between the owner and general contractor). In some cases, the lien limit may be less than the claim, or many lien claimants may be sharing the fund. The trust remedy is not limited under this jurisdiction's legislation.

4. There is certainly a cause of action against Procon, as well as its directors and officers. Procon appears to have received more money on the contract than it paid out to those below. However, if the company is insolvent or its principals cannot be found, Mackenzie may not find it worthwhile to pursue that action.

9.6   HOLDBACK

Holdback requirements are sometimes found in mechanics' lien statutes. **Holdback** (sometimes referred to as retainage) is the term commonly used to describe the percentage of the contract price that the owner must *not* pay the contractor until a specified period after substantial or final completion. The percentages vary from one jurisdiction to another, but typically range from 5 to 15 percent. Some statutes have a sliding scale of percentages that depend on the contract price. The purpose is to designate a portion of the contract price that must be kept out of the hands of the contractor as a reserve to deal with liens at the end of the job.

That is not to say that the holdback funds are kept somewhere in a safe place. In fact, they may not exist at all. Unless the statute requires the holdback funds to be held in trust, there is no guarantee that the lender will disburse them to the owner or that the owner will not use them for another purpose. But it does guarantee that the contractor will not deal with them improperly before the holdback period expires, which provides further security to subcontractors, workers, and suppliers.

Some statutes create a single holdback system, as described earlier, that provides that the owner must hold back a percentage from the general contractor. Other statutes create a multiple holdback system that requires each party to hold back a percentage for all contracts below them. In either system, it is common for contracts with all parties to contain provisions that create a trickle-down effect. The general contractor does not want to finance the holdback and so will usually require its subcontractors to agree to the same holdback percentage.

The release of holdback funds is typically triggered by completion of the contract. It will usually be a specified period following substantial or total completion. The architect's or engineer's certificate will normally be used to determine the completion date. The architect or engineer must act impartially and fairly in making that determination.

9.7   RISK TO THE CONTRACTOR AND OWNER

The general contractor may take all appropriate precautions and disburse all funds received from the owner and yet be faced with liens at the end of the project. This may occur because a subcontractor has breached the trust provisions by failing to pay its employees or suppliers or because a subcontractor has become insolvent.

The general contractor will usually be required under the terms of its contract with the owner to remove all liens at its own expense. If it has already paid all its subcontractors, workers, and suppliers 100 percent of the amounts owed to them, and a second-tier subcontractor files a lien, the general contractor may end up paying twice for the subcontractor's work. Courts in some jurisdictions have held that the contractor becomes a guarantor of its subcontractor's financial obligations in these circumstances.

To avoid getting stung by the same bee twice, precautions are available to the general contractor.[12] One of the more effective precautions is to require the subcontractors to provide performance bonds and labor and material payment bonds. If

---

12.   Many of the following precautions are also available to an owner regarding possible default by the general contractor.

the subcontractor then defaults by failing to pay its workers or suppliers, the surety will be responsible.[13]

Another step often taken by general contractors is to require the subcontractors' managers to submit sworn statements each month as a precondition to payment declaring that to the best of their knowledge all of their financial obligations with respect to the project have been met, including payments to workers, subcontractors, and suppliers and assessments of all authorities having jurisdiction (such as workers' compensation premiums and taxes).[14]

Contractors often conduct their own investigations prior to contracting with a subcontractor so as to determine whether that subcontractor has a reputation for trouble. Further investigations, in the nature of telephone calls to subsubcontractors and suppliers and searching the title to the property for liens, are sometimes undertaken before progress payments are approved in order to catch payment problems as early as possible. If there is any risk that a contractor is not going to pay someone below, joint checks can be issued.

Finally, before payment is made, the contractor may demand from the subcontractor a waiver of liens. This type of waiver is valid only against the party who signs it. For example, if a subcontractor provides the waiver, it does not protect against a lien filed by an employee of the subcontractor.[15] In some cases, these waivers are demanded before any work is performed. This may seem contrary to public policy, but some courts have been known to enforce such waivers if supported by valid consideration.

The owner's liability may be limited to the amount of the holdback, or it may be unlimited, depending on the wording of the statute. In either case, the owner should exercise the same precautions outlined earlier with respect to general contractors. For example, the owner should demand performance and labor and material payment bonds from the general contractor. By employing some common sense as well as elementary precautions, owners and contractors can minimize the risks associated with liens.

9.8   PROBLEMS

1. One of the subcontracts entered into by a general contractor is for final cleanup. The cleaning subcontractor does not begin work on site until substantial completion. The statute requires liens to be filed within thirty days of completion of the prime contract. "Completion" in this jurisdiction is defined as substantial

---

13.   For further discussion, see Chapter 8.

14.   These are called statutory declarations in Canada. They should be drafted by an attorney to ensure they encompass all the financial obligations of the declarant.

15.   In some jurisdictions, a waiver of lien rights is ineffective if given by an individual worker.

rather than total completion. What effect, if any, might it have on the cleaning subcontractor's lien rights?

2. A statute requires claims of lien by workers to be filed not more than thirty days from the last day that the worker performed work on site. An unpaid worker, who has been laid off and who realizes that the thirty-day period has expired, goes to the site and spends an hour doing some touch-up work. He then files a lien for his two months' unpaid wages. Is the lien valid?

10

Delay Claims

10.1 INTRODUCTION

Delay claims are a fact of life on large construction projects. When delays occur, they adversely affect most if not all of the participants. The owner loses revenue or sales, the contractors incur both increased direct costs and extended overhead charges, and the consultants often must provide additional site visits. When significant delays occur, the parties will try to isolate the cause and identify the responsible party and may try to recover damages from that party.

For a party to recover damages for delay, it is necessary to prove at a minimum that (1) a delay occurred, (2) the delay was the fault of some other party (that is, compensable), and (3) the delay cost the claimant money. Delays often occur that are not attributable to the fault of any party. Weather delays are an example. Such delays may or may not be compensable, depending on the wording of the contract. Even if they are not compensable, they may be excusable, in which case the contractor would be entitled to an extension of the contract time and waiver of liquidated damages.

Delays are typically categorized as compensable, excusable, or noncompensable (that is, caused by the contractor). Those categories are explained in this chapter.

The success or failure of a claim for delay may depend on whether the delay affected critical path activities. The critical path is usually determined by the use of a **critical path method (CPM)** network diagram. Other factors that may affect the success or failure of the claim are the existence of concurrent delays, "no damage for delay" clauses, and the availability of documentary evidence needed to prove the claim. In this chapter, all those factors are discussed.

There are consultants who specialize in evaluating, presenting, and negotiating delay claims. These delay claims consultants are often construction professionals who have retired from active participation in the design or building fields and are skilled in schedule manipulation. The emergence of this branch of the consulting industry is evidence of the substantial sums that are often at stake in delay claims.

Delays can be dealt with in one of two ways: The delay can be permitted to extend the time for completion with claims resolved after the fact, or the work can be accelerated in order to make up the period of delay. The costs of **acceleration** can be as great as the costs of delay since acceleration is generally achieved through the use of overtime and additional labor, which can result in a decrease in efficiency. Acceleration claims are treated in much the same way as delay claims.

Directed acceleration claims, in which the owner acknowledges a delay but instructs the contractor to take all steps necessary to meet the contractual completion date, are relatively easy to recognize. However, there is also a category of acceleration claims known as constructive acceleration. **Constructive acceleration** occurs when the contractor has been forced to accelerate the work, without any acknowledgment by the owner that the contractor is required to do so. If the contractor has been delayed by a cause that entitles the contractor to an extension of the contract time, and the contractor's request for an extension is refused, the owner's insistence on the original completion date creates a condition of constructive acceleration and may entitle the contractor to compensation for costs incurred in accelerating the work.

10.2 CRITICAL PATH DELAYS

A critical path schedule is a network diagram that shows the sequence of construction activities as well as the duration of each activity and the start and finish dates of each activity. What differentiates a critical path schedule from a bar chart is the logic diagram (network) that describes the sequence of activities and shows the interrelationship between those activities. Each activity (except for procurement activities and the first construction activity, usually mobilization) will have at least one predecessor activity, and each activity (except for the completion activity, often cleanup) will have at least one successor activity. Because there may be two or more activities that cannot start until their common predecessor is completed, there will be more than one pathway through the network diagram.

Float (also called slack) is an important concept in critical path scheduling. If an activity can be delayed without causing any delay to the final completion date, that activity has float. The number of days of float is equal to the difference between the activity's early start date (the earliest date on which it can start) and its late start date (the latest date it can start without delaying the project completion). Activities with zero float are said to be on the critical path. At least one pathway must exist through the network diagram that contains only activities with zero float. These activities that then form the pathway with the longest aggregate duration from start to finish are called the critical path. (The start and end activities always have no float and always are on the critical path.) Any delay to a critical path activity, unless mitigated, will cause an equal delay to the project completion.

It may not be sufficient for a contractor to prove that a delay occurred that was caused by another party. If the delayed activities are on the critical path, the delay will very likely have a financial impact. However, if the delayed activities all have float, and the period of delay does not exceed the float, it may be difficult or impossible to prove entitlement to damages. Courts consistently rule that delays to activities on the critical path are of primary importance in evaluating delay claims. In fact, it is generally held that a contractor will not be entitled to a time extension for an excusable delay unless the delay extends the duration of the critical path. The question whether the owner or contractor is entitled to the benefit of any float in the schedule has not yet been definitively answered by the courts. If the owner is entitled to it, owner-caused delays that eat up the float are not compensable, and if the contractor is entitled to it, the opposite result is obtained. Another alternative, which is receiving approval in many courts, is that the *project* is entitled to it, in which case the first party to cause a delay that uses the float gets the benefit of that float, and no compensation is made. It is becoming increasingly common for the construction contract to define the right to the float.

There is a good reason the contractor should be entitled to the benefit of the float rather than the owner or the project. To illustrate, suppose that an office tower is being constructed, and the schedule shows that the elevator installation has two weeks of float and therefore is not on the critical path. A temporary hoist is being used during elevator installation, and the hoist is scheduled to be dismantled as soon as the elevators are operational. A delay in the elevator work of less than two weeks will not delay completion but will result in a rental charge of two weeks more for the hoist. If the owner causes such a delay, the contractor should be entitled to compensation. This result is obtained from basic principles of negligence and contract law, without reference to delay claim cases. Of course, the owner can protect against such claims by negotiating into the contract a clause that precludes claims for delay to noncritical activities, as long as the delay does not exceed the float.

It is relatively easy to look at a critical path schedule to determine if a delayed activity was on the critical path at the time the delay occurred. But that is not the whole story. An activity with float, if delayed for a period equal to or greater than the float, will become critical. Such a delay may also have the effect of making previously critical activities noncritical, thus altering the critical path. For that reason, a detailed schedule analysis must be done to properly analyze the effects of any delay.

10.3   COMPENSABLE, EXCUSABLE, AND CONTRACTOR-CAUSED DELAYS

Most construction contracts make some effort to distinguish between excusable compensable (often simply referred to as **compensable**), excusable noncompensable (referred to as **excusable**), and contractor-caused (nonexcusable noncompensable) delays. The CCDC 2 contract contains the following compensable delay provision:

> If the Contractor is delayed in the performance of the Work by an act or omission of the Owner, Consultant, or anyone employed or engaged by them directly or indirectly, contrary to the provisions of the Contract Documents, then the Contract time shall be extended for such reasonable time as the Consultant may decide in consultation with the Contractor. The Contractor shall be reimbursed by the Owner for reasonable costs incurred by the Contractor as the result of such delay.[1]

The AIA document contains a similar provision with respect to extension of time for compensable delay but does not explicitly state that the contractor is to be reimbursed.[2] Rather, a clause provides that the entitlement to an extension of time " ... does not preclude recovery of damages for delay by either party under other provisions of the Contract Documents."[3] Under both contracts, the result will usually be the same as if no clause at all dealt with delays. The law will usually presume, absent any provision to the contrary, that there is an implied term in the agreement that each party will not impede or hinder performance by the other. Under the AIA contract cited, it is arguable that the owner is not liable for the negligence of its independent contractors if a delay is caused by one of them. Even so, the owner will remain liable for the performance of its contractual duties (such as providing design details) even if those duties have been delegated to independent contractors.

The force majeure provision of the CCDC 2 contract provides that the contractor is entitled to an extension of time for delays that are excusable. Those delays include any cause beyond the contractor's control. That provision further provides that "The Contractor shall not be entitled to payment for costs incurred by such delays unless such delays result from actions by the Owner."[4] The AIA Document A201-1987 contains a provision entitling the contractor to an extension of time but does not explicitly preclude a claim for compensation.[5] Yet the result is the same

---

1. Clause GC 6.5.1. See also GC 6.5.2, which contains a compensable delay provision.

2. AIA Document A201-1987, clause 8.3.1.

3. AIA Document A201-1987, clause 8.3.3.

4. Clause GC 6.5.3.

5. Clause 8.3.1.

because the law will not hold parties responsible for acts beyond their control unless the risk of those events is contractually accepted by the party.

With respect to contractor-caused delays, the CCDC 2 delay section does not specifically address the issue; instead, a clause recites what is a basic principle of negligence law:

> If either party to the Contract should suffer damage in any manner because of any wrongful act or neglect of the other party or of anyone for whom the other party is responsible in law, then that party shall be reimbursed by the other party for such damage.[6]

The statement would be true without repeating it in the contract; however, the effect of including it in the contract is to make such a wrongful act or neglect actionable as breach of contract as well as in negligence. Therefore, a contractor-caused delay becomes a breach of contract.

10.4   CONCURRENT DELAYS

In many cases, compensable, excusable, and contractor-caused delays, or two of those three factors, contribute to delay the same activities. For example, the architect may be slow in resolving design discrepancies, a labor disruption may occur, and the contractor's productivity may decline because of poor supervision. This is referred to in the case law as concurrent delay. Thus, concurrent delays are said to occur when two or more independent delays coincide. If the parties are able to isolate the activities affected by each delay and determine the effect of each delay on each activity, in order to remove the concurrency, claims may be proved on an individual basis. Where concurrent delays cannot be apportioned, neither party can recover from the other.

Courts have thus been reluctant to award compensation to the contractor or to enforce liquidated damages provisions in favor of the owner for concurrent delays unless the contract contains a provision that provides for extensions of time for compensable and excusable delays, which allows a court to set-off those delays against contractor-caused delays.

10.5   NO DAMAGE FOR DELAY CLAUSES

Owners will sometimes attempt to negotiate into the contract a "no damages for delay" clause. These clauses are designed to protect the owner from claims for dam-

---

6.   Clause GC 9.2.1.

ages associated with delay and acceleration but do not preclude the contractor from insisting on an extension of time. They are considered to be exculpatory clauses and, consequently, are construed by the courts very strictly against the party they are intended to protect. In extreme cases, courts may refuse to enforce them at all. Such clauses must be construed strictly in limiting a claimant's rights because of the unconscionably harsh result. Only where the language is clear will a court deprive a contractor of the right to damages where the delay is caused by the owner.[7]

No damages for delay clauses come in many shapes and sizes. Some, like the CCDC 2 exclusion of damages for force majeure events, are reasonable in scope and represent a considered allocation of risk.[8] They are generally enforceable. Others are wider in scope and preclude claims for owner-caused delays, where the delay was unintentional. Still others try to exclude all delays, including those caused intentionally by the owner. Some courts will enforce these clauses, whereas others take the position that a contract will be interpreted according to the following rules of interpretation:

1. Words intended to exempt a party from liability because of its own fault are to be construed strictly against it.

2. It is the duty of one party, for whom another is doing work under a contract, to do his or her part to facilitate the work.

3. A contract will not be so construed so as to put one party at the mercy of another.[9]

Allowing the owner to delay the contractor at will, without any recourse for the contractor, puts the contractor at the mercy of the owner and may render the clause unenforceable.

10.6   PROVING A DELAY CLAIM

As with any claim for breach of contract or negligence, it is necessary for the claimant to prove both liability (entitlement) and damages. Entitlement for a delay claim is often easier to prove than damages. The claimant must prove that another party breached a duty owed to the claimant, contractual or otherwise, that caused the claimant delay.

---

7. *Perini Pacific Ltd.* v. *Greater Vancouver Sewerage and Drainage District*, [1967] S.C.R. 189; *Peter Kiewit Sons' Co.* v. *Iowa S. Utilities Co.*, 355 F. Supp 376 (S.D. Iowa 1973).

8. Clause GC 6.5.3.

9. *Wilson and English Constr. Co.* v. *N.Y. Central Railway Co.* (1934), 269 N.Y.S. 874 (N.Y.C.A.).

   Practical difficulties may arise in proving damages for delay. These difficulties are frequently related to lack of adequate documentation. A good understanding of the categories of damages (in Canada these are referred to as heads of damage) ordinarily recovered and the techniques for quantifying damages will enable potential claimants to generate the appropriate documentation to be used in the event of compensable delay.

Heads of Damages

For contractors who have been delayed, the most common head of damage is extended overhead. Overhead is comprised of two components, field overhead and home office overhead. At the time of bid, the contractor anticipates incurring a certain amount of overhead expense, which is proportional to the length of the job.

   Field overhead is relatively easy to calculate. If a delay of two months takes place, some pieces of equipment will be idle for that period. The normal rental rate for that equipment will be a good approximation of the damages attributable to having that equipment sit idle. Of course the contractor would prefer being paid the charge-out rate to the rental rate on the basis that if the equipment had not been idle on this job it could have been earning the charge-out rate on another job. The flaw in that argument is that the contractor could have rented a similar piece of equipment elsewhere and used it on another job. Other field overhead would include temporary power, job site office rental, and the like.

   Job site labor is treated similarly to equipment. Delays do not usually occur with predictable durations or at predictable times. It generally does not make sense to reassign or lay off supervisory staff when delays occur unless it is known in advance that there will be a long and finite period of delay during which no work can be performed. For that reason, the salaries of the job site management team will be included for the period of delay, as well as costs associated with termination and rehiring of hourly labor.

   The contractor's home office overhead will also be increased by a delay. A construction office is generally capable of handling only a certain level of work, and if the level increases beyond capacity, the office, including levels of manpower, must be expanded. The contractor expects that each job will contribute a certain percentage of its revenue to home office overhead. If one job is delayed, the amount of revenue it contributes per month is reduced. The difficulty associated with home office overhead is that not all of it is attributable to the one job that was delayed. It must be apportioned among jobs. The following formula has been developed for calculating the apportionment:[10]

---

10.   It is known as the **Eichleay formula,** named after the claimant Eichleay Corp. in its appeal to the Armed Services Board of Contract Appeals, No. 5183, 60-2 BCA 91, para. 2688.

$$\text{Claimed overhead} = \frac{CA}{TB} \times \frac{P.\ O/H}{P} \times D$$

where   CA   =   the contract amount of the contract that was delayed;

TB   =   the total billing by the contractor during the period P;

P. O/H   =   total home office overhead for the same period P;

D   =   the duration of delay; and

P   =   the period of performance of the contract.

For example, if the contract in question was for $1 million, scheduled to last one year, and the contractor billed $5 million during that year, the fraction CA/TB would be ⅕. That means 20 percent of the contractor's overhead for the year was attributable to this contract. Assuming period overhead for the year (P. O/H) was $500,000, and the period of performance P was 365 days, the fraction (P. O/H)/P would be 500,000/365, or $1,370 per day. Twenty percent of this amount, or $274 per day, is attributable to this contract. If the duration of delay D is 30 days, the claim for home office overhead is 30 × 274, or $8,220.

The Eichleay formula should not be applied blindly. There may be circumstances that would render an unfair result. For example, the contract in question may be the only contract that the contractor has ongoing, because of a downturn in the economy or because the contractor is winding up its operations, which would cause 100 percent of the overhead to be attributed to the contract. Or the contract in question may be close to complete when the delay occurred, resulting in a disproportionately small amount of resources being expended on it during the period of delay. If the contract period is atypical, it may make more sense to use historical data to calculate overhead. Courts may not accept the use of the formula if it would produce an obviously unfair result.

Another common head of damages is loss in productivity. This may occur owing to a number of factors, such as the delay pushing the work into winter conditions, the reduction in productivity associated with loss of momentum caused by repeated stopping and starting, or the loss in productivity caused by performing work out of sequence. Acceleration claims frequently include claims for loss in productivity due to crowding. The contractor chooses an optimum size crew at the time of bid, and adding labor may increase the total output but reduce the average output per worker. These losses are notoriously difficult to quantify.

Delays may cause increases in material and labor prices. Some material (such as cast-in-place concrete) cannot be purchased in advance and stored on site, and the contractor may be forced as well to pay higher labor rates because of delay. These are relatively easy to document once entitlement has been proved.

Delay claims may include a component for loss of profit. These claims may fall under the heading "consequential damages," as discussed in Chapter 2 (under the heading "Damages"), and are likely to be considered too remote. However, if the contractor can prove that the loss of profits is not too speculative, and was reasonably foreseeable by the owner at the time the breach occurred, they may be recoverable.

Required Documentation

The first documents to assemble in preparation for a delay claim are the project schedules. The general contractor should have a bid schedule, ideally in critical path form. It is not uncommon for schedules to be updated either on a regular basis or as significant events affect the schedule. Finally, at the end of the project, the final update (if there is one) should represent the as-built schedule.

Some contractors do not do schedule updates. As long as other forms of project control are in place, failure to update the schedule is not necessarily grounds for criticism unless such updates are contractually required. However, a lack of updated schedules will make it difficult to reconstruct the delays and their effects. The information will have to come from other sources, such as project diaries, correspondence, and photographs.

Various techniques have been developed for schedule manipulation and analysis, but their purpose is usually the same. Each compensable delay is incorporated into the schedule in order to determine what activities are affected and to what extent. It is usually necessary to adjust each update of the schedule accordingly and to remove the effects of noncompensable delays. Unless the schedule is computer generated, the task may be prohibitively expensive. Even using a computer, proving a delay claim is frequently a very costly exercise.

Delay claims consultants may offer advice not only on the effect of delays, but on their compensability as well. However, different types of expertise are required for these two types of advice. If the claim relates to reduction in productivity for an earth-moving operation, for example, the consultant must have expertise in earth moving for the advice to carry any weight (or be admissible in court). Some contractors prefer to hire a claims consultant and not an attorney so as to negotiate a resolution of the claim and avoid the expense of litigation, but if the claim cannot be settled, the consultant's report may be useless or even damaging in a lawsuit. Legal advice should be obtained before the consultant prepares the report, even if it is just to point the consultant in the right direction.

Adequate project records must be maintained as a matter of course, and the best time to start compiling documents to support or defend a claim is at the first indication that a delay may occur, *not* when the claim is made.[11] If a contractor believes

---

11. These documents often include transmittals showing when material was delivered, labor records, correspondence that discusses the delay, diaries, minutes of meetings, photographs, telephone records, and invoices.

that the owner is delaying the project, letters should be written immediately to put the owner on notice. Many contracts contain strict notice requirements for claims, and failure to comply with the contract requirements may in some cases result in the claim being barred.[12] If the claim is large, legal advice should be obtained for the drafting of the notice. Such advice is relatively inexpensive and should preserve the claimant's rights if done in a timely manner. Similarly, an owner should obtain legal advice as soon as notice of a large claim has been made.

Another class of documents needed to prove many delay claims is the productivity and cost reports of the job in question. If the claim includes loss of productivity, it will be necessary to show what productivity was achieved on portions of the job that were not delayed in order to compare them with delayed portions. Contractors track productivity for various purposes, including maintaining a database for estimating future jobs. To be of use in a delay claim, the records should be kept in the ordinary course of business and at regular, frequent intervals. Superintendents may view record keeping and paperwork as a waste of time, but lack of adequate documentation has led to the defeat of many valid and valuable claims. Inexpensive software packages are available commercially that are designed to record productivity data during the progress of a construction project.

Total Cost and Measured Mile Approaches

The **total cost approach** involves taking two "snapshots" of the project cost: one at the beginning and one at the end. The beginning cost is the contractor's estimate, and the end cost is the sum total of all the contractor's costs to perform the work. The contractor then argues that the difference in cost is due to breaches of contract by the owner, such as delay, and attempts to prove that such breaches occurred and that the total increase in the project cost is recoverable as damages.

This approach is fraught with difficulties. It may be tempting to use because it avoids the costly schedule manipulation and compilation of documents required for a detailed individual analysis of delays. But it can result in the entire claim being rejected. The problem arises where there have been increases in cost and delays not caused by the owner. The owner has only to prove that some of the increase in cost is due to other causes, or that the costs would have occurred in the absence of the breaches, and those costs must be deducted from the claim. There are very few cases where the owner cannot point to contractor error and excusable (but noncompensable) causes.

That is not to say that the total cost approach will be rejected every time. Sometimes it is nearly impossible to isolate all the causes and tie each to an increase in

---

12. For example, CCDC 2 clause GC 6.5.4 requires the written notice of claim be made not later than ten working days after commencement of the delay. AIA Document A201-1987 clause 4.3.3 requires written notice be delivered within twenty-one days of the claimant first recognizing the condition giving rise to the claim.

cost. Where such impracticability exists, and as long as the claimant was not substantially responsible for the increase in cost, the approach has a chance of success.

The **measured mile approach** involves using a portion of the contract unaffected by delays as a yardstick to compare productivity for the rest of the contract. The contractor is thus able to demonstrate what could have been achieved in the absence of the owner's breaches. It is still necessary, of course, for the contractor to prove the breaches and tie them to the loss in productivity, and it is still open to the owner to show that other causes were at work. The measured mile approach can also be used defensively by the owner if there is a portion of the contract for which no breach is alleged and for which poor productivity was obtained.

10.7   PROBLEMS

1. The network diagram for construction of an office tower shows two critical paths: one involving completion of the mechanical room and the other involving completion of the elevators. The elevator subcontractor causes a delay of two weeks. The mechanical subcontractor causes a concurrent delay of one week. The owner sues the general contractor for the two-week delay, and the general contractor names the two subcontractors as third parties. The mechanical subcontractor's defense is that its delay did not cause any loss because the delay to the elevators took the mechanical room off the critical path. Should that argument succeed? Explain.

2. A contractor suffers a compensable delay of three months. The contract is for $1 million and is to last one year. During that year, the contractor's billing totaled $10 million. Home office overhead during the year was $500,000. The delay occurred near the end of the project, during the cleanup phase. Discuss calculation of damages.

3. An owner and contractor enter into a contract that states that "the contractor is entitled to an extension but no compensation for delays caused by the owner." The owner suspends work on the site for a period of two months because the delay is advantageous to the owner in its dealings with prospective tenants. The contractor claims compensation. Should the clause be enforceable? Explain.

11

Conflicts of Interest and Ethical Considerations

11.1 OVERVIEW

Many issues of law are not susceptible to precise answers; there are shades of gray in the unsettled areas. This is equally true in the area of conflict of interest although in more recent years guidelines have been developed by various professions dealing with conflicts problems.[1] Conflicts of interest create ethical as well as legal problems. In fact, many disciplinary actions taken against engineers and architects for unprofessional conduct are the result of conflicts of interest. Codes of ethics adopted by professional and trade associations can assist in resolving such problems. Failure to follow these codes of ethics can also give rise to legal liability and disciplinary action against individuals bound by the applicable code.

It has been said that a breach of ethics may be difficult to define, but a person should recognize one when it is present. However, for anyone inexperienced in the

---

1. For example, the State Board of Registration for Professional Engineers and Land Surveyors of Colorado publishes a booklet entitled "Bylaws and Rules of Procedure and Rules of Professional Conduct," which is similar to the guidelines established by the governing bodies in other states.

construction environment, the vague assurance that "you'll know it when you see it" may provide little comfort. Some conflicts of interest are easily recognized because they occur commonly. Others can be recognized because duties are owed to more than one party simultaneously, in which case the issue is to determine which duty is higher.

For certain professions, codes of ethics clearly identify to whom duties are owed and in what priority. Attorneys, for example, have developed very specific rules dealing with conflict of interest between two clients and between the duty owed to the client and the duty owed to the court.[2] Virtually all governing bodies for architects and engineers have similar codes of conduct. Although individuals who are not members of professional bodies are not bound by their rules, the law will sometimes provide a legal remedy for unethical behavior.[3] The following discussion applies to members of professional bodies.

For design professionals, duties to the following parties can usually be found in the applicable code of conduct in each state or province:

- Duty to the public
- Duty to the client
- Duty to the employer
- Duty to the profession

In this chapter, each of these duties is examined together with the interrelationship between the duties. The duty to the public includes the overriding duty to protect the safety and welfare of members of the public, as well as the duty to act with fairness and integrity toward members of the public. The duty to the client includes the avoidance of conflict between personal gain and the client's interest, as well as a duty to maintain confidentiality of certain information. The duty to the employer is similar in some ways to that owed to the client, particularly regarding confidentiality and noncompetition. The duty to the profession is often a formalization of basic principles of common courtesy but may include an obligation to report misconduct of other members.

11.2   THE DUTY TO THE PUBLIC

Professional engineering and architecture registration bodies have been established to protect the public interest, and therefore, it is not surprising that the codes of

---

2. One codification of these rules is found in the American Bar Association Model Rules of Professional Conduct.

3. The law may impose a **fiduciary relationship** on parties in order to protect one of the parties, or it may impose one of the attributes of a fiduciary relationship, such as the requirement not to disclose or make use of confidential information.

ethics recognize the duty to the public as higher than any other.[4] Disregard for public safety can lead to liability in negligence and loss of the right to practice. This duty generally encompasses the duty not to undertake work outside one's area of competence.

Engineers and architects are sometimes called upon by their employers and clients to compromise their professional judgment in order to save money or otherwise further the client's or employer's interest. The engineer or architect in question may be in the role of manager rather than designer. This type of pressure can put the engineer or architect in a further conflict if employment is contingent on the outcome. There is no difficult issue in these cases: Public interest in safety must prevail.[5]

The duty to the public encompasses more than safety. It also includes a duty to act with fairness and integrity. One association obligates its members to act "independently and with fairness and justice to all parties."[6] Another requires its members to be "objective and truthful in professional reports, statement or testimony."[7] Members of the public may rely on professional reports when making investment decisions and are entitled to assume that the author honestly believed the contents of the report.

Engineers and architects are frequently called upon to act as expert witnesses in litigation. They may be retained by one of the parties to assist in the preparation of the case or to give an expert opinion on some technical matter in issue. The professional's obligation is to provide his or her honestly held opinion, whether or not that opinion advances the client's interest.

Not all technical issues are susceptible to only one correct answer. There may be alternative theories that are in accordance with engineering principles that fit the facts. In those circumstances, it is acceptable for the expert witness to present one of those theories, assuming that the witness believes it to be credible, but he or she must be prepared to agree that it is only one of several plausible explanations. It is unprofessional conduct to put forward an unlikely theory as though it were an equally acceptable alternative.

When professionals are sued in negligence, the plaintiff must prove on a balance of probabilities[8] that the defendant failed to meet the standard of care expected of

---

4. The Colorado rules for engineers provide that the duty to protect public safety, health, property, and welfare is "their primary obligation," whereas the Canadian Council of Professional Engineers uses the term *paramount* for that same obligation.

5. The Colorado rules (footnote 1, Rule VI) require engineers to "not permit a client, employer, another person or organization to direct, control or otherwise affect the registrant's exercise of independent professional judgment in rendering professional services for the client."

6. The Association of Professional Engineers, Geologists and Geophysicists of Alberta, Code of Ethics, Rule number 4.

7. Footnote 1, Rule III.

8. The balance of probabilities test means that the claim is more likely true than not. In a criminal case, the **burden of proof** is beyond a reasonable doubt, which is a much more difficult burden to meet.

an average professional in the field and in order to do that must call an expert witness to offer that opinion. It is a very serious allegation for one professional to call unprofessional the work of another, and it should not be done unless the breach is clear.

An expert witness is not a hired gun. The rules of evidence prohibit the admission of opinion evidence except where the subject matter is beyond the knowledge of the average person. The expert is there to assist the court in understanding these technical matters. When the expert takes on the role of advocate, independence is lost.

If the expert witness is paid a fee that is contingent on the outcome of the litigation, there is a strong incentive for the expert to put his or her personal interest before the public interest. Disclosure of such a fee arrangement would render the opinion of the expert of little or no weight and could result in the expert's testimony being rendered inadmissible. The rules governing conduct of attorneys prohibit contingent fees for expert witnesses.[9] Although these rules are binding on attorneys rather than witnesses, such a fee arrangement would still constitute a breach of the expert's duty to remain impartial and independent.[10]

It does not further the client's interest for an expert witness to give an opinion that advances the client's case if that opinion will not stand up to scrutiny. The expert will be cross-examined, and the problems with the opinion are likely to be exposed. The client would be better served by receiving an honestly held opinion in the first instance. If the opinion is unfavorable, the client might be better off settling the case in its early stages rather than incurring substantial legal and expert fees pursuing a losing cause.

11.3   THE CLIENT'S INTEREST

The duty to the client usually ranks above all other duties except the duty to the public. This duty is not always spelled out in detail in the applicable code of conduct, but it includes a duty not to accept financial compensation from any other party whose interest conflicts with an existing client and a duty not to accept any assignment where personal interest may conflict with the client's interest. To illus-

---

9.   Footnote 2, rule 3.4 (b).

10.   An engineer entered into a contingent fee agreement to give expert evidence in a lawsuit. He was disciplined by the APEGBC, and agreed to a stipulated order providing for a three-month suspension. The comments of the Discipline Committee are instructive: "The function of an expert is often to help the understanding and demystifying of complicated technical matters beyond the immediate comprehension of lay people, including members of a judicial court and whoever hired the expert. For this reason it is incumbent upon the engineer, before accepting such an assignment, to carefully evaluate his/her ability, through training and experience, to provide the necessary expertise in the matter. Expert testimony must be factual, unbiased and non-adversarial. These fundamental requirements can be undermined when fee payment for the expert is contingent upon a successful outcome of the trial." For further details, see the report "In the Matter of Roger Hill, P.Eng.," *The BC Professional Engineer,* October 1991.

trate, if an engineer is retained by a client to obtain zoning approval for a development that will decrease surrounding property values, and the engineer owns property in the affected area, a conflict exists between the client's interest and the engineer's personal interest. Approval of the client following full disclosure of the conflict may cure the problem.

During the course of performing his or her duties, the engineer or architect will become aware of certain facts that are confidential. The definition of confidential information may vary from one jurisdiction to another but is generally understood to mean information that is not available from public sources. For example, an architect may be told what the owner's construction budget is; that information must be kept confidential. A contractor bidding or working on the project could make use of it to the owner's disadvantage.

Confidential information may, in some circumstances, include public information. One court described the possibility this way:

> On the other hand, it is perfectly possible to have a confidential document, be it a formula, a plan, a sketch, or something of that kind, which is the result of work done by the maker upon materials which may be available for the use of anybody; but what makes it confidential is the fact that the maker of the document has used his brain and thus produced a result which can only be produced by somebody who goes through the same process.[11]

An exception to the duty of confidentiality is where the duty to the public demands disclosure. The code of ethics in Alberta describes the duty as follows:

> Professional engineers, geologists and geophysicists shall not disclose confidential information without the consent of their clients or employers, unless the withholding of the information is considered contrary to the safety of the public.[12]

11.4   THE EMPLOYER'S INTEREST

An employee is an agent of the employer. One of the attributes of an agency relationship is the duty of fidelity: The employee must be loyal to the employer. Loyalty means that the employee must put the employer's interest ahead of personal interest.

The employee's duty to the employer requires that the employee not accept financial compensation from any other party whose interest conflicts with the employer's interest, nor accept any assignment where personal interest may conflict

---

11. *Saltman Engineering Co. Ltd.* v. *Campbell Engineering Co. Ltd.* (1948), 65 R.P.C. 203, adopted by the Supreme Court of Canada in *Lac Minerals Ltd.* v. *International Corona Resources Ltd.* (1989), 61 D.L.R. (4th) 14 at p. 71.

12. APEGGA Code of Ethics, Rule 6.

with the employer's interest. The most common example of such a conflict arising is an employee competing with the employer either by "moonlighting" or by quitting in order to pursue an opportunity found by the employer. For example, an employee engineer who accepts engineering assignments "on the side," even if the work is performed on weekends or in the evening, is in competition with the employer. As long as it is work that the employer could reasonably perform, accepting the assignment privately would constitute a breach of the employee's duty.

One remedy for such a breach is a "constructive trust."[13] Any profit earned by the employee in competition with the employer is held in trust for the employer, and the employee can be forced to pay damages to the employer equal to those profits. Of course, the employee may obtain the consent of the employer in advance in order to avoid this result.

In addition, there is a duty of confidentiality. The issue of confidentiality often arises when employment is terminated. Any attempt to use client lists or other trade secrets of the employer is a breach of the duty of confidentiality.

It is not uncommon for employers to require employees to agree, either at the time the employee is hired or at the time of termination (if a severance package is being negotiated), that the employee will not compete with the employer for a period of time.[14] The agreement may require that the employee not accept employment in a certain field for a period following termination. Such clauses, if unreasonable in scope, are unenforceable. Courts will not unduly restrict the basic right of individuals to earn a living. If the noncompetition agreement covers too broad an employment field, or too large a geographical area, or too long a time, it will not be enforceable.

11.5 THE DUTY TO THE PROFESSION

The professions of architecture and engineering are self-governing in the sense that once legislation is in place regulating the profession, it is left to the members of that profession to oversee enforcement of the regulations. The members elect a board or council, which in turn sets up committees to conduct investigations and disciplinary proceedings, verify qualifications of new members, draft bylaws, and perform whatever other functions may be necessary.

One of the consequences of self-governance is that members must accept the less than enviable duty of policing each other. It lowers the reputation and quality of the

---

13. A trust is defined in Chapter 9 (section 9.5). A trust may be created by a party intentionally, in which case the trust is called an express trust. It may also be created by statute, as in the case of mechanics' lien legislation. Or it may be implied at law in order to protect the rights of one party in a relationship. This type of trust is called a constructive trust and may be used to protect the rights of the employer if the employee improperly competes with the employer.

14. This is known as a noncompetition agreement.

entire profession to allow members to practice negligently or unprofessionally. For that reason, statutes and bylaws have been enacted that require members to report the unprofessional conduct of their fellow members. Some governing bodies can expel a member for failing to report a malpractice claim against himself or herself.

If an engineer or architect does not have access to all the relevant facts, criticism of the work or opinion of another member of the profession may be considered unprofessional conduct. This may seem like an obvious proposition, but its application can be troublesome. Consider the dilemma faced by an expert witness who is given limited access to documents and other evidence and who is asked to express an opinion based on a set of assumptions and perhaps a few key documents. In fact, this is quite common in construction lawsuits because it is the job of the attorney to place before the court and to prove the facts underlying the opinion. If the expert relies on facts not in evidence, the opinion may be worthless.

The expert must provide an opinion based on a limited set of facts, and that opinion may impugn the professionalism of one of the defendants. To be fair to all parties, the expert should clearly state the assumptions on which the opinion is based and should advise the client that the opinion may change if other facts are shown to be true.

11.6   THE DUAL ROLE OF THE A/E AS OWNER'S AGENT AND IMPARTIAL ARBITER

Certain functions are performed by a design professional that must be done in the client's interest; advice regarding selection of contractors, inspection of the work for deficiencies, and negotiation with regulatory bodies are examples.

The architect of record for a building project is almost always required under the terms of his or her contract to perform the following additional functions, each of which can substantially affect the rights of the contractor:

- Evaluate and certify requests for progress payments.
- Evaluate claims for extra payment and delay.
- Issue the certificate of completion.
- Act as the first arbiter of disputes between the owner and contractor.

In performing these functions, the architect (or engineer, as the case may be) must not allow any perceived or real obligation to the owner to influence his or her decision such that it creates bias or a decision unfair to the contractor.[15]

---

15.   The most recent version of the CCDC 2 contract, clause GC 2.2.6, states explicitly that the consultant must not show favor to either party when interpreting the contract.

Certainly, the architect must not prejudice the owner's position, for example, by certifying an amount for payment that exceeds the value of the work performed. But the tendency is to favor the owner, for a variety of reasons.

Three interests are at work when a dispute arises over a claim for extra payment. The architect owes a duty to the owner to protect against unfounded claims. The contractor may be looking for an extra for work that should have been included in the original bid. The architect also owes a duty to the contractor to act fairly and impartially in evaluating the claim. The third interest is the architect's self-interest.

The architect's self-interest exists because approving a claim for an extra may mean that there was an error or omission in the design. In effect, the architect is being asked to evaluate the adequacy of his or her own design. If the extra is approved where the adequacy of the design is called into question, the owner may sue the architect to recover the extra. At the very least, the implicit admission of an extra will lower the esteem of the designer in the owner's eyes and may affect the likelihood of obtaining future work.

If the architect honestly believes that the contractor is entitled to an extra, regardless of the cause, the claim should be approved. But the architect should be careful not to make any statement that could prejudice his or her insurer's rights. If the contractor's claim raises the possibility of a claim against the architect, the architect should notify his or her insurer and seek legal advice before admitting responsibility.

CASE STUDY
Blecick v. School District No. 18 of Cochise County, Arizona, 406 P.2d 750 (Ariz. C.A. 1965).

A contractor sued the project architect for failing to issue a certificate of completion. The contractor had no direct contract with the architect. The following extract contains a concise summary of the architect's legal position:

> The remaining question as to whether the architects have immunity from suit for refusal to issue a completion certificate must be answered in the affirmative. In the capacity of an arbitrator whose functions require the exercise of judgment, an architect cannot be held liable in damages for failure to exercise care or skill in the performance of his functions. Where a construction contract such as the one herein involved authorizes payments to the builder only after issuance of certificates by the supervising architects and vests the architects with broad supervisory powers, the architects, in making decisions as to the granting of certificates, are acting in the capacity of arbitrators.

Questions

1. Is the architect's immunity absolute?
2. Is another course of action open to the contractor?

Analysis

1. No. If the architect acts in bad faith, there is no immunity. For example, in the case of *Craviolini* v. *Scholer & Fuller*, 357 P.2d 611 (1961), the complainants alleged a conspiracy involving the architects to bankrupt the plaintiff and to interfere with contractual relations.
2. The contractor could seek to appeal the decision of the architect. It is also open to sue the owner for payment in the absence of a certificate although such actions are often unsuccessful because the certificate is a condition precedent to payment.

11.7 PROBLEMS

1. A contractor has entered into an agreement with an owner that contains a "no damages for delay" clause, precluding recovery from the owner for any delay, howsoever caused. The owner causes an intentional delay, which results in severe financial consequences to the contractor. The contractor makes a claim, reasonable in all the circumstances except for the no damages clause, which the architect must evaluate. How should the architect deal with the claim?

2. An engineer is hired as an expert witness for a lawsuit. In the course of investigating the facts, the engineer discovers that his client has defrauded another party. The lawsuit is settled, and as part of the settlement, the parties enter into a confidentiality agreement. The client demands that the engineer keep confidential all facts learned during the investigation. To whom does the engineer owe duties? Which duty prevails?

3. An engineer has designed formwork for a difficult concrete pour. The design is submitted by the engineer to her superior, who suggests that smaller structural members can be used without violating the applicable code. The engineer rechecks her calculations but remains unconvinced. What course of action should the engineer take? Does it make any difference if the superior is not a professional engineer?

4. An engineer employee has invented a new product for use in building construction. The invention was made during the course of employment but has not yet been disclosed to the employer or anyone else. The engineer decides to quit his

job and patent the invention as his own. Is there a breach of any duty? Discuss the ethical issues involved.

5. An environmental engineer is hired by a developer to assess the impact of a proposed project. The engineer concludes that there will be significant environmental problems, and so advises the client. The client advises that she will not use the engineer's report, but will tell the planning authority that there are no significant environmental problems. What are the engineer's obligations?

12

Labor Law

12.1 OVERVIEW

Labor law generally refers to the law that governs the union–management relationship as well as the employee–union relationship, whereas employment law is commonly understood to refer to the law that governs the employee–employer relationship (with no union representation). This chapter is primarily concerned with labor law. A brief discussion of employment law is found in the final section of the chapter.

Labor law is not considered a branch of construction law but is an area of law unto itself. However, construction professionals, particularly those on the contracting side, should possess at least a basic understanding of labor law principles in order to avoid some of the mistakes frequently committed by contractors in dealing with labor issues, avoid committing unfair labor practices, and know when to seek legal advice.

One basic purpose of labor legislation is to promote industrial peace. Another basic purpose was expressed succinctly by Chief Justice Hughes of the U.S. Supreme Court, as follows:

That is a fundamental right. Employees have as clear a right to organize and select their representatives for lawful purposes as the respondent has to organize its business and select its own officers and agents. Discrimination and coercion to prevent free exercise of the right of employees to self-organization and representation is a proper subject for condemnation by competent legislative authority. Long ago we stated the reason for labor organizations. We said that they were organized out of the necessities of the situation; that a single employee was helpless in dealing with an employer; that he was dependent ordinarily on his daily wage for the maintenance of himself and his family; that if the employer refused to pay him the wages that he thought fair, he was nevertheless unable to leave the employ and resist arbitrary and unfair treatment; that union was essential to give laborers opportunity to deal on an equality with their employer.[1]

Before workers began to organize, there was an extreme inequality of bargaining power between employer and worker. That inequality is evident today in countries that either prohibit worker unions or make organization of workers difficult. Such inequality is characterized by subsistence-level wages and unsafe and inhumane working conditions. Although such conditions still exist in the United States and Canada, they are not as prevalent or extreme as during the previous century, prior to the growth of the union movement. The inequality exists (especially during periods of high unemployment) because an employer can usually survive without an individual worker longer than the worker can survive without wages. By bargaining as a group, and threatening to withhold labor as a group, real pressure can be put on the employer during negotiations.

In the United States, labor law is mostly governed by federal legislation.[2] However, some states have enacted labor laws, which are valid unless "preempted" by federal law. The National Labor Relations Act (NLRA) was enacted in 1935 and is one of the primary pieces of federal legislation affecting labor law. Its purpose was to encourage workers to bargain collectively and to protect the right of workers to organize.[3] Other federal labor legislation includes (but is not limited to) the Norris-La Guardia Act (1932) and the Labor Management Relations Act (Taft-Hartley, 1947).

Because of the existence of state legislation (and in Canada, the predominance of provincial legislation), there are variations in the law from one jurisdiction to another though no state law can conflict with federal law in an area addressed by federal law. However, basic principles underlie all labor legislation, and those principles are discussed in this chapter.

---

1. *NLRB* v. *Jones and Laughlin Steel Corp.*, 301 U.S. 1. (1937).

2. In Canada, there is federal labor legislation that covers a relatively small percentage of the work force. Provincial legislation, which may vary substantially from one province to another, predominates.

3. Prior to this Act, organization of workers into unions was considered to be "combination in restraint of trade," which was contrary to the provisions of the Sherman Act (antitrust). In Canada, there is legislation similar to the Sherman Act, entitled The Competition Act. The legal theory behind this application of **antitrust** legislation is that employees who bargain as a group are in essence fixing prices, akin to bid-rigging by contractors, thereby removing competition from the process.

Many issues have arisen out of labor conflict, including the appropriateness of the employer's conduct in resisting an organizing campaign, limitations on the right to picket, resolution of jurisdictional disputes, the legality of secondary boycotts, closed shop agreements, and many others. Some of these issues are of particular relevance to the construction industry and are discussed further in this chapter.

Labor law is an extremely wide field and is considered a complex and specialized area of law; some attorneys limit their practice to a small aspect of labor law, such as injunctions or grievances. Labor disputes can also be very costly, not only in terms of lost production or lost wages, but also in the long term. A union certification can, for example, cause a contractor to become uncompetitive. In the event of a labor dispute or other organized labor activity, contractors should obtain legal advice from an experienced labor attorney *before* taking any action, innocuous as it may seem, such as meeting with employees to discuss the situation.

A union is the sole agent for the employees it represents for the purpose of negotiating and administering the collective agreement. The rules of agency, as explained in Chapter 3 (section 3.3), apply. As agent, the union is authorized to enter into an employment contract with the employer (the third party) on behalf of its principal (the employee). There is one difference, however: Unlike a typical agency relationship, the employer cannot negotiate directly with the employee once union representation is established.[4]

12.2   ESTABLISHING UNION REPRESENTATION

Employees of a company may decide that they need a union to represent them and, thus, approach a union agent. More commonly, a union will determine that those employees could benefit from representation and, thus, begin an organizing drive. In either case, once the union has obtained the support of a majority of employees, it will approach the employer and demand that the employer recognize the union as the bargaining agent for the employees. The employer may either agree or demand an election.

The election is a democratic vote of employees to determine whether this particular union is to be their representative. It is sometimes a matter of dispute who truly falls within the definition of employees.

Definition of Employee

The law distinguishes between employees and independent contractors. The distinction is not always clear. The NLRB in the United States has established a test that considers a number of factors relating to the level of control that the employee (or independent contractor) has over the methods of work. An independent contractor

---

4.   Some states allow an employer to bargain individually with employees.

will usually determine which means and methods will be used to achieve a result (although that result is controlled by the person who has hired the contractor). On the other hand, an employee will not usually determine the means and methods. In some ways, it is similar to the test used to distinguish between an employee and an independent contractor for taxation purposes.[5]

A second category of employee that has caused some difficulty is the supervisory employee. Although a supervisor is an employee in the usual sense of the word, his or her duty to the employer is more likely to come into conflict with the union's interest. For that reason, supervisors may be excluded from the definition of employee based on a categorization of management versus labor. That being said, it is often a difficult question of fact whether a particular employee is truly a supervisor.

There are other exclusions as well, such as government employees. They are not particularly relevant to the construction process.

Organization of employees in the construction industry may be more difficult than in other industries. That is because employees are often hired on a project basis rather than on a permanent basis. When the project is complete, employment is terminated. The union may have obtained less than a majority of support before several projects are complete. In the United States, the unique employment pattern of the construction industry is recognized in s. 8(f) of the NLRA, which allows contractors to enter into a collective agreement with a union without any evidence that the union is supported by a majority of that contractor's employees. However, the obligation to bargain with the union does not extend beyond the expiration of the contract.[6]

CASE STUDY
Castillo v. Givens 704 F.2d 181 (5th Cir. 1983).

The plaintiff Tonche was a field worker who worked for the defendant and obtained and supervised other workers. All were paid less than the minimum wage. The defendant employer maintained that he hired Tonche as an independent contractor and that the other workers were employees of Tonche. At issue was whether the plaintiff (and other workers) were employees for the purposes of the FLSA (Fair Labor Standards Act). The question of status (employee ver-

---

5.   The test used in Canada for both labor relations and taxation purposes is similar.

6.   This was one of the findings in the case of *John Deklewa & Sons*, 282 N.L.R.B. 184. The NLRB ruled that a construction employer could not unilaterally terminate one of these agreements (known as a pre-hire agreement) until the expiration of the agreement or until an election has been held, the result of which was a rejection of the union.

sus independent contractor) would also be relevant to the right to organize in many cases although it was not in this case.

Tonche was also registered as a "farm labor contractor," a fact relied on by the defendant to establish Tonche's status. The court held that he was in fact an employee:

> Defendant places great weight on various specific control elements—defendant did not decide how many or which workers to hire and fire, did not supervise the details of their work, did not furnish the hoes, did not provide transportation, did not decide when the workers arrived at the fields and when they quit, and, defendant argues, did not determine their rate of pay. [This point was in dispute.]
>
> The second factor is the "focal inquiry in the characterization process": whether the individual is or is not, as a matter of economic fact, in business for himself. The record here does not indicate that Tonche had anything that could be called an independent business as distinguished from personal labor. . . . [Other factors were considered as well.]

Questions

1. Why would status make a difference for the purpose of collective bargaining and organizing?
2. What other effects would status as an independent contractor have?
3. What is the relevance of the "control factors" referred to by the court?

Analysis

1. If the workers were independent contractors, organizing for the purpose of setting compensation rates would violate the Sherman Antitrust Act (or in Canada, the Competition Act).
2. It would affect the tax status of the individual, as well as rights and responsibilities under other employer–employee legislation.
3. If an employer sets the hours of work, supervises the work, provides the tools, and otherwise fulfills the traditional functions of an employer, it is more likely that the other party will be seen as an employee, not an independent contractor. One of the more important factors is whether the employee bears the risk of loss and hope of profit or, conversely, is paid the same rate regardless of the result achieved. An independent contractor usually takes some risk of profit or loss though not in all cases.

Employer Resistance to Union Representation

Many employers, when faced with the prospect of union representation, vigorously oppose any effort to organize their employees. Methods used by employers include threats, coercion, increasing pay and benefits, transfer and firing of employees, meetings and discussions with employees, and posting of notices expressing the employer's view. Most of these methods are considered to be unfair labor practices[7] and may result in either invalidation of an election or, in extreme cases, an order requiring the employer to bargain with the union.

It may be less than obvious why increasing pay and benefits, during a union organizing campaign, for example, should be considered an unfair labor practice. The reasoning is that behind the inducement is a veiled threat that these benefits will not be continued if the union is voted in.[8] The fundamental principle is that there should be no interference from anyone in the employees' exercise of their right to organize. Bribery or inducement is considered interference.

This fundamental principle comes into conflict with the constitutional right to freedom of speech in situations where the employer expresses its animosity toward the union. Courts have struggled to determine which principle should prevail, and the answer will depend on whether the employees have been coerced to any degree.[9]

12.3   CRAFT UNIONS AND JURISDICTIONAL DISPUTES

In many industrial settings, one union will represent all the employees. This is typical in some industries. In the construction industry, it is more common for each trade to be represented by a different union.[10] This presents its own set of problems.

Over many years, each craft has carved out a portion of the work it considers to be its own. A union electrician, for example, will not allow a carpenter to lay conduit or pull wire. The specialization of trades is necessary to a degree in order to allow workers to develop greater skill in their trades. But it requires tremendous

---

7. For example, the unfair labor practice provision of the Labour Relations Code in British Columbia provides that an employer shall not "discharge, suspend, transfer, lay off or otherwise discipline an employee, refuse to employ or to continue to employ a person or discriminate against a person in regard to employment or a condition of employment because the person is or proposes to become or seeks to induce another person to become a member or officer of a trade union, or participates in the promotion, formation or administration of a trade union.... " R.S.B.C. 1979, c. 82, s. 6(3). Further examples of unfair labor practices are in the statute.

8. Not all pay or benefit increases will be considered unfair labor practices. If they are pre-established terms of employment, for example, the employer is not required to cancel them.

9. For a summary of cases on this point, see *Labor Relations Law* by Smith et al. (Bobbs-Merrill, 4th ed., 1968).

10. There have been some attempts to establish a common union for all trades in some jurisdictions, but the individual trade union situation is still prevalent.

coordination between the various trades to avoid the inefficiencies associated with many trades working in one area.

Because of the interdependence between the trades, it is possible for one trade to shut down an entire construction project. For example, if the electricians or operating engineers refused to work, the project could come to a halt. A very small minority of workers could cause many others to lose work. To avoid such a scenario, procedures have been put in place to resolve disputes between trades.

A **jurisdictional dispute** is one in which two or more unions each claim that the work in question should properly be performed by its members. For example, the carpenters and plumbers might both claim that the installation of blockouts in formwork for piping runs is their work. Rather than inducing strike action, the two trades would attempt to settle the dispute and, if necessary, submit it to the NLRB for determination. It may be of little interest to the employer which trade performs the work, as long as there is no work stoppage. In making its determination, the NLRB will consider the skills and work involved, company and industry practice, agreements between unions and between employers and unions, and other factors.

12.4   UNION SECURITY AND RIGHT-TO-WORK

Various terms have been used to describe the forms of union security arrangements (or lack thereof), including closed shop, union shop, agency shop, and open shop. A **closed shop** is one in which membership in the union is a precondition to hiring. A union shop requires employees to become union members after they are hired. **Agency shop** is similar to union shop, with the exception that employees are simply required to pay union dues but are not required to join the union. **Open shop** means that union membership or paying of dues is not condition of employment.

Closed shop provisions have been found to be an infringement of the individual's right to freedom of association.[11] In this context, the U.S. Supreme Court has stated:

> The Board recognizes that the hiring hall came into being "to eliminate wasteful, time-consuming, and repetitive scouting for jobs by individual workmen and haphazard uneconomical searches by employers." The hiring hall at times has been a useful adjunct to the closed shop. But Congress may have thought that it need not serve that cause, that in fact it has served well both labor and management—particularly in the maritime field and in the building and construction industry. In the latter the contractor who frequently is a stranger to the area where the work is done requires a "central source" for his employment needs; and a man looking for a job finds in the hiring hall "at least a minimum guarantee of continued employment." Congress has not outlawed the hiring

---

11. Closed shop hiring halls still exist in the construction industry in Canada.

hall, though it has outlawed the closed shop except within the limits prescribed in the provisos to ss. 8(a)(3).[12]

The rationale behind agency shop agreements is that all employees, whether union members or not, benefit from the presence of a union because the union bargaining power raises the level of wages and benefits. Economists call this a "free rider" problem. An individual might see no value in joining the union because the benefit will be realized in any case. However, those who contribute to the union do not wish to subsidize those who don't. As a compromise, nonmembers are not forced to join but are not given a free ride.

The prohibition against closed shops is the minimum level of protection given to nonunion workers. Further protection is given in some states, which have enacted right-to-work legislation. The scope of state laws varies from one jurisdiction to another. Some go so far as to prohibit agency shop agreements.

12.5   WORK STOPPAGES

Strikes and lockouts are the ultimate weapons in a labor dispute. They are costly to both employer and employee. Lost production may be recovered through costly use of overtime, but lost market share may never be recovered. Lost wages for the employee will usually be unrecoverable.

There are circumstances where a lockout may be considered an unfair labor practice, such as when it is without economic justification. But most lockouts (and strikes) occur when there is an impasse in negotiations, and in such circumstances, the lockout or strike may legitimately be used.

There is in general no legal impediment to an employer hiring replacement workers during a work stoppage.[13] Depending on local sentiment, however, there may be practical impediments to continuing operations during a work stoppage. Workers also face no legal impediment to obtaining other employment during a work stoppage.

Picketing is expected during work stoppages. Picketing is protected free speech as long as it is done peacefully and without intimidation. However, just as workers have the right to picket, the public has the right to either respect or ignore a picket line. If the number of pickets is so great as to prevent access to a site, an injunction may be obtained.

---

12.   *International Brotherhood of Teamsters, Local 357* v. *NLRB*, 365 U.S. 667 (1961).

13.   In some provinces, there are restrictions. The Labour Relations Code of British Columbia contains the following provision: "During a lockout or strike authorized by this Code an employer shall not use the services of a person, whether paid or not, who is hired or engaged after the earlier of the date on which the notice to commence collective bargaining is given and the date on which bargaining begins, . . . to perform the work of an employee in the bargaining unit that is on strike or locked out. . . . " RSBC 1979, c. 82, s. 68(1).

Picketing of construction sites creates special problems. The site may be used by a number of employers, some of whom have no relationship or dispute with the union that is picketing. There are two competing rights: the right of the union and its members to picket and the right of the uninterested parties not to be interfered with. In one such construction picketing case, the tribunal made the following comments:

> On the other hand, in the interest of shielding "unoffending employers" from disputes not their own, the Board has taken a more restrictive view of common situs picketing, requiring that it be conducted so as to minimize its impact on neutral employees insofar as this can be done without substantial impairment of the effectiveness of the picketing in reaching the primary employees.[14]

A separate gate is typically used to minimize disruption to neutral parties. Picketing that separate gate was found to be a violation in the preceding case.[15]

12.6   SECONDARY ACTIVITY

To pressure an employer, unions sometimes attempt to bring pressure on neutral parties doing business with that employer. For example, a union may picket a site with the intent to cause others to cease doing business with that employer. However, the NLRA prohibits such secondary pressure where the intent of the pressure is to force one party to cease doing business with another. Cases in this area of the law are somewhat inconsistent, and courts have struggled to balance the competing interests of the union and uninterested parties.

12.7   SUCCESSOR EMPLOYERS
AND SINGLE EMPLOYERS

Where one employer purchases the business or the substantial assets of another company, the purchaser may be found to be a "successor" for the purposes of union bargaining obligations. The U.S. Supreme Court discussed the issue in the *Fall River Dyeing & Finishing Corp.* case:

> This approach, which is primarily factual in nature and based on the totality of the circumstances of a given situation, requires that the Board focus on whether the new com-

---

14. *Building and Construction Trades Council of New Orleans (Markwell & Hartz, Inc.)*, 155 NLRB No. 42 (1965).

15. Footnote 14, *supra*.

pany has "acquired substantial assets of its predecessor and continued, without interruption or substantial change, the predecessor's business operations." Hence the focus is on whether there is "substantial continuity" between the enterprises. Under this approach, the Board examines a number of factors; whether the business of both employers is essentially the same; whether the employees of the new company are doing the same jobs in the same working conditions under the same supervisors; and whether the new entity has the same production process, produces the same products, and basically has the same body of customers.[16]

The implications for a contractor considering the purchase of a business or its assets are obvious: There is a risk that along with the business or its assets will be attached an obligation to bargain with a union.

A further point of the *Fall River* case is that it is not possible for an employer to rid itself of its union obligations by engaging in corporate sleight of hand. A mere change in ownership designed to remove a union will not succeed.

Some employers have taken more drastic measures: closing the operation down or moving it to a different state. It is open to the NLRB to find that various companies with common ownership and control constitute a single employer and, therefore, find that the related employer is liable for unfair labor practices of the primary employer, even if the primary employer has ceased operating.[17] However, practical remedies are difficult to order in such cases.

12.8   ENFORCEMENT OF COLLECTIVE AGREEMENTS

Disputes about the interpretation of collective agreements are not uncommon. Most **collective agreements** contain provisions that require such disputes to be resolved through arbitration. This is not to be confused with the use of arbitration to arrive at a collective agreement (known as interest arbitration). Grievance arbitration is concerned with the determination of rights under an existing collective agreement.

A **grievance** is a complaint either by the union (on behalf of an employee) or by the employer that the other party has breached the collective agreement. Because collective agreements may run for several years, the parties usually anticipate that

---

16.   107 S. Ct. 2225 (1987).

17.   In the United States, single employer status has consequences for secondary boycotts as well as liability for unfair labor practices. However, common direction *and* control is necessary. In the case of *Remke Central Division, Inc.* 227 N.L.R.B. No. 287 (1977), the NLRB repeated an earlier finding that common ownership alone is not sufficient. In some provinces of Canada, companies with common direction (common officers, directors, employees, or headquarters) *or* control (shareholders) may be found to be sufficiently related so as to bind both to the collective agreement. This could have serious implications for anyone who wants to operate both a union and a nonunion company simultaneously. This argument was advanced indirectly in the *Garland Coal & Mining Co.* case (U.S.C.A. 8th Cir. 1985) 121 L.R.R.M. 2029, where the union asked the NLRB to find that one company was the "alter ego" of another.

grievances will occur during the term of the agreement and insert a provision requiring that all grievances be resolved (as a final resort) through arbitration. An independent party or tribunal is appointed to act as judge and jury. The arbitrator may be named in the collective agreement or may be appointed after the grievance has been filed.

12.9   EMPLOYMENT LAW

Unlike labor law, employment law does not have aspects that are unique or particularly troublesome to the construction industry. With the exception of the following introductory remarks, the subject is beyond the scope of this book.

Employment legislation, like labor legislation, addresses the issues of safety and humane working conditions. Federal and state laws protect against various forms of discrimination,[18] set minimum wage levels, regulate payment for overtime, and govern other aspects of the employment relationship. Breaches of human rights and other employment laws can create liability for employers. Damages may include lost wages, reinstatement, and punitive damages and, therefore, can be very high.

The employment relationship, in the absence of a contract (express or implied), is called employment-at-will. This means that either party has the right to terminate the relationship, whether or not just cause for doing so exists. However, implied contracts will be found by courts to exist in many cases, particularly for long-term employees.[19] Representations made by the employer either during the term of employment or to induce the employee to join the company, which could reasonably lead one to believe that employment would not be terminated except for just cause, can form the basis for an implied contract. Similarly, representations found in company literature, such as policy manuals, can serve the same purpose.

Just cause means that the conduct of the employee constitutes a serious enough breach of the employee's obligations, whether those obligations are owed under an express or implied contract, or at common law, to justify termination. In such cases, the employer is not required to give notice or severance pay. If there is no good cause, and there is an implied contract, the employer will likely be required to give adequate notice of termination or severance pay instead of notice. In states that do not recognize implied contracts of employment, state law may still provide for a minimum period of notice or severance.

Many federal and state laws and organizations regulate employment. The Fair Labor Standards Act deals with hours of work and wages. OSHA is responsible for safety and health matters. COBRA is concerned with continuation of medical cov-

18. Protection against discrimination is also found in the constitutions of both the United States and Canada.

19. In many states, the theory of implied contract is used by the courts. In others, the courts refuse to accept it.

erage. The Americans with Disabilities Act protects against certain forms of discrimination. These are but a few examples.[20]

Events that raise liability issues, and should cause both employer and employee to consider the need for legal advice, include termination of employment, discipline, significant changes in working conditions (for example, demotion, reduction in pay, loss of responsibility, transfer), allegations of sexual harassment, discrimination in hiring, discrimination in promotion or transfer, and privacy issues. In some cases, additional remedies may be available through administrative agencies.

12.10   PROBLEMS

1. Several dumptruck drivers have decided to organize in order to bargain for increased compensation. They each own their own rig and have been hired by the same excavation contractor. They are currently being paid $45 per hour, which is intended to cover their truck maintenance and operating costs as well as their wages or profit, as the case may be. They are given direction by the contractor's dispatcher each morning and at each project site by the contractor's superintendents. Are they employees or independent contractors?

2. An employer discovers that a union organizing drive is underway. The employer posts a notice in the plant that states: "If the union succeeds in organizing this company, we will no longer be profitable and will have to shut down in this state. This is not a threat. You are free to choose union representation. However, the economic reality will force us to shut down because we are unwilling to operate at a loss." What legal issues are involved?

---

20. For a more complete list, see *Every Employee's Guide to the Law* by Lewin Joel III (Pantheon Books, 1993).

13

Dispute Resolution

13.1 INTRODUCTION

There are four well-recognized methods of dispute resolution: litigation, arbitration, mediation, and negotiation. There is no ideal method. The appropriate method will depend on the nature of the dispute, the amount of money in dispute, the remedies sought, the willingness of the parties to resolve the dispute, and the nature of the relationship between the parties.

Negotiation is a purely voluntary method. If a party does not wish to negotiate, it would be futile (even if it were possible) to force negotiation. Litigation is at the other extreme. It is involuntary for the defendant. Failure to participate will result in judgment being awarded against the nonparticipant. Failure to pursue a claim by the plaintiff will result in no recovery.

Arbitration is voluntary at the contract negotiation phase; a party can refuse to agree to the inclusion of an arbitration clause in the contract. However, once the clause is agreed to, assuming it is a mandatory arbitration clause, a demand to arbitrate by the other party forces the arbitration, and the court will enforce the arbitration obligation as well as the ruling of the arbitrator.

145

Mediation, like arbitration, may be agreed to in advance or after a dispute has arisen, but unlike binding arbitration, the process is nonbinding. In other words, even though a party may take part in the mediation process, it can refuse to settle the dispute.

13.2   LITIGATION

Litigation is the use of the court system to resolve disputes. There are inherent advantages to litigation. For example, the court can enforce its own orders and its processes. This is particularly important if one of the parties is a reluctant participant. Not all disputes involve good faith disagreements and parties who genuinely desire a fair result. Some lawsuits are caused by a desire by one party to take advantage of another or to delay the performance of recognized obligations (such as the payment of money). Sometimes litigation is the only practical alternative.

There are disadvantages as well. Litigation is costly. Each party must hire an attorney, often an expert witness must be retained, and other disbursements are always incurred for case preparation and trial. Employees of the parties can be inconvenienced or tied up for long periods. A second major disadvantage is delay. It can take years before the matter proceeds to trial, and if appeals are taken, the final result will be delayed further.

The litigation process requires that issues of law and fact that are in dispute be resolved by an independent person or persons. The issues of law are decided by a judge. The issues of fact are decided by a jury or, if the parties prefer, by the judge.[1]

The Pleadings

To commence the litigation process, the plaintiff drafts a complaint, which states the names and addresses of the parties, the allegations that form the basis of the complaint, and the nature of the relief sought.[2] The complaint must be filed in the appropriate court registry and served on the defendants. There is no limit on the number of potential plaintiffs or defendants. On receipt of the complaint, a defendant has a short period in which to file an answer.[3]

The body of the complaint will contain a series of numbered paragraphs, each containing an allegation. A complaint that does not set out a cause of action can be struck (dismissed). Examples of causes of action include breach of contract and

---

1. In Canada, it is unusual for a jury to hear construction or other commercial cases.

2. In Canada, the complaint is called a statement of claim. The answer, as it is called in the United States, is called a statement of defense in Canada.

3. The time limit varies from one jurisdiction to another but will typically be fourteen or twenty-one days. The period may be extended by permission of the court or, in some jurisdictions, by permission of the plaintiff.

negligence. Each cause of action contains a number of elements that must be proved. For example, as explained in Chapter 4, the elements of negligence include existence of a duty, breach of that duty, and damage or loss flowing from the breach. A complaint that alleges a duty but no breach may be struck for failure to allege a cause of action.

The complaint will also state the relief sought. That relief may include general damages, punitive damages, specific performance of a contract, an injunction, or other forms of relief.

The defendant must draft and file an answer containing a denial of all allegations that the defendant plans to contest at trial. Failure to deny an allegation in the answer will be considered admission of that allegation, and that admission may be impossible to retract at a later date.

The plaintiff is, in many jurisdictions, entitled to file a reply on receipt of the answer, but this is not usually done. **Pleadings** may ordinarily be amended after they have been delivered; however, permission of the court may be required.

The pleadings are the only documents that the judge sees prior to the commencement of trial. The pleadings should give the judge a basic understanding of the nature of the dispute.

Because of the technical requirements of drafting pleadings, it is a task best left for attorneys.[4] Furthermore, there are time limitations for filing and serving documents and other procedural requirements that make self-representation a risky proposition. Courts may bend over backward to accommodate lay litigants but may be unwilling or unable to assist if failure to comply has caused prejudice to the other parties.

Counterclaims and Third-Party Claims

A **counterclaim** is a complaint that the defendant makes against the plaintiff. Counterclaims are frequently made by owners who have been sued by their design consultants or contractors for payment of fees. There is no rule limiting the counterclaim to the amount of the original claim, and in practice, counterclaims are sometimes much greater than the original claim.

It is rare for a construction dispute to involve only two parties. More often, a number of other project participants are brought into the litigation by the defendant(s). This is done by "impleading" the other parties.[5] In the United States, there is no obligation for a defendant to implead a third party; instead, the defendant may commence a separate action. In practice, however, it usually makes more sense from a strategic point of view to have the third-party claims heard at the same time.

---

4. There are some courts, most notably small claims courts, in which these technical requirements are not present or are simplified.

5. In Canada, it is called issuing a third-party notice.

To illustrate why, assume that an owner has sued the architect for alleged design errors relating to the structural design of a beam. The architect is contractually responsible to the owner but has subcontracted the structural design to an engineer and, therefore, has a potential third-party claim. The lawsuit between the owner and the architect proceeds on its own, and the architect is found liable because of errors in the structural design. The architect then sues the engineer, who defeats the architect's claim. The engineer was not a party to the first lawsuit and, therefore, is not bound by the result. Furthermore, there may be different witnesses and evidence available at the second trial that can lead to the inconsistent result. To avoid such a result, the architect might prefer to have the engineer named as a third party in the original suit, binding the engineer to findings of fact.

There may be strategic reasons for keeping a potential third party out of a lawsuit. The third party might become hostile to the defendant because the defendant has brought him or her into the litigation. The defendant comes under fire from two sides instead of one.[6]

The Discovery Process

Discovery refers to a number of different procedures available to all parties prior to trial, the purpose of which is to learn as much about the case as possible. The rationale is that if there are no surprises at trial, all parties should be aware of the relative strengths and weaknesses of each party's case before trial, thereby increasing the likelihood of settlement. The goals are to prepare for trial and to promote pretrial settlement.

The procedures available include (but are not limited to) interrogatories, discovery of documents, deposition of witnesses,[7] and inspection of the property.

Interrogatories are a series of written questions sent by one party to another. There are requirements as to form, but otherwise, they are relatively straightforward. They are usually sent shortly after the pleadings phase is complete in order to obtain preliminary answers and to find out which witnesses are knowledgeable about various aspects of the claim.

Discovery of documents is an ongoing process and often continues until shortly before trial. On being served with a subpoena or demand for discovery of documents, a party must produce all documents (except for privileged documents) that

---

6. In Canada, a party who loses a lawsuit is usually required to pay a percentage of the other party's legal costs. This is a strong disincentive to making frivolous claims. A defendant would not implead a third party, faced with cost sanctions, if the third-party claim did not have a good chance of succeeding or unless the potential cost sanctions were dwarfed by the size of the claim. This is not a consideration in the United States, where the general rule is that each party bears his or her own attorney's fees.

7. In the United States, a party is entitled to conduct a deposition of any and all witnesses. In Canada, each party is entitled to only one examination for discovery, as it is called, of a representative of each adverse party. It is not uncommon for a large construction case in the United States to require months of depositions, involving dozens of witnesses.

are relevant to matters at issue in the case. Construction disputes are notorious for generating massive quantities of documents. They will usually include the contract documents (including drawings and specifications), correspondence between the parties and between witnesses, minutes of meetings, diaries, schedules, transmittals, photographs, telephone records, invoices, and depending on the nature of the dispute, any other form of communication (including internal memoranda) that may be considered evidence tending to prove or disprove a fact in dispute.

On large cases, it is not unusual to have tens of thousands of documents produced. Very large cases can generate hundreds of thousands or millions of documents. Each document must be numbered and a list produced describing the documents in some logical sequence. To keep track of the documents and be able to sort and retrieve them, the standard procedure is to enter them into a database, with fields for date, author, recipient, subject matter, and any other field that might help the attorney find a document quickly. The cost of document control alone can be substantial for a large case. Failure to spend the time and money on this task early on in the process can result in greater expense and tactical disadvantage as the trial approaches.

A **deposition** is cross-examination of a witness, under oath, conducted prior to trial. A transcript is made of the questions and answers, and that record may be used at trial as evidence or to impeach (contradict) the witness. The primary purpose of depositions is to obtain the evidence of all witnesses before the trial so as to avoid the possibility of surprise. The element of surprise can never be completely eliminated, but this procedure goes a long way toward that goal. Witnesses who change their evidence from the time of deposition to the time of trial almost always damage their credibility unless there is a very compelling reason for the change.

Parties who represent themselves are at an extreme disadvantage during a deposition. A witness has the right to object to questions because of privilege, relevance, or the form of the question. Failure to object can cause prejudice at trial. Unrepresented parties are often unaware of the proper grounds for objection.

The deposition process is very expensive. For an attorney with a charge-out rate of $150 per hour, a day of deposition will cost the client approximately $1,000 plus expenses, including the cost of the deposition transcript prepared by a court reporter (charges for a day of deposition may easily exceed $500). That does not include the time required for preparation, which may exceed the deposition time itself. Yet it is a necessary and useful procedure.

Inspection of the site is available to all parties even though the site is owned by one party. If the owner of the site refuses access, the court will order that access be given. This is a relatively inexpensive part of the discovery process, and it should not be omitted.

The existence and limits of insurance are discoverable in some jurisdictions although such evidence is generally inadmissible at trial. The purpose of allowing discovery of this evidence is to promote settlement.

Finally, each party must disclose to the other prior to trial the names of all witnesses they intend to call together with a summary of that witness's anticipated evidence. Again, the purpose is to remove the element of surprise and to promote settlement.[8]

Trials

Because most construction trials in the United States are tried by jury, technical, scientific, and engineering matters must be simplified for the jury. Simplification causes the length of the trial to decrease. Experts must explain their opinions in simple terms.

The trial begins with an opening statement by the plaintiff's attorney. The defendant's attorney then has the right to make an opening statement or may choose to "reserve" opening until the plaintiff has completed its case. The plaintiff then introduces evidence, usually by calling witnesses. Each witness gives evidence and is cross-examined. The defendant then goes through the same procedure. There are strict rules for admissibility of evidence. Following the conclusion of the defendant's case, the plaintiff may offer reply (rebuttal) evidence, but only to respond to new points raised by the defendant's case. The parties then present argument that includes summaries of the evidence and case law. At the conclusion of argument, the jury is instructed on the law it must apply and then deliberates in private until a conclusion (verdict) is reached.

Summary

Litigation is often a winner-take-all proposition. It is always risky. Even if a case looks like a sure winner, there is always the risk that the jury may be sympathetic to the other party or that a key witness may change his or her evidence. It is expensive and time consuming, and it does not always produce a fair result. Even though evidence is given under oath, witnesses have been known to contradict each other, and it is not always due to faulty memory. Yet litigation is frequently used to resolve construction disputes though it may be the method of last resort.

Owing to the cost and delay associated with litigation, much interest has been generated in recent years in alternative dispute resolution (known as **ADR**). ADR is generally understood to refer to arbitration and mediation though the organization of an ADR format is limited only by the ingenuity of the parties.

13.3   ARBITRATION

Proponents of ADR claim that arbitration is less expensive and quicker than litigation. It can be but is not necessarily so. Arbitration has been used for many years in

---

8. There is no such requirement in Canada. Surprise witnesses can still give evidence.

other fields, such as labor law. It is used regularly for commercial disputes in other countries. **Arbitration** is best suited for disputes involving parties who have an ongoing business relationship, who would like to maintain that relationship, and who have a genuine desire to resolve the dispute amicably. If one of the parties wants to prolong the dispute, arbitration can prove more expensive than litigation.

An arbitrator is essentially a private judge (and jury because the arbitrator makes findings of fact as well). The parties may choose arbitration as their method of resolving disputes before any dispute has arisen by agreeing to insert an arbitration clause in the contract. Or they may choose to arbitrate after a dispute has occurred.[9] In either case, the parties must decide:

1. Who will act as arbitrator
2. What the terms of reference of the arbitrator will be (that is, what specific questions the arbitrator must answer)
3. What rules of procedure the arbitrator must follow
4. What law is to apply

Several organizations are dedicated to the use of arbitration. In the United States, the American Arbitration Association (AAA) is one such group.[10] The AAA has published a booklet entitled *Construction Industry Arbitration Rules*. If the parties specify these rules in their arbitration clause, the arbitrator must follow them. Other organizations have their own rules, and some jurisdictions have legislation that governs the conduct of an arbitration.[11]

The AAA also provides standard arbitration clauses that may be inserted into contracts or agreed to after the fact. They are found in the introduction to the *Construction Industry Arbitration Rules*. Other clauses are offered by other organizations and may be found in textbooks on the subject.

Several features of arbitration distinguish it from litigation. First, as mentioned, the arbitrator is privately appointed. In the litigation process, the parties have no say in the choice of judge and little say in the choice of jury. Arbitrators are chosen for their reputation and expertise. The parties will usually be aware of a number of people who have the skills to conduct an arbitration and can be counted on to act

---

9.   If the clause is inserted in the contract before any dispute has arisen, it is referred to as mandatory binding arbitration. If the parties agree to arbitrate after the dispute has arisen, it is called voluntary binding arbitration. Nonbinding arbitration requires the arbitrator to give an advisory opinion. All references to arbitration in this chapter refer to binding arbitration unless noted otherwise.

10.   The AAA has offices throughout the United States. Its headquarters are at 140 W. 51st St., New York, NY 10020.

11.   Parties considering the use of an arbitration clause should be aware of the legislation that will govern the arbitration. The Commercial Arbitration Act in B.C., RSBC 1979 c. 3, s. 22 provides that unless the parties otherwise agree, the rules of the B.C. International Arbitration Centre will apply to the conduct of the arbitration.

impartially. If the parties cannot agree on an arbitrator, any one of the arbitration organizations can provide a list of candidates.

Organizations such as the AAA have established fee schedules for their services. In addition to these fees, which may be a percentage of the amount in dispute, the arbitrator, unlike a judge, must be paid. It may also be necessary to rent facilities in which to hold the hearing. Most arbitration agreements provide that the parties will bear equally the costs of the arbitrator(s) unless the arbitrator(s) makes an award of costs against one party. These costs can be substantial.

The arbitrator's schedule is another factor to consider. Many construction arbitrators are practicing professionals—attorneys, contractors, engineers, or architects— and scheduling a long hearing may necessitate either considerable delay or breaking up the hearing into several parts. If the hearing takes longer than scheduled, the parties may have to come back for a day at a time to suit everyone's schedule.

One advantage to the arbitration process is its privacy. Unlike court proceedings that are open to the public, an arbitration is a private hearing. This may not be of particular importance in some cases, but in others, there may be a particular need for privacy. For example, the evidence may include trade secrets, such as productivity data or profit and overhead figures that, if made available to competitors, could affect success in bidding on future work.

Another advantage is the arbitrator's expertise. The parties can choose an arbitrator with training or experience in the field of construction that is the subject matter of the case. One effect of doing so is that technical evidence can be canvassed more quickly and in greater depth because there is no need to explain the basics. Care must be taken, however, that the arbitrator(s) not make assumptions based on experience rather than evidence.

There is one serious disadvantage to the arbitration process. It concerns the third-party problem described in the "Litigation" section of this chapter. Because arbitration is a voluntary process, the parties cannot force a third party to take part (except as a witness, subject to the laws in the jurisdiction) unless that party is signatory to the arbitration clause. One cannot simply implead a reluctant third party. As a consequence, third-party claims may have to be heard separately, in another forum, with the risk of inconsistent findings. The AIA Document A201-1987 (General Conditions of the Contract for Construction) contains the following clause:

> *Limitation on Consolidation or Joinder.* No arbitration arising out of or relating to the Contract Documents shall include, by consolidation or joinder in any other manner, the Architect, the Architect's employees or consultants, except by written consent containing specific reference to the Agreement and signed by the Architect, Owner, Contractor and any other person or entity sought to be joined. No arbitration shall include, by consolidation or joinder or in any other manner, parties other than the Owner, Contractor, a separate contractor as described in Article 6 and other persons substantially involved in a common question of fact or law whose presence is required if complete relief is to be accorded in arbitration. . . . [12]

---

12. Article 4.5.5.

If the contractor believes that some of the allegations are the responsibility of the architect, and the architect refuses to agree to be joined in the arbitration, the architect cannot be joined. The parties might face inconsistent findings in separate proceedings. Yet the owner and contractor would be forced to arbitrate because of Article 4.5.1:

> *Controversies and Claims Subject to Arbitration.* Any controversy or Claim arising out of or related to the Contract, or the breach thereof, shall be settled by arbitration in accordance with the Construction Industry Arbitration Rules of the American Arbitration Association. . . . Such controversies or Claims upon which the Architect has given notice and rendered a decision as provided in Subparagraph 4.4.4 shall be subject to arbitration upon written demand of either party.[13]

The rules of evidence and procedure are less formal in an arbitration than in a court of law. Almost all arbitration associations specify in their rules that formal rules of evidence need not be followed. In general, this means that the rules are used but are relaxed to some degree. Hearsay or opinion evidence that might be inadmissible in court can be heard by the arbitrator, for example, though the arbitrator should be careful as to the weight given to such evidence. It is essential that the fundamental principles of fairness be adhered to, whether or not the arbitrator chooses to follow the formal rules that would apply in court. This means that each party must be given adequate notice of the hearing, an opportunity to be heard, an opportunity to test the evidence of the other parties, and an impartial and unbiased decision maker.

Finally, some claims are not capable of being arbitrated because of the form of relief sought. In some jurisdictions, for example, legislation requires that a mechanics' lien claim be proved in court.

13.4   NEGOTIATION

There are no hard and fast rules to negotiation. Many books intended to teach the reader to become an effective negotiator have been written on the subject. Technique and strategy vary from one person to another and from case to case. It is more of an art than a science. Negotiating skill may be improved through study, but in the final analysis, it is best learned through experience.

There are always alternatives to a negotiated settlement. Litigation is almost always an alternative. Doing nothing is another. For that reason, negotiation should be approached with an understanding of the alternatives so that no settlement will be agreed to that is worse than the alternatives.

Negotiated settlements have two clear advantages to litigation and arbitration: The process is usually much less costly, and the uncertainty is eliminated. A $50,000

---

13.   AIA Document A201-1987.

settlement may be preferable, if a party is risk-averse, to litigating a $100,000 claim that has a 50 percent probability of success. Further, the mere existence of a contingent liability can impair the ability of a person or company to carry on business, making a negotiated settlement that much more attractive.

13.5   MEDIATION

Mediation is an assisted negotiation process in which the settlement discussions are facilitated by a neutral third party. It has proved effective in complex multiparty disputes as well as simple ones. To succeed, the parties must have a genuine desire to reach a settlement, the mediation should be attended by a representative of each party with authority to conclude a settlement, and the mediator should have the trust of all parties.

One of the ground rules for mediation is that if no settlement is reached, everything said by all the parties and by the mediator is privileged, which means that it cannot be used as evidence in subsequent proceedings.[14] This allows the parties to be more open with each other and improves the likelihood of settlement.

One of the functions of the mediator is to provide a reality check for the parties. For example, one of the parties may have received advice from its attorney that a particular argument is very likely to succeed at trial. The party would be reluctant to compromise further based on that assessment. The attorney may honestly believe that assessment, but objectivity can be lost after long periods of involvement in the case. In addition, the mediator may be made aware of facts that the party is unaware of.

The first phase of a mediation is an exchange of opening statements by each of the parties. It is like the opening argument at trial, only briefer. The mediator then meets separately with each party, discussing the strengths and weaknesses of each position, in an attempt to bring the parties closer together. Unlike a judge or arbitrator, the mediator is allowed to meet with one party in the absence of the others to discuss the case.

During the separate meetings, a party can request that certain information be kept confidential. In this instance, the mediator is not allowed to disclose the information to any other party. The mediator will receive confidential information from each party—including, in many cases, the bottom-line settlement figure—and must ensure that such information is not disclosed without consent.

If settlement is reached, the mediator or one of the parties will accept the task of recording the terms of settlement in the form of a settlement agreement, which is then signed by the parties.

---

14.   This rule applies during negotiations as well; statements and offers made during settlement discussions are protected by privilege.

13.6   OTHER DISPUTE RESOLUTION METHODS

There are other methods of dispute resolution that are similar to mediation, including minitrials and settlement conferences. In some jurisdictions, it is a mandatory
step in the litigation process for the parties to attempt to settle the case through
mediation or settlement conference. A settlement conference is an informal meeting with a judge in order that the judge might assist the parties to settle the case. A
minitrial is a condensed version of a trial in front of a judge alone. Evidence may be
presented, or in some minitrials, rather than call witnesses, anticipated evidence
may be summarized in written form. The judge makes a nonbinding ruling, which
should give the parties a realistic idea of the probable outcome of a complete trial.

There are many variations of these methods, including binding mediation (media-
tion/arbitration), court-appointed masters and referees, summary jury trials, and
partnering. Parties considering these processes should evaluate the following factors: cost; time (delay); whether an independent party is involved and, if so, the
qualifications of the party and how he or she is chosen; whether the process is binding; and the right or lack of right to appeal an unfavorable decision to a higher
authority or court.

APPENDIX A

AIA Document A201-1987

General Conditions of the Contract for Construction

Provided by the American Institute of Architects, whose permission to
reproduce the document here is gratefully acknowledged. Copies of this
document are available from the AIA, 1735 New York Avenue N.W.,
Washington, DC 20006.

AIA Document A201

General Conditions of the Contract for Construction

THIS DOCUMENT HAS IMPORTANT LEGAL CONSEQUENCES; CONSULTATION WITH AN ATTORNEY IS ENCOURAGED WITH RESPECT TO ITS MODIFICATION

1987 EDITION
TABLE OF ARTICLES

1. GENERAL PROVISIONS

2. OWNER

3. CONTRACTOR

4. ADMINISTRATION OF THE CONTRACT

5. SUBCONTRACTORS

6. CONSTRUCTION BY OWNER OR BY SEPARATE CONTRACTORS

7. CHANGES IN THE WORK

8. TIME

9. PAYMENTS AND COMPLETION

10. PROTECTION OF PERSONS AND PROPERTY

11. INSURANCE AND BONDS

12. UNCOVERING AND CORRECTION OF WORK

13. MISCELLANEOUS PROVISIONS

14. TERMINATION OR SUSPENSION OF THE CONTRACT

This document has been approved and endorsed by the Associated General Contractors of America.

INDEX

Acceptance of Nonconforming Work 9.6.6, 9.9.3, **12.3**
Acceptance of Work 9.6.6, 9.8.2, 9.9.3, 9.10.1, 9.10.3
Access to Work **3.16**, 6.2.1, 12.1
Accident Prevention 4.2.3, 10
Acts and Omissions . . . 3.2.1, 3.2.2, 3.3.2, 3.12.8, 3.18, 4.2.3, 4.3.2,
4.3.9, 8.3.1, 10.1.4, 10.2.5, 13.4.2, 13.7, 14.1
Addenda 1.1.1, 3.11
Additional Cost, Claims for 4.3.6, 4.3.7, 4.3.9, 6.1.1, 10.3
Additional Inspections and Testing 4.2.6, 9.8.2, 12.2.1, 13.5
Additional Time, Claims for 4.3.6, 4.3.8, 4.3.9, 8.3.2
ADMINISTRATION OF THE CONTRACT 3.3.3, **4**, 9.4, 9.5
Advertisement or Invitation to Bid 1.1.1
Aesthetic Effect 4.2.13, 4.5.1
Allowances **3.8**
All-risk Insurance 11.3.1.1
Applications for Payment . . 4.2.5, 7.3.7, 9.2, **9.3**, 9.4, 9.5.1, 9.6.3,
9.8.3, 9.10.1, 9.10.3, 9.10.4, 11.1.3, 14.2.4
Approvals . . . . 2.4, 3.3.3, 3.5, 3.10.2, 3.12.4 through 3.12.8, 3.18.3,
4.2.7, 9.3.2, 11.3.1.4, 13.4.2, 13.5
Arbitration 4.1.4, 4.3.2, 4.3.4, 4.4.4, 4.5,
8.3.1, 10.1.2, 11.3.9, 11.3.10
Architect 4.1
Architect, Definition of 4.1.1
Architect, Extent of Authority 2.4, 3.12.6, 4.2, 4.3.2, 4.3.6,
4.4, 5.2, 6.3, 7.1.2, 7.2.1, 7.3.6, 7.4, 9.2, 9.3.1,
9.4, 9.5, 9.6.3, 9.8.2, 9.8.3, 9.10.1, 10.1.2, 12.1, 12.2.1,
13.5.1, 13.5.2, 14.2.2, 14.2.4
Architect, Limitations of Authority and Responsibility . . 3.3.3, 3.12.8,
3.12.11, 4.1.2, 4.2.1, 4.2.2, 4.2.3, 4.2.6, 4.2.7, 4.2.10, 4.2.12,
4.2.13, 4.3.2, 5.2.1, 7.4, 9.4.2, 9.6.4, 9.6.6
Architect's Additional Services and Expenses 2.4, 9.8.2,
11.3.1.1, 12.2.1, 12.2.4, 13.5.2, 13.5.3, 14.2.4
Architect's Administration of the Contract 4.2, 4.3.6,
4.3.7, 4.4, 9.4, 9.5
Architect's Approvals . . 2.4, 3.5.1, 3.10.2, 3.12.6, 3.12.8, 3.18.3, 4.2.7
Architect's Authority to Reject Work 3.5.1, 4.2.6, 12.1.2, 12.2.1
Architect's Copyright 1.3
Architect's Decisions 4.2.6, 4.2.7, 4.2.11, 4.2.12, 4.2.13,
4.3.2, 4.3.6, 4.4.1, 4.4.4, 4.5, 6.3, 7.3.6, 7.3.8, 8.1.3, 8.3.1,
9.2, 9.4, 9.5.1, 9.8.2, 9.9.1, 10.1.2, 13.5.2, 14.2.2, 14.2.4
Architect's Inspections 4.2.2, 4.2.9, 4.3.6, 9.4.2, 9.8.2,
9.9.2, 9.10.1, 13.5
Architect's Instructions . . 4.2.6, 4.2.7, 4.2.8, 4.3.7, 7.4.1, 12.1, 13.5.2
Architect's Interpretations 4.2.11, 4.2.12, 4.3.7
Architect's On-Site Observations 4.2.2, 4.2.5, 4.3.6, 9.4.2,
9.5.1, 9.10.1, 13.5
Architect's Project Representative 4.2.10
Architect's Relationship with Contractor 1.1.2, 3.2.1, 3.2.2,
3.3.3, 3.5.1, 3.7.3, 3.11, 3.12.8, 3.12.11, 3.16, 3.18, 4.2.3, 4.2.4,
4.2.6, 4.2.12, 5.2, 6.2.2, 7.3.4, 9.8.2, 11.3.7, 12.1, 13.5
Architect's Relationship with Subcontractors . . . 1.1.2, 4.2.3, 4.2.4,
4.2.6, 9.6.3, 9.6.4, 11.3.7
Architect's Representations 9.4.2, 9.5.1, 9.10.1
Architect's Site Visits 4.2.2, 4.2.5, 4.2.9, 4.3.6, 9.4.2, 9.5.1,
9.8.2, 9.9.2, 9.10.1, 13.5
Asbestos 10.1
Attorneys' Fees 3.18.1, 9.10.2, 10.1.4
Award of Separate Contracts 6.1.1
**Award of Subcontracts and Other Contracts for
Portions of the Work** **5.2**
Basic Definitions **1.1**
Bidding Requirements 1.1.1, 1.1.7, 5.2.1, 11.4.1
Boiler and Machinery Insurance **11.3.2**
Bonds, Lien 9.10.2
Bonds, Performance and Payment 7.3.6.4, 9.10.3, 11.3.9, 11.4

Building Permit 3.7.1
Capitalization **1.4**
Certificate of Substantial Completion 9.8.2
Certificates for Payment 4.2.5, 4.2.9, 9.3.3, **9.4**, 9.5, 9.6.1,
9.6.6, 9.7.1, 9.8.3, 9.10.1, 9.10.3, 13.7, 14.1.1.3, 14.2.4
Certificates of Inspection, Testing or Approval 3.12.11, 13.5.4
Certificates of Insurance 9.3.2, 9.10.2, 11.1.3
Change Orders 1.1.1, 2.4.1, 3.8.2.4, 3.11, 4.2.8, 4.3.3, 5.2.3,
7.1, **7.2**, 7.3.2, 8.3.1, 9.3.1.1, 9.10.3, 11.3.1.2,
11.3.4, 11.3.9, 12.1.2
Change Orders, Definition of 7.2.1
Changes **7.1**
CHANGES IN THE WORK 3.11, 4.2.8, **7**, 8.3.1, 9.3.1.1, 10.1.3
Claim, Definition of **4.3.1**
Claims and Disputes **4.3**, 4.4, 4.5, 6.2.5, 8.3.2,
9.3.1.2, 9.3.3, 9.10.4, 10.1.4
Claims and Timely Assertion of Claims 4.5.6
Claims for Additional Cost 4.3.6, **4.3.7**, 4.3.9, 6.1.1, 10.3
Claims for Additional Time 4.3.6, **4.3.8**, 4.3.9, 8.3.2
Claims for Concealed or Unknown Conditions 4.3.6
Claims for Damages . . . 3.18, 4.3.9, 6.1.1, 6.2.5, 8.3.2, 9.5.1.2, 10.1.4
Claims Subject to Arbitration 4.3.2, 4.4.4, 4.5.1
Cleaning Up **3.15**, 6.3
Commencement of Statutory Limitation Period 13.7
Commencement of the Work, Conditions Relating to 2.1.2,
2.2.1, 3.2.1, 3.2.2, 3.7.1, 3.10.1, 3.12.6, 4.3.7, 5.2.1,
6.2.2, 8.1.2, 8.2.2, 9.2, 11.1.3, 11.3.6, 11.4.1
Commencement of the Work, Definition of 8.1.2
Communications Facilitating Contract
Administration 3.9.1, 4.2.4, 5.2.1
Completion, Conditions Relating to 3.11, 3.15, 4.2.2, 4.2.9,
4.3.2, 9.4.2, 9.8, 9.9.1, 9.10, 11.3.5, 12.2.2, 13.7
COMPLETION, PAYMENTS AND **9**
Completion, Substantial 4.2.9, 4.3.5.2, 8.1.1, 8.1.3, 8.2.3,
9.8, 9.9.1, 12.2.2, 13.7
Compliance with Laws 1.3, 3.6, 3.7, 3.13, 4.1.1, 10.2.2, 11.1,
11.3, 13.1, 13.5.1, 13.5.2, 13.6, 14.1.1, 14.2.1.3
Concealed or Unknown Conditions 4.3.6
Conditions of the Contract 1.1.1, 1.1.7, 6.1.1
Consent, Written 1.3.1, 3.12.8, 3.14.2, 4.1.2,
4.3.4, 4.5.5, 9.3.2, 9.8.2, 9.9.1, 9.10.2, 9.10.3, 10.1.2, 10.1.3,
11.3.1, 11.3.1.4, 11.3.11, 13.2, 13.4.2
**CONSTRUCTION BY OWNER OR BY SEPARATE
CONTRACTORS** 1.1.4, **6**
Construction Change Directive, Definition of 7.3.1
Construction Change Directives 1.1.1, 4.2.8, 7.1, **7.3**, 9.3.1.1
Construction Schedules, Contractor's 3.10, 6.1.3
Contingent Assignment of Subcontracts **5.4**
Continuing Contract Performance **4.3.4**
Contract, Definition of 1.1.2
**CONTRACT, TERMINATION OR
SUSPENSION OF THE** 4.3.7, 5.4.1.1, **14**
Contract Administration 3.3.3, 4, 9.4, 9.5
Contract Award and Execution, Conditions Relating to 3.7.1,
3.10, 5.2, 9.2, 11.1.3, 11.3.6, 11.4.1
Contract Documents, The **1.1**, 1.2, 7
Contract Documents, Copies Furnished and Use of . . . 1.3, 2.2.5, 5.3
Contract Documents, Definition of 1.1.1
Contract Performance During Arbitration 4.3.4, 4.5.3
Contract Sum 3.8, 4.3.6, 4.3.7, 4.4.4, 5.2.3,
6.1.3, 7.2, 7.3, **9.1**, 9.7, 11.3.1, 12.2.4, 12.3, 14.2.4
Contract Sum, Definition of **9.1**
Contract Time 4.3.6, 4.3.8, 4.4.4, 7.2.1.3, 7.3,
8.2.1, 8.3.1, 9.7, 12.1.1
Contract Time, **Definition** of **8.1.1**

159

CONTRACTOR 3
Contractor, **Definition** of **3.1**, 6.1.2
Contractor's Bid 1.1.1
Contractor's Construction Schedules **3.10**, 6.1.3
Contractor's Employees 3.3.2, 3.4.2, 3.8.1, 3.9, 3.18, 4.2.3,
    4.2.6, 8.1.2, 10.2, 10.3, 11.1.1, 14.2.1.1
Contractor's Liability Insurance **11.1**
Contractor's Relationship with Separate Contractors
    and Owner's Forces 2.2.6, 3.12.5, 3.14.2, 4.2.4, 6, 12.2.5
Contractor's Relationship with Subcontractors 1.2.4, 3.3.2,
    3.18.1, 3.18.2, 5.2, 5.3, 5.4, 9.6.2, 11.3.7, 11.3.8, 14.2.1.2
Contractor's Relationship with the Architect 1.1.2, 3.2.1, 3.2.2,
    3.3.3, 3.5.1, 3.7.3, 3.11, 3.12.8 3.16, 3.18, 4.2.3, 4.2.4, 4.2.6,
    4.2.12, 5.2, 6.2.2, 7.3.4, 9.8.2, 11.3.7, 12.1, 13.5
Contractor's Representations .. 1.2.2, 3.5.1, 3.12.7, 6.2.2, 8.2.1, 9.3.3
Contractor's Responsibility for Those
    Performing the Work 3.3.2, 3.18, 4.2.3, 10
Contractor's Review of Contract Documents 1.2.2, 3.2, 3.7.3
Contractor's Right to Stop the Work 9.7
Contractor's Right to Terminate the Contract 14.1
Contractor's Submittals 3.10, 3.11, 3.12, 4.2.7, 5.2.1, 5.2.3,
    7.3.6, 9.2, 9.3.1, 9.8.2, 9.9.1, 9.9.2, 9.9.3,
    9.10.2, 9.10.3, 10.1.2, 11.4.2, 11.4.3
Contractor's Superintendent 3.9, 10.2.6
Contractor's Supervision and Construction Procedures ... 1.2.4,
    3.3, 3.4, 4.2.3, 8.2.2, 8.2.3, 10
Contractual Liability Insurance 11.1.1.7, 11.2.1
Coordination and Correlation 1.2, 1.2.2, 1.2.4, 3.3.1,
    3.10, 3.12.7, 6.1.3, 6.2.1
Copies Furnished of Drawings and Specifications ... 1.3, 2.2.5, 3.11
Correction of Work 2.3, 2.4, 4.2.1, 9.8.2,
    9.9.1, 12.1.2, 12.2, 13.7.1.3
Cost, Definition of 7.3.6, 14.3.5
Costs 2.4, 3.2.1, 3.7.4, 3.8.2, 3.15.2, 4.3.6, 4.3.7, 4.3.8.1, 5.2.3,
    6.1.1, 6.2.3, 6.3, 7.3.3.3, 7.3.6, 7.3.7, 9.7, 9.8.2, 9.10.2, 11.3.1.2,
    11.3.1.3, 11.3.4, 11.3.9, 12.1, 12.2.1, 12.2.4, 12.2.5, 13.5, 14
Cutting and Patching **3.14**, 6.2.6
Damage to Construction of Owner or Separate Contractors 3.14.2,
    6.2.4, 9.5.1.5, 10.2.1.2, 10.2.5, 10.3, 11.1, 11.3, 12.2.5
Damage to the Work 3.14.2, 9.9.1, 10.2.1.2, 10.2.5, 10.3
Damages, Claims for .. 3.18, 4.3.9, 6.1.1, 6.2.5, 8.3.2, 9.5.1.2, 10.1.4
Damages for Delay 6.1.1, 8.3.3, 9.5.1.6, 9.7
Date of Commencement of the Work, Definition of 8.1.2
Date of Substantial Completion, Definition of 8.1.3
Day, Definition of 8.1.4
Decisions of the Architect 4.2.6, 4.2.7, 4.2.11, 4.2.12, 4.2.13,
    4.3.2, 4.3.6, 4.4.1, 4.4.4, 4.5, 6.3, 7.3.6, 7.3.8, 8.1.3, 8.3.1, 9.2,
    9.4, 9.5.1, 9.8.2, 9.9.1, 10.1.2, 13.5.2, 14.2.2, 14.2.4
Decisions to Withhold Certification **9.5**, 9.7, 14.1.1.3
Defective or Nonconforming Work, Acceptance,
    Rejection and Correction of 2.3, 2.4, 3.5.1, 4.2.1,
    4.2.6, 4.3.5, 9.5.2, 9.8.2, 9.9.1, 10.2.5, 12, 13.7.1.3
Defective Work, Definition of 3.5.1
Definitions 1.1, 2.1.1, 3.1, 3.5.1, 3.12.1, 3.12.2, 3.12.3, 4.1.1,
    4.3.1, 5.1, 6.1.2, 7.2.1, 7.3.1, 7.3.6, 8.1, 9.1, 9.8.1
Delays and Extensions of Time 4.3.1, 4.3.8.1, 4.3.8.2,
    6.1.1, 6.2.3, 7.2.1, 7.3.1, 7.3.4, 7.3.5, 7.3.8,
    7.3.9, 8.1.1, **8.3**, 10.3.1, 14.1.1.4
Disputes 4.1.4, 4.3, 4.4, 4.5, 6.2.5, 6.3, 7.3.8, 9.3.1.2
Documents and Samples at the Site 3.11
Drawings, Definition of 1.1.5
Drawings and Specifications, Use and Ownership of.... 1.1.1, 1.3,
    2.2.5, 3.11, 5.3
Duty to Review Contract Documents and Field Conditions 3.2
Effective Date of Insurance 8.2.2, 11.1.2

Emergencies 4.3.7, **10.3**
Employees, Contractor's 3.3.2, 3.4.2, 3.8.1, 3.9, 3.18.1,
    3.18.2, 4.2.3, 4.2.6, 8.1.2, 10.2, 10.3, 11.1.1, 14.2.1.1
Equipment, Labor, Materials and 1.1.3, 1.1.6, 3.4, 3.5.1,
    3.8.2, 3.12.3, 3.12.7, 3.12.11, 3.13, 3.15.1, 4.2.7,
    6.2.1, 7.3.6, 9.3.2, 9.3.3, 11.3, 12.2.4, 14
Execution and Progress of the Work 1.1.3, 1.2.3, 3.2, 3.4.1,
    3.5.1, 4.2.2, 4.2.3, 4.3.4, 4.3.8, 6.2.2, 7.1.3,
    7.3.9, 8.2, 8.3, 9.5, 9.9.1, 10.2, 14.2, 14.3
Execution, Correlation and Intent of the
    Contract Documents **1.2**, 3.7.1
Extensions of Time 4.3.1, 4.3.8, 7.2.1.3, 8.3, 10.3.1
Failure of Payment by Contractor 9.5.1.3, 14.2.1.2
Failure of Payment by Owner 4.3.7, 9.7, 14.1.3
Faulty Work (See Defective or Nonconforming Work)
Final Completion and Final Payment 4.2.1, 4.2.9, 4.3.2,
    4.3.5, **9.10**, 11.1.2, 11.1.3, 11.3.5, 12.3.1, 13.7
Financial Arrangements, Owner's 2.2.1
Fire and Extended Coverage Insurance 11.3
GENERAL PROVISIONS **1**
Governing Law **13.1**
Guarantees (See Warranty and Warranties)
Hazardous Materials 10.1, 10.2.4
Identification of Contract Documents 1.2.1
Identification of Subcontractors and Suppliers 5.2.1
Indemnification 3.17, **3.18**, 9.10.2, 10.1.4, 11.3.1.2, 11.3.7
Information and Services Required of the Owner 2.1.2, **2.2**,
    4.3.4, 6.1.3, 6.1.4, 6.2.6, 9.3.2, 9.6.1, 9.6.4, 9.8.3, 9.9.2,
    9.10.3, 10.1.4, 11.2, 11.3, 13.5.1, 13.5.2
Injury or Damage to Person or Property **4.3.9**
Inspections 3.3.3, 3.3.4, 3.7.1, 4.2.2,
    4.2.6, 4.2.9, 4.3.6, 9.4.2, 9.8.2, 9.9.2, 9.10.1, 13.5
Instructions to Bidders 1.1.1
Instructions to the Contractor 3.8.1, 4.2.8, 5.2.1, 7, 12.1, 13.5.2
Insurance 4.3.9, 6.1.1, 7.3.6.4, 9.3.2, 9.8.2, 9.9.1, 9.10.2, 11
Insurance, Boiler and Machinery **11.3.2**
Insurance, Contractor's Liability **11.1**
Insurance, Effective Date of 8.2.2, 11.1.2
Insurance, Loss of Use **11.3.3**
Insurance, Owner's Liability **11.2**
Insurance, Property 10.2.5, **11.3**
Insurance, Stored Materials 9.3.2, 11.3.1.4
INSURANCE AND BONDS **11**
Insurance Companies, Consent to Partial Occupancy .. 9.9.1, 11.3.11
Insurance Companies, Settlement with 11.3.10
Intent of the Contract Documents 1.2.3, 3.12.4,
    4.2.6, 4.2.7, 4.2.12, 4.2.13, 7.4
Interest **13.6**
Interpretation 1.2.5, 1.4, **1.5**, 4.1.1, 4.3.1, 5.1, 6.1.2, 8.1.4
Interpretations, Written 4.2.11, 4.2.12, 4.3.7
Joinder and Consolidation of Claims Required 4.5.6
Judgment on Final Award 4.5.1, 4.5.4.1, **4.5.7**
Labor and Materials, Equipment 1.1.3, 1.1.6, **3.4**, 3.5.1, 3.8.2,
    3.12.2, 3.12.3, 3.12.7, 3.12.11, 3.13, 3.15.1,
    4.2.7, 6.2.1, 7.3.6, 9.3.2, 9.3.3, 12.2.4, 14
Labor Disputes 8.3.1
Laws and Regulations 1.3, 3.6, 3.7, 3.13, 4.1.1, 4.5.5, 4.5.7,
    9.9.1, 10.2.2, 11.1, 11.3, 13.1, 13.4, 13.5.1, 13.5.2, 13.6
Liens 2.1.2, 4.3.2, 4.3.5.1, 8.2.2, 9.3.3, 9.10.2
Limitation on Consolidation or Joinder **4.5.5**
Limitations, Statutes of 4.5.4.2, 12.2.6, 13.7
Limitations of Authority 3.3.1, 4.1.2, 4.2.1,
    4.2.3, 4.2.7, 4.2.10, 5.2.2, 5.2.4, 7.4, 11.3.10

160

Limitations of Liability 2.3, 3.2.1, 3.5.1, 3.7.3, 3.12.8, 3.12.11,
   3.17, 3.18, 4.2.6, 4.2.7, 4.2.12, 6.2.2, 9.4.2, 9.6.4, 9.10.4,
   10.1.4, 10.2.5, 11.1.2, 11.2.1, 11.3.7, 13.4.2, 13.5.2
Limitations of Time, General 2.2.1, 2.2.4, 3.2.1, 3.7.3,
   3.8.2, 3.10, 3.12.5, 3.15.1, 4.2.1, 4.2.7, 4.2.11, 4.3.2,
   4.3.3, 4.3.4,4.3.6, 4.3.9, 4.5.4.2, 5.2.1, 5.2.3, 6.2.4, 7.3.4, 7.4,
   8.2, 9.5, 9.6.2, 9.8, 9.9, 9.10, 11.1.3, 11.3.1, 11.3.2, 11.3.5,
   11.3.6, 12.2.1, 12.2.2, 13.5, 13.7
Limitations of Time, Specific 2.1.2, 2.2.1, 2.4, 3.10, 3.11,
   3.15.1, 4.2.1, 4.2.11, 4.3, 4.4, 4.5, 5.3, 5.4, 7.3.5, 7.3.9, 8.2,
   9.2, 9.3.1, 9.3.3, 9.4.1, 9.6.1, 9.7, 9.8.2, 9.10.2, 11.1.3, 11.3.6,
   11.3.10, 11.3.11, 12.2.2, 12.2.4, 12.2.6, 13.5, 13.7
Loss of Use Insurance **11.3.3**
Material Suppliers 1.3.1, 3.12.1, 4.2.4, 4.2.6, 5.2.1,
   9.3.1, 9.3.1.2, 9.3.3, 9.4.2, 9.6.5, 9.10.4
Materials, Hazardous 10.1, 10.2.4
Materials, Labor, Equipment and 1.1.3, 1.1.6, 3.4, 3.5.1, 3.8.2,
   3.12.2, 3.12.3, 3.12.7, 3.12.11, 3.13, 3.15.1, 4.2.7, 6.2.1,
   7.3.6, 9.3.2, 9.3.3, 12.2.4, 14
Means, Methods, Techniques, Sequences and
   Procedures of Construction 3.3.1, 4.2.3, 4.2.7, 9.4.2
Minor Changes in the Work 1.1.1, 4.2.8, 4.3.7, 7.1, 7.4
MISCELLANEOUS PROVISIONS **13**
Modifications, Definition of 1.1.1
Modifications to the Contract 1.1.1, 1.1.2, 3.7.3, 3.11,
   4.1.2, 4.2.1, 5.2.3, 7, 8.3.1, 9.7
Mutual Responsibility **6.2**
Nonconforming Work, Acceptance of **12.3**
Nonconforming Work, Rejection and Correction of 2.3.1,
   4.3.5, 9.5.2, 9.8.2, 12, 13.7.1.3
Notice 2.3, 2.4, 3.2.1, 3.2.2, 3.7.3, 3.7.4, 3.9, 3.12.8,
   3.12.9, 3.17, 4.3, 4.4.4, 4.5, 5.2.1, 5.3, 5.4.1.1, 8.2.2, 9.4.1,
   9.5.1, 9.6.1, 9.7, 9.10, 10.1.2, 10.2.6, 11.1.3, 11.3, 12.2.2,
   12.2.4, 13.3, 13.5.1, 13.5.2, 14
Notice, Written 2.3, 2.4, 3.9, 3.12.8, 3.12.9, 4.3,
   4.4.4, 4.5, 5.2.1, 5.3, 5.4.1.1, 8.2.2, 9.4.1, 9.5.1, 9.7, 9.10,
   10.1.2, 10.2.6, 11.1.3, 11.3, 12.2.2, 12.2.4, **13.3**, 13.5.2, 14
Notice of Testing and Inspections 13.5.1, 13.5.2
Notice to Proceed 8.2.2
Notices, Permits, Fees and 2.2.3, **3.7**, 3.13, 7.3.6.4, 10.2.2
Observations, Architect's On-Site 4.2.2, 4.2.5,
   4.3.6, 9.4.2, 9.5.1, 9.10.1, 13.5
Observations, Contractor's 1.2.2, 3.2.2
Occupancy 9.6.6, 9.8.1, 9.9, 11.3.11
On-Site Inspections by the Architect 4.2.2, 4.2.9, 4.3.6,
   9.4.2, 9.8.2, 9.9.2, 9.10.1
On-Site Observations by the Architect 4.2.2, 4.2.5, 4.3.6,
   9.4.2, 9.5.1, 9.10.1, 13.5
Orders, Written 2.3, 3.9, 4.3.7, 7, 8.2.2, 11.3.9, 12.1,
   12.2, 13.5.2, 14.3.1

OWNER **2**
Owner, **Definition** of **2.1**
Owner, Information and Services Required of the 2.1.2,
   2.2, 4.3.4, 6, 9, 10.1.4, 11.2, 11.3, 13.5.1, 14.1.1.5, 14.1.3
Owner's Authority 3.8.1, 4.1.3, 4.2.9, 5.2.1, 5.2.4, 5.4.1,
   7.3.1, 8.2.2, 9.3.1, 9.3.2, 11.4.1, 12.2.4, 13.5.2, 14.2, 14.3.1
Owner's Financial Capability 2.2.1, 14.1.1.5
Owner's Liability Insurance **11.2**
Owner's Loss of Use Insurance 11.3.3
Owner's Relationship with Subcontractors 1.1.2,
   5.2.1, 5.4.1, 9.6.4
Owner's Right to Carry Out the Work 2.4, 12.2.4, 14.2.2.2
Owner's Right to Clean Up **6.3**

Owner's Right to Perform Construction and to
   Award Separate Contracts **6.1**
Owner's Right to Stop the Work **2.3**, 4.3.7
Owner's Right to Suspend the Work 14.3
Owner's Right to Terminate the Contract 14.2
Ownership and Use of Architect's Drawings, Specifications
   and Other Documents 1.1.1, **1.3**, 2.2.5, 5.3
Partial Occupancy or Use 9.6.6, **9.9**, 11.3.11
Patching, Cutting and **3.14**, 6.2.6
Patents, Royalties and **3.17**
Payment, Applications for 4.2.5, 9.2, **9.3**, 9.4,
   9.5.1, 9.8.3, 9.10.1, 9.10.3, 9.10.4, 14.2.4
Payment, Certificates for 4.2.5, 4.2.9, 9.3.3, **9.4**, 9.5,
   9.6.1, 9.6.6, 9.7.1, 9.8.3, 9.10.1, 9.10.3, 13.7, 14.1.1.3, 14.2.4
Payment, Failure of 4.3.7, 9.5.1.3,
   9.7, 9.10.2, 14.1.1.3, 14.2.1.2
Payment, Final 4.2.1, 4.2.9, 4.3.2, 4.3.5, 9.10, 11.1.2,
   11.1.3, 11.3.5, 12.3.1
Payment Bond, Performance Bond and 7.3.6.4,
   9.10.3, 11.3.9, **11.4**
Payments, Progress 4.3.4, 9.3, 9.6,
   9.8.3, 9.10.3, 13.6, 14.2.3
PAYMENTS AND COMPLETION **9**, 14
Payments to Subcontractors 5.4.2, 9.5.1.3,
   9.6.2, 9.6.3, 9.6.4, 11.3.8, 14.2.1.2
PCB 10.1
Performance Bond and Payment Bond 7.3.6.4,
   9.10.3, 11.3.9, 11.4
Permits, Fees and Notices 2.2.3, **3.7**, 3.13, 7.3.6.4, 10.2.2
PERSONS AND PROPERTY, PROTECTION OF **10**
Polychlorinated Biphenyl 10.1
Product Data, Definition of 3.12.2
Product Data and Samples, Shop Drawings 3.11, **3.12**, 4.2.7
Progress and Completion 4.2.2, 4.3.4, **8.2**
Progress Payments 4.3.4, 9.3,
   9.6, 9.8.3, 9.10.3, 13.6, 14.2.3
Project, Definition of the **1.1.4**
Project Manual, Definition of the **1.1.7**
Project Manuals 2.2.5
Project Representatives 4.2.10
Property Insurance 10.2.5, **11.3**
PROTECTION OF PERSONS AND PROPERTY **10**
Regulations and Laws 1.3, 3.6, 3.7, 3.13, 4.1.1, 4.5.5,
   4.5.7, 10.2.2, 11.1, 11.3, 13.1, 13.4, 13.5.1, 13.5.2, 13.6, 14
Rejection of Work 3.5.1, 4.2.6, 12.2
Releases of Waivers and Liens 9.10.2
Representations 1.2.2, 3.5.1, 3.12.7,
   6.2.2, 8.2.1, 9.3.3, 9.4.2, 9.5.1, 9.8.2, 9.10.1
Representatives 2.1.1, 3.1.1, 3.9,
   4.1.1, 4.2.1, 4.2.10, 5.1.1, 5.1.2, 13.2.1
Resolution of Claims and Disputes **4.4**, 4.5
Responsibility for Those Performing the Work 3.3.2,
   4.2.3, 6.1.3, 6.2, 10
Retainage 9.3.1, 9.6.2, 9.8.3, 9.9.1, 9.10.2, 9.10.3
Review of Contract Documents and Field
   Conditions by Contractor 1.2.2, **3.2**, 3.7.3, 3.12.7
Review of Contractor's Submittals by
   Owner and Architect 3.10.1, 3.10.2, 3.11, 3.12,
   4.2.7, 4.2.9, 5.2.1, 5.2.3, 9.2, 9.8.2
Review of Shop Drawings, Product Data
   and Samples by Contractor 3.12.5
Rights and Remedies 1.1.2, 2.3, 2.4, 3.5.1, 3.15.2,
   4.2.6, 4.3.6, 4.5, 5.3, 6.1, 6.3, 7.3.1, 8.3.1, 9.5.1, 9.7, 10.2.5,
   10.3, 12.2.2, 12.2.4, **13.4**, 14
Royalties and Patents **3.17**

161

Rules and Notices for Arbitration **4.5.2**
Safety of Persons and Property **10.2**
Safety Precautions and Programs 4.2.3, 4.2.7, **10.1**
Samples, Definition of 3.12.3
Samples, Shop Drawings, Product Data and . . . 3.11, **3.12**, 4.2.7
Samples at the Site, Documents and **3.11**
Schedule of Values **9.2**, 9.3.1
Schedules, Construction 3.10
Separate Contracts and Contractors 1.1.4, 3.14.2, 4.2.4,
    4.5.5, 6, 11.3.7, 12.1.2, 12.2.5
Shop Drawings, Definition of 3.12.1
Shop Drawings, Product Data and Samples 3.11, **3.12**, 4.2.7
Site, Use of **3.13**, 6.1.1, 6.2.1
Site Inspections . . . 1.2.2, 3.3.4, 4.2.2, 4.2.9, 4.3.6, 9.8.2, 9.10.1, 13.5
Site Visits, Architect's 4.2.2, 4.2.5, 4.2.9, 4.3.6,
    9.4.2, 9.5.1, 9.8.2, 9.9.2, 9.10.1, 13.5
Special Inspections and Testing 4.2.6, 12.2.1, 13.5
Specifications, Definition of the 1.1.6
Specifications, The 1.1.1, **1.1.6**, 1.1.7, 1.2.4, 1.3.1, 3.11
Statutes of Limitations 4.5.4.2, 12.2.6, 13.7
Stopping the Work 2.3, 4.3.7, 9.7, 10.1.2, 10.3, 14.1
Stored Materials 6.2.1, 9.3.2, 10.2.1.2, 10.2.4, 11.3.1.4
Subcontractor, Definition of 5.1.1
SUBCONTRACTORS **5**
Subcontractors, Work by 1.2.4, 3.3.2, 3.12.1,
    4.2.3, 5.3, 5.4
Subcontractual Relations 5.3, 5.4, 9.3.1.2, 9.6.2,
    9.6.3, 9.6.4, 10.2.1, 11.3.7, 11.3.8, 14.1.1, 14.2.1.2, 14.3.2
Submittals 1.3, 3.2.3, 3.10, 3.11, 3.12, 4.2.7, 5.2.1, 5.2.3,
    7.3.6, 9.2, 9.3.1, 9.8.2, 9.9.1, 9.10.2, 9.10.3, 10.1.2, 11.1.3
Subrogation, Waivers of 6.1.1, 11.3.5, **11.3.7**
Substantial Completion 4.2.9, 4.3.5.2, 8.1.1, 8.1.3,
    8.2.3, **9.8**, 9.9.1, 12.2.1, 12.2.2, 13.7
Substantial Completion, Definition of 9.8.1
Substitution of Subcontractors 5.2.3, 5.2.4
Substitution of the Architect 4.1.3
Substitutions of Materials 3.5.1
Sub-subcontractor, Definition of 5.1.2
Subsurface Conditions 4.3.6
Successors and Assigns **13.2**
Superintendent **3.9**, 10.2.6
Supervision and Construction Procedures 1.2.4, **3.3**, 3.4,
    4.2.3, 4.3.4, 6.1.3, 6.2.4, 7.1.3, 7.3.4, 8.2, 8.3.1, 10, 12, 14
Surety 4.4.1, 4.4.4, 5.4.1.2, 9.10.2, 9.10.3, 14.2.2
Surety, Consent of 9.9.1, 9.10.2, 9.10.3
Surveys 2.2.2, 3.18.3

Suspension by the Owner for Convenience **14.3**
Suspension of the Work 4.3.7, 5.4.2, 14.1.1.4, 14.3
Suspension or Termination of the Contract 4.3.7, 5.4.1.1, 14
Taxes **3.6**, 7.3.6.4
Termination by the Contractor **14.1**
Termination by the Owner for Cause 5.4.1.1, **14.2**
Termination of the Architect 4.1.3
Termination of the Contractor 14.2.2
TERMINATION OR SUSPENSION OF THE CONTRACT **14**
Tests and Inspections 3.3.3, 4.2.6, 4.2.9, 9.4.2, 12.2.1, **13.5**
TIME **8**
Time, Delays and Extensions of 4.3.8, 7.2.1, **8.3**
Time Limits, Specific 2.1.2, 2.2.1, 2.4, 3.10, 3.11, 3.15.1,
    4.2.1, 4.2.11, 4.3, 4.4, 4.5, 5.3, 5.4, 7.3.5, 7.3.9, 8.2, 9.2, 9.3.1,
    9.3.3, 9.4.1, 9.6.1, 9.7, 9.8.2, 9.10.2, 11.1.3, 11.3.6, 11.3.10,
    11.3.11, 12.2.2, 12.2.4, 12.2.6, 13.7, 14
Time Limits on Claims 4.3.2, **4.3.3**, 4.3.6, 4.3.9, 4.4, 4.5
Title to Work 9.3.2, 9.3.3
UNCOVERING AND CORRECTION OF WORK **12**
Uncovering of Work **12.1**
Unforeseen Conditions 4.3.6, 8.3.1, 10.1
Unit Prices 7.1.4, 7.3.3.2
Use of Documents 1.1.1, 1.3, 2.2.5, 3.12.7, 5.3
Use of Site **3.13**, 6.1.1, 6.2.1
Values, Schedule of **9.2**, 9.3.1
Waiver of Claims: Final Payment **4.3.5**, 4.5.1, 9.10.3
Waiver of Claims by the Architect 13.4.2
Waiver of Claims by the Contractor 9.10.4, 11.3.7, 13.4.2
Waiver of Claims by the Owner 4.3.5, 4.5.1, 9.9.3,
    9.10.3, 11.3.3, 11.3.5, 11.3.7, 13.4.2
Waiver of Liens 9.10.2
Waivers of Subrogation 6.1.1, 11.3.5, 11.3.7
Warranty and Warranties **3.5**, 4.2.9,
    4.3.5.3, 9.3.3, 9.8.2, 9.9.1, 12.2.2, 13.7.1.3
Weather Delays 4.3.8.2
When Arbitration May Be Demanded **4.5.4**
Work, Definition of 1.1.3
Written Consent 1.3.1, 3.12.8, 3.14.2, 4.1.2, 4.3.4,
    4.5.5, 9.3.2, 9.8.2, 9.9.1, 9.10.2, 9.10.3, 10.1.2, 10.1.3,
    11.3.1, 11.3.1.4, 11.3.11, 13.2, 13.4.2
Written Interpretations 4.2.11, 4.2.12, 4.3.7
Written Notice 2.3, 2.4, 3.9, 3.12.8, 3.12.9, 4.3, 4.4.4,
    4.5, 5.2.1, 5.3, 5.4.1.1, 8.2.2, 9.4.1, 9.5.1, 9.7, 9.10, 10.1.2,
    10.2.6, 11.1.3, 11.3, 12.2.2, 12.2.4, **13.3**, 13.5.2, 14
Written Orders 2.3, 3.9, 4.3.7,
    7, 8.2.2, 11.3.9, 12.1, 12.2, 13.5.2, 14.3.1

162

ARTICLE 1

GENERAL PROVISIONS

1.1 BASIC DEFINITIONS

1.1.1 THE CONTRACT DOCUMENTS

The Contract Documents consist of the Agreement between Owner and Contractor (hereinafter the Agreement), Conditions of the Contract (General, Supplementary and other Conditions), Drawings, Specifications, addenda issued prior to execution of the Contract, other documents listed in the Agreement and Modifications issued after execution of the Contract. A Modification is (1) a written amendment to the Contract signed by both parties, (2) a Change Order, (3) a Construction Change Directive or (4) a written order for a minor change in the Work issued by the Architect. Unless specifically enumerated in the Agreement, the Contract Documents do not include other documents such as bidding requirements (advertisement or invitation to bid, Instructions to Bidders, sample forms, the Contractor's bid or portions of addenda relating to bidding requirements).

1.1.2 THE CONTRACT

The Contract Documents form the Contract for Construction. The Contract represents the entire and integrated agreement between the parties hereto and supersedes prior negotiations, representations or agreements, either written or oral. The Contract may be amended or modified only by a Modification. The Contract Documents shall not be construed to create a contractual relationship of any kind (1) between the Architect and Contractor, (2) between the Owner and a Subcontractor or Subsubcontractor or (3) between any persons or entities other than the Owner and Contractor. The Architect shall, however, be entitled to performance and enforcement of obligations under the Contract intended to facilitate performance of the Architect's duties.

1.1.3 THE WORK

The term ''Work'' means the construction and services required by the Contract Documents, whether completed or partially completed, and includes all other labor, materials, equipment and services provided or to be provided by the Contractor to fulfill the Contractor's obligations. The Work may constitute the whole or a part of the Project.

1.1.4 THE PROJECT

The Project is the total construction of which the Work performed under the Contract Documents may be the whole or a part and which may include construction by the Owner or by separate contractors.

1.1.5 THE DRAWINGS

The Drawings are the graphic and pictorial portions of the Contract Documents, wherever located and whenever issued, showing the design, location and dimensions of the Work, generally including plans, elevations, sections, details, schedules and diagrams.

1.1.6 THE SPECIFICATIONS

The Specifications are that portion of the Contract Documents consisting of the written requirements for materials, equip-

ment, construction systems, standards and workmanship for the Work, and performance of related services.

1.1.7 THE PROJECT MANUAL

The Project Manual is the volume usually assembled for the Work which may include the bidding requirements, sample forms, Conditions of the Contract and Specifications.

1.2 EXECUTION, CORRELATION AND INTENT

1.2.1 The Contract Documents shall be signed by the Owner and Contractor as provided in the Agreement. If either the Owner or Contractor or both do not sign all the Contract Documents, the Architect shall identify such unsigned Documents upon request.

1.2.2 Execution of the Contract by the Contractor is a representation that the Contractor has visited the site, become familiar with local conditions under which the Work is to be performed and correlated personal observations with requirements of the Contract Documents.

1.2.3 The intent of the Contract Documents is to include all items necessary for the proper execution and completion of the Work by the Contractor. The Contract Documents are complementary, and what is required by one shall be as binding as if required by all; performance by the Contractor shall be required only to the extent consistent with the Contract Documents and reasonably inferable from them as being necessary to produce the intended results.

1.2.4 Organization of the Specifications into divisions, sections and articles, and arrangement of Drawings shall not control the Contractor in dividing the Work among Subcontractors or in establishing the extent of Work to be performed by any trade.

1.2.5 Unless otherwise stated in the Contract Documents, words which have well-known technical or construction industry meanings are used in the Contract Documents in accordance with such recognized meanings.

1.3 OWNERSHIP AND USE OF ARCHITECT'S DRAWINGS, SPECIFICATIONS AND OTHER DOCUMENTS

1.3.1 The Drawings, Specifications and other documents prepared by the Architect are instruments of the Architect's service through which the Work to be executed by the Contractor is described. The Contractor may retain one contract record set. Neither the Contractor nor any Subcontractor, Subsubcontractor or material or equipment supplier shall own or claim a copyright in the Drawings, Specifications and other documents prepared by the Architect, and unless otherwise indicated the Architect shall be deemed the author of them and will retain all common law, statutory and other reserved rights, in addition to the copyright. All copies of them, except the Contractor's record set, shall be returned or suitably accounted for to the Architect, on request, upon completion of the Work. The Drawings, Specifications and other documents prepared by the Architect, and copies thereof furnished to the Contractor, are for use solely with respect to this Project. They are not to be used by the Contractor or any Subcontractor, Subsubcontractor or material or equipment supplier on other projects or for additions to this Project outside the scope of the

Work without the specific written consent of the Owner and Architect. The Contractor, Subcontractors, Sub-subcontractors and material or equipment suppliers are granted a limited license to use and reproduce applicable portions of the Drawings, Specifications and other documents prepared by the Architect appropriate to and for use in the execution of their Work under the Contract Documents. All copies made under this license shall bear the statutory copyright notice, if any, shown on the Drawings, Specifications and other documents prepared by the Architect. Submittal or distribution to meet official regulatory requirements or for other purposes in connection with this Project is not to be construed as publication in derogation of the Architect's copyright or other reserved rights.

1.4 CAPITALIZATION

1.4.1 Terms capitalized in these General Conditions include those which are (1) specifically defined, (2) the titles of numbered articles and identified references to Paragraphs, Subparagraphs and Clauses in the document or (3) the titles of other documents published by the American Institute of Architects.

1.5 INTERPRETATION

1.5.1 In the interest of brevity the Contract Documents frequently omit modifying words such as "all" and "any" and articles such as "the" and "an," but the fact that a modifier or an article is absent from one statement and appears in another is not intended to affect the interpretation of either statement.

ARTICLE 2

OWNER

2.1 DEFINITION

2.1.1 The Owner is the person or entity identified as such in the Agreement and is referred to throughout the Contract Documents as if singular in number. The term "Owner" means the Owner or the Owner's authorized representative.

2.1.2 The Owner upon reasonable written request shall furnish to the Contractor in writing information which is necessary and relevant for the Contractor to evaluate, give notice of or enforce mechanic's lien rights. Such information shall include a correct statement of the record legal title to the property on which the Project is located, usually referred to as the site, and the Owner's interest therein at the time of execution of the Agreement and, within five days after any change, information of such change in title, recorded or unrecorded.

2.2 INFORMATION AND SERVICES REQUIRED OF THE OWNER

2.2.1 The Owner shall, at the request of the Contractor, prior to execution of the Agreement and promptly from time to time thereafter, furnish to the Contractor reasonable evidence that financial arrangements have been made to fulfill the Owner's obligations under the Contract. *[Note: Unless such reasonable evidence were furnished on request prior to the execution of the Agreement, the prospective contractor would not be required to execute the Agreement or to commence the Work.]*

2.2.2 The Owner shall furnish surveys describing physical characteristics, legal limitations and utility locations for the site of the Project, and a legal description of the site.

2.2.3 Except for permits and fees which are the responsibility of the Contractor under the Contract Documents, the Owner shall secure and pay for necessary approvals, easements, assess-ments and charges required for construction, use or occupancy of permanent structures or for permanent changes in existing facilities.

2.2.4 Information or services under the Owner's control shall be furnished by the Owner with reasonable promptness to avoid delay in orderly progress of the Work.

2.2.5 Unless otherwise provided in the Contract Documents, the Contractor will be furnished, free of charge, such copies of Drawings and Project Manuals as are reasonably necessary for execution of the Work.

2.2.6 The foregoing are in addition to other duties and responsibilities of the Owner enumerated herein and especially those in respect to Article 6 (Construction by Owner or by Separate Contractors), Article 9 (Payments and Completion) and Article 11 (Insurance and Bonds).

2.3 OWNER'S RIGHT TO STOP THE WORK

2.3.1 If the Contractor fails to correct Work which is not in accordance with the requirements of the Contract Documents as required by Paragraph 12.2 or persistently fails to carry out Work in accordance with the Contract Documents, the Owner, by written order signed personally or by an agent specifically so empowered by the Owner in writing, may order the Contractor to stop the Work, or any portion thereof, until the cause for such order has been eliminated; however, the right of the Owner to stop the Work shall not give rise to a duty on the part of the Owner to exercise this right for the benefit of the Contractor or any other person or entity, except to the extent required by Subparagraph 6.1.3.

2.4 OWNER'S RIGHT TO CARRY OUT THE WORK

2.4.1 If the Contractor defaults or neglects to carry out the Work in accordance with the Contract Documents and fails within a seven-day period after receipt of written notice from the Owner to commence and continue correction of such default or neglect with diligence and promptness, the Owner may after such seven-day period give the Contractor a second written notice to correct such deficiencies within a second seven-day period. If the Contractor within such second seven-day period after receipt of such second notice fails to commence and continue to correct any deficiencies, the Owner may, without prejudice to other remedies the Owner may have, correct such deficiencies. In such case an appropriate Change Order shall be issued deducting from payments then or thereafter due the Contractor the cost of correcting such deficiencies, including compensation for the Architect's additional services and expenses made necessary by such default, neglect or failure. Such action by the Owner and amounts charged to the Contractor are both subject to prior approval of the Architect. If payments then or thereafter due the Contractor are not sufficient to cover such amounts, the Contractor shall pay the difference to the Owner.

ARTICLE 3

CONTRACTOR

3.1 DEFINITION

3.1.1 The Contractor is the person or entity identified as such in the Agreement and is referred to throughout the Contract Documents as if singular in number. The term "Contractor" means the Contractor or the Contractor's authorized representative.

164

3.2 REVIEW OF CONTRACT DOCUMENTS AND FIELD CONDITIONS BY CONTRACTOR

3.2.1 The Contractor shall carefully study and compare the Contract Documents with each other and with information furnished by the Owner pursuant to Subparagraph 2.2.2 and shall at once report to the Architect errors, inconsistencies or omissions discovered. The Contractor shall not be liable to the Owner or Architect for damage resulting from errors, inconsistencies or omissions in the Contract Documents unless the Contractor recognized such error, inconsistency or omission and knowingly failed to report it to the Architect. If the Contractor performs any construction activity knowing it involves a recognized error, inconsistency or omission in the Contract Documents without such notice to the Architect, the Contractor shall assume appropriate responsibility for such performance and shall bear an appropriate amount of the attributable costs for correction.

3.2.2 The Contractor shall take field measurements and verify field conditions and shall carefully compare such field measurements and conditions and other information known to the Contractor with the Contract Documents before commencing activities. Errors, inconsistencies or omissions discovered shall be reported to the Architect at once.

3.2.3 The Contractor shall perform the Work in accordance with the Contract Documents and submittals approved pursuant to Paragraph 3.12.

3.3 SUPERVISION AND CONSTRUCTION PROCEDURES

3.3.1 The Contractor shall supervise and direct the Work, using the Contractor's best skill and attention. The Contractor shall be solely responsible for and have control over construction means, methods, techniques, sequences and procedures and for coordinating all portions of the Work under the Contract, unless Contract Documents give other specific instructions concerning these matters.

3.3.2 The Contractor shall be responsible to the Owner for acts and omissions of the Contractor's employees, Subcontractors and their agents and employees, and other persons performing portions of the Work under a contract with the Contractor.

3.3.3 The Contractor shall not be relieved of obligations to perform the Work in accordance with the Contract Documents either by activities or duties of the Architect in the Architect's administration of the Contract, or by tests, inspections or approvals required or performed by persons other than the Contractor.

3.3.4 The Contractor shall be responsible for inspection of portions of Work already performed under this Contract to determine that such portions are in proper condition to receive subsequent Work.

3.4 LABOR AND MATERIALS

3.4.1 Unless otherwise provided in the Contract Documents, the Contractor shall provide and pay for labor, materials, equipment, tools, construction equipment and machinery, water, heat, utilities, transportation, and other facilities and services necessary for proper execution and completion of the Work, whether temporary or permanent and whether or not incorporated or to be incorporated in the Work.

3.4.2 The Contractor shall enforce strict discipline and good order among the Contractor's employees and other persons carrying out the Contract. The Contractor shall not permit employment of unfit persons or persons not skilled in tasks assigned to them.

3.5 WARRANTY

3.5.1 The Contractor warrants to the Owner and Architect that materials and equipment furnished under the Contract will be of good quality and new unless otherwise required or permitted by the Contract Documents, that the Work will be free from defects not inherent in the quality required or permitted, and that the Work will conform with the requirements of the Contract Documents. Work not conforming to these requirements, including substitutions not properly approved and authorized, may be considered defective. The Contractor's warranty excludes remedy for damage or defect caused by abuse, modifications not executed by the Contractor, improper or insufficient maintenance, improper operation, or normal wear and tear under normal usage. If required by the Architect, the Contractor shall furnish satisfactory evidence as to the kind and quality of materials and equipment.

3.6 TAXES

3.6.1 The Contractor shall pay sales, consumer, use and similar taxes for the Work or portions thereof provided by the Contractor which are legally enacted when bids are received or negotiations concluded, whether or not yet effective or merely scheduled to go into effect.

3.7 PERMITS, FEES AND NOTICES

3.7.1 Unless otherwise provided in the Contract Documents, the Contractor shall secure and pay for the building permit and other permits and governmental fees, licenses and inspections necessary for proper execution and completion of the Work which are customarily secured after execution of the Contract and which are legally required when bids are received or negotiations concluded.

3.7.2 The Contractor shall comply with and give notices required by laws, ordinances, rules, regulations and lawful orders of public authorities bearing on performance of the Work.

3.7.3 It is not the Contractor's responsibility to ascertain that the Contract Documents are in accordance with applicable laws, statutes, ordinances, building codes, and rules and regulations. However, if the Contractor observes that portions of the Contract Documents are at variance therewith, the Contractor shall promptly notify the Architect and Owner in writing, and necessary changes shall be accomplished by appropriate Modification.

3.7.4 If the Contractor performs Work knowing it to be contrary to laws, statutes, ordinances, building codes, and rules and regulations without such notice to the Architect and Owner, the Contractor shall assume full responsibility for such Work and shall bear the attributable costs.

3.8 ALLOWANCES

3.8.1 The Contractor shall include in the Contract Sum all allowances stated in the Contract Documents. Items covered by allowances shall be supplied for such amounts and by such persons or entities as the Owner may direct, but the Contractor shall not be required to employ persons or entities against which the Contractor makes reasonable objection.

3.8.2 Unless otherwise provided in the Contract Documents:

    .1 materials and equipment under an allowance shall be selected promptly by the Owner to avoid delay in the Work;

    .2 allowances shall cover the cost to the Contractor of materials and equipment delivered at the site and all required taxes, less applicable trade discounts;

.3 Contractor's costs for unloading and handling at the site, labor, installation costs, overhead, profit and other expenses contemplated for stated allowance amounts shall be included in the Contract Sum and not in the allowances;

.4 whenever costs are more than or less than allowances, the Contract Sum shall be adjusted accordingly by Change Order. The amount of the Change Order shall reflect (1) the difference between actual costs and the allowances under Clause 3.8.2.2 and (2) changes in Contractor's costs under Clause 3.8.2.3.

3.9 SUPERINTENDENT

3.9.1 The Contractor shall employ a competent superintendent and necessary assistants who shall be in attendance at the Project site during performance of the Work. The superintendent shall represent the Contractor, and communications given to the superintendent shall be as binding as if given to the Contractor. Important communications shall be confirmed in writing. Other communications shall be similarly confirmed on written request in each case.

3.10 CONTRACTOR'S CONSTRUCTION SCHEDULES

3.10.1 The Contractor, promptly after being awarded the Contract, shall prepare and submit for the Owner's and Architect's information a Contractor's construction schedule for the Work. The schedule shall not exceed time limits current under the Contract Documents, shall be revised at appropriate intervals as required by the conditions of the Work and Project, shall be related to the entire Project to the extent required by the Contract Documents, and shall provide for expeditious and practicable execution of the Work.

3.10.2 The Contractor shall prepare and keep current, for the Architect's approval, a schedule of submittals which is coordinated with the Contractor's construction schedule and allows the Architect reasonable time to review submittals.

3.10.3 The Contractor shall conform to the most recent schedules.

3.11 DOCUMENTS AND SAMPLES AT THE SITE

3.11.1 The Contractor shall maintain at the site for the Owner one record copy of the Drawings, Specifications, addenda, Change Orders and other Modifications, in good order and marked currently to record changes and selections made during construction, and in addition approved Shop Drawings, Product Data, Samples and similar required submittals. These shall be available to the Architect and shall be delivered to the Architect for submittal to the Owner upon completion of the Work.

3.12 SHOP DRAWINGS, PRODUCT DATA AND SAMPLES

3.12.1 Shop Drawings are drawings, diagrams, schedules and other data specially prepared for the Work by the Contractor or a Subcontractor, Sub-subcontractor, manufacturer, supplier or distributor to illustrate some portion of the Work.

3.12.2 Product Data are illustrations, standard schedules, performance charts, instructions, brochures, diagrams and other information furnished by the Contractor to illustrate materials or equipment for some portion of the Work.

3.12.3 Samples are physical examples which illustrate materials, equipment or workmanship and establish standards by which the Work will be judged.

3.12.4 Shop Drawings, Product Data, Samples and similar submittals are not Contract Documents. The purpose of their submittal is to demonstrate for those portions of the Work for

which submittals are required the way the Contractor proposes to conform to the information given and the design concept expressed in the Contract Documents. Review by the Architect is subject to the limitations of Subparagraph 4.2.7.

3.12.5 The Contractor shall review, approve and submit to the Architect Shop Drawings, Product Data, Samples and similar submittals required by the Contract Documents with reasonable promptness and in such sequence as to cause no delay in the Work or in the activities of the Owner or of separate contractors. Submittals made by the Contractor which are not required by the Contract Documents may be returned without action.

3.12.6 The Contractor shall perform no portion of the Work requiring submittal and review of Shop Drawings, Product Data, Samples or similar submittals until the respective submittal has been approved by the Architect. Such Work shall be in accordance with approved submittals.

3.12.7 By approving and submitting Shop Drawings, Product Data, Samples and similar submittals, the Contractor represents that the Contractor has determined and verified materials, field measurements and field construction criteria related thereto, or will do so, and has checked and coordinated the information contained within such submittals with the requirements of the Work and of the Contract Documents.

3.12.8 The Contractor shall not be relieved of responsibility for deviations from requirements of the Contract Documents by the Architect's approval of Shop Drawings, Product Data, Samples or similar submittals unless the Contractor has specifically informed the Architect in writing of such deviation at the time of submittal and the Architect has given written approval to the specific deviation. The Contractor shall not be relieved of responsibility for errors or omissions in Shop Drawings, Product Data, Samples or similar submittals by the Architect's approval thereof.

3.12.9 The Contractor shall direct specific attention, in writing or on resubmitted Shop Drawings, Product Data, Samples or similar submittals, to revisions other than those requested by the Architect on previous submittals.

3.12.10 Informational submittals upon which the Architect is not expected to take responsive action may be so identified in the Contract Documents.

3.12.11 When professional certification of performance criteria of materials, systems or equipment is required by the Contract Documents, the Architect shall be entitled to rely upon the accuracy and completeness of such calculations and certifications.

3.13 USE OF SITE

3.13.1 The Contractor shall confine operations at the site to areas permitted by law, ordinances, permits and the Contract Documents and shall not unreasonably encumber the site with materials or equipment.

3.14 CUTTING AND PATCHING

3.14.1 The Contractor shall be responsible for cutting, fitting or patching required to complete the Work or to make its parts fit together properly.

3.14.2 The Contractor shall not damage or endanger a portion of the Work or fully or partially completed construction of the Owner or separate contractors by cutting, patching or otherwise altering such construction, or by excavation. The Contractor shall not cut or otherwise alter such construction by the

Owner or a separate contractor except with written consent of the Owner and of such separate contractor; such consent shall not be unreasonably withheld. The Contractor shall not unreasonably withhold from the Owner or a separate contractor the Contractor's consent to cutting or otherwise altering the Work.

3.15 CLEANING UP

3.15.1 The Contractor shall keep the premises and surrounding area free from accumulation of waste materials or rubbish caused by operations under the Contract. At completion of the Work the Contractor shall remove from and about the Project waste materials, rubbish, the Contractor's tools, construction equipment, machinery and surplus materials.

3.15.2 If the Contractor fails to clean up as provided in the Contract Documents, the Owner may do so and the cost thereof shall be charged to the Contractor.

3.16 ACCESS TO WORK

3.16.1 The Contractor shall provide the Owner and Architect access to the Work in preparation and progress wherever located.

3.17 ROYALTIES AND PATENTS

3.17.1 The Contractor shall pay all royalties and license fees. The Contractor shall defend suits or claims for infringement of patent rights and shall hold the Owner and Architect harmless from loss on account thereof, but shall not be responsible for such defense or loss when a particular design, process or product of a particular manufacturer or manufacturers is required by the Contract Documents. However, if the Contractor has reason to believe that the required design, process or product is an infringement of a patent, the Contractor shall be responsible for such loss unless such information is promptly furnished to the Architect.

3.18 INDEMNIFICATION

3.18.1 To the fullest extent permitted by law, the Contractor shall indemnify and hold harmless the Owner, Architect, Architect's consultants, and agents and employees of any of them from and against claims, damages, losses and expenses, including but not limited to attorneys' fees; arising out of or resulting from performance of the Work, provided that such claim, damage, loss or expense is attributable to bodily injury, sickness, disease or death, or to injury to or destruction of tangible property (other than the Work itself) including loss of use resulting therefrom, but only to the extent caused in whole or in part by negligent acts or omissions of the Contractor, a Subcontractor, anyone directly or indirectly employed by them or anyone for whose acts they may be liable, regardless of whether or not such claim, damage, loss or expense is caused in part by a party indemnified hereunder. Such obligation shall not be construed to negate, abridge, or reduce other rights or obligations of indemnity which would otherwise exist as to a party or person described in this Paragraph 3.18.

3.18.2 In claims against any person or entity indemnified under this Paragraph 3.18 by an employee of the Contractor, a Subcontractor, anyone directly or indirectly employed by them or anyone for whose acts they may be liable, the indemnification obligation under this Paragraph 3.18 shall not be limited by a limitation on amount or type of damages, compensation or benefits payable by or for the Contractor or a Subcontractor under workers' or workmen's compensation acts, disability benefit acts or other employee benefit acts.

3.18.3 The obligations of the Contractor under this Paragraph 3.18 shall not extend to the liability of the Architect, the Archi-

tect's consultants, and agents and employees of any of them arising out of (1) the preparation or approval of maps, drawings, opinions, reports, surveys, Change Orders, designs or specifications, or (2) the giving of or the failure to give directions or instructions by the Architect, the Architect's consultants, and agents and employees of any of them provided such giving or failure to give is the primary cause of the injury or damage.

ARTICLE 4

ADMINISTRATION OF THE CONTRACT

4.1 ARCHITECT

4.1.1 The Architect is the person lawfully licensed to practice architecture or an entity lawfully practicing architecture identified as such in the Agreement and is referred to throughout the Contract Documents as if singular in number. The term "Architect" means the Architect or the Architect's authorized representative.

4.1.2 Duties, responsibilities and limitations of authority of the Architect as set forth in the Contract Documents shall not be restricted, modified or extended without written consent of the Owner, Contractor and Architect. Consent shall not be unreasonably withheld.

4.1.3 In case of termination of employment of the Architect, the Owner shall appoint an architect against whom the Contractor makes no reasonable objection and whose status under the Contract Documents shall be that of the former architect.

4.1.4 Disputes arising under Subparagraphs 4.1.2 and 4.1.3 shall be subject to arbitration.

4.2 ARCHITECT'S ADMINISTRATION OF THE CONTRACT

4.2.1 The Architect will provide administration of the Contract as described in the Contract Documents, and will be the Owner's representative (1) during construction, (2) until final payment is due and (3) with the Owner's concurrence, from time to time during the correction period described in Paragraph 12.2. The Architect will advise and consult with the Owner. The Architect will have authority to act on behalf of the Owner only to the extent provided in the Contract Documents, unless otherwise modified by written instrument in accordance with other provisions of the Contract.

4.2.2 The Architect will visit the site at intervals appropriate to the stage of construction to become generally familiar with the progress and quality of the completed Work and to determine in general if the Work is being performed in a manner indicating that the Work, when completed, will be in accordance with the Contract Documents. However, the Architect will not be required to make exhaustive or continuous on-site inspections to check quality or quantity of the Work. On the basis of on-site observations as an architect, the Architect will keep the Owner informed of progress of the Work, and will endeavor to guard the Owner against defects and deficiencies in the Work.

4.2.3 The Architect will not have control over or charge of and will not be responsible for construction means, methods, techniques, sequences or procedures, or for safety precautions and programs in connection with the Work, since these are solely the Contractor's responsibility as provided in Paragraph 3.3. The Architect will not be responsible for the Contractor's failure to carry out the Work in accordance with the Contract Documents. The Architect will not have control over or charge of and will not be responsible for acts or omissions of the Contractor, Subcontractors, or their agents or employees, or of any other persons performing portions of the Work.

4.2.4 Communications Facilitating Contract Administration. Except as otherwise provided in the Contract Documents or when direct communications have been specially authorized, the Owner and Contractor shall endeavor to communicate through the Architect. Communications by and with the Architect's consultants shall be through the Architect. Communications by and with Subcontractors and material suppliers shall be through the Contractor. Communications by and with separate contractors shall be through the Owner.

4.2.5 Based on the Architect's observations and evaluations of the Contractor's Applications for Payment, the Architect will review and certify the amounts due the Contractor and will issue Certificates for Payment in such amounts.

4.2.6 The Architect will have authority to reject Work which does not conform to the Contract Documents. Whenever the Architect considers it necessary or advisable for implementation of the intent of the Contract Documents, the Architect will have authority to require additional inspection or testing of the Work in accordance with Subparagraphs 13.5.2 and 13.5.3, whether or not such Work is fabricated, installed or completed. However, neither this authority of the Architect nor a decision made in good faith either to exercise or not to exercise such authority shall give rise to a duty or responsibility of the Architect to the Contractor, Subcontractors, material and equipment suppliers, their agents or employees, or other persons performing portions of the Work.

4.2.7 The Architect will review and approve or take other appropriate action upon the Contractor's submittals such as Shop Drawings, Product Data and Samples, but only for the limited purpose of checking for conformance with information given and the design concept expressed in the Contract Documents. The Architect's action will be taken with such reasonable promptness as to cause no delay in the Work or in the activities of the Owner, Contractor or separate contractors, while allowing sufficient time in the Architect's professional judgment to permit adequate review. Review of such submittals is not conducted for the purpose of determining the accuracy and completeness of other details such as dimensions and quantities, or for substantiating instructions for installation or performance of equipment or systems, all of which remain the responsibility of the Contractor as required by the Contract Documents. The Architect's review of the Contractor's submittals shall not relieve the Contractor of the obligations under Paragraphs 3.3, 3.5 and 3.12. The Architect's review shall not constitute approval of safety precautions or, unless otherwise specifically stated by the Architect, of any construction means, methods, techniques, sequences or procedures. The Architect's approval of a specific item shall not indicate approval of an assembly of which the item is a component.

4.2.8 The Architect will prepare Change Orders and Construction Change Directives, and may authorize minor changes in the Work as provided in Paragraph 7.4.

4.2.9 The Architect will conduct inspections to determine the date or dates of Substantial Completion and the date of final completion, will receive and forward to the Owner for the Owner's review and records written warranties and related documents required by the Contract and assembled by the Contractor, and will issue a final Certificate for Payment upon compliance with the requirements of the Contract Documents.

4.2.10 If the Owner and Architect agree, the Architect will provide one or more project representatives to assist in carrying out the Architect's responsibilities at the site. The duties, responsibilities and limitations of authority of such project representatives shall be as set forth in an exhibit to be incorporated in the Contract Documents.

4.2.11 The Architect will interpret and decide matters concerning performance under and requirements of the Contract Documents on written request of either the Owner or Contractor. The Architect's response to such requests will be made with reasonable promptness and within any time limits agreed upon. If no agreement is made concerning the time within which interpretations required of the Architect shall be furnished in compliance with this Paragraph 4.2, then delay shall not be recognized on account of failure by the Architect to furnish such interpretations until 15 days after written request is made for them.

4.2.12 Interpretations and decisions of the Architect will be consistent with the intent of and reasonably inferable from the Contract Documents and will be in writing or in the form of drawings. When making such interpretations and decisions, the Architect will endeavor to secure faithful performance by both Owner and Contractor, will not show partiality to either and will not be liable for results of interpretations or decisions so rendered in good faith.

4.2.13 The Architect's decisions on matters relating to aesthetic effect will be final if consistent with the intent expressed in the Contract Documents.

4.3   CLAIMS AND DISPUTES

4.3.1 Definition. A Claim is a demand or assertion by one of the parties seeking, as a matter of right, adjustment or interpretation of Contract terms, payment of money, extension of time or other relief with respect to the terms of the Contract. The term "Claim" also includes other disputes and matters in question between the Owner and Contractor arising out of or relating to the Contract. Claims must be made by written notice. The responsibility to substantiate Claims shall rest with the party making the Claim.

4.3.2 Decision of Architect. Claims, including those alleging an error or omission by the Architect, shall be referred initially to the Architect for action as provided in Paragraph 4.4. A decision by the Architect, as provided in Subparagraph 4.4.4, shall be required as a condition precedent to arbitration or litigation of a Claim between the Contractor and Owner as to all such matters arising prior to the date final payment is due, regardless of (1) whether such matters relate to execution and progress of the Work or (2) the extent to which the Work has been completed. The decision by the Architect in response to a Claim shall not be a condition precedent to arbitration or litigation in the event (1) the position of Architect is vacant, (2) the Architect has not received evidence or has failed to render a decision within agreed time limits, (3) the Architect has failed to take action required under Subparagraph 4.4.4 within 30 days after the Claim is made, (4) 45 days have passed after the Claim has been referred to the Architect or (5) the Claim relates to a mechanic's lien.

4.3.3 Time Limits on Claims. Claims by either party must be made within 21 days after occurrence of the event giving rise to such Claim or within 21 days after the claimant first recognizes the condition giving rise to the Claim, whichever is later. Claims must be made by written notice. An additional Claim made after the initial Claim has been implemented by Change Order will not be considered unless submitted in a timely manner.

4.3.4 Continuing Contract Performance. Pending final resolution of a Claim including arbitration, unless otherwise agreed in writing the Contractor shall proceed diligently with performance of the Contract and the Owner shall continue to make payments in accordance with the Contract Documents.

4.3.5 Waiver of Claims: Final Payment. The making of final payment shall constitute a waiver of Claims by the Owner except those arising from:

    .1 liens, Claims, security interests or encumbrances arising out of the Contract and unsettled;

    .2 failure of the Work to comply with the requirements of the Contract Documents; or

    .3 terms of special warranties required by the Contract Documents.

4.3.6 Claims for Concealed or Unknown Conditions. If conditions are encountered at the site which are (1) subsurface or otherwise concealed physical conditions which differ materially from those indicated in the Contract Documents or (2) unknown physical conditions of an unusual nature, which differ materially from those ordinarily found to exist and generally recognized as inherent in construction activities of the character provided for in the Contract Documents, then notice by the observing party shall be given to the other party promptly before conditions are disturbed and in no event later than 21 days after first observance of the conditions. The Architect will promptly investigate such conditions and, if they differ materially and cause an increase or decrease in the Contractor's cost of, or time required for, performance of any part of the Work, will recommend an equitable adjustment in the Contract Sum or Contract Time, or both. If the Architect determines that the conditions at the site are not materially different from those indicated in the Contract Documents and that no change in the terms of the Contract is justified, the Architect shall so notify the Owner and Contractor in writing, stating the reasons. Claims by either party in opposition to such determination must be made within 21 days after the Architect has given notice of the decision. If the Owner and Contractor cannot agree on an adjustment in the Contract Sum or Contract Time, the adjustment shall be referred to the Architect for initial determination, subject to further proceedings pursuant to Paragraph 4.4.

4.3.7 Claims for Additional Cost. If the Contractor wishes to make Claim for an increase in the Contract Sum, written notice as provided herein shall be given before proceeding to execute the Work. Prior notice is not required for Claims relating to an emergency endangering life or property arising under Paragraph 10.3. If the Contractor believes additional cost is involved for reasons including but not limited to (1) a written interpretation from the Architect, (2) an order by the Owner to stop the Work where the Contractor was not at fault, (3) a written order for a minor change in the Work issued by the Architect, (4) failure of payment by the Owner, (5) termination of the Contract by the Owner, (6) Owner's suspension or (7) other reasonable grounds, Claim shall be filed in accordance with the procedure established herein.

4.3.8 Claims for Additional Time

4.3.8.1 If the Contractor wishes to make Claim for an increase in the Contract Time, written notice as provided herein shall be given. The Contractor's Claim shall include an estimate of cost and of probable effect of delay on progress of the Work. In the case of a continuing delay only one Claim is necessary.

4.3.8.2 If adverse weather conditions are the basis for a Claim for additional time, such Claim shall be documented by data substantiating that weather conditions were abnormal for the period of time and could not have been reasonably anticipated, and that weather conditions had an adverse effect on the scheduled construction.

4.3.9 Injury or Damage to Person or Property. If either party to the Contract suffers injury or damage to person or property because of an act or omission of the other party, of any of the other party's employees or agents, or of others for whose acts such party is legally liable, written notice of such injury or damage, whether or not insured, shall be given to the other party within a reasonable time not exceeding 21 days after first observance. The notice shall provide sufficient detail to enable the other party to investigate the matter. If a Claim for additional cost or time related to this Claim is to be asserted, it shall be filed as provided in Subparagraphs 4.3.7 or 4.3.8.

4.4   RESOLUTION OF CLAIMS AND DISPUTES

4.4.1 The Architect will review Claims and take one or more of the following preliminary actions within ten days of receipt of a Claim: (1) request additional supporting data from the claimant, (2) submit a schedule to the parties indicating when the Architect expects to take action, (3) reject the Claim in whole or in part, stating reasons for rejection, (4) recommend approval of the Claim by the other party or (5) suggest a compromise. The Architect may also, but is not obligated to, notify the surety, if any, of the nature and amount of the Claim.

4.4.2 If a Claim has been resolved, the Architect will prepare or obtain appropriate documentation.

4.4.3 If a Claim has not been resolved, the party making the Claim shall, within ten days after the Architect's preliminary response, take one or more of the following actions: (1) submit additional supporting data requested by the Architect, (2) modify the initial Claim or (3) notify the Architect that the initial Claim stands.

4.4.4 If a Claim has not been resolved after consideration of the foregoing and of further evidence presented by the parties or requested by the Architect, the Architect will notify the parties in writing that the Architect's decision will be made within seven days, which decision shall be final and binding on the parties but subject to arbitration. Upon expiration of such time period, the Architect will render to the parties the Architect's written decision relative to the Claim, including any change in the Contract Sum or Contract Time or both. If there is a surety and there appears to be a possibility of a Contractor's default, the Architect may, but is not obligated to, notify the surety and request the surety's assistance in resolving the controversy.

4.5   ARBITRATION

4.5.1 Controversies and Claims Subject to Arbitration. Any controversy or Claim arising out of or related to the Contract, or the breach thereof, shall be settled by arbitration in accordance with the Construction Industry Arbitration Rules of the American Arbitration Association, and judgment upon the award rendered by the arbitrator or arbitrators may be entered in any court having jurisdiction thereof, except controversies or Claims relating to aesthetic effect and except those waived as provided for in Subparagraph 4.3.5. Such controversies or Claims upon which the Architect has given notice and rendered a decision as provided in Subparagraph 4.4.4 shall be subject to arbitration upon written demand of either party. Arbitration may be commenced when 45 days have passed after a Claim has been referred to the Architect as provided in Paragraph 4.3 and no decision has been rendered.

4.5.2 Rules and Notices for Arbitration. Claims between the Owner and Contractor not resolved under Paragraph 4.4 shall, if subject to arbitration under Subparagraph 4.5.1, be decided by arbitration in accordance with the Construction Industry Arbitration Rules of the American Arbitration Association currently in effect, unless the parties mutually agree otherwise. Notice of demand for arbitration shall be filed in writing with the other party to the Agreement between the Owner and Contractor and with the American Arbitration Association, and a copy shall be filed with the Architect.

4.5.3 Contract Performance During Arbitration. During arbitration proceedings, the Owner and Contractor shall comply with Subparagraph 4.3.4.

4.5.4 When Arbitration May Be Demanded. Demand for arbitration of any Claim may not be made until the earlier of (1) the date on which the Architect has rendered a final written decision on the Claim, (2) the tenth day after the parties have presented evidence to the Architect or have been given reasonable opportunity to do so, if the Architect has not rendered a final written decision by that date, or (3) any of the five events described in Subparagraph 4.3.2.

4.5.4.1 When a written decision of the Architect states that (1) the decision is final but subject to arbitration and (2) a demand for arbitration of a Claim covered by such decision must be made within 30 days after the date on which the party making the demand receives the final written decision, then failure to demand arbitration within said 30 days' period shall result in the Architect's decision becoming final and binding upon the Owner and Contractor. If the Architect renders a decision after arbitration proceedings have been initiated, such decision may be entered as evidence, but shall not supersede arbitration proceedings unless the decision is acceptable to all parties concerned.

4.5.4.2 A demand for arbitration shall be made within the time limits specified in Subparagraphs 4.5.1 and 4.5.4 and Clause 4.5.4.1 as applicable, and in other cases within a reasonable time after the Claim has arisen, and in no event shall it be made after the date when institution of legal or equitable proceedings based on such Claim would be barred by the applicable statute of limitations as determined pursuant to Paragraph 13.7.

4.5.5 Limitation on Consolidation or Joinder. No arbitration arising out of or relating to the Contract Documents shall include, by consolidation or joinder or in any other manner, the Architect, the Architect's employees or consultants, except by written consent containing specific reference to the Agreement and signed by the Architect, Owner, Contractor and any other person or entity sought to be joined. No arbitration shall include, by consolidation or joinder or in any other manner, parties other than the Owner, Contractor, a separate contractor as described in Article 6 and other persons substantially involved in a common question of fact or law whose presence is required if complete relief is to be accorded in arbitration. No person or entity other than the Owner, Contractor or a separate contractor as described in Article 6 shall be included as an original third party or additional third party to an arbitration whose interest or responsibility is insubstantial. Consent to arbitration involving an additional person or entity shall not constitute consent to arbitration of a dispute not described therein or with a person or entity not named or described therein. The foregoing agreement to arbitrate and other agreements to arbitrate with an additional person or entity duly consented to by parties to the Agreement shall be specifically enforceable under applicable law in any court having jurisdiction thereof.

4.5.6 Claims and Timely Assertion of Claims. A party who files a notice of demand for arbitration must assert in the demand all Claims then known to that party on which arbitration is permitted to be demanded. When a party fails to include a Claim through oversight, inadvertence or excusable neglect, or when a Claim has matured or been acquired subsequently, the arbitrator or arbitrators may permit amendment.

4.5.7 Judgment on Final Award. The award rendered by the arbitrator or arbitrators shall be final, and judgment may be entered upon it in accordance with applicable law in any court having jurisdiction thereof.

ARTICLE 5

SUBCONTRACTORS

5.1   DEFINITIONS

5.1.1 A Subcontractor is a person or entity who has a direct contract with the Contractor to perform a portion of the Work at the site. The term "Subcontractor" is referred to throughout the Contract Documents as if singular in number and means a Subcontractor or an authorized representative of the Subcontractor. The term "Subcontractor" does not include a separate contractor or subcontractors of a separate contractor.

5.1.2 A Sub-subcontractor is a person or entity who has a direct or indirect contract with a Subcontractor to perform a portion of the Work at the site. The term "Sub-subcontractor" is referred to throughout the Contract Documents as if singular in number and means a Sub-subcontractor or an authorized representative of the Sub-subcontractor.

5.2   AWARD OF SUBCONTRACTS AND OTHER CONTRACTS FOR PORTIONS OF THE WORK

5.2.1 Unless otherwise stated in the Contract Documents or the bidding requirements, the Contractor, as soon as practicable after award of the Contract, shall furnish in writing to the Owner through the Architect the names of persons or entities (including those who are to furnish materials or equipment fabricated to a special design) proposed for each principal portion of the Work. The Architect will promptly reply to the Contractor in writing stating whether or not the Owner or the Architect, after due investigation, has reasonable objection to any such proposed person or entity. Failure of the Owner or Architect to reply promptly shall constitute notice of no reasonable objection.

5.2.2 The Contractor shall not contract with a proposed person or entity to whom the Owner or Architect has made reasonable and timely objection. The Contractor shall not be required to contract with anyone to whom the Contractor has made reasonable objection.

5.2.3 If the Owner or Architect has reasonable objection to a person or entity proposed by the Contractor, the Contractor shall propose another to whom the Owner or Architect has no reasonable objection. The Contract Sum shall be increased or decreased by the difference in cost occasioned by such change and an appropriate Change Order shall be issued. However, no increase in the Contract Sum shall be allowed for such change unless the Contractor has acted promptly and responsively in submitting names as required.

5.2.4 The Contractor shall not change a Subcontractor, person or entity previously selected if the Owner or Architect makes reasonable objection to such change.

5.3 SUBCONTRACTUAL RELATIONS

5.3.1 By appropriate agreement, written where legally required for validity, the Contractor shall require each Subcontractor, to the extent of the Work to be performed by the Subcontractor, to be bound to the Contractor by terms of the Contract Documents, and to assume toward the Contractor all the obligations and responsibilities which the Contractor, by these Documents, assumes toward the Owner and Architect. Each subcontract agreement shall preserve and protect the rights of the Owner and Architect under the Contract Documents with respect to the Work to be performed by the Subcontractor so that subcontracting thereof will not prejudice such rights, and shall allow to the Subcontractor, unless specifically provided otherwise in the subcontract agreement, the benefit of all rights, remedies and redress against the Contractor that the Contractor, by the Contract Documents, has against the Owner. Where appropriate, the Contractor shall require each Subcontractor to enter into similar agreements with Sub-sub-contractors. The Contractor shall make available to each proposed Subcontractor, prior to the execution of the subcontract agreement, copies of the Contract Documents to which the Subcontractor will be bound, and, upon written request of the Subcontractor, identify to the Subcontractor terms and conditions of the proposed subcontract agreement which may be at variance with the Contract Documents. Subcontractors shall similarly make copies of applicable portions of such documents available to their respective proposed Sub-subcontractors.

5.4 CONTINGENT ASSIGNMENT OF SUBCONTRACTS

5.4.1 Each subcontract agreement for a portion of the Work is assigned by the Contractor to the Owner provided that:

> **.1** assignment is effective only after termination of the Contract by the Owner for cause pursuant to Paragraph 14.2 and only for those subcontract agreements which the Owner accepts by notifying the Subcontractor in writing; and

> **.2** assignment is subject to the prior rights of the surety, if any, obligated under bond relating to the Contract.

5.4.2 If the Work has been suspended for more than 30 days, the Subcontractor's compensation shall be equitably adjusted.

ARTICLE 6

CONSTRUCTION BY OWNER OR BY SEPARATE CONTRACTORS

6.1 OWNER'S RIGHT TO PERFORM CONSTRUCTION AND TO AWARD SEPARATE CONTRACTS

6.1.1 The Owner reserves the right to perform construction or operations related to the Project with the Owner's own forces, and to award separate contracts in connection with other portions of the Project or other construction or operations on the site under Conditions of the Contract identical or substantially similar to these including those portions related to insurance and waiver of subrogation. If the Contractor claims that delay or additional cost is involved because of such action by the Owner, the Contractor shall make such Claim as provided elsewhere in the Contract Documents.

6.1.2 When separate contracts are awarded for different portions of the Project or other construction or operations on the site, the term "Contractor" in the Contract Documents in each case shall mean the Contractor who executes each separate Owner-Contractor Agreement.

6.1.3 The Owner shall provide for coordination of the activities of the Owner's own forces and of each separate contractor with the Work of the Contractor, who shall cooperate with them. The Contractor shall participate with other separate contractors and the Owner in reviewing their construction schedules when directed to do so. The Contractor shall make any revisions to the construction schedule and Contract Sum deemed necessary after a joint review and mutual agreement. The construction schedules shall then constitute the schedules to be used by the Contractor, separate contractors and the Owner until subsequently revised.

6.1.4 Unless otherwise provided in the Contract Documents, when the Owner performs construction or operations related to the Project with the Owner's own forces, the Owner shall be deemed to be subject to the same obligations and to have the same rights which apply to the Contractor under the Conditions of the Contract, including, without excluding others, those stated in Article 3, this Article 6 and Articles 10, 11 and 12.

6.2 MUTUAL RESPONSIBILITY

6.2.1 The Contractor shall afford the Owner and separate contractors reasonable opportunity for introduction and storage of their materials and equipment and performance of their activities and shall connect and coordinate the Contractor's construction and operations with theirs as required by the Contract Documents.

6.2.2 If part of the Contractor's Work depends for proper execution or results upon construction or operations by the Owner or a separate contractor, the Contractor shall, prior to proceeding with that portion of the Work, promptly report to the Architect apparent discrepancies or defects in such other construction that would render it unsuitable for such proper execution and results. Failure of the Contractor so to report shall constitute an acknowledgment that the Owner's or separate contractors' completed or partially completed construction is fit and proper to receive the Contractor's Work, except as to defects not then reasonably discoverable.

6.2.3 Costs caused by delays or by improperly timed activities or defective construction shall be borne by the party responsible therefor.

6.2.4 The Contractor shall promptly remedy damage wrongfully caused by the Contractor to completed or partially completed construction or to property of the Owner or separate contractors as provided in Subparagraph 10.2.5.

6.2.5 Claims and other disputes and matters in question between the Contractor and a separate contractor shall be subject to the provisions of Paragraph 4.3 provided the separate contractor has reciprocal obligations.

6.2.6 The Owner and each separate contractor shall have the same responsibilities for cutting and patching as are described for the Contractor in Paragraph 3.14.

6.3 OWNER'S RIGHT TO CLEAN UP

6.3.1 If a dispute arises among the Contractor, separate contractors and the Owner as to the responsibility under their respective contracts for maintaining the premises and surrounding area free from waste materials and rubbish as described in Paragraph 3.15, the Owner may clean up and allocate the cost among those responsible as the Architect determines to be just.

ARTICLE 7

CHANGES IN THE WORK

7.1 CHANGES

7.1.1 Changes in the Work may be accomplished after execution of the Contract, and without invalidating the Contract, by Change Order, Construction Change Directive or order for a minor change in the Work, subject to the limitations stated in this Article 7 and elsewhere in the Contract Documents.

7.1.2 A Change Order shall be based upon agreement among the Owner, Contractor and Architect; a Construction Change Directive requires agreement by the Owner and Architect and may or may not be agreed to by the Contractor; an order for a minor change in the Work may be issued by the Architect alone.

7.1.3 Changes in the Work shall be performed under applicable provisions of the Contract Documents, and the Contractor shall proceed promptly, unless otherwise provided in the Change Order, Construction Change Directive or order for a minor change in the Work.

7.1.4 If unit prices are stated in the Contract Documents or subsequently agreed upon, and if quantities originally contemplated are so changed in a proposed Change Order or Construction Change Directive that application of such unit prices to quantities of Work proposed will cause substantial inequity to the Owner or Contractor, the applicable unit prices shall be equitably adjusted.

7.2 CHANGE ORDERS

7.2.1 A Change Order is a written instrument prepared by the Architect and signed by the Owner, Contractor and Architect, stating their agreement upon all of the following:

.1 a change in the Work;

.2 the amount of the adjustment in the Contract Sum, if any; and

.3 the extent of the adjustment in the Contract Time, if any.

7.2.2 Methods used in determining adjustments to the Contract Sum may include those listed in Subparagraph 7.3.3.

7.3 CONSTRUCTION CHANGE DIRECTIVES

7.3.1 A Construction Change Directive is a written order prepared by the Architect and signed by the Owner and Architect, directing a change in the Work and stating a proposed basis for adjustment, if any, in the Contract Sum or Contract Time, or both. The Owner may by Construction Change Directive, without invalidating the Contract, order changes in the Work within the general scope of the Contract consisting of additions, deletions or other revisions, the Contract Sum and Contract Time being adjusted accordingly.

7.3.2 A Construction Change Directive shall be used in the absence of total agreement on the terms of a Change Order.

7.3.3 If the Construction Change Directive provides for an adjustment to the Contract Sum, the adjustment shall be based on one of the following methods:

.1 mutual acceptance of a lump sum properly itemized and supported by sufficient substantiating data to permit evaluation;

.2 unit prices stated in the Contract Documents or subsequently agreed upon;

.3 cost to be determined in a manner agreed upon by the parties and a mutually acceptable fixed or percentage fee; or

.4 as provided in Subparagraph 7.3.6.

7.3.4 Upon receipt of a Construction Change Directive, the Contractor shall promptly proceed with the change in the Work involved and advise the Architect of the Contractor's agreement or disagreement with the method, if any, provided in the Construction Change Directive for determining the proposed adjustment in the Contract Sum or Contract Time.

7.3.5 A Construction Change Directive signed by the Contractor indicates the agreement of the Contractor therewith, including adjustment in Contract Sum and Contract Time or the method for determining them. Such agreement shall be effective immediately and shall be recorded as a Change Order.

7.3.6 If the Contractor does not respond promptly or disagrees with the method for adjustment in the Contract Sum, the method and the adjustment shall be determined by the Architect on the basis of reasonable expenditures and savings of those performing the Work attributable to the change, including, in case of an increase in the Contract Sum, a reasonable allowance for overhead and profit. In such case, and also under Clause 7.3.3.3, the Contractor shall keep and present, in such form as the Architect may prescribe, an itemized accounting together with appropriate supporting data. Unless otherwise provided in the Contract Documents, costs for the purposes of this Subparagraph 7.3.6 shall be limited to the following:

.1 costs of labor, including social security, old age and unemployment insurance, fringe benefits required by agreement or custom, and workers' or workmen's compensation insurance;

.2 costs of materials, supplies and equipment, including cost of transportation, whether incorporated or consumed;

.3 rental costs of machinery and equipment, exclusive of hand tools, whether rented from the Contractor or others;

.4 costs of premiums for all bonds and insurance, permit fees, and sales, use or similar taxes related to the Work; and

.5 additional costs of supervision and field office personnel directly attributable to the change.

7.3.7 Pending final determination of cost to the Owner, amounts not in dispute may be included in Applications for Payment. The amount of credit to be allowed by the Contractor to the Owner for a deletion or change which results in a net decrease in the Contract Sum shall be actual net cost as confirmed by the Architect. When both additions and credits covering related Work or substitutions are involved in a change, the allowance for overhead and profit shall be figured on the basis of net increase, if any, with respect to that change.

7.3.8 If the Owner and Contractor do not agree with the adjustment in Contract Time or the method for determining it, the adjustment or the method shall be referred to the Architect for determination.

7.3.9 When the Owner and Contractor agree with the determination made by the Architect concerning the adjustments in the Contract Sum and Contract Time, or otherwise reach agreement upon the adjustments, such agreement shall be effective immediately and shall be recorded by preparation and execution of an appropriate Change Order.

172

7.4 MINOR CHANGES IN THE WORK

7.4.1 The Architect will have authority to order minor changes in the Work not involving adjustment in the Contract Sum or extension of the Contract Time and not inconsistent with the intent of the Contract Documents. Such changes shall be effected by written order and shall be binding on the Owner and Contractor. The Contractor shall carry out such written orders promptly.

ARTICLE 8

TIME

8.1 DEFINITIONS

8.1.1 Unless otherwise provided, Contract Time is the period of time, including authorized adjustments, allotted in the Contract Documents for Substantial Completion of the Work.

8.1.2 The date of commencement of the Work is the date established in the Agreement. The date shall not be postponed by the failure to act of the Contractor or of persons or entities for whom the Contractor is responsible.

8.1.3 The date of Substantial Completion is the date certified by the Architect in accordance with Paragraph 9.8.

8.1.4 The term "day" as used in the Contract Documents shall mean calendar day unless otherwise specifically defined.

8.2 PROGRESS AND COMPLETION

8.2.1 Time limits stated in the Contract Documents are of the essence of the Contract. By executing the Agreement the Contractor confirms that the Contract Time is a reasonable period for performing the Work.

8.2.2 The Contractor shall not knowingly, except by agreement or instruction of the Owner in writing, prematurely commence operations on the site or elsewhere prior to the effective date of insurance required by Article 11 to be furnished by the Contractor. The date of commencement of the Work shall not be changed by the effective date of such insurance. Unless the date of commencement is established by a notice to proceed given by the Owner, the Contractor shall notify the Owner in writing not less than five days or other agreed period before commencing the Work to permit the timely filing of mortgages, mechanic's liens and other security interests.

8.2.3 The Contractor shall proceed expeditiously with adequate forces and shall achieve Substantial Completion within the Contract Time.

8.3 DELAYS AND EXTENSIONS OF TIME

8.3.1 If the Contractor is delayed at any time in progress of the Work by an act or neglect of the Owner or Architect, or of an employee of either, or of a separate contractor employed by the Owner, or by changes ordered in the Work, or by labor disputes, fire, unusual delay in deliveries, unavoidable casualties or other causes beyond the Contractor's control, or by delay authorized by the Owner pending arbitration, or by other causes which the Architect determines may justify delay, then the Contract Time shall be extended by Change Order for such reasonable time as the Architect may determine.

8.3.2 Claims relating to time shall be made in accordance with applicable provisions of Paragraph 4.3.

8.3.3 This Paragraph 8.3 does not preclude recovery of damages for delay by either party under other provisions of the Contract Documents.

ARTICLE 9

PAYMENTS AND COMPLETION

9.1 CONTRACT SUM

9.1.1 The Contract Sum is stated in the Agreement and, including authorized adjustments, is the total amount payable by the Owner to the Contractor for performance of the Work under the Contract Documents.

9.2 SCHEDULE OF VALUES

9.2.1 Before the first Application for Payment, the Contractor shall submit to the Architect a schedule of values allocated to various portions of the Work, prepared in such form and supported by such data to substantiate its accuracy as the Architect may require. This schedule, unless objected to by the Architect, shall be used as a basis for reviewing the Contractor's Applications for Payment.

9.3 APPLICATIONS FOR PAYMENT

9.3.1 At least ten days before the date established for each progress payment the Contractor shall submit to the Architect an itemized Application for Payment for operations completed in accordance with the schedule of values. Such application shall be notarized, if required, and supported by such data substantiating the Contractor's right to payment as the Owner or Architect may require, such as copies of requisitions from Subcontractors and material suppliers, and reflecting retainage if provided for elsewhere in the Contract Documents.

9.3.1.1 Such applications may include requests for payment on account of changes in the Work which have been properly authorized by Construction Change Directives but not yet included in Change Orders.

9.3.1.2 Such applications may not include requests for payment of amounts the Contractor does not intend to pay to a Subcontractor or material supplier because of a dispute or other reason.

9.3.2 Unless otherwise provided in the Contract Documents, payments shall be made on account of materials and equipment delivered and suitably stored at the site for subsequent incorporation in the Work. If approved in advance by the Owner, payment may similarly be made for materials and equipment suitably stored off the site at a location agreed upon in writing. Payment for materials and equipment stored on or off the site shall be conditioned upon compliance by the Contractor with procedures satisfactory to the Owner to establish the Owner's title to such materials and equipment or otherwise protect the Owner's interest, and shall include applicable insurance, storage and transportation to the site for such materials and equipment stored off the site.

9.3.3 The Contractor warrants that title to all Work covered by an Application for Payment will pass to the Owner no later than the time of payment. The Contractor further warrants that upon submittal of an Application for Payment all Work for which Certificates for Payment have been previously issued and payments received from the Owner shall, to the best of the Contractor's knowledge, information and belief, be free and clear of liens, claims, security interests or encumbrances in favor of the Contractor, Subcontractors, material suppliers, or other persons or entities making a claim by reason of having provided labor, materials and equipment relating to the Work.

9.4 CERTIFICATES FOR PAYMENT

9.4.1 The Architect will, within seven days after receipt of the Contractor's Application for Payment, either issue to the

173

Owner a Certificate for Payment, with a copy to the Contractor, for such amount as the Architect determines is properly due, or notify the Contractor and Owner in writing of the Architect's reasons for withholding certification in whole or in part as provided in Subparagraph 9.5.1.

9.4.2 The issuance of a Certificate for Payment will constitute a representation by the Architect to the Owner, based on the Architect's observations at the site and the data comprising the Application for Payment, that the Work has progressed to the point indicated and that, to the best of the Architect's knowledge, information and belief, quality of the Work is in accordance with the Contract Documents. The foregoing representations are subject to an evaluation of the Work for conformance with the Contract Documents upon Substantial Completion, to results of subsequent tests and inspections, to minor deviations from the Contract Documents correctable prior to completion and to specific qualifications expressed by the Architect. The issuance of a Certificate for Payment will further constitute a representation that the Contractor is entitled to payment in the amount certified. However, the issuance of a Certificate for Payment will not be a representation that the Architect has (1) made exhaustive or continuous on-site inspections to check the quality or quantity of the Work, (2) reviewed construction means, methods, techniques, sequences or procedures, (3) reviewed copies of requisitions received from Subcontractors and material suppliers and other data requested by the Owner to substantiate the Contractor's right to payment or (4) made examination to ascertain how or for what purpose the Contractor has used money previously paid on account of the Contract Sum.

9.5   DECISIONS TO WITHHOLD CERTIFICATION

9.5.1 The Architect may decide not to certify payment and may withhold a Certificate for Payment in whole or in part, to the extent reasonably necessary to protect the Owner, if in the Architect's opinion the representations to the Owner required by Subparagraph 9.4.2 cannot be made. If the Architect is unable to certify payment in the amount of the Application, the Architect will notify the Contractor and Owner as provided in Subparagraph 9.4.1. If the Contractor and Architect cannot agree on a revised amount, the Architect will promptly issue a Certificate for Payment for the amount for which the Architect is able to make such representations to the Owner. The Architect may also decide not to certify payment or, because of subsequently discovered evidence or subsequent observations, may nullify the whole or a part of a Certificate for Payment previously issued, to such extent as may be necessary in the Architect's opinion to protect the Owner from loss because of:

.1 defective Work not remedied;

.2 third party claims filed or reasonable evidence indicating probable filing of such claims;

.3 failure of the Contractor to make payments properly to Subcontractors or for labor, materials or equipment;

.4 reasonable evidence that the Work cannot be completed for the unpaid balance of the Contract Sum;

.5 damage to the Owner or another contractor;

.6 reasonable evidence that the Work will not be completed within the Contract Time, and that the unpaid balance would not be adequate to cover actual or liquidated damages for the anticipated delay; or

.7 persistent failure to carry out the Work in accordance with the Contract Documents.

9.5.2 When the above reasons for withholding certification are removed, certification will be made for amounts previously withheld.

9.6   PROGRESS PAYMENTS

9.6.1 After the Architect has issued a Certificate for Payment, the Owner shall make payment in the manner and within the time provided in the Contract Documents, and shall so notify the Architect.

9.6.2 The Contractor shall promptly pay each Subcontractor, upon receipt of payment from the Owner, out of the amount paid to the Contractor on account of such Subcontractor's portion of the Work, the amount to which said Subcontractor is entitled, reflecting percentages actually retained from payments to the Contractor on account of such Subcontractor's portion of the Work. The Contractor shall, by appropriate agreement with each Subcontractor, require each Subcontractor to make payments to Subsubcontractors in similar manner.

9.6.3 The Architect will, on request, furnish to a Subcontractor, if practicable, information regarding percentages of completion or amounts applied for by the Contractor and action taken thereon by the Architect and Owner on account of portions of the Work done by such Subcontractor.

9.6.4 Neither the Owner nor Architect shall have an obligation to pay or to see to the payment of money to a Subcontractor except as may otherwise be required by law.

9.6.5 Payment to material suppliers shall be treated in a manner similar to that provided in Subparagraphs 9.6.2, 9.6.3 and 9.6.4.

9.6.6 A Certificate for Payment, a progress payment, or partial or entire use or occupancy of the Project by the Owner shall not constitute acceptance of Work not in accordance with the Contract Documents.

9.7   FAILURE OF PAYMENT

9.7.1 If the Architect does not issue a Certificate for Payment, through no fault of the Contractor, within seven days after receipt of the Contractor's Application for Payment, or if the Owner does not pay the Contractor within seven days after the date established in the Contract Documents the amount certified by the Architect or awarded by arbitration, then the Contractor may, upon seven additional days' written notice to the Owner and Architect, stop the Work until payment of the amount owing has been received. The Contract Time shall be extended appropriately and the Contract Sum shall be increased by the amount of the Contractor's reasonable costs of shut-down, delay and start-up, which shall be accomplished as provided in Article 7.

9.8   SUBSTANTIAL COMPLETION

9.8.1 Substantial Completion is the stage in the progress of the Work when the Work or designated portion thereof is sufficiently complete in accordance with the Contract Documents so the Owner can occupy or utilize the Work for its intended use.

9.8.2 When the Contractor considers that the Work, or a portion thereof which the Owner agrees to accept separately, is substantially complete, the Contractor shall prepare and submit to the Architect a comprehensive list of items to be completed or corrected. The Contractor shall proceed promptly to complete and correct items on the list. Failure to include an item on such list does not alter the responsibility of the Contractor to complete all Work in accordance with the Contract Documents. Upon receipt of the Contractor's list, the Architect will make an inspection to determine whether the Work or designated portion thereof is substantially complete. If the Architect's inspection discloses any item, whether or not included on the Contractor's list, which is not in accordance with the requirements of the Contract Documents, the Contractor shall, before issuance of the Certificate of Substantial Completion, complete or correct such item upon notification by the Architect. The Contractor shall then submit a request for another inspection by the Architect to determine Substantial Completion. When the Work or designated portion thereof is substantially complete, the Architect will prepare a Certificate of Substantial Completion which shall establish the date of Substantial Completion, shall establish responsibilities of the Owner and Contractor for security, maintenance, heat, utilities, damage to the Work and insurance, and shall fix the time within which the Contractor shall finish all items on the list accompanying the Certificate. Warranties required by the Contract Documents shall commence on the date of Substantial Completion of the Work or designated portion thereof unless otherwise provided in the Certificate of Substantial Completion. The Certificate of Substantial Completion shall be submitted to the Owner and Contractor for their written acceptance of responsibilities assigned to them in such Certificate.

9.8.3 Upon Substantial Completion of the Work or designated portion thereof and upon application by the Contractor and certification by the Architect, the Owner shall make payment, reflecting adjustment in retainage, if any, for such Work or portion thereof as provided in the Contract Documents.

9.9   PARTIAL OCCUPANCY OR USE

9.9.1 The Owner may occupy or use any completed or partially completed portion of the Work at any stage when such portion is designated by separate agreement with the Contractor, provided such occupancy or use is consented to by the insurer as required under Subparagraph 11.3.11 and authorized by public authorities having jurisdiction over the Work. Such partial occupancy or use may commence whether or not the portion is substantially complete, provided the Owner and Contractor have accepted in writing the responsibilities assigned to each of them for payments, retainage if any, security, maintenance, heat, utilities, damage to the Work and insurance, and have agreed in writing concerning the period for correction of the Work and commencement of warranties required by the Contract Documents. When the Contractor considers a portion substantially complete, the Contractor shall prepare and submit a list to the Architect as provided under Subparagraph 9.8.2. Consent of the Contractor to partial occupancy or use shall not be unreasonably withheld. The stage of the progress of the Work shall be determined by written agreement between the Owner and Contractor or, if no agreement is reached, by decision of the Architect.

9.9.2 Immediately prior to such partial occupancy or use, the Owner, Contractor and Architect shall jointly inspect the area to be occupied or portion of the Work to be used in order to determine and record the condition of the Work.

9.9.3 Unless otherwise agreed upon, partial occupancy or use of a portion or portions of the Work shall not constitute acceptance of Work not complying with the requirements of the Contract Documents.

9.10   FINAL COMPLETION AND FINAL PAYMENT

9.10.1 Upon receipt of written notice that the Work is ready for final inspection and acceptance and upon receipt of a final Application for Payment, the Architect will promptly make

such inspection and, when the Architect finds the Work acceptable under the Contract Documents and the Contract fully performed, the Architect will promptly issue a final Certificate for Payment stating that to the best of the Architect's knowledge, information and belief, and on the basis of the Architect's observations and inspections, the Work has been completed in accordance with terms and conditions of the Contract Documents and that the entire balance found to be due the Contractor and noted in said final Certificate is due and payable. The Architect's final Certificate for Payment will constitute a further representation that conditions listed in Subparagraph 9.10.2 as precedent to the Contractor's being entitled to final payment have been fulfilled.

9.10.2 Neither final payment nor any remaining retained percentage shall become due until the Contractor submits to the Architect (1) an affidavit that payrolls, bills for materials and equipment, and other indebtedness connected with the Work for which the Owner or the Owner's property might be responsible or encumbered (less amounts withheld by Owner) have been paid or otherwise satisfied, (2) a certificate evidencing that insurance required by the Contract Documents to remain in force after final payment is currently in effect and will not be cancelled or allowed to expire until at least 30 days' prior written notice has been given to the Owner, (3) a written statement that the Contractor knows of no substantial reason that the insurance will not be renewable to cover the period required by the Contract Documents, (4) consent of surety, if any, to final payment and (5), if required by the Owner, other data establishing payment or satisfaction of obligations, such as receipts, releases and waivers of liens, claims, security interests or encumbrances arising out of the Contract, to the extent and in such form as may be designated by the Owner. If a Subcontractor refuses to furnish a release or waiver required by the Owner, the Contractor may furnish a bond satisfactory to the Owner to indemnify the Owner against such lien. If such lien remains unsatisfied after payments are made, the Contractor shall refund to the Owner all money that the Owner may be compelled to pay in discharging such lien, including all costs and reasonable attorneys' fees.

9.10.3 If, after Substantial Completion of the Work, final completion thereof is materially delayed through no fault of the Contractor or by issuance of Change Orders affecting final completion, and the Architect so confirms, the Owner shall, upon application by the Contractor and certification by the Architect, and without terminating the Contract, make payment of the balance due for that portion of the Work fully completed and accepted. If the remaining balance for Work not fully completed or corrected is less than retainage stipulated in the Contract Documents, and if bonds have been furnished, the written consent of surety to payment of the balance due for that portion of the Work fully completed and accepted shall be submitted by the Contractor to the Architect prior to certification of such payment. Such payment shall be made under terms and conditions governing final payment, except that it shall not constitute a waiver of claims. The making of final payment shall constitute a waiver of claims by the Owner as provided in Subparagraph 4.3.5.

9.10.4 Acceptance of final payment by the Contractor, a Subcontractor or material supplier shall constitute a waiver of claims by that payee except those previously made in writing and identified by that payee as unsettled at the time of final Application for Payment. Such waivers shall be in addition to the waiver described in Subparagraph 4.3.5.

175

ARTICLE 10

PROTECTION OF PERSONS AND PROPERTY

10.1 SAFETY PRECAUTIONS AND PROGRAMS

10.1.1 The Contractor shall be responsible for initiating, maintaining and supervising all safety precautions and programs in connection with the performance of the Contract.

10.1.2 In the event the Contractor encounters on the site material reasonably believed to be asbestos or polychlorinated biphenyl (PCB) which has not been rendered harmless, the Contractor shall immediately stop Work in the area affected and report the condition to the Owner and Architect in writing. The Work in the affected area shall not thereafter be resumed except by written agreement of the Owner and Contractor if in fact the material is asbestos or polychlorinated biphenyl (PCB) and has not been rendered harmless. The Work in the affected area shall be resumed in the absence of asbestos or polychlorinated biphenyl (PCB), or when it has been rendered harmless, by written agreement of the Owner and Contractor, or in accordance with final determination by the Architect on which arbitration has not been demanded, or by arbitration under Article 4.

10.1.3 The Contractor shall not be required pursuant to Article 7 to perform without consent any Work relating to asbestos or polychlorinated biphenyl (PCB).

10.1.4 To the fullest extent permitted by law, the Owner shall indemnify and hold harmless the Contractor, Architect, Architect's consultants and agents and employees of any of them from and against claims, damages, losses and expenses, including but not limited to attorneys' fees, arising out of or resulting from performance of the Work in the affected area if in fact the material is asbestos or polychlorinated biphenyl (PCB) and has not been rendered harmless, provided that such claim, damage, loss or expense is attributable to bodily injury, sickness, disease or death, or to injury to or destruction of tangible property (other than the Work itself) including loss of use resulting therefrom, but only to the extent caused in whole or in part by negligent acts or omissions of the Owner, anyone directly or indirectly employed by the Owner or anyone for whose acts the Owner may be liable, regardless of whether or not such claim, damage, loss or expense is caused in part by a party indemnified hereunder. Such obligation shall not be construed to negate, abridge, or reduce other rights or obligations of indemnity which would otherwise exist as to a party or person described in this Subparagraph 10.1.4.

10.2 SAFETY OF PERSONS AND PROPERTY

10.2.1 The Contractor shall take reasonable precautions for safety of, and shall provide reasonable protection to prevent damage, injury or loss to:

    .1 employees on the Work and other persons who may be affected thereby;

    .2 the Work and materials and equipment to be incorporated therein, whether in storage on or off the site, under care, custody or control of the Contractor or the Contractor's Subcontractors or Sub-subcontractors; and

    .3 other property at the site or adjacent thereto, such as trees, shrubs, lawns, walks, pavements, roadways, structures and utilities not designated for removal, relocation or replacement in the course of construction.

10.2.2 The Contractor shall give notices and comply with applicable laws, ordinances, rules, regulations and lawful orders of public authorities bearing on safety of persons or property or their protection from damage, injury or loss.

10.2.3 The Contractor shall erect and maintain, as required by existing conditions and performance of the Contract, reasonable safeguards for safety and protection, including posting danger signs and other warnings against hazards, promulgating safety regulations and notifying owners and users of adjacent sites and utilities.

10.2.4 When use or storage of explosives or other hazardous materials or equipment or unusual methods are necessary for execution of the Work, the Contractor shall exercise utmost care and carry on such activities under supervision of properly qualified personnel.

10.2.5 The Contractor shall promptly remedy damage and loss (other than damage or loss insured under property insurance required by the Contract Documents) to property referred to in Clauses 10.2.1.2 and 10.2.1.3 caused in whole or in part by the Contractor, a Subcontractor, a Sub-subcontractor, or anyone directly or indirectly employed by any of them, or by anyone for whose acts they may be liable and for which the Contractor is responsible under Clauses 10.2.1.2 and 10.2.1.3, except damage or loss attributable to acts or omissions of the Owner or Architect or anyone directly or indirectly employed by either of them, or by anyone for whose acts either of them may be liable, and not attributable to the fault or negligence of the Contractor. The foregoing obligations of the Contractor are in addition to the Contractor's obligations under Paragraph 3.18.

10.2.6 The Contractor shall designate a responsible member of the Contractor's organization at the site whose duty shall be the prevention of accidents. This person shall be the Contractor's superintendent unless otherwise designated by the Contractor in writing to the Owner and Architect.

10.2.7 The Contractor shall not load or permit any part of the construction or site to be loaded so as to endanger its safety.

10.3 EMERGENCIES

10.3.1 In an emergency affecting safety of persons or property, the Contractor shall act, at the Contractor's discretion, to prevent threatened damage, injury or loss. Additional compensation or extension of time claimed by the Contractor on account of an emergency shall be determined as provided in Paragraph 4.3 and Article 7.

ARTICLE 11

INSURANCE AND BONDS

11.1 CONTRACTOR'S LIABILITY INSURANCE

11.1.1 The Contractor shall purchase from and maintain in a company or companies lawfully authorized to do business in the jurisdiction in which the Project is located such insurance as will protect the Contractor from claims set forth below which may arise out of or result from the Contractor's operations under the Contract and for which the Contractor may be legally liable, whether such operations be by the Contractor or by a Subcontractor or by anyone directly or indirectly employed by any of them, or by anyone for whose acts any of them may be liable:

    .1 claims under workers' or workmen's compensation, disability benefit and other similar employee benefit acts which are applicable to the Work to be performed;

176

.2 claims for damages because of bodily injury, occupational sickness or disease, or death of the Contractor's employees;

.3 claims for damages because of bodily injury, sickness or disease, or death of any person other than the Contractor's employees;

.4 claims for damages insured by usual personal injury liability coverage which are sustained (1) by a person as a result of an offense directly or indirectly related to employment of such person by the Contractor, or (2) by another person;

.5 claims for damages, other than to the Work itself, because of injury to or destruction of tangible property, including loss of use resulting therefrom;

.6 claims for damages because of bodily injury, death of a person or property damage arising out of ownership, maintenance or use of a motor vehicle; and

.7 claims involving contractual liability insurance applicable to the Contractor's obligations under Paragraph 3.18.

11.1.2 The insurance required by Subparagraph 11.1.1 shall be written for not less than limits of liability specified in the Contract Documents or required by law, whichever coverage is greater. Coverages, whether written on an occurrence or claims-made basis, shall be maintained without interruption from date of commencement of the Work until date of final payment and termination of any coverage required to be maintained after final payment.

11.1.3 Certificates of Insurance acceptable to the Owner shall be filed with the Owner prior to commencement of the Work. These Certificates and the insurance policies required by this Paragraph 11.1 shall contain a provision that coverages afforded under the policies will not be cancelled or allowed to expire until at least 30 days' prior written notice has been given to the Owner. If any of the foregoing insurance coverages are required to remain in force after final payment and are reasonably available, an additional certificate evidencing continuation of such coverage shall be submitted with the final Application for Payment as required by Subparagraph 9.10.2. Information concerning reduction of coverage shall be furnished by the Contractor with reasonable promptness in accordance with the Contractor's information and belief.

11.2 OWNER'S LIABILITY INSURANCE

11.2.1 The Owner shall be responsible for purchasing and maintaining the Owner's usual liability insurance. Optionally, the Owner may purchase and maintain other insurance for self-protection against claims which may arise from operations under the Contract. The Contractor shall not be responsible for purchasing and maintaining this optional Owner's liability insurance unless specifically required by the Contract Documents.

11.3 PROPERTY INSURANCE

11.3.1 Unless otherwise provided, the Owner shall purchase and maintain, in a company or companies lawfully authorized to do business in the jurisdiction in which the Project is located, property insurance in the amount of the initial Contract Sum as well as subsequent modifications thereto for the entire Work at the site on a replacement cost basis without voluntary deductibles. Such property insurance shall be maintained, unless otherwise provided in the Contract Documents or otherwise agreed in writing by all persons and entities who are beneficiaries of such insurance, until final payment has been made as provided in Paragraph 9.10 or until no person or entity

other than the Owner has an insurable interest in the property required by this Paragraph 11.3 to be covered, whichever is earlier. This insurance shall include interests of the Owner, the Contractor, Subcontractors and Sub-subcontractors in the Work.

11.3.1.1 Property insurance shall be on an all-risk policy form and shall insure against the perils of fire and extended coverage and physical loss or damage including, without duplication of coverage, theft, vandalism, malicious mischief, collapse, falsework, temporary buildings and debris removal including demolition occasioned by enforcement of any applicable legal requirements, and shall cover reasonable compensation for Architect's services and expenses required as a result of such insured loss. Coverage for other perils shall not be required unless otherwise provided in the Contract Documents.

11.3.1.2 If the Owner does not intend to purchase such property insurance required by the Contract and with all of the coverages in the amount described above, the Owner shall so inform the Contractor in writing prior to commencement of the Work. The Contractor may then effect insurance which will protect the interests of the Contractor, Subcontractors and Sub-subcontractors in the Work, and by appropriate Change Order the cost thereof shall be charged to the Owner. If the Contractor is damaged by the failure or neglect of the Owner to purchase or maintain insurance as described above, without so notifying the Contractor, then the Owner shall bear all reasonable costs properly attributable thereto.

11.3.1.3 If the property insurance requires minimum deductibles and such deductibles are identified in the Contract Documents, the Contractor shall pay costs not covered because of such deductibles. If the Owner or insurer increases the required minimum deductibles above the amounts so identified or if the Owner elects to purchase this insurance with voluntary deductible amounts, the Owner shall be responsible for payment of the additional costs not covered because of such increased or voluntary deductibles. If deductibles are not identified in the Contract Documents, the Owner shall pay costs not covered because of deductibles.

11.3.1.4 Unless otherwise provided in the Contract Documents, this property insurance shall cover portions of the Work stored off the site after written approval of the Owner at the value established in the approval, and also portions of the Work in transit.

11.3.2 Boiler and Machinery Insurance. The Owner shall purchase and maintain boiler and machinery insurance required by the Contract Documents or by law, which shall specifically cover such insured objects during installation and until final acceptance by the Owner; this insurance shall include interests of the Owner, Contractor, Subcontractors and Sub-subcontractors in the Work, and the Owner and Contractor shall be named insureds.

11.3.3 Loss of Use Insurance. The Owner, at the Owner's option, may purchase and maintain such insurance as will insure the Owner against loss of use of the Owner's property due to fire or other hazards, however caused. The Owner waives all rights of action against the Contractor for loss of use of the Owner's property, including consequential losses due to fire or other hazards however caused.

11.3.4 If the Contractor requests in writing that insurance for risks other than those described herein or for other special hazards be included in the property insurance policy, the Owner shall, if possible, include such insurance, and the cost thereof shall be charged to the Contractor by appropriate Change Order.

177

11.3.5 If during the Project construction period the Owner insures properties, real or personal or both, adjoining or adjacent to the site by property insurance under policies separate from those insuring the Project, or if after final payment property insurance is to be provided on the completed Project through a policy or policies other than those insuring the Project during the construction period, the Owner shall waive all rights in accordance with the terms of Subparagraph 11.3.7 for damages caused by fire or other perils covered by this separate property insurance. All separate policies shall provide this waiver of subrogation by endorsement or otherwise.

11.3.6 Before an exposure to loss may occur, the Owner shall file with the Contractor a copy of each policy that includes insurance coverages required by this Paragraph 11.3. Each policy shall contain all generally applicable conditions, definitions, exclusions and endorsements related to this Project. Each policy shall contain a provision that the policy will not be cancelled or allowed to expire until at least 30 days' prior written notice has been given to the Contractor.

11.3.7 Waivers of Subrogation. The Owner and Contractor waive all rights against (1) each other and any of their subcontractors, sub-subcontractors, agents and employees, each of the other, and (2) the Architect, Architect's consultants, separate contractors described in Article 6, if any, and any of their subcontractors, sub-subcontractors, agents and employees for damages caused by fire or other perils to the extent covered by property insurance obtained pursuant to this Paragraph 11 or other property insurance applicable to the Work, except such rights as they have to proceeds of such insurance held by the Owner as fiduciary. The Owner or Contractor, as appropriate, shall require of the Architect, Architect's consultants, separate contractors described in Article 6, if any, and the subcontractors, sub-subcontractors, agents and employees of any of them, by appropriate agreements, written where legally required for validity, similar waivers each in favor of other parties enumerated herein. The policies shall provide such waivers of subrogation by endorsement or otherwise. A waiver of subrogation shall be effective as to a person or entity even though that person or entity would otherwise have a duty of indemnification, contractual or otherwise, did not pay the insurance premium directly or indirectly, and whether or not the person or entity had an insurable interest in the property damaged.

11.3.8 A loss insured under Owner's property insurance shall be adjusted by the Owner as fiduciary and made payable to the Owner as fiduciary for the insureds, as their interests may appear, subject to requirements of any applicable mortgagee clause and of Subparagraph 11.3.10. The Contractor shall pay Subcontractors their just shares of insurance proceeds received by the Contractor, and by appropriate agreements, written where legally required for validity, shall require Subcontractors to make payments to their Sub-subcontractors in similar manner.

11.3.9 If required in writing by a party in interest, the Owner as fiduciary shall, upon occurrence of an insured loss, give bond for proper performance of the Owner's duties. The cost of required bonds shall be charged against proceeds received as fiduciary. The Owner shall deposit in a separate account proceeds so received, which the Owner shall distribute in accordance with such agreement as the parties in interest may reach, or in accordance with an arbitration award in which case the procedure shall be as provided in Paragraph 4.5. If after such loss no other special agreement is made, replacement of damaged property shall be covered by appropriate Change Order.

11.3.10 The Owner as fiduciary shall have power to adjust and settle a loss with insurers unless one of the parties in interest shall object in writing within five days after occurrence of loss to the Owner's exercise of this power; if such objection be made, arbitrators shall be chosen as provided in Paragraph 4.5. The Owner as fiduciary shall, in that case, make settlement with insurers in accordance with directions of such arbitrators. If distribution of insurance proceeds by arbitration is required, the arbitrators will direct such distribution.

11.3.11 Partial occupancy or use in accordance with Paragraph 9.9 shall not commence until the insurance company or companies providing property insurance have consented to such partial occupancy or use by endorsement or otherwise. The Owner and the Contractor shall take reasonable steps to obtain consent of the insurance company or companies and shall, without mutual written consent, take no action with respect to partial occupancy or use that would cause cancellation, lapse or reduction of insurance.

11.4 PERFORMANCE BOND AND PAYMENT BOND

11.4.1 The Owner shall have the right to require the Contractor to furnish bonds covering faithful performance of the Contract and payment of obligations arising thereunder as stipulated in bidding requirements or specifically required in the Contract Documents on the date of execution of the Contract.

11.4.2 Upon the request of any person or entity appearing to be a potential beneficiary of bonds covering payment of obligations arising under the Contract, the Contractor shall promptly furnish a copy of the bonds or shall permit a copy to be made.

ARTICLE 12

UNCOVERING AND CORRECTION OF WORK

12.1 UNCOVERING OF WORK

12.1.1 If a portion of the Work is covered contrary to the Architect's request or to requirements specifically expressed in the Contract Documents, it must, if required in writing by the Architect, be uncovered for the Architect's observation and be replaced at the Contractor's expense without change in the Contract Time.

12.1.2 If a portion of the Work has been covered which the Architect has not specifically requested to observe prior to its being covered, the Architect may request to see such Work and it shall be uncovered by the Contractor. If such Work is in accordance with the Contract Documents, costs of uncovering and replacement shall, by appropriate Change Order, be charged to the Owner. If such Work is not in accordance with the Contract Documents, the Contractor shall pay such costs unless the condition was caused by the Owner or a separate contractor in which event the Owner shall be responsible for payment of such costs.

12.2 CORRECTION OF WORK

12.2.1 The Contractor shall promptly correct Work rejected by the Architect or failing to conform to the requirements of the Contract Documents, whether observed before or after Substantial Completion and whether or not fabricated, installed or completed. The Contractor shall bear costs of correcting such rejected Work, including additional testing and inspections and compensation for the Architect's services and expenses made necessary thereby.

12.2.2 If, within one year after the date of Substantial Completion of the Work or designated portion thereof, or after the date for commencement of warranties established under Subparagraph 9.9.1, or by terms of an applicable special warranty required by the Contract Documents, any of the Work is found to be not in accordance with the requirements of the Contract Documents, the Contractor shall correct it promptly after receipt of written notice from the Owner to do so unless the Owner has previously given the Contractor a written acceptance of such condition. This period of one year shall be extended with respect to portions of Work first performed after Substantial Completion by the period of time between Substantial Completion and the actual performance of the Work. This obligation under this Subparagraph 12.2.2 shall survive acceptance of the Work under the Contract and termination of the Contract. The Owner shall give such notice promptly after discovery of the condition.

12.2.3 The Contractor shall remove from the site portions of the Work which are not in accordance with the requirements of the Contract Documents and are neither corrected by the Contractor nor accepted by the Owner.

12.2.4 If the Contractor fails to correct nonconforming Work within a reasonable time, the Owner may correct it in accordance with Paragraph 2.4. If the Contractor does not proceed with correction of such nonconforming Work within a reasonable time fixed by written notice from the Architect, the Owner may remove it and store the salvable materials or equipment at the Contractor's expense. If the Contractor does not pay costs of such removal and storage within ten days after written notice, the Owner may upon ten additional days' written notice sell such materials and equipment at auction or at private sale and shall account for the proceeds thereof, after deducting costs and damages that should have been borne by the Contractor, including compensation for the Architect's services and expenses made necessary thereby. If such proceeds of sale do not cover costs which the Contractor should have borne, the Contract Sum shall be reduced by the deficiency. If payments then or thereafter due the Contractor are not sufficient to cover such amount, the Contractor shall pay the difference to the Owner.

12.2.5 The Contractor shall bear the cost of correcting destroyed or damaged construction, whether completed or partially completed, of the Owner or separate contractors caused by the Contractor's correction or removal of Work which is not in accordance with the requirements of the Contract Documents.

12.2.6 Nothing contained in this Paragraph 12.2 shall be construed to establish a period of limitation with respect to other obligations which the Contractor might have under the Contract Documents. Establishment of the time period of one year as described in Subparagraph 12.2.2 relates only to the specific obligation of the Contractor to correct the Work, and has no relationship to the time within which the obligation to comply with the Contract Documents may be sought to be enforced, nor to the time within which proceedings may be commenced to establish the Contractor's liability with respect to the Contractor's obligations other than specifically to correct the Work.

12.3 ACCEPTANCE OF NONCONFORMING WORK

12.3.1 If the Owner prefers to accept Work which is not in accordance with the requirements of the Contract Documents, the Owner may do so instead of requiring its removal and correction, in which case the Contract Sum will be reduced as appropriate and equitable. Such adjustment shall be effected whether or not final payment has been made.

ARTICLE 13

MISCELLANEOUS PROVISIONS

13.1 GOVERNING LAW

13.1.1 The Contract shall be governed by the law of the place where the Project is located.

13.2 SUCCESSORS AND ASSIGNS

13.2.1 The Owner and Contractor respectively bind themselves, their partners, successors, assigns and legal representatives to the other party hereto and to partners, successors, assigns and legal representatives of such other party in respect to covenants, agreements and obligations contained in the Contract Documents. Neither party to the Contract shall assign the Contract as a whole without written consent of the other. If either party attempts to make such an assignment without such consent, that party shall nevertheless remain legally responsible for all obligations under the Contract.

13.3 WRITTEN NOTICE

13.3.1 Written notice shall be deemed to have been duly served if delivered in person to the individual or a member of the firm or entity or to an officer of the corporation for which it was intended, or if delivered at or sent by registered or certified mail to the last business address known to the party giving notice.

13.4 RIGHTS AND REMEDIES

13.4.1 Duties and obligations imposed by the Contract Documents and rights and remedies available thereunder shall be in addition to and not a limitation of duties, obligations, rights and remedies otherwise imposed or available by law.

13.4.2 No action or failure to act by the Owner, Architect or Contractor shall constitute a waiver of a right or duty afforded them under the Contract, nor shall such action or failure to act constitute approval of or acquiescence in a breach thereunder, except as may be specifically agreed in writing.

13.5 TESTS AND INSPECTIONS

13.5.1 Tests, inspections and approvals of portions of the Work required by the Contract Documents or by laws, ordinances, rules, regulations or orders of public authorities having jurisdiction shall be made at an appropriate time. Unless otherwise provided, the Contractor shall make arrangements for such tests, inspections and approvals with an independent testing laboratory or entity acceptable to the Owner, or with the appropriate public authority, and shall bear all related costs of tests, inspections and approvals. The Contractor shall give the Architect timely notice of when and where tests and inspections are to be made so the Architect may observe such procedures. The Owner shall bear costs of tests, inspections or approvals which do not become requirements until after bids are received or negotiations concluded.

13.5.2 If the Architect, Owner or public authorities having jurisdiction determine that portions of the Work require additional testing, inspection or approval not included under Subparagraph 13.5.1, the Architect will, upon written authorization from the Owner, instruct the Contractor to make arrangements for such additional testing, inspection or approval by an entity acceptable to the Owner, and the Contractor shall give timely notice to the Architect of when and where tests and inspections are to be made so the Architect may observe such procedures.

179

The Owner shall bear such costs except as provided in Subparagraph 13.5.3.

13.5.3 If such procedures for testing, inspection or approval under Subparagraphs 13.5.1 and 13.5.2 reveal failure of the portions of the Work to comply with requirements established by the Contract Documents, the Contractor shall bear all costs made necessary by such failure including those of repeated procedures and compensation for the Architect's services and expenses.

13.5.4 Required certificates of testing, inspection or approval shall, unless otherwise required by the Contract Documents, be secured by the Contractor and promptly delivered to the Architect.

13.5.5 If the Architect is to observe tests, inspections or approvals required by the Contract Documents, the Architect will do so promptly and, where practicable, at the normal place of testing.

13.5.6 Tests or inspections conducted pursuant to the Contract Documents shall be made promptly to avoid unreasonable delay in the Work.

13.6   INTEREST

13.6.1 Payments due and unpaid under the Contract Documents shall bear interest from the date payment is due at such rate as the parties may agree upon in writing or, in the absence thereof, at the legal rate prevailing from time to time at the place where the Project is located.

13.7   COMMENCEMENT OF STATUTORY LIMITATION PERIOD

13.7.1 As between the Owner and Contractor:

 .1 Before Substantial Completion. As to acts or failures to act occurring prior to the relevant date of Substantial Completion, any applicable statute of limitations shall commence to run and any alleged cause of action shall be deemed to have accrued in any and all events not later than such date of Substantial Completion;

 .2 Between Substantial Completion and Final Certificate for Payment. As to acts or failures to act occurring subsequent to the relevant date of Substantial Completion and prior to issuance of the final Certificate for Payment, any applicable statute of limitations shall commence to run and any alleged cause of action shall be deemed to have accrued in any and all events not later than the date of issuance of the final Certificate for Payment; and

 .3 After Final Certificate for Payment. As to acts or failures to act occurring after the relevant date of issuance of the final Certificate for Payment, any applicable statute of limitations shall commence to run and any alleged cause of action shall be deemed to have accrued in any and all events not later than the date of any act or failure to act by the Contractor pursuant to any warranty provided under Paragraph 3.5, the date of any correction of the Work or failure to correct the Work by the Contractor under Paragraph 12.2, or the date of actual commission of any other act or failure to perform any duty or obligation by the Contractor or Owner, whichever occurs last.

ARTICLE 14

TERMINATION OR SUSPENSION OF THE CONTRACT

14.1   TERMINATION BY THE CONTRACTOR

14.1.1 The Contractor may terminate the Contract if the Work is stopped for a period of 30 days through no act or fault of the Contractor or a Subcontractor, Sub-subcontractor or their agents or employees or any other persons performing portions of the Work under contract with the Contractor, for any of the following reasons:

 .1 issuance of an order of a court or other public authority having jurisdiction;

 .2 an act of government, such as a declaration of national emergency, making material unavailable;

 .3 because the Architect has not issued a Certificate for Payment and has not notified the Contractor of the reason for withholding certification as provided in Subparagraph 9.4.1, or because the Owner has not made payment on a Certificate for Payment within the time stated in the Contract Documents;

 .4 if repeated suspensions, delays or interruptions by the Owner as described in Paragraph 14.3 constitute in the aggregate more than 100 percent of the total number of days scheduled for completion, or 120 days in any 365-day period, whichever is less; or

 .5 the Owner has failed to furnish to the Contractor promptly, upon the Contractor's request, reasonable evidence as required by Subparagraph 2.2.1.

14.1.2 If one of the above reasons exists, the Contractor may, upon seven additional days' written notice to the Owner and Architect, terminate the Contract and recover from the Owner payment for Work executed and for proven loss with respect to materials, equipment, tools, and construction equipment and machinery, including reasonable overhead, profit and damages.

14.1.3 If the Work is stopped for a period of 60 days through no act or fault of the Contractor or a Subcontractor or their agents or employees or any other persons performing portions of the Work under contract with the Contractor because the Owner has persistently failed to fulfill the Owner's obligations under the Contract Documents with respect to matters important to the progress of the Work, the Contractor may, upon seven additional days' written notice to the Owner and the Architect, terminate the Contract and recover from the Owner as provided in Subparagraph 14.1.2.

14.2   TERMINATION BY THE OWNER FOR CAUSE

14.2.1 The Owner may terminate the Contract if the Contractor:

 .1 persistently or repeatedly refuses or fails to supply enough properly skilled workers or proper materials;

 .2 fails to make payment to Subcontractors for materials or labor in accordance with the respective agreements between the Contractor and the Subcontractors;

 .3 persistently disregards laws, ordinances, or rules, regulations or orders of a public authority having jurisdiction; or

 .4 otherwise is guilty of substantial breach of a provision of the Contract Documents.

14.2.2 When any of the above reasons exist, the Owner, upon certification by the Architect that sufficient cause exists to justify such action, may without prejudice to any other rights or remedies of the Owner and after giving the Contractor and the Contractor's surety, if any, seven days' written notice, terminate employment of the Contractor and may, subject to any prior rights of the surety:

.1 take possession of the site and of all materials, equipment, tools, and construction equipment and machinery thereon owned by the Contractor;

.2 accept assignment of subcontracts pursuant to Paragraph 5.4; and

.3 finish the Work by whatever reasonable method the Owner may deem expedient.

14.2.3 When the Owner terminates the Contract for one of the reasons stated in Subparagraph 14.2.1, the Contractor shall not be entitled to receive further payment until the Work is finished.

14.2.4 If the unpaid balance of the Contract Sum exceeds costs of finishing the Work, including compensation for the Architect's services and expenses made necessary thereby, such excess shall be paid to the Contractor. If such costs exceed the unpaid balance, the Contractor shall pay the difference to the Owner. The amount to be paid to the Contractor or Owner, as the case may be, shall be certified by the Architect, upon application, and this obligation for payment shall survive termination of the Contract.

**14.3   SUSPENSION BY THE OWNER
          FOR CONVENIENCE**

14.3.1 The Owner may, without cause, order the Contractor in writing to suspend, delay or interrupt the Work in whole or in part for such period of time as the Owner may determine.

14.3.2 An adjustment shall be made for increases in the cost of performance of the Contract, including profit on the increased cost of performance, caused by suspension, delay or interruption. No adjustment shall be made to the extent:

.1 that performance is, was or would have been so suspended, delayed or interrupted by another cause for which the Contractor is responsible; or

.2 that an equitable adjustment is made or denied under another provision of this Contract.

14.3.3 Adjustments made in the cost of performance may have a mutually agreed fixed or percentage fee.

181

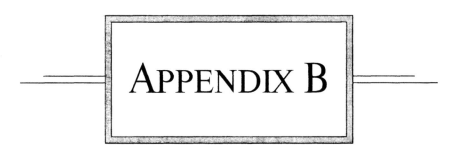

APPENDIX B

AIA Document B141-1987

Standard Form of Agreement Between Owner and Architect

Provided by the American Institute of Architects, whose permission to reproduce the document here is gratefully acknowledged. Copies of this document are available from the AIA, 1735 New York Avenue N.W., Washington, DC 20006.

AIA Document B141

Standard Form of Agreement Between Owner and Architect

1987 EDITION

THIS DOCUMENT HAS IMPORTANT LEGAL CONSEQUENCES; CONSULTATION WITH AN ATTORNEY IS ENCOURAGED WITH RESPECT TO ITS COMPLETION OR MODIFICATION.

AGREEMENT

made as of the
Nineteen Hundred and

day of

in the year of

BETWEEN the Owner:
(Name and address)

and the Architect:
(Name and address)

For the following Project:
(Include detailed description of Project, location, address and scope.)

The Owner and Architect agree as set forth below.

ARTICLE 1

ARCHITECT'S RESPONSIBILITIES

1.1 ARCHITECT'S SERVICES

1.1.1 The Architect's services consist of those services performed by the Architect, Architect's employees and Architect's consultants as enumerated in Articles 2 and 3 of this Agreement and any other services included in Article 12.

1.1.2 The Architect's services shall be performed as expeditiously as is consistent with professional skill and care and the orderly progress of the Work. Upon request of the Owner, the Architect shall submit for the Owner's approval a schedule for the performance of the Architect's services which may be adjusted as the Project proceeds, and shall include allowances for periods of time required for the Owner's review and for approval of submissions by authorities having jurisdiction over the Project. Time limits established by this schedule approved by the Owner shall not, except for reasonable cause, be exceeded by the Architect or Owner.

1.1.3 The services covered by this Agreement are subject to the time limitations contained in Subparagraph 11.5.1.

ARTICLE 2

SCOPE OF ARCHITECT'S BASIC SERVICES

2.1 DEFINITION

2.1.1 The Architect's Basic Services consist of those described in Paragraphs 2.2 through 2.6 and any other services identified in Article 12 as part of Basic Services, and include normal structural, mechanical and electrical engineering services.

2.2 SCHEMATIC DESIGN PHASE

2.2.1 The Architect shall review the program furnished by the Owner to ascertain the requirements of the Project and shall arrive at a mutual understanding of such requirements with the Owner.

2.2.2 The Architect shall provide a preliminary evaluation of the Owner's program, schedule and construction budget requirements, each in terms of the other, subject to the limitations set forth in Subparagraph 5.2.1.

2.2.3 The Architect shall review with the Owner alternative approaches to design and construction of the Project.

2.2.4 Based on the mutually agreed-upon program, schedule and construction budget requirements, the Architect shall prepare, for approval by the Owner, Schematic Design Documents consisting of drawings and other documents illustrating the scale and relationship of Project components.

2.2.5 The Architect shall submit to the Owner a preliminary estimate of Construction Cost based on current area, volume or other unit costs.

2.3 DESIGN DEVELOPMENT PHASE

2.3.1 Based on the approved Schematic Design Documents and any adjustments authorized by the Owner in the program,

schedule or construction budget, the Architect shall prepare, for approval by the Owner, Design Development Documents consisting of drawings and other documents to fix and describe the size and character of the Project as to architectural, structural, mechanical and electrical systems, materials and such other elements as may be appropriate.

2.3.2 The Architect shall advise the Owner of any adjustments to the preliminary estimate of Construction Cost.

2.4 CONSTRUCTION DOCUMENTS PHASE

2.4.1 Based on the approved Design Development Documents and any further adjustments in the scope or quality of the Project or in the construction budget authorized by the Owner, the Architect shall prepare, for approval by the Owner, Construction Documents consisting of Drawings and Specifications setting forth in detail the requirements for the construction of the Project.

2.4.2 The Architect shall assist the Owner in the preparation of the necessary bidding information, bidding forms, the Conditions of the Contract, and the form of Agreement between the Owner and Contractor.

2.4.3 The Architect shall advise the Owner of any adjustments to previous preliminary estimates of Construction Cost indicated by changes in requirements or general market conditions.

2.4.4 The Architect shall assist the Owner in connection with the Owner's responsibility for filing documents required for the approval of governmental authorities having jurisdiction over the Project.

2.5 BIDDING OR NEGOTIATION PHASE

2.5.1 The Architect, following the Owner's approval of the Construction Documents and of the latest preliminary estimate of Construction Cost, shall assist the Owner in obtaining bids or negotiated proposals and assist in awarding and preparing contracts for construction.

2.6 CONSTRUCTION PHASE—ADMINISTRATION OF THE CONSTRUCTION CONTRACT

2.6.1 The Architect's responsibility to provide Basic Services for the Construction Phase under this Agreement commences with the award of the Contract for Construction and terminates at the earlier of the issuance to the Owner of the final Certificate for Payment or 60 days after the date of Substantial Completion of the Work, unless extended under the terms of Subparagraph 10.3.3.

2.6.2 The Architect shall provide administration of the Contract for Construction as set forth below and in the edition of AIA Document A201, General Conditions of the Contract for Construction, current as of the date of this Agreement, unless otherwise provided in this Agreement.

2.6.3 Duties, responsibilities and limitations of authority of the Architect shall not be restricted, modified or extended without written agreement of the Owner and Architect with consent of the Contractor, which consent shall not be unreasonably withheld.

185

2.6.4 The Architect shall be a representative of and shall advise and consult with the Owner (1) during construction until final payment to the Contractor is due, and (2) as an Additional Service at the Owner's direction from time to time during the correction period described in the Contract for Construction. The Architect shall have authority to act on behalf of the Owner only to the extent provided in this Agreement unless otherwise modified by written instrument.

2.6.5 The Architect shall visit the site at intervals appropriate to the stage of construction or as otherwise agreed by the Owner and Architect in writing to become generally familiar with the progress and quality of the Work completed and to determine in general if the Work is being performed in a manner indicating that the Work when completed will be in accordance with the Contract Documents. However, the Architect shall not be required to make exhaustive or continuous on-site inspections to check the quality or quantity of the Work. On the basis of on-site observations as an architect, the Architect shall keep the Owner informed of the progress and quality of the Work, and shall endeavor to guard the Owner against defects and deficiencies in the Work. *(More extensive site representation may be agreed to as an Additional Service, as described in Paragraph 3.2.)*

2.6.6 The Architect shall not have control over or charge of and shall not be responsible for construction means, methods, techniques, sequences or procedures, or for safety precautions and programs in connection with the Work, since these are solely the Contractor's responsibility under the Contract for Construction. The Architect shall not be responsible for the Contractor's schedules or failure to carry out the Work in accordance with the Contract Documents. The Architect shall not have control over or charge of acts or omissions of the Contractor, Subcontractors, or their agents or employees, or of any other persons performing portions of the Work.

2.6.7 The Architect shall at all times have access to the Work wherever it is in preparation or progress.

2.6.8 Except as may otherwise be provided in the Contract Documents or when direct communications have been specially authorized, the Owner and Contractor shall communicate through the Architect. Communications by and with the Architect's consultants shall be through the Architect.

2.6.9 Based on the Architect's observations and evaluations of the Contractor's Applications for Payment, the Architect shall review and certify the amounts due the Contractor.

2.6.10 The Architect's certification for payment shall constitute a representation to the Owner, based on the Architect's observations at the site as provided in Subparagraph 2.6.5 and on the data comprising the Contractor's Application for Payment, that the Work has progressed to the point indicated and that, to the best of the Architect's knowledge, information and belief, quality of the Work is in accordance with the Contract Documents. The foregoing representations are subject to an evaluation of the Work for conformance with the Contract Documents upon Substantial Completion, to results of subsequent tests and inspections, to minor deviations from the Contract Documents correctable prior to completion and to specific qualifications expressed by the Architect. The issuance of a Certificate for Payment shall further constitute a representation that the Contractor is entitled to payment in the amount certified. However, the issuance of a Certificate for Payment shall not be a representation that the Architect has (1) made exhaustive or continuous on-site inspections to check the quality or

quantity of the Work, (2) reviewed construction means, methods, techniques, sequences or procedures, (3) reviewed copies of requisitions received from Subcontractors and material suppliers and other data requested by the Owner to substantiate the Contractor's right to payment or (4) ascertained how or for what purpose the Contractor has used money previously paid on account of the Contract Sum.

2.6.11 The Architect shall have authority to reject Work which does not conform to the Contract Documents. Whenever the Architect considers it necessary or advisable for implementation of the intent of the Contract Documents, the Architect will have authority to require additional inspection or testing of the Work in accordance with the provisions of the Contract Documents, whether or not such Work is fabricated, installed or completed. However, neither this authority of the Architect nor a decision made in good faith either to exercise or not to exercise such authority shall give rise to a duty or responsibility of the Architect to the Contractor, Subcontractors, material and equipment suppliers, their agents or employees or other persons performing portions of the Work.

2.6.12 The Architect shall review and approve or take other appropriate action upon Contractor's submittals such as Shop Drawings, Product Data and Samples, but only for the limited purpose of checking for conformance with information given and the design concept expressed in the Contract Documents. The Architect's action shall be taken with such reasonable promptness as to cause no delay in the Work or in the construction of the Owner or of separate contractors, while allowing sufficient time in the Architect's professional judgment to permit adequate review. Review of such submittals is not conducted for the purpose of determining the accuracy and completeness of other details such as dimensions and quantities or for substantiating instructions for installation or performance of equipment or systems designed by the Contractor, all of which remain the responsibility of the Contractor to the extent required by the Contract Documents. The Architect's review shall not constitute approval of safety precautions or, unless otherwise specifically stated by the Architect, of construction means, methods, techniques, sequences or procedures. The Architect's approval of a specific item shall not indicate approval of an assembly of which the item is a component. When professional certification of performance characteristics of materials, systems or equipment is required by the Contract Documents, the Architect shall be entitled to rely upon such certification to establish that the materials, systems or equipment will meet the performance criteria required by the Contract Documents.

2.6.13 The Architect shall prepare Change Orders and Construction Change Directives, with supporting documentation and data if deemed necessary by the Architect as provided in Subparagraphs 3.1.1 and 3.3.3, for the Owner's approval and execution in accordance with the Contract Documents, and may authorize minor changes in the Work not involving an adjustment in the Contract Sum or an extension of the Contract Time which are not inconsistent with the intent of the Contract Documents.

2.6.14 The Architect shall conduct inspections to determine the date or dates of Substantial Completion and the date of final completion, shall receive and forward to the Owner for the Owner's review and records written warranties and related documents required by the Contract Documents and assembled by the Contractor, and shall issue a final Certificate for Payment upon compliance with the requirements of the Contract Documents.

2.6.15 The Architect shall interpret and decide matters concerning performance of the Owner and Contractor under the requirements of the Contract Documents on written request of either the Owner or Contractor. The Architect's response to such requests shall be made with reasonable promptness and within any time limits agreed upon.

2.6.16 Interpretations and decisions of the Architect shall be consistent with the intent of and reasonably inferable from the Contract Documents and shall be in writing or in the form of drawings. When making such interpretations and initial decisions, the Architect shall endeavor to secure faithful performance by both Owner and Contractor, shall not show partiality to either, and shall not be liable for results of interpretations or decisions so rendered in good faith.

2.6.17 The Architect's decisions on matters relating to aesthetic effect shall be final if consistent with the intent expressed in the Contract Documents.

2.6.18 The Architect shall render written decisions within a reasonable time on all claims, disputes or other matters in question between the Owner and Contractor relating to the execution or progress of the Work as provided in the Contract Documents.

2.6.19 The Architect's decisions on claims, disputes or other matters, including those in question between the Owner and Contractor, except for those relating to aesthetic effect as provided in Subparagraph 2.6.17, shall be subject to arbitration as provided in this Agreement and in the Contract Documents.

ARTICLE 3
ADDITIONAL SERVICES

3.1 GENERAL

3.1.1 The services described in this Article 3 are not included in Basic Services unless so identified in Article 12, and they shall be paid for by the Owner as provided in this Agreement, in addition to the compensation for Basic Services. The services described under Paragraphs 3.2 and 3.4 shall only be provided if authorized or confirmed in writing by the Owner. If services described under Contingent Additional Services in Paragraph 3.3 are required due to circumstances beyond the Architect's control, the Architect shall notify the Owner prior to commencing such services. If the Owner deems that such services described under Paragraph 3.3 are not required, the Owner shall give prompt written notice to the Architect. If the Owner indicates in writing that all or part of such Contingent Additional Services are not required, the Architect shall have no obligation to provide those services.

3.2 PROJECT REPRESENTATION BEYOND BASIC SERVICES

3.2.1 If more extensive representation at the site than is described in Subparagraph 2.6.5 is required, the Architect shall provide one or more Project Representatives to assist in carrying out such additional on-site responsibilities.

3.2.2 Project Representatives shall be selected, employed and directed by the Architect, and the Architect shall be compensated therefor as agreed by the Owner and Architect. The duties, responsibilities and limitations of authority of Project Representatives shall be as described in the edition of AIA Document B352 current as of the date of this Agreement, unless otherwise agreed.

3.2.3 Through the observations by such Project Representatives, the Architect shall endeavor to provide further protection for the Owner against defects and deficiencies in the Work, but the furnishing of such project representation shall not modify the rights, responsibilities or obligations of the Architect as described elsewhere in this Agreement.

3.3 CONTINGENT ADDITIONAL SERVICES

3.3.1 Making revisions in Drawings, Specifications or other documents when such revisions are:

  .1 inconsistent with approvals or instructions previously given by the Owner, including revisions made necessary by adjustments in the Owner's program or Project budget;

  .2 required by the enactment or revision of codes, laws or regulations subsequent to the preparation of such documents; or

  .3 due to changes required as a result of the Owner's failure to render decisions in a timely manner.

3.3.2 Providing services required because of significant changes in the Project including, but not limited to, size, quality, complexity, the Owner's schedule, or the method of bidding or negotiating and contracting for construction, except for services required under Subparagraph 5.2.5.

3.3.3 Preparing Drawings, Specifications and other documentation and supporting data, evaluating Contractor's proposals, and providing other services in connection with Change Orders and Construction Change Directives.

3.3.4 Providing services in connection with evaluating substitutions proposed by the Contractor and making subsequent revisions to Drawings, Specifications and other documentation resulting therefrom.

3.3.5 Providing consultation concerning replacement of Work damaged by fire or other cause during construction, and furnishing services required in connection with the replacement of such Work.

3.3.6 Providing services made necessary by the default of the Contractor, by major defects or deficiencies in the Work of the Contractor, or by failure of performance of either the Owner or Contractor under the Contract for Construction.

3.3.7 Providing services in evaluating an extensive number of claims submitted by the Contractor or others in connection with the Work.

3.3.8 Providing services in connection with a public hearing, arbitration proceeding or legal proceeding except where the Architect is party thereto.

3.3.9 Preparing documents for alternate, separate or sequential bids or providing services in connection with bidding, negotiation or construction prior to the completion of the Construction Documents Phase.

3.4 OPTIONAL ADDITIONAL SERVICES

3.4.1 Providing analyses of the Owner's needs and programming the requirements of the Project.

3.4.2 Providing financial feasibility or other special studies.

3.4.3 Providing planning surveys, site evaluations or comparative studies of prospective sites.

3.4.4 Providing special surveys, environmental studies and submissions required for approvals of governmental authorities or others having jurisdiction over the Project.

3.4.5 Providing services relative to future facilities, systems and equipment.

3.4.6 Providing services to investigate existing conditions or facilities or to make measured drawings thereof.

3.4.7 Providing services to verify the accuracy of drawings or other information furnished by the Owner.

3.4.8 Providing coordination of construction performed by separate contractors or by the Owner's own forces and coordination of services required in connection with construction performed and equipment supplied by the Owner.

3.4.9 Providing services in connection with the work of a construction manager or separate consultants retained by the Owner.

3.4.10 Providing detailed estimates of Construction Cost.

3.4.11 Providing detailed quantity surveys or inventories of material, equipment and labor.

3.4.12 Providing analyses of owning and operating costs.

3.4.13 Providing interior design and other similar services required for or in connection with the selection, procurement or installation of furniture, furnishings and related equipment.

3.4.14 Providing services for planning tenant or rental space.

3.4.15 Making investigations, inventories of materials or equipment, or valuations and detailed appraisals of existing facilities.

3.4.16 Preparing a set of reproducible record drawings showing significant changes in the Work made during construction based on marked-up prints, drawings and other data furnished by the Contractor to the Architect.

3.4.17 Providing assistance in the utilization of equipment or systems such as testing, adjusting and balancing, preparation of operation and maintenance manuals, training personnel for operation and maintenance, and consultation during operation.

3.4.18 Providing services after issuance to the Owner of the final Certificate for Payment, or in the absence of a final Certificate for Payment, more than 60 days after the date of Substantial Completion of the Work.

3.4.19 Providing services of consultants for other than architectural, structural, mechanical and electrical engineering portions of the Project provided as a part of Basic Services.

3.4.20 Providing any other services not otherwise included in this Agreement or not customarily furnished in accordance with generally accepted architectural practice.

ARTICLE 4
OWNER'S RESPONSIBILITIES

4.1 The Owner shall provide full information regarding requirements for the Project, including a program which shall set forth the Owner's objectives, schedule, constraints and criteria, including space requirements and relationships, flexibility, expandability, special equipment, systems and site requirements.

4.2 The Owner shall establish and update an overall budget for the Project, including the Construction Cost, the Owner's other costs and reasonable contingencies related to all of these costs.

4.3 If requested by the Architect, the Owner shall furnish evidence that financial arrangements have been made to fulfill the Owner's obligations under this Agreement.

4.4 The Owner shall designate a representative authorized to act on the Owner's behalf with respect to the Project. The Owner or such authorized representative shall render decisions in a timely manner pertaining to documents submitted by the Architect in order to avoid unreasonable delay in the orderly and sequential progress of the Architect's services.

4.5 The Owner shall furnish surveys describing physical characteristics, legal limitations and utility locations for the site of the Project, and a written legal description of the site. The surveys and legal information shall include, as applicable, grades and lines of streets, alleys, pavements and adjoining property and structures; adjacent drainage; rights-of-way, restrictions, easements, encroachments, zoning, deed restrictions, boundaries and contours of the site; locations, dimensions and necessary data pertaining to existing buildings, other improvements and trees; and information concerning available utility services and lines, both public and private, above and below grade, including inverts and depths. All the information on the survey shall be referenced to a project benchmark.

4.6 The Owner shall furnish the services of geotechnical engineers when such services are requested by the Architect. Such services may include but are not limited to test borings, test pits, determinations of soil bearing values, percolation tests, evaluations of hazardous materials, ground corrosion and resistivity tests, including necessary operations for anticipating subsoil conditions, with reports and appropriate professional recommendations.

4.6.1 The Owner shall furnish the services of other consultants when such services are reasonably required by the scope of the Project and are requested by the Architect.

4.7 The Owner shall furnish structural, mechanical, chemical, air and water pollution tests, tests for hazardous materials, and other laboratory and environmental tests, inspections and reports required by law or the Contract Documents.

4.8 The Owner shall furnish all legal, accounting and insurance counseling services as may be necessary at any time for the Project, including auditing services the Owner may require to verify the Contractor's Applications for Payment or to ascertain how or for what purposes the Contractor has used the money paid by or on behalf of the Owner.

4.9 The services, information, surveys and reports required by Paragraphs 4.5 through 4.8 shall be furnished at the Owner's expense, and the Architect shall be entitled to rely upon the accuracy and completeness thereof.

4.10 Prompt written notice shall be given by the Owner to the Architect if the Owner becomes aware of any fault or defect in the Project or nonconformance with the Contract Documents.

4.11 The proposed language of certificates or certifications requested of the Architect or Architect's consultants shall be submitted to the Architect for review and approval at least 14 days prior to execution. The Owner shall not request certifications that would require knowledge or services beyond the scope of this Agreement.

188

ARTICLE 5
CONSTRUCTION COST

5.1 DEFINITION

5.1.1 The Construction Cost shall be the total cost or estimated cost to the Owner of all elements of the Project designed or specified by the Architect.

5.1.2 The Construction Cost shall include the cost at current market rates of labor and materials furnished by the Owner and equipment designed, specified, selected or specially provided for by the Architect, plus a reasonable allowance for the Contractor's overhead and profit. In addition, a reasonable allowance for contingencies shall be included for market conditions at the time of bidding and for changes in the Work during construction.

5.1.3 Construction Cost does not include the compensation of the Architect and Architect's consultants, the costs of the land, rights-of-way, financing or other costs which are the responsibility of the Owner as provided in Article 4.

5.2 RESPONSIBILITY FOR CONSTRUCTION COST

5.2.1 Evaluations of the Owner's Project budget, preliminary estimates of Construction Cost and detailed estimates of Construction Cost, if any, prepared by the Architect, represent the Architect's best judgment as a design professional familiar with the construction industry. It is recognized, however, that neither the Architect nor the Owner has control over the cost of labor, materials or equipment, over the Contractor's methods of determining bid prices, or over competitive bidding, market or negotiating conditions. Accordingly, the Architect cannot and does not warrant or represent that bids or negotiated prices will not vary from the Owner's Project budget or from any estimate of Construction Cost or evaluation prepared or agreed to by the Architect.

5.2.2 No fixed limit of Construction Cost shall be established as a condition of this Agreement by the furnishing, proposal or establishment of a Project budget, unless such fixed limit has been agreed upon in writing and signed by the parties hereto. If such a fixed limit has been established, the Architect shall be permitted to include contingencies for design, bidding and price escalation, to determine what materials, equipment, component systems and types of construction are to be included in the Contract Documents, to make reasonable adjustments in the scope of the Project and to include in the Contract Documents alternate bids to adjust the Construction Cost to the fixed limit. Fixed limits, if any, shall be increased in the amount of an increase in the Contract Sum occurring after execution of the Contract for Construction.

5.2.3 If the Bidding or Negotiation Phase has not commenced within 90 days after the Architect submits the Construction Documents to the Owner, any Project budget or fixed limit of Construction Cost shall be adjusted to reflect changes in the general level of prices in the construction industry between the date of submission of the Construction Documents to the Owner and the date on which proposals are sought.

5.2.4 If a fixed limit of Construction Cost (adjusted as provided in Subparagraph 5.2.3) is exceeded by the lowest bona fide bid or negotiated proposal, the Owner shall:

    .1 give written approval of an increase in such fixed limit;

    .2 authorize rebidding or renegotiating of the Project within a reasonable time;

    .3 if the Project is abandoned, terminate in accordance with Paragraph 8.3; or

    .4 cooperate in revising the Project scope and quality as required to reduce the Construction Cost.

5.2.5 If the Owner chooses to proceed under Clause 5.2.4.4, the Architect, without additional charge, shall modify the Contract Documents as necessary to comply with the fixed limit, if established as a condition of this Agreement. The modification of Contract Documents shall be the limit of the Architect's responsibility arising out of the establishment of a fixed limit. The Architect shall be entitled to compensation in accordance with this Agreement for all services performed whether or not the Construction Phase is commenced.

ARTICLE 6
USE OF ARCHITECT'S DRAWINGS, SPECIFICATIONS AND OTHER DOCUMENTS

6.1 The Drawings, Specifications and other documents prepared by the Architect for this Project are instruments of the Architect's service for use solely with respect to this Project and, unless otherwise provided, the Architect shall be deemed the author of these documents and shall retain all common law, statutory and other reserved rights, including the copyright. The Owner shall be permitted to retain copies, including reproducible copies, of the Architect's Drawings, Specifications and other documents for information and reference in connection with the Owner's use and occupancy of the Project. The Architect's Drawings, Specifications or other documents shall not be used by the Owner or others on other projects, for additions to this Project or for completion of this Project by others, unless the Architect is adjudged to be in default under this Agreement, except by agreement in writing and with appropriate compensation to the Architect.

6.2 Submission or distribution of documents to meet official regulatory requirements or for similar purposes in connection with the Project is not to be construed as publication in derogation of the Architect's reserved rights.

ARTICLE 7
ARBITRATION

7.1 Claims, disputes or other matters in question between the parties to this Agreement arising out of or relating to this Agreement or breach thereof shall be subject to and decided by arbitration in accordance with the Construction Industry Arbitration Rules of the American Arbitration Association currently in effect unless the parties mutually agree otherwise.

7.2 Demand for arbitration shall be filed in writing with the other party to this Agreement and with the American Arbitration Association. A demand for arbitration shall be made within a reasonable time after the claim, dispute or other matter in question has arisen. In no event shall the demand for arbitration be made after the date when institution of legal or equitable proceedings based on such claim, dispute or other matter in question would be barred by the applicable statutes of limitations.

7.3 No arbitration arising out of or relating to this Agreement shall include, by consolidation, joinder or in any other manner, an additional person or entity not a party to this Agreement,

189

except by written consent containing a specific reference to this Agreement signed by the Owner, Architect, and any other person or entity sought to be joined. Consent to arbitration involving an additional person or entity shall not constitute consent to arbitration of any claim, dispute or other matter in question not described in the written consent or with a person or entity not named or described therein. The foregoing agreement to arbitrate and other agreements to arbitrate with an additional person or entity duly consented to by the parties to this Agreement shall be specifically enforceable in accordance with applicable law in any court having jurisdiction thereof.

7.4 The award rendered by the arbitrator or arbitrators shall be final, and judgment may be entered upon it in accordance with applicable law in any court having jurisdiction thereof.

ARTICLE 8
TERMINATION, SUSPENSION OR ABANDONMENT

8.1 This Agreement may be terminated by either party upon not less than seven days' written notice should the other party fail substantially to perform in accordance with the terms of this Agreement through no fault of the party initiating the termination.

8.2 If the Project is suspended by the Owner for more than 30 consecutive days, the Architect shall be compensated for services performed prior to notice of such suspension. When the Project is resumed, the Architect's compensation shall be equitably adjusted to provide for expenses incurred in the interruption and resumption of the Architect's services.

8.3 This Agreement may be terminated by the Owner upon not less than seven days' written notice to the Architect in the event that the Project is permanently abandoned. If the Project is abandoned by the Owner for more than 90 consecutive days, the Architect may terminate this Agreement by giving written notice.

8.4 Failure of the Owner to make payments to the Architect in accordance with this Agreement shall be considered substantial nonperformance and cause for termination.

8.5 If the Owner fails to make payment when due the Architect for services and expenses, the Architect may, upon seven days' written notice to the Owner, suspend performance of services under this Agreement. Unless payment in full is received by the Architect within seven days of the date of the notice, the suspension shall take effect without further notice. In the event of a suspension of services, the Architect shall have no liability to the Owner for delay or damage caused the Owner because of such suspension of services.

8.6 In the event of termination not the fault of the Architect, the Architect shall be compensated for services performed prior to termination, together with Reimbursable Expenses then due and all Termination Expenses as defined in Paragraph 8.7.

8.7 Termination Expenses are in addition to compensation for Basic and Additional Services, and include expenses which are directly attributable to termination. Termination Expenses shall be computed as a percentage of the total compensation for Basic Services and Additional Services earned to the time of termination, as follows:

    .1 Twenty percent of the total compensation for Basic and Additional Services earned to date if termination occurs before or during the predesign, site analysis, or Schematic Design Phases; or

    .2 Ten percent of the total compensation for Basic and Additional Services earned to date if termination occurs during the Design Development Phase; or

    .3 Five percent of the total compensation for Basic and Additional Services earned to date if termination occurs during any subsequent phase.

ARTICLE 9
MISCELLANEOUS PROVISIONS

9.1 Unless otherwise provided, this Agreement shall be governed by the law of the principal place of business of the Architect.

9.2 Terms in this Agreement shall have the same meaning as those in AIA Document A201, General Conditions of the Contract for Construction, current as of the date of this Agreement.

9.3 Causes of action between the parties to this Agreement pertaining to acts or failures to act shall be deemed to have accrued and the applicable statutes of limitations shall commence to run not later than either the date of Substantial Completion for acts or failures to act occurring prior to Substantial Completion or the date of issuance of the final Certificate for Payment for acts or failures to act occurring after Substantial Completion.

9.4 The Owner and Architect waive all rights against each other and against the contractors, consultants, agents and employees of the other for damages, but only to the extent covered by property insurance during construction, except such rights as they may have to the proceeds of such insurance as set forth in the edition of AIA Document A201, General Conditions of the Contract for Construction, current as of the date of this Agreement. The Owner and Architect each shall require similar waivers from their contractors, consultants and agents.

9.5 The Owner and Architect, respectively, bind themselves, their partners, successors, assigns and legal representatives to the other party to this Agreement and to the partners, successors, assigns and legal representatives of such other party with respect to all covenants of this Agreement. Neither Owner nor Architect shall assign this Agreement without the written consent of the other.

9.6 This Agreement represents the entire and integrated agreement between the Owner and Architect and supersedes all prior negotiations, representations or agreements, either written or oral. This Agreement may be amended only by written instrument signed by both Owner and Architect.

9.7 Nothing contained in this Agreement shall create a contractual relationship with or a cause of action in favor of a third party against either the Owner or Architect.

9.8 Unless otherwise provided in this Agreement, the Architect and Architect's consultants shall have no responsibility for the discovery, presence, handling, removal or disposal of or exposure of persons to hazardous materials in any form at the Project site, including but not limited to asbestos, asbestos products, polychlorinated biphenyl (PCB) or other toxic substances.

9.9 The Architect shall have the right to include representations of the design of the Project, including photographs of the exterior and interior, among the Architect's promotional and professional materials. The Architect's materials shall not include the Owner's confidential or proprietary information if the Owner has previously advised the Architect in writing of the specific information considered by the Owner to be confidential or proprietary. The Owner shall provide professional credit for the Architect on the construction sign and in the promotional materials for the Project.

ARTICLE 10
PAYMENTS TO THE ARCHITECT

10.1 DIRECT PERSONNEL EXPENSE

10.1.1 Direct Personnel Expense is defined as the direct salaries of the Architect's personnel engaged on the Project and the portion of the cost of their mandatory and customary contributions and benefits related thereto, such as employment taxes and other statutory employee benefits, insurance, sick leave, holidays, vacations, pensions and similar contributions and benefits.

10.2 REIMBURSABLE EXPENSES

10.2.1 Reimbursable Expenses are in addition to compensation for Basic and Additional Services and include expenses incurred by the Architect and Architect's employees and consultants in the interest of the Project, as identified in the following Clauses.

10.2.1.1 Expense of transportation in connection with the Project; expenses in connection with authorized out-of-town travel; long-distance communications; and fees paid for securing approval of authorities having jurisdiction over the Project.

10.2.1.2 Expense of reproductions, postage and handling of Drawings, Specifications and other documents.

10.2.1.3 If authorized in advance by the Owner, expense of overtime work requiring higher than regular rates.

10.2.1.4 Expense of renderings, models and mock-ups requested by the Owner.

10.2.1.5 Expense of additional insurance coverage or limits, including professional liability insurance, requested by the Owner in excess of that normally carried by the Architect and Architect's consultants.

10.2.1.6 Expense of computer-aided design and drafting equipment time when used in connection with the Project.

10.3 PAYMENTS ON ACCOUNT OF BASIC SERVICES

10.3.1 An initial payment as set forth in Paragraph 11.1 is the minimum payment under this Agreement.

10.3.2 Subsequent payments for Basic Services shall be made monthly and, where applicable, shall be in proportion to services performed within each phase of service, on the basis set forth in Subparagraph 11.2.2.

10.3.3 If and to the extent that the time initially established in Subparagraph 11.5.1 of this Agreement is exceeded or extended through no fault of the Architect, compensation for any services rendered during the additional period of time shall be computed in the manner set forth in Subparagraph 11.3.2.

10.3.4 When compensation is based on a percentage of Construction Cost and any portions of the Project are deleted or otherwise not constructed, compensation for those portions of the Project shall be payable to the extent services are performed on those portions, in accordance with the schedule set forth in Subparagraph 11.2.2, based on (1) the lowest bona fide bid or negotiated proposal, or (2) if no such bid or proposal is received, the most recent preliminary estimate of Construction Cost or detailed estimate of Construction Cost for such portions of the Project.

10.4 PAYMENTS ON ACCOUNT OF ADDITIONAL SERVICES

10.4.1 Payments on account of the Architect's Additional Services and for Reimbursable Expenses shall be made monthly upon presentation of the Architect's statement of services rendered or expenses incurred.

10.5 PAYMENTS WITHHELD

10.5.1 No deductions shall be made from the Architect's compensation on account of penalty, liquidated damages or other sums withheld from payments to contractors, or on account of the cost of changes in the Work other than those for which the Architect has been found to be liable.

10.6 ARCHITECT'S ACCOUNTING RECORDS

10.6.1 Records of Reimbursable Expenses and expenses pertaining to Additional Services and services performed on the basis of a multiple of Direct Personnel Expense shall be available to the Owner or the Owner's authorized representative at mutually convenient times.

ARTICLE 11
BASIS OF COMPENSATION

The Owner shall compensate the Architect as follows:

11.1 AN INITIAL PAYMENT of   Dollars ($)
shall be made upon execution of this Agreement and credited to the Owner's account at final payment.

11.2 BASIC COMPENSATION

11.2.1 FOR BASIC SERVICES, as described in Article 2, and any other services included in Article 12 as part of Basic Services, Basic Compensation shall be computed as follows:

(Insert basis of compensation, including stipulated sums, multiples or percentages, and identify phases to which particular methods of compensation apply, if necessary.)

191

11.2.2 Where compensation is based on a stipulated sum or percentage of Construction Cost, progress payments for Basic Services in each phase shall total the following percentages of the total Basic Compensation payable:

(Insert additional phases as appropriate.)

Schematic Design Phase:	percent (%)
Design Development Phase:	percent (%)
Construction Documents Phase:	percent (%)
Bidding or Negotiation Phase:	percent (%)
Construction Phase:	percent (%)
Total Basic Compensation:	one hundred percent (100%)

11.3 COMPENSATION FOR ADDITIONAL SERVICES

11.3.1 FOR PROJECT REPRESENTATION BEYOND BASIC SERVICES, as described in Paragraph 3.2, compensation shall be computed as follows:

11.3.2 FOR ADDITIONAL SERVICES OF THE ARCHITECT, as described in Articles 3 and 12, other than (1) Additional Project Representation, as described in Paragraph 3.2, and (2) services included in Article 12 as part of Additional Services, but excluding services of consultants, compensation shall be computed as follows:

(Insert basis of compensation, including rates and/or multiples of Direct Personnel Expense for Principals and employees, and identify Principals and classify employees, if required. Identify specific services to which particular methods of compensation apply, if necessary.)

11.3.3 FOR ADDITIONAL SERVICES OF CONSULTANTS, including additional structural, mechanical and electrical engineering services and those provided under Subparagraph 3.4.19 or identified in Article 12 as part of Additional Services, a multiple of ( ) times the amounts billed to the Architect for such services.

(Identify specific types of consultants in Article 12, if required.)

11.4 REIMBURSABLE EXPENSES

11.4.1 FOR REIMBURSABLE EXPENSES, as described in Paragraph 10.2, and any other items included in Article 12 as Reimbursable Expenses, a multiple of ( ) times the expenses incurred by the Architect, the Architect's employees and consultants in the interest of the Project.

11.5 ADDITIONAL PROVISIONS

11.5.1 IF THE BASIC SERVICES covered by this Agreement have not been completed within ( ) months of the date hereof, through no fault of the Architect, extension of the Architect's services beyond that time shall be compensated as provided in Subparagraphs 10.3.3 and 11.3.2.

11.5.2 Payments are due and payable ( ) days from the date of the Architect's invoice. Amounts unpaid ( ) days after the invoice date shall bear interest at the rate entered below, or in the absence thereof at the legal rate prevailing from time to time at the principal place of business of the Architect.

(Insert rate of interest agreed upon.)

(Usury laws and requirements under the Federal Truth in Lending Act, similar state and local consumer credit laws and other regulations at the Owner's and Architect's principal places of business, the location of the Project and elsewhere may affect the validity of this provision. Specific legal advice should be obtained with respect to deletions or modifications, and also regarding requirements such as written disclosures or waivers.)

11.5.3 The rates and multiples set forth for Additional Services shall be annually adjusted in accordance with normal salary review practices of the Architect.

ARTICLE 12
OTHER CONDITIONS OR SERVICES

(Insert descriptions of other services, identify Additional Services included within Basic Compensation and modifications to the payment and compensation terms included in this Agreement.)

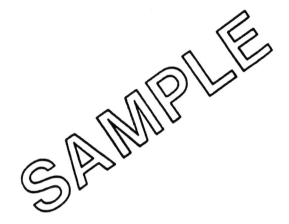

This Agreement entered into as of the day and year first written above.

OWNER   ARCHITECT

_____   _____
(Signature)   *(Signature)*

_____   _____
(Printed name and title)   *(Printed name and title)*

APPENDIX C

AIA Document A310-1970

Bid Bond

THE AMERICAN INSTITUTE OF ARCHITECTS

AIA Document A310

Bid Bond

KNOW ALL MEN BY THESE PRESENTS, that we

(Here insert full name and address or legal title of Contractor)

as Principal, hereinafter called the Principal, and

(Here insert full name and address or legal title of Surety)

a corporation duly organized under the laws of the State of
as Surety, hereinafter called the Surety, are held and firmly bound unto

(Here insert full name and address or legal title of Owner)

as Obligee, hereinafter called the Obligee, in the sum of

Dollars ($),

for the payment of which sum well and truly to be made, the said Principal and the said Surety, bind ourselves, our heirs, executors, administrators, successors and assigns, jointly and severally, firmly by these presents.

WHEREAS, the Principal has submitted a bid for

(Here insert full name, address and description of project)

NOW, THEREFORE, if the Obligee shall accept the bid of the Principal and the Principal shall enter into a Contract with the Obligee in accordance with the terms of such bid, and give such bond or bonds as may be specified in the bidding or Contract Documents with good and sufficient surety for the faithful performance of such Contract and for the prompt payment of labor and material furnished in the prosecution thereof, or in the event of the failure of the Principal to enter such Contract and give such bond or bonds, if the Principal shall pay to the Obligee the difference not to exceed the penalty hereof between the amount specified in said bid and such larger amount for which the Obligee may in good faith contract with another party to perform the Work covered by said bid, then this obligation shall be null and void, otherwise to remain in full force and effect.

Signed and sealed this   day of   19

_____   { _____ (Principal)   (Seal)
        (Witness)

                                                        _____
                                                                (Title)

_____   { _____ (Surety)   (Seal)
        (Witness)

                                                        _____
                                                                (Title)

APPENDIX D

AIA Document A311-1970

Performance Bond and Labor and Material Payment Bond

THE AMERICAN INSTITUTE OF ARCHITECTS

AIA Document A311

Performance Bond

KNOW ALL MEN BY THESE PRESENTS: that

(Here insert full name and address or legal title of Contractor)

as Principal, hereinafter called Contractor, and,

(Here insert full name and address or legal title of Surety)

as Surety, hereinafter called Surety, are held and firmly bound unto

(Here insert full name and address or legal title of Owner)

as Obligee, hereinafter called Owner, in the amount of

Dollars ($),

for the payment whereof Contractor and Surety bind themselves, their heirs, executors, administrators, successors and assigns, jointly and severally, firmly by these presents.

WHEREAS,

Contractor has by written agreement dated   19   , entered into a contract with Owner for
(Here insert full name, address and description of project)

in accordance with Drawings and Specifications prepared by

(Here insert full name and address or legal title of Architect)

which contract is by reference made a part hereof, and is hereinafter referred to as the Contract.

PERFORMANCE BOND

NOW, THEREFORE, THE CONDITION OF THIS OBLIGATION is such that, if Contractor shall promptly and faithfully perform said Contract, then this obligation shall be null and void; otherwise it shall remain in full force and effect.

The Surety hereby waives notice of any alteration or extension of time made by the Owner.

Whenever Contractor shall be, and declared by Owner to be in default under the Contract, the Owner having performed Owner's obligations thereunder, the Surety may promptly remedy the default, or shall promptly

1) Complete the Contract in accordance with its terms and conditions, or

2) Obtain a bid or bids for completing the Contract in accordance with its terms and conditions, and upon determination by Surety of the lowest responsible bidder, or, if the Owner elects, upon determination by the Owner and the Surety jointly of the lowest responsible bidder, arrange for a contract between such bidder and Owner, and make available as Work progresses (even though there should be a default or a succession of defaults under the contract or contracts of completion arranged under this paragraph) sufficient funds to pay the cost of completion less the balance of the contract price; but not exceeding, including other costs and damages for which the Surety may be liable hereunder, the amount set forth in the first paragraph hereof. The term "balance of the contract price," as used in this paragraph, shall mean the total amount payable by Owner to Contractor under the Contract and any amendments thereto, less the amount properly paid by Owner to Contractor.

Any suit under this bond must be instituted before the expiration of two (2) years from the date on which final payment under the Contract falls due.

No right of action shall accrue on this bond to or for the use of any person or corporation other than the Owner named herein or the heirs, executors, administrators or successors of the Owner.

Signed and sealed this   day of   19

_____
(Witness)

                (Principal)   (Seal)

                (Title)

_____
(Witness)

                (Surety)   (Seal)

                (Title)

THE AMERICAN INSTITUTE OF ARCHITECTS

AIA Document A311

Labor and Material Payment Bond

THIS BOND IS ISSUED SIMULTANEOUSLY WITH PERFORMANCE BOND IN FAVOR OF THE
OWNER CONDITIONED ON THE FULL AND FAITHFUL PERFORMANCE OF THE CONTRACT

KNOW ALL MEN BY THESE PRESENTS: that

(Here insert full name and address or legal title of Contractor)

as Principal, hereinafter called Principal, and,

(Here insert full name and address or legal title of Surety)

as Surety, hereinafter called Surety, are held and firmly bound unto

(Here insert full name and address or legal title of Owner)

as Obligee, hereinafter called Owner, for the use and benefit of claimants as hereinbelow defined, in the

amount of

(Here insert a sum equal to at least one-half of the contract price)   Dollars ($),

for the payment whereof Principal and Surety bind themselves, their heirs, executors, administrators,
successors and assigns, jointly and severally, firmly by these presents.

WHEREAS,

Principal has by written agreement dated   19   , entered into a contract with Owner for
(Here insert full name, address and description of project)

in accordance with Drawings and Specifications prepared by

(Here insert full name and address or legal title of Architect)

which contract is by reference made a part hereof, and is hereinafter referred to as the Contract.

200

LABOR AND MATERIAL PAYMENT BOND

NOW, THEREFORE, THE CONDITION OF THIS OBLIGATION is such that, if Principal shall promptly make payment to all claimants as hereinafter defined, for all labor and material used or reasonably required for use in the performance of the Contract, then this obligation shall be void; otherwise it shall remain in full force and effect, subject, however, to the following conditions:

1. A claimant is defined as one having a direct contract with the Principal or with a Subcontractor of the Principal for labor, material, or both, used or reasonably required for use in the performance of the Contract, labor and material being construed to include that part of water, gas, power, light, heat, oil, gasoline, telephone service or rental of equipment directly applicable to the Contract.

2. The above named Principal and Surety hereby jointly and severally agree with the Owner that every claimant as herein defined, who has not been paid in full before the expiration of a period of ninety (90) days after the date on which the last of such claimant's work or labor was done or performed, or materials were furnished by such claimant, may sue on this bond for the use of such claimant, prosecute the suit to final judgment for such sum or sums as may be justly due claimant, and have execution thereon. The Owner shall not be liable for the payment of any costs or expenses of any such suit.

3. No suit or action shall be commenced hereunder by any claimant:

a) Unless claimant, other than one having a direct contract with the Principal, shall have given written notice to any two of the following: the Principal, the Owner, or the Surety above named, within ninety (90) days after such claimant did or performed the last of the work or labor, or furnished the last of the materials for which said claim is made, stating with substantial

accuracy the amount claimed and the name of the party to whom the materials were furnished, or for whom the work or labor was done or performed. Such notice shall be served by mailing the same by registered mail or certified mail, postage prepaid, in an envelope addressed to the Principal, Owner or Surety, at any place where an office is regularly maintained for the transaction of business, or served in any manner in which legal process may be served in the state in which the aforesaid project is located, save that such service need not be made by a public officer.

b) After the expiration of one (1) year following the date on which Principal ceased Work on said Contract, it being understood, however, that if any limitation embodied in this bond is prohibited by any law controlling the construction hereof such limitation shall be deemed to be amended so as to be equal to the minimum period of limitation permitted by such law.

c) Other than in a state court of competent jurisdiction in and for the county or other political subdivision of the state in which the Project, or any part thereof, is situated, or in the United States District Court for the district in which the Project, or any part thereof, is situated, and not elsewhere.

4. The amount of this bond shall be reduced by and to the extent of any payment or payments made in good faith hereunder, inclusive of the payment by Surety of mechanics' liens which may be filed of record against said improvement, whether or not claim for the amount of such lien be presented under and against this bond.

Signed and sealed this   day of   19

_____
(Witness)

{
(Principal)   (Seal)

(Title)
}

_____
(Witness)

{
(Surety)   (Seal)

(Title)
}

201

APPENDIX E

CCDC 2—1994

Stipulated Price Contract

2

Stipulated price contract

Project:

 Canadian construction documents committee

TABLE OF CONTENTS

AGREEMENT BETWEEN OWNER AND CONTRACTOR
A-1 The Work
A-2 Agreements and Amendments
A-3 Contract Documents
A-4 Contract Price
A-5 Payment
A-6 Receipt of and Addresses for Notices
A-7 Language of the Contract
A-8 Succession

DEFINITIONS
1. Contract
2. Contract Documents
3. Owner
4. Contractor
5. Subcontractor
6. Supplier
7. Consultant
8. Project
9. Work
10. Place of the Work
11. Product
12. Provide
13. Contract Price
14. Contract Time
15. Working Day
16. Supplemental Instruction
17. Change Order
18. Change Directive
19. Substantial Performance of the Work
20. Value Added Taxes

GENERAL CONDITIONS OF THE STIPULATED PRICE CONTRACT

PART 1   GENERAL PROVISIONS
GC 1.1 Contract Documents
GC 1.2 Law of the Contract
GC 1.3 Rights and Remedies
GC 1.4 Assignment

PART 2   ADMINISTRATION OF THE CONTRACT
GC 2.1 Authority of the Consultant
GC 2.2 Role of the Consultant
GC 2.3 Review and Inspection of the Work
GC 2.4 Defective Work

PART 3   EXECUTION OF THE WORK
GC 3.1 Control of the Work
GC 3.2 Construction by Owner or Other Contractors
GC 3.3 Temporary Supports, Structures, and Facilities
GC 3.4 Document Review
GC 3.5 Construction Schedule
GC 3.6 Construction Safety
GC 3.7 Supervisor
GC 3.8 Subcontractors and Suppliers
GC 3.9 Labour and Products
GC 3.10 Documents at the Site
GC 3.11 Shop Drawings
GC 3.12 Use of the Work
GC 3.13 Cutting and Remedial Work
GC 3.14 Cleanup

PART 4   ALLOWANCES
GC 4.1 Cash Allowances
GC 4.2 Contingency Allowance

PART 5   PAYMENT
GC 5.1 Financing Information Required of the Owner
GC 5.2 Applications for Progress Payment
GC 5.3 Progress Payment
GC 5.4 Substantial Performance of the Work
GC 5.5 Payment of Holdback upon Substantial Performance of the Work
GC 5.6 Progressive Release of Holdback
GC 5.7 Final Payment
GC 5.8 Withholding of Payment
GC 5.9 Non-conforming Work

PART 6   CHANGES IN THE WORK
GC 6.1 Changes
GC 6.2 Change Order
GC 6.3 Change Directive
GC 6.4 Concealed or Unknown Conditions
GC 6.5 Delays

PART 7   DEFAULT NOTICE
GC 7.1 Owner's Right to Perform the Work, Stop the Work, or Terminate the Contract
GC 7.2 Contractor's Right to Stop the Work or Terminate the Contract

PART 8   DISPUTE RESOLUTION
GC 8.1 Authority of the Consultant
GC 8.2 Negotiation, Mediation, and Arbitration
GC 8.3 Retention of Rights

PART 9   PROTECTION OF PERSONS AND PROPERTY
GC 9.1 Protection of Work and Property
GC 9.2 Damages and Mutual Responsibility
GC 9.3 Toxic and Hazardous Substances and Materials

PART 10   GOVERNING REGULATIONS
GC 10.1 Taxes and Duties
GC 10.2 Laws, Notices, Permits, and Fees
GC 10.3 Patent Fees
GC 10.4 Workers' Compensation

PART 11   INSURANCE — BONDS
GC 11.1 Insurance
GC 11.2 Bonds

PART 12   INDEMNIFICATION — WAIVER — WARRANTY
GC 12.1 Indemnification
GC 12.2 Waiver of Claims
GC 12.3 Warranty

CCDC

205

AGREEMENT BETWEEN OWNER AND CONTRACTOR
For use when a stipulated price is the basis of payment.

This Agreement made on the _____ day of _____

in the year _____

by and between

_____

_____

hereinafter called the *"Owner"*

and

_____

_____

hereinafter called the *"Contractor"*

The *Owner* and the *Contractor* agree as follows:

ARTICLE A-1   THE WORK

The *Contractor* shall:

1.1   perform the *Work* required by the *Contract Documents* for _____

_____
insert above the title of the Work

    located at _____
insert above the Place of the Work

    which have been signed by the parties, and for which _____

_____
insert above the name of the Consultant

    is acting as and is hereinafter called the *"Consultant"* and

1.2   do and fulfill everything indicated by this Agreement, and

1.3   commence the *Work* by the _____ day of _____ in the year _____

    and, subject to adjustment in *Contract Time* as provided for in the *Contract Documents*, attain *Substantial*

    Performance of the Work, by the _____ day of _____ in the year _____.

ARTICLE A-2 AGREEMENTS AND AMENDMENTS

2.1   The *Contract* supersedes all prior negotiations, representations, or agreements, either written or oral, relating in any manner to the *Work*, including the bidding documents that are not expressly listed in Article A-3 of the Agreement - CONTRACT DOCUMENTS.

2.2   The *Contract* may be amended only as provided in the *Contract Documents*.

ARTICLE A-3   CONTRACT DOCUMENTS

3.1   The following are the *Contract Documents* referred to in Article A-1 of the Agreement - THE WORK:

- Agreement Between *Owner* and *Contractor*
- Definitions
- The General Conditions of the Stipulated Price Contract
- *

---

*   *(Insert here, attaching additional pages if required, a list identifying all other Contract Documents e.g. Supplementary Conditions; Specifications, giving a list of contents with section numbers and titles, number of pages, and date; Drawings, giving drawing number, title, date, revision date or mark; Addenda, giving title, number, date)*

ARTICLE A-4   CONTRACT PRICE

4.1   The *Contract Price*, which excludes *Value Added Taxes*, is:

_____

_____ dollars

and _____ cents. $ _____

4.2   *Value Added Taxes* (of _____ %) payable by the *Owner* to the Contractor are:

_____

_____ dollars

and _____ cents. $ _____

4.3   Total amount payable by the *Owner* to the *Contractor* for the construction of the *Work* is:

_____

_____ dollars

and _____ cents. $ _____

4.4   All amounts are in Canadian funds.

4.5   These amounts shall be subject to adjustments as provided in the *Contract Documents*.

ARTICLE A-5   PAYMENT

5.1   Subject to the provisions of the *Contract Documents*, and in accordance with legislation and statutory regulations respecting holdback percentages and, where such legislation or regulations do not exist or apply, subject to a holdback of _____ percent (_____ %), the *Owner* shall in Canadian funds:

    .1   make progress payments to the *Contractor* on account of the *Contract Price* when due in the amount certified by the *Consultant* together with such *Value Added Taxes* as may be applicable to such payment, and

    .2   upon *Substantial Performance of the Work*, pay to the *Contractor* the unpaid balance of the holdback amount when due together with such *Value Added Taxes* as may be applicable to such payment, and

    .3   upon the issuance of the final certificate for payment, pay to the *Contractor* the unpaid balance of the *Contract Price* when due together with such *Value Added Taxes* as may be applicable to such payment.

5.2   In the event of loss or damage occurring where payment becomes due under the property and boiler insurance policies, payments shall be made to the *Contractor* in accordance with the provisions of GC 11.1 - INSURANCE.

5.3   Interest

    .1   Should either party fail to make payments as they become due under the terms of the *Contract* or in an award by arbitration or court, interest at _____ percent (_____ %) per annum above the bank rate on such unpaid amounts shall also become due and payable until payment. Such interest shall be compounded on a monthly basis. The bank rate shall be the rate established by the Bank of Canada as the minimum rate at which the Bank of Canada makes short term advances to the chartered banks.

    .2   Interest shall apply at the rate and in the manner prescribed by paragraph 5.3.1 of this Article on the amount of any claim settled pursuant to Part 8 of the General Conditions - DISPUTE RESOLUTION from the date the amount would have been due and payable under the *Contract*, had it not been in dispute, until the date it is paid.

ARTICLE A-6   RECEIPT OF AND ADDRESSES FOR NOTICES

6.1   Notices in writing between the parties or between them and the *Consultant* shall be considered to have been received by the addressee on the date of delivery if delivered to the individual, or to a member of the firm, or to an officer of the corporation for whom they are intended by hand or by registered post; or if sent by regular post, to have been delivered within 5 *Working Days* of the date of mailing when addressed as follows:

The *Owner* at _____

street and number and postal box number if applicable

_____

post office or district, province, postal code

_____

The *Contractor* at _____

street and number and postal box number if applicable

_____

post office or district, province, postal code

_____

The *Consultant* at _____

street and number and postal box number if applicable

_____

post office or district, province, postal code

_____

ARTICLE A-7   LANGUAGE OF THE CONTRACT

7.1   When the *Contract Documents* are prepared in both the English and French languages, it is agreed that in the event of any apparent discrepancy between the English and French versions, the English/French* language shall prevail.

 * *Complete this statement by striking out inapplicable term.*

7.2   This Agreement is drawn in English at the request of the parties hereto. La présente convention est rédigée en anglais à la demande des parties.

ARTICLE A-8   SUCCESSION

8.1   The *Contract Documents* are to be read into and form part of this Agreement and the whole shall constitute the *Contract* between the parties, and subject to the law and the provisions of the *Contract Documents* shall enure to the benefit of and be binding upon the parties hereto, their respective heirs, legal representatives, successors, and assigns.

In witness whereof the parties hereto have executed this Agreement and by the hands of their duly authorized representatives.

SIGNED AND DELIVERED
in the presence of:

OWNER

_____
name of owner

_____
signature

WITNESS

_____
name and title of person signing

_____   _____
signature   *signature*

_____   _____
name and title of person signing   *name and title of person signing*

CONTRACTOR

_____
name of contractor

_____
signature

WITNESS

_____
name and title of person signing

_____   _____
signature   *signature*

_____   _____
name and title of person signing   *name and title of person signing*

N.B.   Where legal jurisdiction, local practice, or Owner or Contractor requirement calls for:
(a)   proof of authority to execute this document, attach such proof of authority in the form of a certified copy of a resolution naming the representative(s) authorized to sign the Agreement for and on behalf of the corporation or partnership; or
(b)   the affixing of a corporate seal, this Agreement should be properly sealed.

DEFINITIONS

The following Definitions shall apply to all *Contract Documents*.

1. **Contract**
   The *Contract* is the undertaking by the parties to perform their respective duties, responsibilities, and obligations as prescribed in the *Contract Documents* and represents the entire agreement between the parties.

2. **Contract Documents**
   The *Contract Documents* consist of those documents listed in Article A-3 of the Agreement - CONTRACT DOCUMENTS and amendments agreed upon between the parties.

3. **Owner**
   The *Owner* is the person or entity identified as such in the Agreement. The term *Owner* means the *Owner* or the *Owner*'s authorized agent or representative as designated to the *Contractor* in writing, but does not include the *Consultant*.

4. **Contractor**
   The *Contractor* is the person or entity identified as such in the Agreement. The term *Contractor* means the *Contractor* or the *Contractor*'s authorized representative as designated to the *Owner* in writing.

5. **Subcontractor**
   A *Subcontractor* is a person or entity having a direct contract with the *Contractor* to perform a part or parts of the *Work*, or to supply *Products* worked to a special design for the *Work*.

6. **Supplier**
   A *Supplier* is a person or entity having a direct contract with the *Contractor* to supply *Products* not worked to a special design for the *Work*.

7. **Consultant**
   The *Consultant* is the person or entity identified as such in the Agreement. The *Consultant* is the Architect, the Engineer, or entity licensed to practice in the province or territory of the *Place of the Work*. The term *Consultant* means the *Consultant* or the *Consultant*'s authorized representative.

8. **Project**
   The *Project* means the total construction contemplated of which the *Work* may be the whole or a part.

9. **Work**
   The *Work* means the total construction and related services required by the *Contract Documents*.

10. **Place of the Work**
    The *Place of the Work* is the designated site or location of the *Work* identified in Article A-1 of the Agreement - THE WORK.

11. **Product**
    Product or Products means material, machinery, equipment, and fixtures forming the *Work*, but does not include machinery and equipment used to prepare, fabricate, convey, or erect the *Work*, which are referred to as construction machinery and equipment.

12. **Provide**
    Provide means to supply and install.

13. **Contract Price**

The *Contract Price* is the amount stipulated in Article A-4 of the Agreement - CONTRACT PRICE.

14. **Contract Time**

The *Contract Time* is the time stipulated in paragraph 1.3 of Article A-1 of the Agreement - THE WORK from commencement of the *Work* to *Substantial Performance of the Work.*

15. **Working Day**

Working Day means a day other than a Saturday, Sunday, or a holiday which is observed by the construction industry in the area of the *Place of the Work.*

16. **Supplemental Instruction**

A *Supplemental Instruction* is an instruction, not involving adjustment in the *Contract Price* or *Contract Time*, in the form of specifications, drawings, schedules, samples, models or written instructions, consistent with the intent of the *Contract Documents*. It is to be issued by the *Consultant* to supplement the *Contract Documents* as required for the performance of the *Work.*

17. **Change Order**

A *Change Order* is a written amendment to the *Contract* prepared by the *Consultant* and signed by the *Owner* and the *Contractor* stating their agreement upon:
- a change in the *Work*;
- the method of adjustment or the amount of the adjustment in the *Contract Price*, if any; and
- the extent of the adjustment in the *Contract Time*, if any.

18. **Change Directive**

A *Change Directive* is a written instruction prepared by the *Consultant* and signed by the *Owner* directing a change in the *Work* within the general scope of the *Contract Documents.*

19. **Substantial Performance of the Work**

Substantial Performance of the Work is as defined in the lien legislation applicable to the *Place of the Work.* If such legislation is not in force or does not contain such definition, *Substantial Performance of the Work* shall have been reached when the *Work* is ready for use or is being used for the purpose intended and is so certified by the *Consultant.*

20. **Value Added Taxes**

Value Added Taxes means such sum as shall be levied upon the *Contract Price* by the Federal or any Provincial Government and is computed as a percentage of the *Contract Price* and includes the Goods and Services Tax, the Quebec Sales Tax and any similar tax, the payment or collection of which is by the legislation imposing such tax an obligation of the *Contractor.*

GENERAL CONDITIONS OF THE STIPULATED PRICE CONTRACT

PART 1 GENERAL PROVISIONS

GC 1.1 CONTRACT DOCUMENTS

1.1.1   The intent of the *Contract Documents* is to include the labour, *Products*, and services necessary for the performance of the *Work* by the *Contractor* in accordance with these documents. It is not intended, however, that the *Contractor* shall supply products or perform work not consistent with, not covered by, or not properly inferable from the *Contract Documents*.

1.1.2   Nothing contained in the *Contract Documents* shall create any contractual relationship between:

    .1   the *Owner* and a *Subcontractor*, a *Supplier*, or their agent, employee, or other person performing any of the *Work*.

    .2   the *Consultant* and the *Contractor*, a *Subcontractor*, a *Supplier*, or their agent, employee, or other person performing any of the *Work*.

1.1.3   The *Contract Documents* are complementary, and what is required by any one shall be as binding as if required by all.

1.1.4   Words and abbreviations which have well known technical or trade meanings are used in the *Contract Documents* in accordance with such recognized meanings.

1.1.5   References in the *Contract Documents* to the singular shall be considered to include the plural as the context requires.

1.1.6   The specifications are that portion of the *Contract Documents*, wherever located and whenever issued, consisting of the written requirements and standards for *Products*, systems, workmanship, and the services necessary for the performance of the *Work*.

1.1.7   The drawings are the graphic and pictorial portions of the *Contract Documents*, wherever located and whenever issued, showing the design, location, and dimensions of the *Work*, generally including plans, elevations, sections, details, schedules, and diagrams.

1.1.8   Neither the organization of the specifications into divisions, sections, and parts nor the arrangement of drawings shall control the *Contractor* in dividing the work among *Subcontractors* and *Suppliers* or in establishing the extent of the work to be performed by a trade.

1.1.9   If there is a conflict within *Contract Documents*:

    .1   the order of priority of documents, from highest to lowest, shall be
        • the Agreement between the *Owner* and the *Contractor*,
        • the Definitions,
        • Supplementary Conditions,
        • the General Conditions,
        • Division 1 of the specifications,
        • Divisions 2 through 16 of the specifications,
        • material and finishing schedules,
        • drawings.

.2   drawings of larger scale shall govern over those of smaller scale of the same date.

.3   dimensions shown on drawings shall govern over dimensions scaled from drawings.

.4   later dated documents shall govern over earlier documents of the same type.

1.1.10   The *Owner* shall provide the *Contractor*, without charge, sufficient copies of the *Contract Documents* to perform the *Work*.

1.1.11   Specifications, drawings, models, and copies thereof furnished by the *Consultant* are and shall remain the *Consultant*'s property, with the exception of the signed *Contract* sets, which shall belong to each party to the *Contract*. All specifications, drawings, and models furnished by the *Consultant* are to be used only with respect to the *Work* and are not to be used on other work. These specifications, drawings, and models are not to be copied or altered in any manner without the written authorization of the *Consultant*.

1.1.12   Models furnished by the *Contractor* at the *Owner*'s expense are the property of the *Owner*.

GC 1.2 LAW OF THE CONTRACT

1.2.1   The law of the *Place of the Work* shall govern the interpretation of the *Contract*.

GC 1.3 RIGHTS AND REMEDIES

1.3.1   Except as expressly provided in the *Contract Documents*, the duties and obligations imposed by the *Contract Documents* and the rights and remedies available thereunder shall be in addition to and not a limitation of any duties, obligations, rights, and remedies otherwise imposed or available by law.

1.3.2   No action or failure to act by the *Owner*, *Consultant*, or *Contractor* shall constitute a waiver of any right or duty afforded any of them under the *Contract*, nor shall any such action or failure to act constitute an approval of or acquiescence in any breach thereunder, except as may be specifically agreed in writing.

GC 1.4 ASSIGNMENT

1.4.1   Neither party to the *Contract* shall assign the *Contract* or a portion thereof without the written consent of the other, which consent shall not be unreasonably withheld.

PART 2 ADMINISTRATION OF THE CONTRACT

GC 2.1 AUTHORITY OF THE CONSULTANT

2.1.1   The *Consultant* will have authority to act on behalf of the *Owner* only to the extent provided in the *Contract Documents*, unless otherwise modified by written agreement as provided in paragraph 2.1.2.

2.1.2   The duties, responsibilities, and limitations of authority of the *Consultant* as set forth in the *Contract Documents* shall be modified or extended only with the written consent of the *Owner*, the *Contractor*, and the *Consultant*.

2.1.3   If the *Consultant*'s employment is terminated, the *Owner* shall immediately appoint or reappoint a *Consultant* against whom the *Contractor* makes no reasonable objection and whose status under the *Contract Documents* shall be that of the former *Consultant*.

GC 2.2 ROLE OF THE CONSULTANT

2.2.1   The *Consultant* will provide administration of the *Contract* as described in the *Contract Documents* during construction until issuance of the final certificate for payment, and subject to GC 2.1 - AUTHORITY OF THE CONSULTANT and with the *Owner*'s concurrence, from time to time until the completion of any correction of defects as provided in paragraph 12.3.3 of GC 12.3 - WARRANTY.

2.2.2   The *Consultant* will visit the *Place of the Work* at intervals appropriate to the progress of construction to become familiar with the progress and quality of the work and to determine if the *Work* is proceeding in general conformity with the *Contract Documents*.

2.2.3   If the *Owner* and the *Consultant* agree, the *Consultant* will provide at the *Place of the Work*, one or more project representatives to assist in carrying out the *Consultant*'s responsibilities. The duties, responsibilities, and limitations of authority of such project representatives shall be as set forth in writing to the *Contractor*.

2.2.4   Based on the *Consultant*'s observations and evaluation of the *Contractor*'s applications for payment, the *Consultant* will determine the amounts owing to the *Contractor* under the *Contract* and will issue certificates for payment as provided in Article A-5 of the Agreement - PAYMENT, GC 5.3 - PROGRESS PAYMENT, and GC 5.7 - FINAL PAYMENT.

2.2.5   The *Consultant* will not be responsible for and will not have control, charge, or supervision of construction means, methods, techniques, sequences, or procedures, or for safety precautions and programs required in connection with the *Work* in accordance with the applicable construction safety legislation, other regulations, or general construction practice. The *Consultant* will not be responsible for the *Contractor*'s failure to carry out the *Work* in accordance with the *Contract Documents*. The *Consultant* will not have control over, charge of, or be responsible for the acts or omissions of the *Contractor*, *Subcontractors*, *Suppliers*, or their agents, employees, or any other persons performing portions of the *Work*.

2.2.6   The *Consultant* will be, in the first instance, the interpreter of the requirements of the *Contract Documents* and shall make findings as to the performance thereunder by both parties to the *Contract*, except with respect to GC 5.1 - FINANCING INFORMATION REQUIRED OF THE OWNER. Interpretations and findings of the *Consultant* shall be consistent with the intent of the *Contract Documents*. When making such interpretations and findings the *Consultant* will not show partiality to either the *Owner* or the *Contractor*.

2.2.7   Claims, disputes, and other matters in question relating to the performance of the *Work* or the interpretation of the *Contract Documents*, except for GC 5.1 - FINANCING INFORMATION REQUIRED OF THE OWNER, shall be referred initially to the *Consultant* by notice in writing given to the *Consultant* and to the other party for the *Consultant*'s interpretation and finding which will be given by notice in writing to the parties within a reasonable time.

2.2.8   The *Consultant* will have authority to reject work which in the *Consultant*'s opinion does not conform to the requirements of the *Contract Documents*. Whenever the *Consultant* considers it necessary or advisable, the *Consultant* will have authority to require inspection or testing of work, whether or not such work is fabricated, installed, or completed. However, neither the authority of the *Consultant* to act nor any decision either to exercise or not to exercise such authority shall give rise to any duty or responsibility of the *Consultant* to the *Contractor*, *Subcontractors*, *Suppliers*, or their agents, employees, or other persons performing any of the *Work*.

2.2.9   During the progress of the *Work* the *Consultant* will furnish *Supplemental Instructions* to the *Contractor* with reasonable promptness or in accordance with a schedule for such instructions agreed to by the *Consultant* and the *Contractor*.

2.2.10 The *Consultant* will review and take appropriate action upon such *Contractor*'s submittals as shop drawings, *Product* data, and samples, as provided in the *Contract Documents*.

2.2.11 The *Consultant* will prepare *Change Orders* and *Change Directives* as provided in GC 6.2 - CHANGE ORDER and GC 6.3 - CHANGE DIRECTIVE.

2.2.12 The *Consultant* will conduct reviews of the *Work* to determine the date of *Substantial Performance of the Work* as provided in GC 5.4 - SUBSTANTIAL PERFORMANCE OF THE WORK.

2.2.13 All certificates issued by the *Consultant* shall be to the best of the *Consultant*'s knowledge, information, and belief. By issuing any certificate, the *Consultant* does not guarantee the *Work* is correct or complete.

2.2.14 The *Consultant* will receive and review written warranties and related documents required by the *Contract* and provided by the *Contractor* and will forward such warranties and documents to the *Owner* for the *Owner*'s acceptance.

GC 2.3 REVIEW AND INSPECTION OF THE WORK

2.3.1 The *Owner* and the *Consultant* shall have access to the *Work* at all times. The *Contractor* shall provide sufficient, safe, and proper facilities at all times for the review of the *Work* by the *Consultant* and the inspection of the *Work* by authorized agencies. If parts of the *Work* are in preparation at locations other than the *Place of the Work*, the *Owner* and the *Consultant* shall be given access to such work whenever it is in progress.

2.3.2 If work is designated for tests, inspections, or approvals in the *Contract Documents*, or by the *Consultant*'s instructions, or the laws or ordinances of the *Place of the Work*, the *Contractor* shall give the *Consultant* reasonable notice of when the work will be ready for review and inspection. The *Contractor* shall arrange for and shall give the *Consultant* reasonable notice of the date and time of inspections by other authorities.

2.3.3 The *Contractor* shall furnish promptly to the *Consultant* two copies of certificates and inspection reports relating to the *Work*.

2.3.4 If the *Contractor* covers, or permits to be covered, work that has been designated for special tests, inspections, or approvals before such special tests, inspections, or approvals are made, given or completed, the *Contractor* shall, if so directed, uncover such work, have the inspections or tests satisfactorily completed, and make good covering work at the *Contractor*'s expense.

2.3.5 The *Consultant* may order any portion or portions of the *Work* to be examined to confirm that such work is in accordance with the requirements of the *Contract Documents*. If the work is not in accordance with the requirements of the *Contract Documents*, the *Contractor* shall correct the work and pay the cost of examination and correction. If the work is in accordance with the requirements of the *Contract Documents*, the *Owner* shall pay the cost of examination and restoration.

GC 2.4 DEFECTIVE WORK

2.4.1 The *Contractor* shall promptly remove from the *Place of the Work* and replace or re-execute defective work that has been rejected by the *Consultant* as failing to conform to the *Contract Documents* whether or not the defective work has been incorporated in the *Work* and whether or not the defect is the result of poor workmanship, use of defective products, or damage through carelessness or other act or omission of the *Contractor*.

2.4.2 The *Contractor* shall make good promptly other contractors' work destroyed or damaged by such removals or replacements at the *Contractor*'s expense.

2.4.3 If in the opinion of the *Consultant* it is not expedient to correct defective work or work not performed as provided in the *Contract Documents*, the *Owner* may deduct from the amount otherwise due to the *Contractor* the difference in value between the work as performed and that called for by the *Contract*

Documents. If the *Owner* and the *Contractor* do not agree on the difference in value, they shall refer the matter to the *Consultant* for a determination.

PART 3 EXECUTION OF THE WORK

GC 3.1 CONTROL OF THE WORK

3.1.1 The *Contractor* shall have total control of the *Work* and shall effectively direct and supervise the *Work* so as to ensure conformity with the *Contract Documents*.

3.1.2 The *Contractor* shall be solely responsible for construction means, methods, techniques, sequences, and procedures and for co-ordinating the various parts of the *Work* under the *Contract*.

GC 3.2 CONSTRUCTION BY OWNER OR OTHER CONTRACTORS

3.2.1 The *Owner* reserves the right to award separate contracts in connection with other parts of the *Project* to other contractors and to perform work with own forces.

3.2.2 When separate contracts are awarded for other parts of the *Project*, or when work is performed by the *Owner*'s own forces, the *Owner* shall:

   .1 provide for the co-ordination of the activities and work of other contractors and *Owner*'s own forces with the *Work* of the *Contract*;

   .2 assume overall responsibility for compliance with the applicable health and construction safety legislation at the *Place of the Work*;

   .3 enter into separate contracts with other contractors under conditions of contract which are compatible with the conditions of the *Contract*;

   .4 ensure that insurance coverage is provided to the same requirements as are called for in GC 11.1 - INSURANCE and co-ordinate such insurance with the insurance coverage of the *Contractor* as it affects the *Work*; and

   .5 take all reasonable precautions to avoid labour disputes or other disputes on the *Project* arising from the work of other contractors or the *Owner*'s own forces.

3.2.3 When separate contracts are awarded for other parts of the *Project*, or when work is performed by the *Owner*'s own forces, the *Contractor* shall:

   .1 afford the *Owner* and other contractors reasonable opportunity to introduce and store their products and use their construction machinery and equipment to execute their work;

   .2 co-ordinate and schedule the *Work* with the work of other contractors and *Owner*'s own forces and connect as specified or shown in the *Contract Documents*;

   .3 participate with other contractors and the *Owner* in reviewing their construction schedules when directed to do so; and

   .4 where part of the *Work* is affected by or depends upon for its proper execution the work of other contractors or *Owner*'s own forces, promptly report to the *Consultant* in writing and prior to proceeding with that part of the *Work*, any apparent deficiencies in such work. Failure by the *Contractor* to so report shall invalidate any claims against the *Owner* by reason of the deficiencies in the work of other contractors or *Owner*'s own forces except those deficiencies not then reasonably discoverable.

3.2.4 Where a change in the *Work* is required as a result of the co-ordination and connection of the work of other contractors or *Owner*'s own forces with the *Work*, the changes shall be authorized and valued as provided in GC 6.1 - CHANGES, GC 6.2 - CHANGE ORDER, and GC 6.3 - CHANGE DIRECTIVE.

3.2.5 Claims, disputes, and other matters in question between the *Contractor* and other contractors shall be dealt with as provided in Part 8 of the General Conditions - DISPUTE RESOLUTION provided the other contractors have reciprocal obligations. The *Contractor* shall be deemed to have consented to arbitration of any dispute with any other contractor whose contract with the *Owner* contains a similar agreement to arbitrate.

GC 3.3 TEMPORARY SUPPORTS, STRUCTURES, AND FACILITIES

3.3.1 The *Contractor* shall have the sole responsibility for the design, erection, operation, maintenance, and removal of temporary supports, structures, and facilities and the design and execution of construction methods required in their use.

3.3.2 The *Contractor* shall engage and pay for registered professional engineering personnel skilled in the appropriate disciplines to perform those functions referred to in paragraph 3.3.1 where required by law or by the *Contract Documents* and in all cases where such temporary supports, structures, and facilities and their method of construction are of such a nature that professional engineering skill is required to produce safe and satisfactory results.

3.3.3 Notwithstanding the provisions of GC 3.1 - CONTROL OF THE WORK, paragraph 3.3.1, and paragraph 3.3.2 or provisions to the contrary elsewhere in the *Contract Documents* where such *Contract Documents* include designs for temporary supports, structures, and facilities or specify a method of construction in whole or in part, such facilities and methods shall be considered to be part of the design of the *Work* and the *Contractor* shall not be held responsible for that part of the design or the specified method of construction. The *Contractor* shall, however, be responsible for the execution of such design or specified method of construction in the same manner as for the execution of the *Work*.

GC 3.4 DOCUMENT REVIEW

3.4.1 The *Contractor* shall review the *Contract Documents* and shall report promptly to the *Consultant* any error, inconsistency, or omission the *Contractor* may discover. Such review by the *Contractor* shall be to the best of the *Contractor*'s knowledge, information, and belief and in making such review the *Contractor* does not assume any responsibility to the *Owner* or the *Consultant* for the accuracy of the review. The *Contractor* shall not be liable for damage or costs resulting from such errors, inconsistencies, or omissions in the *Contract Documents*, which the *Contractor* did not discover. If the *Contractor* does discover any error, inconsistency, or omission in the *Contract Documents*, the *Contractor* shall not proceed with the work affected until the *Contractor* has received corrected or missing information from the *Consultant*.

GC 3.5 CONSTRUCTION SCHEDULE

3.5.1 The *Contractor* shall:

.1 prepare and submit to the *Owner* and the *Consultant* prior to the first application for payment, a construction schedule that indicates the timing of the major activities of the *Work* and provides sufficient detail of the critical events and their inter-relationship to demonstrate the *Work* will be performed in conformity with the *Contract Time*;

219

.2   monitor the progress of the *Work* relative to the construction schedule and update the schedule on a monthly basis or as stipulated by the *Contract Documents*; and

.3   advise the *Consultant* of any revisions required to the schedule as the result of extensions of the *Contract Time* as provided in Part 6 of the General Conditions - CHANGES IN THE WORK.

GC 3.6 CONSTRUCTION SAFETY

3.6.1   Subject to paragraph 3.2.2.2 of GC 3.2 - CONSTRUCTION BY OWNER OR OTHER CONTRACTORS, the *Contractor* shall be solely responsible for construction safety at the *Place of the Work* and for compliance with the rules, regulations, and practices required by the applicable construction health and safety legislation and shall be responsible for initiating, maintaining, and supervising all safety precautions and programs in connection with the performance of the *Work*.

GC 3.7 SUPERVISOR

3.7.1   The *Contractor* shall employ a competent supervisor and necessary assistants who shall be in attendance at the *Place of the Work* while work is being performed. The supervisor shall not be changed except for valid reason.

3.7.2   The supervisor shall represent the *Contractor* at the *Place of the Work* and notices and instructions given to the supervisor by the *Consultant* shall be held to have been received by the *Contractor*.

GC 3.8 SUBCONTRACTORS AND SUPPLIERS

3.8.1   The *Contractor* shall preserve and protect the rights of the parties under the *Contract* with respect to work to be performed under subcontract, and shall:

.1   enter into contracts or written agreements with *Subcontractors* and *Suppliers* to require them to perform their work as provided in the *Contract Documents*;

.2   incorporate the terms and conditions of the *Contract Documents* into all contracts or written agreements with *Subcontractors* and *Suppliers*; and

.3   be as fully responsible to the *Owner* for acts and omissions of *Subcontractors*, *Suppliers*, and of persons directly or indirectly employed by them as for acts and omissions of persons directly employed by the *Contractor*.

3.8.2   The *Contractor* shall indicate in writing, at the request of the *Owner*, those *Subcontractors* or *Suppliers* whose bids have been received by the *Contractor* which the *Contractor* would be prepared to accept for the performance of a portion of the *Work*. Should the *Owner* not object before signing the *Contract*, the *Contractor* shall employ those *Subcontractors* or *Suppliers* so identified by the *Contractor* in writing for the performance of that portion of the *Work* to which their bid applies.

3.8.3   The *Owner* may, for reasonable cause, at any time before the *Owner* has signed the *Contract*, object to the use of a proposed *Subcontractor* or *Supplier* and require the *Contractor* to employ one of the other subcontract bidders.

3.8.4   If the *Owner* requires the *Contractor* to change a proposed *Subcontractor* or *Supplier*, the *Contract Price* and *Contract Time* shall be adjusted by the differences occasioned by such required change.

3.8.5   The *Contractor* shall not be required to employ as a *Subcontractor* or *Supplier*, a person or firm to whom the *Contractor* may reasonably object.

3.8.6   The *Owner*, through the *Consultant*, may provide to a *Subcontractor* or *Supplier* information as to the percentage of the *Subcontractor*'s or *Supplier*'s work which has been certified for payment.

GC 3.9 LABOUR AND PRODUCTS

3.9.1   The *Contractor* shall provide and pay for labour, *Products*, tools, construction machinery and equipment, water, heat, light, power, transportation, and other facilities and services necessary for the performance of the *Work* in accordance with the *Contract*.

3.9.2   *Products* provided shall be new. *Products* which are not specified shall be of a quality consistent with those specified and their use acceptable to the *Consultant*.

3.9.3   The *Contractor* shall maintain good order and discipline among the *Contractor*'s employees engaged on the *Work* and shall not employ on the *Work* anyone not skilled in the tasks assigned.

GC 3.10 DOCUMENTS AT THE SITE

3.10.1   The *Contractor* shall keep one copy of current *Contract Documents*, submittals, reports, and records of meetings at the *Place of the Work*, in good order and available to the *Owner* and the *Consultant*.

GC 3.11 SHOP DRAWINGS

3.11.1   Shop drawings are drawings, diagrams, illustrations, schedules, performance charts, brochures, *Product*, and other data which the *Contractor* provides to illustrate details of a portion of the *Work*.

3.11.2   The *Contractor* shall provide shop drawings as described in the *Contract Documents* or as the *Consultant* may reasonably request.

3.11.3   The *Contractor* shall review all shop drawings prior to submission to the *Consultant*. The *Contractor* represents by this review that: the *Contractor* has determined and verified all field measurements and field construction conditions, or will do so; *Product* requirements; catalogue numbers; and similar data and that the *Contractor* has checked and co-ordinated each shop drawing with the requirements of the *Work* and of the *Contract Documents*. The *Contractor* shall confirm this review of each shop drawing by stamp, date, and signature of the person responsible. At the time of submission the *Contractor* shall notify the *Consultant* in writing of any deviations in the shop drawings from the requirements of the *Contract Documents*.

3.11.4   The *Contractor* shall submit shop drawings to the *Consultant* to review in orderly sequence and sufficiently in advance so as to cause no delay in the *Work* or in the work of other contractors. Upon request of the *Contractor* or the *Consultant*, they jointly shall prepare a schedule of the dates for submission and return of shop drawings. Shop drawings which require approval of any legally constituted authority having jurisdiction shall be submitted to such authority by the *Contractor* for approval.

3.11.5   The *Contractor* shall submit shop drawings in the form specified or as the *Consultant* may direct. The *Consultant* will review and return shop drawings in accordance with the schedule agreed upon, or otherwise with reasonable promptness so as to cause no delay. The *Consultant*'s review is for conformity to the design concept and for general arrangement only. The *Consultant*'s review shall not relieve the *Contractor* of responsibility for errors or omissions in the shop drawings or for meeting all requirements of the *Contract Documents* unless the *Consultant* expressly notes the acceptance of a deviation on the shop drawings.

3.11.6   Upon the *Consultant*'s request, the *Contractor* shall revise and resubmit shop drawings which the *Consultant* rejects as inconsistent with the *Contract Documents* unless otherwise directed by the *Consultant*. The

Contractor shall notify the *Consultant* in writing of any revisions to the resubmission other than those requested by the *Consultant*.

GC 3.12 USE OF THE WORK

3.12.1   The *Contractor* shall confine construction machinery and equipment, storage of *Products*, and operations of employees to limits indicated by laws, ordinances, permits, or the *Contract Documents* and shall not unreasonably encumber the *Work* with *Products*.

3.12.2   The *Contractor* shall not load or permit to be loaded any part of the *Work* with a weight or force that will endanger the safety of the *Work*.

GC 3.13 CUTTING AND REMEDIAL WORK

3.13.1   The *Contractor* shall do the cutting and remedial work required to make the several parts of the *Work* come together properly.

3.13.2   The *Contractor* shall co-ordinate the *Work* to ensure that this requirement is kept to a minimum.

3.13.3   Should the *Owner*, the *Consultant*, other contractors or anyone employed by them be responsible for ill-timed work necessitating cutting or remedial work to be performed, the cost of such cutting or remedial work shall be valued as provided in GC 6.1 - CHANGES, GC 6.2 - CHANGE ORDER, and GC 6.3 - CHANGE DIRECTIVE.

3.13.4   Cutting and remedial work shall be performed by specialists familiar with the *Products* affected and shall be performed in a manner to neither damage nor endanger the *Work*.

GC 3.14 CLEANUP

3.14.1   The *Contractor* shall maintain the *Work* in a tidy condition and free from the accumulation of waste products and debris, other than that caused by the *Owner*, other contractors or their employees.

3.14.2   The *Contractor* shall remove waste products and debris, other than that resulting from the work of the *Owner*, other contractors or their employees, and shall leave the *Work* clean and suitable for occupancy by the *Owner* before attainment of *Substantial Performance of the Work*. The *Contractor* shall remove products, tools, construction machinery, and equipment not required for the performance of the remaining work.

3.14.3   Prior to application for the final certificate for payment, the *Contractor* shall remove products, tools, construction machinery and equipment, and waste products and debris, other than that resulting from the work of the *Owner*, other contractors or their employees.

PART 4 ALLOWANCES

GC 4.1 CASH ALLOWANCES

4.1.1   The *Contract Price* includes cash allowances stated in the *Contract Documents*, which allowances shall be expended as the *Owner* directs through the *Consultant*.

4.1.2   Cash allowances cover the net cost to the *Contractor* of services, *Products*, construction machinery and equipment, freight, unloading, handling, storage, installation, and other authorized expenses incurred in performing the work stipulated under the cash allowances but do not include any *Value Added Taxes* payable by the *Owner* to the *Contractor*.

4.1.3   The *Contract Price*, and not the cash allowances, includes the *Contractor*'s overhead and profit in connection with such cash allowances.

4.1.4   Where costs under a cash allowance exceed the amount of the allowance, the *Contractor* shall be compensated for any excess incurred and substantiated plus an amount for overhead and profit as set out in the *Contract Documents*.

4.1.5   The *Contract Price* shall be adjusted by *Change Order* to provide for any difference between the actual cost and each cash allowance.

4.1.6   The value of the work performed under a cash allowance is eligible to be included in progress payments.

4.1.7   The *Contractor* and the *Consultant* shall jointly prepare a schedule that shows when the *Consultant* and *Owner* must authorize ordering of items called for under cash allowances to avoid delaying the progress of the *Work*.

GC 4.2 CONTINGENCY ALLOWANCE

4.2.1   The *Contract Price* includes the contingency allowance, if any, stated in the *Contract Documents*.

4.2.2   Expenditures under the contingency allowance shall be authorized and valued as provided in GC 6.1 - CHANGES, GC 6.2 - CHANGE ORDER, and GC 6.3 - CHANGE DIRECTIVE.

4.2.3   The *Contract Price* shall be adjusted by *Change Order* to provide for any difference between the expenditures authorized under paragraph 4.2.2 and the contingency allowance.

PART 5 PAYMENT

GC 5.1 FINANCING INFORMATION REQUIRED OF THE OWNER

5.1.1   The *Owner* shall, at the request of the *Contractor*, prior to execution of the Agreement, and/or promptly from time to time thereafter, furnish to the *Contractor* reasonable evidence that financial arrangements have been made to fulfill the *Owner*'s obligations under the *Contract*.

5.1.2   The *Owner* shall notify the *Contractor* in writing of any material change in the *Owner*'s financial arrangements during the performance of the *Contract*.

GC 5.2 APPLICATIONS FOR PROGRESS PAYMENT

5.2.1   Applications for payment on account as provided in Article A-5 of the Agreement - PAYMENT may be made monthly as the *Work* progresses.

5.2.2   Applications for payment shall be dated the last day of the agreed monthly payment period and the amount claimed shall be for the value, proportionate to the amount of the *Contract*, of work performed and *Products* delivered to the *Place of the Work* at that date.

5.2.3   The *Contractor* shall submit to the *Consultant*, at least 14 days before the first application for payment, a schedule of values for the parts of the *Work*, aggregating the total amount of the *Contract Price*, so as to facilitate evaluation of applications for payment.

5.2.4　The schedule of values shall be made out in such form and supported by such evidence as the *Consultant* may reasonably direct and when accepted by the *Consultant*, shall be used as the basis for applications for payment, unless it is found to be in error.

5.2.5　The *Contractor* shall include a statement based on the schedule of values with each application for payment.

5.2.6　Claims for *Products* delivered to the *Place of the Work* but not yet incorporated into the *Work* shall be supported by such evidence as the *Consultant* may reasonably require to establish the value and delivery of the *Products*.

GC 5.3 PROGRESS PAYMENT

5.3.1　The *Consultant* will issue to the *Owner*, no later than 10 days after the receipt of an application for payment from the *Contractor* submitted in accordance with GC 5.2 - APPLICATIONS FOR PROGRESS PAYMENT, a certificate for payment in the amount applied for or in such other amount as the *Consultant* determines to be properly due. If the *Consultant* amends the application, the *Consultant* will promptly notify the *Contractor* in writing giving reasons for the amendment.

5.3.2　The *Owner* shall make payment to the *Contractor* on account as provided in Article A-5 of the Agreement - PAYMENT no later than 5 days after the date of a certificate for payment issued by the *Consultant*.

GC 5.4 SUBSTANTIAL PERFORMANCE OF THE WORK

5.4.1　When the *Contractor* considers that the *Work* is substantially performed, or if permitted by the lien legislation applicable to the *Place of the Work* a designated portion thereof which the *Owner* agrees to accept separately is substantially performed, the *Contractor* shall prepare and submit to the *Consultant* a comprehensive list of items to be completed or corrected and apply for a review by the *Consultant* to establish *Substantial Performance of the Work* or substantial performance of the designated portion of the *Work*. Failure to include an item on the list does not alter the responsibility of the *Contractor* to complete the *Contract*.

5.4.2　No later than 10 days after the receipt of the *Contractor*'s list and application, the *Consultant* will review the *Work* to verify the validity of the application, and no later than 7 days after completing the review, will notify the *Contractor* whether the *Work* or the designated portion of the *Work* is substantially performed.

5.4.3　The *Consultant* shall state the date of *Substantial Performance of the Work* or designated portion of the *Work* in a certificate.

5.4.4　Immediately following the issuance of the certificate of *Substantial Performance of the Work*, the *Contractor*, in consultation with the *Consultant*, will establish a reasonable date for finishing the *Work*.

GC 5.5 PAYMENT OF HOLDBACK UPON SUBSTANTIAL PERFORMANCE OF THE WORK

5.5.1　After the issuance of the certificate of *Substantial Performance of the Work*, the *Contractor* shall:

　.1　submit an application for payment of the holdback amount,

　.2　submit a sworn statement that all accounts for labour, subcontracts, *Products*, construction machinery and equipment, and other indebtedness which may have been incurred by the *Contractor* in the *Substantial Performance of the Work* and for which the *Owner* might in any way be held responsible have been paid in full, except for amounts properly retained as a holdback or as an identified amount in dispute.

5.5.2   After the receipt of an application for payment from the *Contractor* and the sworn statement as provided in paragraph 5.5.1, the *Consultant* will issue a certificate for payment of the holdback amount.

5.5.3   Where the holdback amount has not been placed in a separate holdback account, the *Owner* shall, 10 days prior to the expiry of the holdback period stipulated in the lien legislation applicable to the *Place of the Work*, place the holdback amount in a bank account in the joint names of the *Owner* and the *Contractor*.

5.5.4   The holdback amount authorized by the certificate for payment of the holdback amount is due and payable on the day following the expiration of the holdback period stipulated in the lien legislation applicable to the *Place of the Work*. Where lien legislation does not exist or apply, the holdback amount shall be due and payable in accordance with other legislation, industry practice, or provisions which may be agreed to between the parties. The *Owner* may retain out of the holdback amount any sums required by law to satisfy any liens against the *Work* or, if permitted by the lien legislation applicable to the *Place of the Work*, other third party monetary claims against the *Contractor* which are enforceable against the *Owner*.

GC 5.6 PROGRESSIVE RELEASE OF HOLDBACK

5.6.1   Where legislation permits and where, upon application by the *Contractor*, the *Consultant* has certified that the work of a *Subcontractor* or *Supplier* has been performed prior to *Substantial Performance of the Work*, the *Owner* shall pay the *Contractor* the holdback amount retained for such subcontract work, or the *Products* supplied by such *Supplier*, on the day following the expiration of the holdback period for such work stipulated in the lien legislation applicable to the *Place of the Work*.

5.6.2   Notwithstanding the provisions of the preceding paragraph, and notwithstanding the wording of such certificates, the *Contractor* shall ensure that such subcontract work or *Products* is protected pending the issuance of a final certificate for payment and be responsible for the correction of defects or work not performed regardless of whether or not such was apparent when such certificates were issued.

GC 5.7 FINAL PAYMENT

5.7.1   When the *Contractor* considers that the *Work* is completed, the *Contractor* shall submit an application for final payment.

5.7.2   The *Consultant* will, no later than 10 days after the receipt of an application from the *Contractor* for final payment, review the *Work* to verify the validity of the application. The *Consultant* will, no later than 7 days after reviewing the *Work*, notify the *Contractor* that the application is valid or give reasons why it is not valid.

5.7.3   When the *Consultant* finds the *Contractor*'s application for final payment valid, the *Consultant* will issue a final certificate for payment.

5.7.4   Subject to the provision of paragraph 10.4.1 of GC 10.4 - WORKERS' COMPENSATION, and any lien legislation applicable to the *Place of the Work*, the *Owner* shall, no later than 5 days after the issuance of a final certificate for payment, pay the *Contractor* as provided in Article A-5 of the Agreement - PAYMENT.

GC 5.8 WITHHOLDING OF PAYMENT

5.8.1   If because of climatic or other conditions reasonably beyond the control of the *Contractor*, there are items of work that cannot be performed, payment in full for that portion of the *Work* which has been performed as certified by the *Consultant* shall not be withheld or delayed by the *Owner* on account thereof, but the *Owner* may withhold, until the remaining portion of the *Work* is finished, only such an amount that the *Consultant* determines is sufficient and reasonable to cover the cost of performing such remaining work.

GC 5.9 NON-CONFORMING WORK

5.9.1 No payment by the *Owner* under the *Contract* nor partial or entire use or occupancy of the *Work* by the *Owner* shall constitute an acceptance of any portion of the *Work* or *Products* which are not in accordance with the requirements of the *Contract Documents*.

PART 6 CHANGES IN THE WORK

GC 6.1 CHANGES

6.1.1 The *Owner*, through the *Consultant*, without invalidating the *Contract*, may make changes in the *Work* consisting of additions, deletions, or other revisions to the *Work* by *Change Order* or *Change Directive*.

6.1.2 The *Contractor* shall not perform a change in the *Work* without a *Change Order* or a *Change Directive*.

GC 6.2 CHANGE ORDER

6.2.1 When a change in the *Work* is proposed or required, the *Consultant* shall provide a notice describing the proposed change in the *Work* to the *Contractor*. The *Contractor* shall present, in a form acceptable to the *Consultant*, a method of adjustment or an amount of adjustment for the *Contract Price*, if any, and the adjustment in the *Contract Time*, if any, for the proposed change in the *Work*.

6.2.2 When the *Owner* and the *Contractor* agree to the adjustments in the *Contract Price* and *Contract Time* or to the method to be used to determine the adjustments, such agreement shall be effective immediately and shall be recorded in a *Change Order*, signed by *Owner* and *Contractor*. The value of the work performed as the result of a *Change Order* shall be included in applications for progress payment.

GC 6.3 CHANGE DIRECTIVE

6.3.1 If the *Owner* requires the *Contractor* to proceed with a change in the *Work* prior to the *Owner* and the *Contractor* agreeing upon the adjustment in *Contract Price* and *Contract Time*, the *Owner*, through the *Consultant*, shall issue a *Change Directive*.

6.3.2 Upon receipt of a *Change Directive*, the *Contractor* shall proceed promptly with the change in the *Work*. The adjustment in the *Contract Price* for a change carried out by way of a *Change Directive* shall be determined on the basis of the cost of expenditures and savings to perform the work attributable to the change. If a change in the *Work* results in a net increase in the *Contract Price*, an allowance for overhead and profit shall be included.

6.3.3 If a change in the *Work* results in a net decrease in the *Contract Price*, the amount of the credit shall be the net cost, without deduction for overhead or profit. When both additions and deletions covering related work or substitutions are involved in a change in the *Work*, the allowance for overhead and profit shall be calculated on the basis of the net increase, if any, with respect to that change in the *Work*.

6.3.4 The *Contractor* shall keep and present, in such form as the *Consultant* may require, an itemized accounting of the cost of expenditures and savings referred to in paragraph 6.3.2 together with supporting data. The cost of performing the work attributable to the *Change Directive* shall be limited to the actual cost of all of the following:

.1 wages and benefits paid for labour in the direct employ of the *Contractor* under applicable collective bargaining agreements, or under a salary or wage schedule agreed upon by the *Owner* and *Contractor*;

.2   salaries, wages, and benefits of the *Contractor*'s office personnel engaged in a technical capacity and other personnel at shops or on the road, engaged in expediting the production or transportation of materials or equipment;

.3   contributions, assessments, or taxes incurred for such items as unemployment insurance, provincial health insurance, workers' compensation, and Canada or Quebec Pension Plan, insofar as such cost is based on wages, salaries, or other remuneration paid to employees of the *Contractor* and included in the cost of the work as provided in paragraphs 6.3.4.1 and 6.3.4.2;

.4   travel and subsistence expenses of the *Contractor*'s personnel described in paragraphs 6.3.4.1 and 6.3.4.2;

.5   the cost of all *Products* including cost of transportation thereof;

.6   the cost of materials, supplies, equipment, temporary services and facilities, and hand tools not owned by the workers, including transportation and maintenance thereof, which are consumed; and cost less salvage value on such items used but not consumed, which remain the property of the *Contractor*;

.7   rental cost of all tools, machinery, and equipment, exclusive of hand tools, whether rented from or provided by the *Contractor* or others, including installation, minor repairs and replacements, dismantling, removal, transportation and delivery cost thereof;

.8   deposits lost;

.9   the amounts of all subcontracts;

.10   the cost of quality assurance such as independent inspection and testing services;

.11   charges levied by authorities having jurisdiction at the *Place of the Work*;

.12   royalties, patent license fees, and damages for infringement of patents and cost of defending suits therefor subject always to the *Contractor*'s obligations to indemnify the *Owner* as provided in paragraph 10.3.1 of GC 10.3 - PATENT FEES;

.13   any adjustment in premiums for all bonds and insurance which the *Contractor* is required, by the *Contract Documents*, to purchase and maintain;

.14   any adjustment in taxes and duties for which the *Contractor* is liable;

.15   charges for long distance telephone and facsimile communications, courier services, expressage, and petty cash items incurred;

.16   the cost of removal and disposal of waste products and debris;

.17   cost incurred due to emergencies affecting the safety of persons or property;

6.3.5   Pending determination of the final amount of a *Change Directive*, the undisputed value of the work performed as the result of a *Change Directive* is eligible to be included in progress payments.

6.3.6   If the *Owner* and *Contractor* do not agree on the proposed adjustment in the *Contract Time* or the method of determining it, the adjustment shall be referred to the *Consultant* for determination.

6.3.7   If at any time after the start of the work directed by a *Change Directive*, the *Owner* and the *Contractor* reach agreement on the adjustment to the *Contract Price* and to the *Contract Time*, this agreement shall be recorded in a *Change Order* signed by *Owner* and *Contractor*.

227

GC 6.4 CONCEALED OR UNKNOWN CONDITIONS

6.4.1   If the *Owner* or the *Contractor* discover conditions at the *Place of the Work* which are:

    .1   subsurface or otherwise concealed physical conditions which existed before the commencement of the *Work* which differ materially from those indicated in the *Contract Documents*; or

    .2   physical conditions of a nature which differ materially from those ordinarily found to exist and generally recognized as inherent in construction activities of the character provided for in the *Contract Documents*;

then the observing party shall notify the other party in writing before conditions are disturbed and in no event later than 5 *Working Days* after first observance of the conditions.

6.4.2   The *Consultant* will promptly investigate such conditions and make a finding. If the finding is that the conditions differ materially and this would cause an increase or decrease in the *Contractor*'s cost or time to perform the *Work*, the *Consultant*, with the *Owner*'s approval, shall issue appropriate instructions for a change in the *Work* as provided in GC 6.2 - CHANGE ORDER or GC 6.3 - CHANGE DIRECTIVE.

6.4.3   If the *Consultant* finds that the conditions at the *Place of the Work* are not materially different or that no change in the *Contract Price* or the *Contract Time* is justified, the *Consultant* shall report the reasons for this finding to the *Owner* and the *Contractor* in writing.

GC 6.5 DELAYS

6.5.1   If the *Contractor* is delayed in the performance of the *Work* by an action or omission of the *Owner*, *Consultant*, or anyone employed or engaged by them directly or indirectly, contrary to the provisions of the *Contract Documents*, then the *Contract Time* shall be extended for such reasonable time as the *Consultant* may recommend in consultation with the *Contractor*. The *Contractor* shall be reimbursed by the *Owner* for reasonable costs incurred by the *Contractor* as the result of such delay.

6.5.2   If the *Contractor* is delayed in the performance of the *Work* by a stop work order issued by a court or other public authority and providing that such order was not issued as the result of an act or fault of the *Contractor* or any person employed or engaged by the *Contractor* directly or indirectly, then the *Contract Time* shall be extended for such reasonable time as the *Consultant* may recommend in consultation with the *Contractor*. The *Contractor* shall be reimbursed by the *Owner* for reasonable costs incurred by the *Contractor* as the result of such delay.

6.5.3   If the *Contractor* is delayed in the performance of the *Work* by labour disputes, strikes, lock-outs (including lock-outs decreed or recommended for its members by a recognized contractors' association, of which the *Contractor* is a member or to which the *Contractor* is otherwise bound), fire, unusual delay by common carriers or unavoidable casualties, or without limit to any of the foregoing, by a cause beyond the *Contractor*'s control, then the *Contract Time* shall be extended for such reasonable time as the *Consultant* may recommend in consultation with the *Contractor*. The extension of time shall not be less than the time lost as the result of the event causing the delay, unless the *Contractor* agrees to a shorter extension. The *Contractor* shall not be entitled to payment for costs incurred by such delays unless such delays result from actions by the *Owner*.

6.5.4   No extension shall be made for delay unless notice in writing of claim is given to the *Consultant* not later than 10 *Working Days* after the commencement of delay, providing however, that in the case of a continuing cause of delay only one notice of claim shall be necessary.

6.5.5   If no schedule is made under paragraph 2.2.9 of GC 2.2 - ROLE OF THE CONSULTANT, no claim for delay shall be allowed because of failure of the *Consultant* to furnish instructions until 10 *Working Days* after demand for such instructions has been made and not then, unless the claim is reasonable.

PART 7 DEFAULT NOTICE

GC 7.1 OWNER'S RIGHT TO PERFORM THE WORK, STOP THE WORK, OR TERMINATE THE CONTRACT

7.1.1   If the *Contractor* should be adjudged bankrupt, or makes a general assignment for the benefit of creditors because of the *Contractor*'s insolvency, or if a receiver is appointed because of the *Contractor*'s insolvency, the *Owner* may, without prejudice to any other right or remedy the *Owner* may have, by giving the *Contractor* or receiver or trustee in bankruptcy notice in writing, terminate the *Contract*.

7.1.2   If the *Contractor* should neglect to prosecute the *Work* properly or otherwise fails to comply with the requirements of the *Contract* to a substantial degree and if the *Consultant* has given a written statement to the *Owner* and *Contractor* that sufficient cause exists to justify such action, the *Owner* may, without prejudice to any other right or remedy the *Owner* may have, notify the *Contractor* in writing that the *Contractor* is in default of the *Contractor*'s contractual obligations and instruct the *Contractor* to correct the default in the 5 *Working Days* immediately following the receipt of such notice.

7.1.3   If the default cannot be corrected in the 5 *Working Days* specified, the *Contractor* shall be in compliance with the *Owner*'s instructions if the *Contractor*:

   .1   commences the correction of the default within the specified time, and

   .2   provides the *Owner* with an acceptable schedule for such correction, and

   .3   corrects the default in accordance with such schedule.

7.1.4   If the *Contractor* fails to correct the default in the time specified or subsequently agreed upon, without prejudice to any other right or remedy the *Owner* may have, the *Owner* may:

   .1   correct such default and deduct the cost thereof from any payment then or thereafter due the *Contractor* provided the *Consultant* has certified such cost to the *Owner* and the *Contractor*, or

   .2   terminate the *Contractor*'s right to continue with the *Work* in whole or in part or terminate the *Contract*.

7.1.5   If the *Owner* terminates the *Contractor*'s right to continue with the *Work* as provided in paragraphs 7.1.1 and 7.1.4, the *Owner* shall be entitled to:

   .1   take possession of the *Work* and *Products*; utilize the construction machinery and equipment; subject to the rights of third parties, finish the *Work* by whatever method the *Owner* may consider expedient, but without undue delay or expense; and

   .2   withhold further payment to the *Contractor* until a final certificate for payment is issued; and

   .3   charge the *Contractor* the amount by which the full cost of finishing the *Work* as certified by the *Consultant*, including compensation to the *Consultant* for the *Consultant*'s additional services and a reasonable allowance as determined by the *Consultant* to cover the cost of corrections to work performed by the *Contractor* that may be required under GC 12.3 - WARRANTY, exceeds the unpaid balance of the *Contract Price*; however, if such cost of finishing the *Work* is less than the unpaid balance of the *Contract Price*, the *Owner* shall pay the *Contractor* the difference; and

   .4   on expiry of the warranty period, charge the *Contractor* the amount by which the cost of corrections to the *Contractor*'s work under GC 12.3 - WARRANTY exceeds the allowance provided for such corrections, or if the cost of such corrections is less than the allowance, pay the *Contractor* the difference.

7.1.6   The *Contractor*'s obligation under the *Contract* as to quality, correction, and warranty of the work performed by the *Contractor* up to the time of termination shall continue in force after such termination.

GC 7.2 CONTRACTOR'S RIGHT TO STOP THE WORK OR TERMINATE THE CONTRACT

7.2.1   If the *Owner* should be adjudged bankrupt, or makes a general assignment for the benefit of creditors because of the *Owner*'s insolvency, or if a receiver is appointed because of the *Owner*'s insolvency, the *Contractor* may, without prejudice to any other right or remedy the *Contractor* may have, by giving the *Owner* or receiver or trustee in bankruptcy notice in writing, terminate the *Contract*.

7.2.2   If the *Work* should be stopped or otherwise delayed for a period of 30 days or more under an order of a court or other public authority and providing that such order was not issued as the result of an act or fault of the *Contractor* or of anyone directly or indirectly employed or engaged by the *Contractor*, the *Contractor* may, without prejudice to any other right or remedy the *Contractor* may have, by giving the *Owner* notice in writing, terminate the *Contract*.

7.2.3   The *Contractor* may notify the *Owner* in writing, with a copy to the *Consultant*, that the *Owner* is in default of the *Owner*'s contractual obligations if:

    .1   the *Owner* fails to furnish, when so requested by the *Contractor*, reasonable evidence that financial arrangements have been made to fulfill the *Owner*'s obligations under the *Contract*, or

    .2   the *Consultant* fails to issue a certificate as provided in GC 5.3 PROGRESS PAYMENT, or

    .3   the *Owner* fails to pay the *Contractor* when due the amounts certified by the *Consultant* or awarded by arbitration or court, or

    .4   the *Owner* violates the requirements of the *Contract* to a substantial degree and the *Consultant*, except for GC 5.1 - FINANCING INFORMATION REQUIRED OF THE OWNER, confirms by written statement to the *Contractor* that sufficient cause exists.

7.2.4   The *Contractor*'s notice in writing to the *Owner* provided under paragraph 7.2.3 shall advise that if the default is not corrected within 5 *Working Days* following the receipt of the notice in writing, the *Contractor* may, without prejudice to any other right or remedy the *Contractor* may have, stop the *Work* or terminate the *Contract*.

7.2.5   If the *Contractor* terminates the *Contract* under the conditions set out above, the *Contractor* shall be entitled to be paid for all work performed including reasonable profit, for loss sustained upon *Products* and construction machinery and equipment, and such other damages as the *Contractor* may have sustained as a result of the termination of the *Contract*.

PART 8   DISPUTE RESOLUTION

GC 8.1 AUTHORITY OF THE CONSULTANT

8.1.1   Differences between the parties to the *Contract* as to the interpretation, application or administration of the *Contract* or any failure to agree where agreement between the parties is called for, herein collectively called disputes, which are not resolved in the first instance by findings of the *Consultant* as provided in GC 2.2 - ROLE OF THE CONSULTANT, shall be settled in accordance with the requirements of Part 8 of the General Conditions - DISPUTE RESOLUTION.

8.1.2   If a dispute arises under the *Contract* in respect of a matter in which the *Consultant* has no authority under the *Contract* to make a finding, the procedures set out in paragraph 8.1.3 and paragraphs 8.2.3 to 8.2.8 of

GC 8.2 - NEGOTIATION, MEDIATION, AND ARBITRATION, and in GC 8.3 - RETENTION OF RIGHTS apply to that dispute with the necessary changes to detail as may be required.

8.1.3   If a dispute is not resolved promptly, the *Consultant* shall give such instructions as in the *Consultant*'s opinion are necessary for the proper performance of the *Work* and to prevent delays pending settlement of the dispute. The parties shall act immediately according to such instructions, it being understood that by so doing neither party will jeopardize any claim the party may have. If it is subsequently determined that such instructions were in error or at variance with the *Contract Documents*, the *Owner* shall pay the *Contractor* costs incurred by the *Contractor* in carrying out such instructions which the *Contractor* was required to do beyond what the *Contract Documents* correctly understood and interpreted would have required, including costs resulting from interruption of the *Work*.

GC 8.2 NEGOTIATION, MEDIATION, AND ARBITRATION

8.2.1   In accordance with the latest edition of the Rules for Mediation of CCDC 2 Construction Disputes, the parties shall appoint a Project Mediator

     .1   within 30 days after the *Contract* was awarded, or

     .2   if the parties neglected to make an appointment within the 30 day period, within 15 days after either party by notice in writing requests that the Project Mediator be appointed.

8.2.2   A party shall be conclusively deemed to have accepted a finding of the *Consultant* under GC 2.2 - ROLE OF THE CONSULTANT and to have expressly waived and released the other party from any claims in respect of the particular matter dealt with in that finding unless, within 15 *Working Days* after receipt of that finding, the party sends a notice in writing of dispute to the other party and to the *Consultant*, which contains the particulars of the matter in dispute and the relevant provisions of the *Contract Documents*. The responding party shall send a notice in writing of reply to the dispute within 10 *Working Days* after receipt of the notice of dispute setting out particulars of this response and any relevant provisions of the *Contract Documents*.

8.2.3   The parties shall make all reasonable efforts to resolve their dispute by amicable negotiations and agree to provide, without prejudice, frank, candid and timely disclosure of relevant facts, information, and documents to facilitate these negotiations.

8.2.4   After a period of 10 *Working Days* following receipt of a responding party's notice in writing of reply under paragraph 8.2.2, the parties shall request the Project Mediator to assist the parties to reach agreement on any unresolved dispute. The mediated negotiations shall be conducted in accordance with the latest edition of the Rules for Mediation of CCDC 2 Construction Disputes.

8.2.5   If the dispute has not been resolved within 10 *Working Days* after the Project Mediator was requested under paragraph 8.2.4 or within such further period agreed by the parties, the Project Mediator shall terminate the mediated negotiations by giving notice in writing to both parties.

8.2.6   By giving a notice in writing to the other party, not later than 10 *Working Days* after the date of termination of the mediated negotiations under paragraph 8.2.5, either party may refer the dispute to be finally resolved by arbitration under the latest edition of the Rules for Arbitration of CCDC 2 Construction Disputes. The arbitration shall be conducted in the jurisdiction of the *Place of the Work*.

8.2.7   On expiration of the 10 *Working Days*, the arbitration agreement under paragraph 8.2.6 is not binding on the parties and, if a notice is not given under paragraph 8.2.6 within the required time, the parties may refer the unresolved dispute to the courts or to any other form of dispute resolution, including arbitration, which they have agreed to use.

8.2.8   If neither party requires by notice in writing given within 10 *Working Days* of the date of notice requesting arbitration in paragraph 8.2.6 that a dispute be arbitrated immediately, all disputes referred to arbitration as provided in paragraph 8.2.6 shall be

    .1   held in abeyance until
        (1)   *Substantial Performance of the Work*,
        (2)   the *Contract* has been terminated, or
        (3)   the *Contractor* has abandoned the *Work*,
       whichever is earlier, and

    .2   consolidated into a single arbitration under the rules governing the arbitration under paragraph 8.2.6.

GC 8.3 RETENTION OF RIGHTS

8.3.1   It is agreed that no act by either party shall be construed as a renunciation or waiver of any rights or recourses, provided the party has given the notices required under Part 8 of the General Conditions - DISPUTE RESOLUTION and has carried out the instructions as provided in paragraph 8.1.3.

8.3.2   Nothing in Part 8 of the General Conditions - DISPUTE RESOLUTION shall be construed in any way to limit a party from asserting any statutory right to a lien under applicable lien legislation of the jurisdiction of the *Place of the Work* and the assertion of such right by initiating judicial proceedings is not to be construed as a waiver of any right that party may have under paragraph 8.2.6 to proceed by way of arbitration to adjudicate the merits of the claim upon which such a lien is based.

PART 9 PROTECTION OF PERSONS AND PROPERTY

GC 9.1 PROTECTION OF WORK AND PROPERTY

9.1.1   The *Contractor* shall protect the *Work* and the *Owner*'s property and property adjacent to the *Place of the Work* from damage which may arise as the result of the *Contractor*'s operations under the *Contract*, and shall be responsible for such damage, except damage which occurs as the result of:

    .1   errors in the *Contract Documents*;

    .2   acts or omissions by the *Owner*, the *Consultant*, other contractors, their agents and employees.

9.1.2   Should the *Contractor* in the performance of the *Contract* damage the *Work*, the *Owner*'s property, or property adjacent to the *Place of the Work*, the *Contractor* shall be responsible for the making good such damage at the *Contractor*'s expense.

9.1.3   Should damage occur to the *Work* or *Owner*'s property for which the *Contractor* is not responsible, as provided in paragraph 9.1.1, the *Contractor* shall make good such damage to the *Work* and, if the *Owner* so directs, to the *Owner*'s property. The *Contract Price* and *Contract Time* shall be adjusted as provided in GC 6.1 - CHANGES, GC 6.2 - CHANGE ORDER, and GC 6.3 - CHANGE DIRECTIVE.

GC 9.2 DAMAGES AND MUTUAL RESPONSIBILITY

9.2.1   If either party to the *Contract* should suffer damage in any manner because of any wrongful act or neglect of the other party or of anyone for whom the other party is responsible in law, then that party shall be reimbursed by the other party for such damage. The reimbursing party shall be subrogated to the rights of the other party in respect of such wrongful act or neglect if it be that of a third party.

9.2.2 Claims for damage under paragraph 9.2.1 shall be made in writing to the party liable within reasonable time after the first observance of such damage and if undisputed shall be confirmed by *Change Order*. Disputed claims shall be resolved as set out in Part 8 of the General Conditions - DISPUTE RESOLUTION.

9.2.3 If the *Contractor* has caused damage to the work of another contractor on the *Project*, the *Contractor* agrees upon due notice to settle with the other contractor by negotiation or arbitration. If the other contractor makes a claim against the *Owner* on account of damage alleged to have been so sustained, the *Owner* shall notify the *Contractor* and may require the *Contractor* to defend the action at the *Contractor*'s expense. The *Contractor* shall satisfy a final order or judgment against the *Owner* and pay the costs incurred by the *Owner* arising from such action.

9.2.4 If the *Contractor* becomes liable to pay or satisfy a final order, judgment, or award against the *Owner*, then the *Contractor*, upon undertaking to indemnify the *Owner* against any and all liability for costs, shall have the right to appeal in the name of the *Owner* such final order or judgment to any and all courts of competent jurisdiction.

GC 9.3 TOXIC AND HAZARDOUS SUBSTANCES AND MATERIALS

9.3.1 For the purposes of applicable environmental legislation, the *Owner* shall be deemed to have control and management of the *Place of the Work* with respect to existing conditions.

9.3.2 Prior to the *Contractor* commencing the *Work*, the *Owner* shall

.1 take all reasonable steps to determine whether any toxic or hazardous substances or materials are present at the *Place of the Work*, and

.2 provide the *Consultant* and the *Contractor* with a written list of any such substances and materials.

9.3.3 The *Owner* shall take all reasonable steps to ensure that no person suffers injury, sickness, or death and that no property is injured or destroyed as a result of exposure to, or the presence of, toxic or hazardous substances or materials which were at the *Place of the Work* prior to the *Contractor* commencing the *Work*.

9.3.4 Unless the *Contract* expressly provides otherwise, the *Owner* shall be responsible for taking all necessary steps, in accordance with legal requirements, to dispose of, store or otherwise render harmless toxic or hazardous substances or materials which were present at the *Place of the Work* prior to the *Contractor* commencing the *Work*.

9.3.5 If the *Contractor*

.1 encounters toxic or hazardous substances or materials at the *Place of the Work*, or

.2 has reasonable grounds to believe that toxic or hazardous substances or materials are present at the *Place of the Work*,

which were not disclosed by the *Owner*, as required under paragraph 9.3.2, or which were disclosed but have not been dealt with as required under paragraph 9.3.4, the *Contractor* shall

.3 take all reasonable steps, including stopping the *Work*, to ensure that no person suffers injury, sickness, or death and that no property is injured or destroyed as a result of exposure to or the presence of the substances or materials, and

.4 immediately report the circumstances to the *Consultant* and the *Owner* in writing.

9.3.6   If the *Contractor* is delayed in performing the *Work* or incurs additional costs as a result of taking steps required under paragraph 9.3.5.3, the *Contract Time* shall be extended for such reasonable time as the *Consultant* may recommend in consultation with the *Contractor* and the *Contractor* shall be reimbursed for reasonable costs incurred as a result of the delay and as a result of taking those steps.

9.3.7   Notwithstanding paragraphs 2.2.6 and 2.2.7 of GC 2.2 - ROLE OF THE CONSULTANT, or paragraph 8.1.1 of GC 8.1 - AUTHORITY OF THE CONSULTANT, the *Consultant* may select and rely upon the advice of an independent expert in a dispute under paragraph 9.3.6 and, in that case, the expert shall be deemed to have been jointly retained by the *Owner* and the *Contractor* and shall be jointly paid by them.

9.3.8   The *Owner* shall indemnify and hold harmless the *Contractor*, the *Consultant*, their agents and employees, from and against claims, demands, losses, costs, damages, actions, suits, or proceedings arising out of or resulting from exposure to, or the presence of, toxic or hazardous substances or materials which were at the *Place of the Work* prior to the *Contractor* commencing the *Work*. This obligation shall not be construed to negate, abridge, or reduce other rights or obligations of indemnity set out in GC 12.1 - INDEMNIFICATION or which otherwise exist respecting a person or party described in this paragraph.

9.3.9   GC 9.3 - TOXIC AND HAZARDOUS SUBSTANCES AND MATERIALS shall govern over the provisions of paragraph 1.3.1 of GC 1.3 - RIGHTS AND REMEDIES or GC 9.2 - DAMAGES AND MUTUAL RESPONSIBILITY.

PART 10   GOVERNING REGULATIONS

GC 10.1   TAXES AND DUTIES

10.1.1   The *Contract Price* shall include all taxes and customs duties in effect at the time of the bid closing except for *Value Added Taxes* payable by the *Owner* to the *Contractor* as stipulated in Article A-4 of the Agreement - CONTRACT PRICE.

10.1.2   Any increase or decrease in costs to the *Contractor* due to changes in such included taxes and duties after the time of the bid closing shall increase or decrease the *Contract Price* accordingly.

GC 10.2   LAWS, NOTICES, PERMITS, AND FEES

10.2.1   The laws of the *Place of the Work* shall govern the *Work*.

10.2.2   The *Owner* shall obtain and pay for the building permit, permanent easements, and rights of servitude. The *Contractor* shall be responsible for permits, licenses, or certificates necessary for the performance of the *Work* which were in force at the date of bid closing.

10.2.3   The *Contractor* shall give the required notices and comply with the laws, ordinances, rules, regulations, or codes which are or become in force during the performance of the *Work* and which relate to the *Work*, to the preservation of the public health, and to construction safety.

10.2.4   The *Contractor* shall not be responsible for verifying that the *Contract Documents* are in compliance with the applicable laws, ordinances, rules, regulations, or codes relating to the *Work*. If the *Contract Documents* are at variance therewith, or if, subsequent to the date of bid closing, changes are made to the applicable laws, ordinances, rules, regulations, or codes which require modification to the *Contract Documents*, the *Contractor* shall notify the *Consultant* in writing requesting direction immediately upon such variance or change becoming known. The *Consultant* will make the changes required to the *Contract Documents* as provided in GC 6.1 - CHANGES, GC 6.2 - CHANGE ORDER, and GC 6.3 - CHANGE DIRECTIVE.

10.2.5 If the *Contractor* fails to notify the *Consultant* in writing; and fails to obtain direction as required in paragraph 10.2.4; and performs work knowing it to be contrary to any laws, ordinances, rules, regulations, or codes; the *Contractor* shall be responsible for and shall correct the violations thereof; and shall bear the costs, expenses, and damages attributable to the failure to comply with the provisions of such laws, ordinances, rules, regulations, or codes.

GC 10.3 PATENT FEES

10.3.1 The *Contractor* shall pay the royalties and patent licence fees required for the performance of the *Contract*. The *Contractor* shall hold the *Owner* harmless from and against claims, demands, losses, costs, damages, actions, suits, or proceedings arising out of the *Contractor*'s performance of the *Contract* which are attributable to an infringement or an alleged infringement of a patent of invention by the *Contractor* or anyone for whose acts the *Contractor* may be liable.

10.3.2 The *Owner* shall hold the *Contractor* harmless against claims, demands, losses, costs, damages, actions, suits, or proceedings arising out of the *Contractor*'s performance of the *Contract* which are attributable to an infringement or an alleged infringement of a patent of invention in executing anything for the purpose of the *Contract*, the model, plan, or design of which was supplied to the *Contractor* as part of the *Contract Documents*.

GC 10.4 WORKERS' COMPENSATION

10.4.1 Prior to commencing the *Work*, *Substantial Performance of the Work*, and the issuance of the final certificate for payment, the *Contractor* shall provide evidence of compliance with workers' compensation legislation at the *Place of the Work*, including payments due thereunder.

10.4.2 At any time during the term of the *Contract*, when requested by the *Owner*, the *Contractor* shall provide such evidence of compliance by the *Contractor* and *Subcontractors*.

PART 11 INSURANCE — BONDS

GC 11.1 INSURANCE

11.1.1 Without restricting the generality of GC 12.1 - INDEMNIFICATION, the *Contractor* shall provide, maintain, and pay for the insurance coverages specified in GC 11.1 - INSURANCE. Unless otherwise stipulated, the duration of each insurance policy shall be from the date of commencement of the *Work* until the date of the final certificate for payment. Prior to commencement of the *Work* and upon the placement, renewal, amendment, or extension of all or any part of the insurance, the *Contractor* shall promptly provide the *Owner* with confirmation of coverage and, if required, a certified true copy of the policies certified by an authorized representative of the insurer together with copies of any amending endorsements.

.1 **General Liability Insurance:**

General liability insurance shall be in the joint names of the *Contractor*, the *Owner*, and the *Consultant*, with limits of not less than $2,000,000 per occurrence and with a property damage deductible not exceeding $2,500. The insurance coverage shall not be less than the insurance required by IBC Form 2100, or its equivalent replacement, provided that IBC Form 2100 shall contain the latest edition of the relevant CCDC endorsement form. To achieve the desired limit, umbrella, or excess liability insurance may be used. All liability coverage shall be maintained for completed operations hazards from the date of *Substantial Performance of the Work*, as set out in the certificate of *Substantial Performance of the Work*, on an ongoing basis for a period of 6 years following *Substantial Performance of the Work*. Where the *Contractor* maintains a single, blanket policy, the addition of the *Owner* and the *Consultant* is limited to liability arising out of the *Project* and all operations necessary or incidental thereto. The policy shall be endorsed to provide the *Owner* with not less than 30 days notice in writing in advance of any cancellation, and of change or amendment restricting coverage.

.2   Automobile Liability Insurance:

Automobile liability insurance in respect of licensed vehicles shall have limits of not less than $2,000,000 inclusive per occurrence for bodily injury, death, and damage to property, covering all licensed vehicles owned or leased by the *Contractor*, and endorsed to provide the *Owner* with not less than 15 days notice in writing in advance of any cancellation, change or amendment restricting coverage. Where the policy has been issued pursuant to a government-operated automobile insurance system, the *Contractor* shall provide the *Owner* with confirmation of automobile insurance coverage for all automobiles registered in the name of the *Contractor*.

.3   Aircraft and Watercraft Liability Insurance:

Aircraft and watercraft liability insurance with respect to owned or non-owned aircraft and watercraft if used directly or indirectly in the performance of the *Work*, including use of additional premises, shall be subject to limits of not less than $2,000,000 inclusive per occurrence for bodily injury, death, and damage to property including loss of use thereof and limits of not less than $2,000,000 for aircraft passenger hazard. Such insurance shall be in a form acceptable to the *Owner*. The policies shall be endorsed to provide the *Owner* with not less than 15 days notice in writing in advance of cancellation, change, or amendment restricting coverage.

.4   Property and Boiler and Machinery Insurance:

(1)   "All risks" property insurance shall be in the joint names of the *Contractor*, the *Owner*, and the *Consultant*, insuring not less than the sum of the amount of the *Contract Price* and the full value, as stated in the Supplementary Conditions, of *Products* that are specified to be provided by the *Owner* for incorporation into the *Work*, with a deductible not exceeding $2,500. The insurance coverage shall not be less than the insurance required by IBC Form 4042 or its equivalent replacement, provided that IBC Form 4042 shall contain the latest edition of the relevant CCDC endorsement form. The coverage shall be maintained continuously until 10 days after the date of the final certificate for payment.

(2)   Boiler and machinery insurance shall be in the joint names of the *Contractor*, the *Owner*, and the *Consultant* for not less than the replacement value of the boilers, pressure vessels, and other insurable objects forming part of the *Work*. The insurance provided shall not be less than the insurance provided by the "Comprehensive Boiler and Machinery Form" and shall be maintained continuously from commencement of use or operation of the property insured and until 10 days after the date of the final certificate for payment.

(3)   The policies shall allow for partial or total use or occupancy of the *Work*. If because of such use or occupancy the *Contractor* is unable to provide coverage, the *Contractor* shall notify the *Owner* in writing. Prior to such use or occupancy the *Owner* shall provide, maintain, and pay for property and boiler insurance insuring the full value of the *Work*, as in sub-paragraphs (1) and (2), including coverage for such use or occupancy and shall provide the *Contractor* with proof of such insurance. The *Contractor* shall refund to the *Owner* the unearned premiums applicable to the *Contractor*'s policies upon termination of coverage.

(4)   The policies shall provide that, in the case of a loss or damage, payment shall be made to the *Owner* and the *Contractor* as their respective interests may appear. The *Contractor* shall act on behalf of the *Owner* for the purpose of adjusting the amount of such loss or damage payment with the insurers. When the extent of the loss or damage is determined, the *Contractor* shall proceed to restore the *Work*. Loss or damage shall not affect the rights and obligations of either party under the *Contract* except that the *Contractor* shall be entitled to

236

such reasonable extension of *Contract Time* relative to the extent of the loss or damage as the *Consultant* may recommend in consultation with the *Contractor*.

(5)   The *Contractor* shall be entitled to receive from the *Owner*, in addition to the amount due under the *Contract*, the amount at which the *Owner*'s interest in restoration of the *Work* has been appraised, such amount to be paid as the restoration of the *Work* proceeds and as provided in GC 5.2 - APPLICATIONS FOR PROGRESS PAYMENT and GC 5.3 - PROGRESS PAYMENT. In addition the *Contractor* shall be entitled to receive from the payments made by the insurer the amount of the *Contractor*'s interest in the restoration of the *Work*.

(6)   In the case of loss or damage to the *Work* arising from the work of another contractor, or *Owner*'s own forces, the *Owner*, in accordance with the *Owner*'s obligations under paragraph 3.2.2.4 of GC 3.2 - CONSTRUCTION BY OWNER OR OTHER CONTRACTORS, shall pay the *Contractor* the cost of restoring the *Work* as the restoration of the *Work* proceeds and as provided in GC 5.2 - APPLICATIONS FOR PROGRESS PAYMENT and GC 5.3 - PROGRESS PAYMENT.

.5   **Contractors' Equipment Insurance:**

"All risks" contractors' equipment insurance covering construction machinery and equipment used by the *Contractor* for the performance of the *Work*, including boiler insurance on temporary boilers and pressure vessels, shall be in a form acceptable to the *Owner* and shall not allow subrogation claims by the insurer against the *Owner*. The policies shall be endorsed to provide the *Owner* with not less than 15 days notice in writing in advance of cancellation, change, or amendment restricting coverage. Subject to satisfactory proof of financial capability by the *Contractor* for self-insurance, the *Owner* agrees to waive the equipment insurance requirement.

11.1.2   The *Contractor* shall be responsible for deductible amounts under the policies except where such amounts may be excluded from the *Contractor*'s responsibility by the terms of GC 9.1 - PROTECTION OF WORK AND PROPERTY and GC 9.2 - DAMAGES AND MUTUAL RESPONSIBILITY.

11.1.3   Where the full insurable value of the *Work* is substantially less than the *Contract Price*, the *Owner* may reduce the amount of insurance required or waive the course of construction insurance requirement.

11.1.4   If the *Contractor* fails to provide or maintain insurance as required by the *Contract Documents*, then the *Owner* shall have the right to provide and maintain such insurance and give evidence to the *Contractor* and the *Consultant*. The *Contractor* shall pay the cost thereof to the *Owner* on demand or the *Owner* may deduct the amount which is due or may become due to the *Contractor*.

11.1.5   All required insurance policies shall be with insurers licensed to underwrite insurance in the jurisdiction of the *Place of the Work*.

GC 11.2 BONDS

11.2.1   The *Contractor* shall, prior to commencement of the *Work* or within the specified time, provide to the *Owner* any surety bonds required by the *Contract*.

11.2.2   Such bonds shall be issued by a duly licensed surety company authorized to transact a business of suretyship in the province or territory of the *Place of the Work* and shall be maintained in good standing until the fulfilment of the *Contract*. The form of such bonds shall be in accordance with the latest edition of the CCDC approved bond forms.

PART 12 INDEMNIFICATION — WAIVER — WARRANTY

GC 12.1 INDEMNIFICATION

12.1.1 The *Contractor* shall indemnify and hold harmless the *Owner* and the *Consultant*, their agents and employees from and against claims, demands, losses, costs, damages, actions, suits, or proceedings (hereinafter called "claims"), by third parties that arise out of, or are attributable to, the *Contractor's* performance of the *Contract* provided such claims are:

    .1   attributable to bodily injury, sickness, disease, or death, or to injury to or destruction of tangible property, and

    .2   caused by negligent acts or omissions of the *Contractor* or anyone for whose acts the *Contractor* may be liable, and

    .3   made in writing within a period of 6 years from the date of *Substantial Performance of the Work* as set out in the certificate of *Substantial Performance of the Work*, or within such shorter period as may be prescribed by any limitation statute of the province or territory of the *Place of the Work*.

The *Owner* expressly waives the right to indemnity for claims other than those stated above.

12.1.2 The obligation of the *Contractor* to indemnify hereunder shall be limited to $2,000,000 per occurrence from the commencement of the *Work* until *Substantial Performance of the Work* and thereafter to an aggregate limit of $2,000,000.

12.1.3 The *Owner* shall indemnify and hold harmless the *Contractor*, the *Contractor's* agents and employees from and against claims, demands, losses, costs, damages, actions, suits, or proceedings arising out of the *Contractor's* performance of the *Contract* which are attributable to a lack of or defect in title or an alleged lack of or defect in title to the *Place of the Work*.

12.1.4 GC 12.1 - INDEMNIFICATION shall govern over the provisions of paragraph 1.3.1 of GC 1.3 - RIGHTS AND REMEDIES or GC 9.2 - DAMAGES AND MUTUAL RESPONSIBILITY.

GC 12.2 WAIVER OF CLAIMS

12.2.1 Waiver of Claims by *Owner*

As of the date of the final certificate for payment, the *Owner* expressly waives and releases the *Contractor* from all claims against the *Contractor* including without limitation those that might arise from the negligence or breach of contract by the *Contractor* except one or more of the following:

    .1   those made in writing prior to the date of the final certificate for payment and still unsettled;

    .2   those arising from the provisions of GC 12.1 - INDEMNIFICATION or GC 12.3 - WARRANTY;

    .3   those arising from the provisions of paragraph 9.3.5 of GC 9.3 - TOXIC AND HAZARDOUS SUBSTANCES AND MATERIALS and those arising from the *Contractor* bringing or introducing any toxic or hazardous substances and materials to the *Place of the Work* after the *Contractor* commences the *Work*.

In the Common Law provinces GC 12.2.1.4 shall read as follows:

    .4   those made in writing within a period of 6 years from the date of *Substantial Performance of the Work*, as set out in the certificate of *Substantial Performance of the Work*, or within such shorter period as may be prescribed by any limitation statute of the province or territory of the *Place of the Work* and those arising from any liability of the *Contractor* for damages resulting from the *Contractor's* performance of the *Contract* with respect to substantial defects or deficiencies in the *Work* for which the *Contractor* is proven responsible.

As used herein "substantial defects or deficiencies" means those defects or deficiencies in the *Work* which affect the *Work* to such an extent or in such a manner that a significant part or the whole of the *Work* is unfit for the purpose intended by the *Contract Documents*.

In the Province of Quebec GC 12.2.1.4 shall read as follows:

.4 those arising under the provisions of Article 2118 of the Civil Code of Quebec.

12.2.2 Waiver of Claims by *Contractor*

As of the date of the final certificate for payment, the *Contractor* expressly waives and releases the *Owner* from all claims against the *Owner* including without limitation those that might arise from the negligence or breach of contract by the *Owner* except:

.1 those made in writing prior to the *Contractor's* application for final payment and still unsettled; and

.2 those arising from the provisions of GC 9.3 - TOXIC AND HAZARDOUS SUBSTANCES AND MATERIALS or GC 10.3 - PATENT FEES.

12.2.3 GC 12.2 - WAIVER OF CLAIMS shall govern over the provisions of paragraph 1.3.1 of GC 1.3 - RIGHTS AND REMEDIES or GC 9.2 - DAMAGES AND MUTUAL RESPONSIBILITY.

GC 12.3 WARRANTY

12.3.1 The warranty period with regard to the *Contract* is one year from the date of *Substantial Performance of the Work* or those periods specified in the *Contract Documents* for certain portions of the *Work* or *Products*.

12.3.2 The *Contractor* shall be responsible for the proper performance of the *Work* to the extent that the design and *Contract Documents* permit such performance.

12.3.3 Except for the provisions of paragraph 12.3.6 and subject to paragraph 12.3.2, the *Contractor* shall correct promptly, at the *Contractor's* expense, defects or deficiencies in the *Work* which appear prior to and during the warranty periods specified in the *Contract Documents*.

12.3.4 The *Owner*, through the *Consultant*, shall promptly give the *Contractor* notice in writing of observed defects and deficiencies that occur during the warranty period.

12.3.5 The *Contractor* shall correct or pay for damage resulting from corrections made under the requirements of paragraph 12.3.3.

12.3.6 The *Contractor* shall be responsible for obtaining *Product* warranties in excess of one year on behalf of the *Owner* from the manufacturer. These *Product* warranties shall be issued by the manufacturer to the benefit of the *Owner*.

APPENDIX F

CCDC 3—1986

Cost Plus Contract

Cost plus contract

(Percentage or fixed fee)

Project

 Canadian construction documents committee

The Canadian Construction Documents Committee is a joint committee composed of representatives appointed by:

The Association of Consulting Engineers of Canada
The Canadian Construction Association
The Canadian Council of Professional Engineers
Construction Specifications Canada
The Royal Architectural Institute of Canada

Committee policy and procedures are directed and approved by the constituent associations.

This document has been endorsed by each of the above organizations.

Enquiries should be directed to:

The Secretary,
Canadian Construction Documents Committee,
85 Albert Street,
Ottawa, Ontario, Canada   K1P 6A4.

CCDC 3-86

NOTE: The apportionment of risk and benefit to both the Owner and the Contractor under this Cost Plus Contract form are significantly different from those arising under other different contracting methods. Parties using this method should have a clear understanding of their roles and the terms and conditions set out herein.

CONTENTS

AGREEMENT BETWEEN
OWNER AND CONTRACTOR

DEFINITIONS

GENERAL CONDITIONS OF THE
COST PLUS CONTRACT

	GC NO.
General	
Documents	1
Additional Instructions	2
Consultant	3
Delays	4
Owner's Right to Perform Work or Stop the Work or Terminate Contract	5
Contractor's Right to Stop the Work or Terminate Contract	6
Disputes	7
Assignment	8
Other Contractors	9
Subcontractors	10
Changes	
Changes in the Work	11
Valuation and Certification of Changes in the Work	12
Payment	
Applications for Payment	13
Certificates and Payments	14
Governing Regulations	
Taxes and Duties	15
Laws, Notices, Permits and Fees	16
Patent Fees	17
Workers' Compensation Insurance	18
Insurance, Protection and Damages	
Indemnification	19
Insurance	20
Protection of Work and Property	21
Damages and Mutual Responsibility	22
Performance Protection	
Bonds	23
Warranty	24
Execution of the Work	
Contractor's Responsibilities and Control of the Work	25
Superintendence	26
Labour and Products	27
Subsurface Conditions	28
Use of the Work	29
Cleanup and Final Cleaning of the Work	30
Cutting and Remedial Work	31
Inspection of the Work	32
Rejected Work	33
Shop Drawings	34

AGREEMENT BETWEEN OWNER AND CONTRACTOR
for use when cost of work plus a fee form the basis of payment
and to be used only with the General Conditions of the Cost Plus
Contract.

This Agreement made on the .... day of ....

in the year nineteen hundred and ....

by and between

....

....

hereinafter called the "Owner"

and

....

....

hereinafter called the "Contractor"

witnesses: that the parties agree as follows

ARTICLE A-1 THE WORK

The Contractor shall:

(a) perform the Work required by the Contract Documents for ....
(insert here the title of the Work and the Project)

....

which have been signed by the parties, and which were prepared by ....

.... acting as and hereinafter called the "Consultant" and

(b) do and fulfill everything indicated by this Agreement, and

(c) commence the Work by the .... day of ....

19 .... and, subject only to adjustment as provided for in the Contract Documents, attain Substantial

Performance of the Work, as certified by the Consultant, by the ....

day of .... 19 ....

244

ARTICLE A-2 CONTRACT DOCUMENTS

The following is an exact list of the Contract Documents referred to in Article A-1 of this Agreement and as defined in item 2 of DEFINITIONS. This list is subject to subsequent amendments in accordance with the provisions of the Contract and agreed upon between the parties. Terms used in the Contract Documents which are defined in the attached DEFINITIONS shall have the meanings designated in those DEFINITIONS.

(Insert here, attaching additional pages if required, a list identifying the Contract Documents including: the Agreement; Definitions; General Conditions; Supplementary Conditions; drawings, giving drawing number, title, date, revision date or mark; specifications, giving a list of contents with section numbers and titles, number of pages, and date or revision marks; wage schedule; schedule of head office or other personnel as referred to in Article A-9 paragraph (b), including the method of determining such costs; method of calculating financing costs as referred to in Article A-9 paragraph (u); method of calculating computer costs as referred to in Article A-9 paragraph (w); and schedule providing for advance or special payments.)

ARTICLE A-3 CONTRACT FEE

In consideration of the performance of the Contract, the Owner agrees to pay the Contractor in Canadian funds a Contract Fee as follows:

* A percentage fee of _____ percent (%) of the Cost of the Work, earned as the gross Cost of the Work accrues.

* A fixed fee of ....

   .... dollars

   ($ ....), earned as follows:

   ....

   ....

   ....

   ....

   ....

* *Delete inapplicable section.*

The Contract Fee shall be subject to adjustment as may be required in accordance with the provisions of the Contract Documents. Such adjustments shall be made in the following manner:

   ....

   ....

   ....

   ....

   ....

ARTICLE A-4 PAYMENT

(a) Subject to applicable legislation and the provisions of the Contract Documents, and in accordance with legislation and statutory regulations respecting holdback percentages and, where such legislation or regulations do not exist or apply, subject to a holdback of _____ percent (_____ %), the Owner shall:

   (1) make monthly payments to the Contractor in Canadian funds on account of the Cost of the Work performed to date and products delivered to the Place of the Work or other locations designated by the Owner, the amounts of such payments to be as certified by the Consultant, and

   (2) make monthly payments to the Contractor of the portion of the CONTRACT FEE earned as described in Article A-3 CONTRACT FEE of this Agreement, and

   (3) upon Substantial Performance of the Work as certified by the Consultant pay to the Contractor the unpaid balance of holdback monies when due in accordance with paragraph 14.4 of GC 14 - CERTIFICATES AND PAYMENTS, and

   (4) upon Total Performance of the Work as certified by the Consultant pay to the Contractor the unpaid monies when due in accordance with paragraphs 14.7 and 14.8 of GC 14 — CERTIFICATES AND PAYMENTS.

(b) In the event of loss or damage occurring where payment becomes due under the property and boiler insurance policies, payments shall be made to the Contractor in accordance with the provisions of GC 20 — INSURANCE.

(c) If the Owner fails to make payments to the Contractor as they become due under the terms of this Contract or in an award by arbitration or court, interest of _____ percent (_____ %) per annum on such unpaid amounts shall also become due and payable until payment. Such interest shall be calculated and added to any unpaid amounts monthly.

ARTICLE A-5 RIGHTS AND REMEDIES

(a) The duties and obligations imposed by the Contract Documents and the rights and remedies available thereunder shall be in addition to and not a limitation of any duties, obligations, rights and remedies otherwise imposed or available by law.

(b) No action or failure to act by the Owner, Consultant or Contractor shall constitute a waiver of any right or duty afforded any of them under the Contract, nor shall any such action or failure to act constitute an approval of or acquiescence in any breach thereunder, except as may be specifically agreed in writing.

ARTICLE A-6 RECEIPT OF AND ADDRESSES FOR NOTICES

Communications in writing between the parties or between them and the Consultant shall be considered to have been received by the addressee on the date of delivery if delivered by hand to the individual or to a member of the firm or to an officer of the corporation for whom they are intended or if sent by post or by telegram, to have been delivered within five (5) working days of the date of mailing, dispatch or of delivery to the telegraph company when addressed as follows:

The Owner at ....
street and number and postal box number if applicable

....
post office or district, province, postal code

The Contractor at ....
street and number and postal box number if applicable

....
post office or district, province, postal code

The Consultant at ....
street and number and postal box number if applicable

....
post office or district, province, postal code

ARTICLE A-7 LAW OF THE CONTRACT
The law of the Place of the Work shall govern the interpretation of the Contract.

ARTICLE A-8 LANGUAGE OF THE CONTRACT
When the Contract Documents are prepared in both the English and French languages, it is agreed that in the event of any apparent discrepancy between the English and French versions, the * *English* / *French* language shall prevail.

This Agreement is drawn in English at the request of all parties hereto; ce marché est rédigé en anglais à la demande de toutes les parties.

* Complete this statement by striking out the inapplicable term if the Contract Documents have been prepared and issued in both official languages of Canada.

ARTICLE A-9   COST OF THE WORK

As provided in Article A-4 PAYMENT of this Agreement, the Owner agrees to pay the Contractor for the Cost of the Work in addition to the Contract Fee stipulated in Article A-3 CONTRACT FEE of this Agreement. The Cost of the Work shall be at rates prevailing in the locality of the Place of the Work, except with the prior consent of the Owner, and shall include:

(a) wages and benefits paid for labour in the direct employ of the Contractor in the performance of the Work under applicable collective bargaining agreements, or under a salary or wage schedule agreed upon by the Owner and Contractor and included in Article A-2 CONTRACT DOCUMENTS of this Agreement;

(b) salaries, wages and benefits of the Contractor's personnel, when stationed at the field office, in whatever capacity employed; salaries, wages and benefits of personnel engaged at shops, or on the road, in expediting the production or transportation of materials or equipment, for that portion of their time spent on the Work; salaries, wages and benefits of head office or other personnel listed in Article A-2 CONTRACT DOCUMENTS of this Agreement, for that portion of their time spent on the Work;

(c) contributions, assessments or taxes incurred during the performance of the Work for such items as unemployment insurance, workers' compensation, and Canada or Quebec Pension Plan, insofar as such costs are based on wages, salaries, or other remuneration paid to employees of the Contractor and included in the Cost of the Work under paragraphs (a) and (b) above;

(d) the portion of travel and subsistence expenses of the Contractor or of his officers or employees incurred while travelling in discharge of duties connected with the Work;

(e) the cost of all materials, products, supplies and equipment incorporated into the Work, including costs of transportation thereof;

(f) the cost of materials, products, supplies, equipment, temporary services and facilities, and hand tools not owned by the workers, including transportation and maintenance thereof, which are consumed in the performance of the Work, and cost less salvage value on such items used, but not consumed, which remain the property of the Contractor;

(g) rental costs of all tools, machinery, and equipment, exclusive of hand tools, used in the performance of the Work, whether rented from the Contractor or others, including installation, minor repairs and replacements, dismantling, removal, transportation and delivery costs thereof;

(h) deposits lost;

(i) the amounts of all subcontracts and the costs to the Contractor that result from any Subcontractor's insolvency or failure to perform;

(j) the cost of quality assurance such as independant inspection and testing services;

(k) charges levied by authorities having jurisdiction at the Place of the Work;

(l) royalties, patent licence fees, and damages for infringement of patents and costs of defending suits therefor subject always to the Contractor's obligations to indemnify the Owner pursuant to paragraph 17.1 of GC 17 — PATENT FEES;

(m) premiums for all bonds and insurance which the Contractor is required, by the Contract Documents, to purchase and maintain;

(n) taxes and duties related to the Work and for which the Contractor is liable;

(o) losses and expenses sustained by the Contractor for matters which are the subject of insurance under the policies prescribed in GC 20 — INSURANCE when such losses and expenses are not recoverable because the amounts are in excess of collectible amounts or within the deductible amounts;

(p) charges for telegrams, telexes, telephones, courier services, expressage, and petty cash items incurred in connection with the Work;

(q) the cost of removal and disposal of waste products and debris;

(r) costs incurred due to emergencies affecting the safety of persons or property;

(s) legal costs, incurred by the Contractor, arising out of the execution of the Work in accordance with the Contract Documents;

(t) costs incurred by the Contractor for the correction of defects or deficiencies in the Work other than those defects or deficiencies to be corrected at the Contractor's own expense pursuant to the provisions of GC 33 REJECTED WORK;

(u) the cost of financing the Work in accordance with the method determined by the parties and identified in Article A-2 CONTRACT DOCUMENTS of this Agreement;

(v) the cost of auditing when requested by the Owner;

(w) the cost of computer time and usage in accordance with the method determined by the parties and identified in Article A-2 CONTRACT DOCUMENTS of this Agreement; and

(x) other costs incurred in the performance of the Work as listed below:

....

....

....

....

....

....

....

....

....

Notwithstanding the foregoing and any provisions contained in the General Conditions of the Contract, it is the intention of the parties that the Cost of the Work referred to herein shall cover and include any and all contingencies other than those which are the result of or occasioned by any failure on the part of the Contractor to exercise reasonable care and diligence in his attention to the Work. Any cost due to failure on the part of the Contractor to exercise reasonable care and diligence in his attention to the Work shall be borne by him.

ARTICLE A-10 DISCOUNTS, REBATES AND REFUNDS

All cash discounts shall accrue to the Contractor unless the Owner deposits funds with the Contractor with which to make payments, or where the Owner pays the costs of financing the Work, in which case the cash discounts shall accrue to the Owner. All trade discounts, rebates and refunds, and all returns from sale of surplus materials and equipment applicable to the Work shall accrue to the Owner, and the Contractor shall make provisions so that they can be secured.

ARTICLE A-11 ACCOUNTING AND AUDIT

(a) The Contractor shall keep full and detailed accounts and records necessary for the documentation of the Cost of the Work.

(b) The Owner or his designated representative shall be afforded access to all of the Contractor's books, records, correspondence, instructions, drawings, receipts, vouchers and memoranda relating to this Contract, and for this purpose the Contractor shall preserve all such records for a period of one (1) year from the date of Total Performance of the Work.

ARTICLE A-12 PRIOR NEGOTIATIONS, REPRESENTATIONS OR AGREEMENTS

The Contract supersedes all prior negotiations, representations or agreements, either written or oral, including the bidding documents. The Contract may be amended only as provided in the General Conditions of the Contract.

ARTICLE A-13 SUCCESSION

The General Conditions of the Cost Plus Contract hereto annexed, and the other aforesaid Contract Documents, are to be read into and form part of this Agreement and the whole shall constitute the Contract between the parties and subject to law and the provisions of the Contract Documents shall enure to the benefit of and be binding upon the parties hereto, their respective heirs, legal representatives, successors and assigns.

251

In witness whereof the parties hereto have executed this Agreement under their respective corporate seals and by the hands of their proper officers thereunto duly authorized.

SIGNED, SEALED AND DELIVERED
in the presence of:

OWNER

. . . .
name

. . . .

. . . .
signature

. . . .
name and title

. . . .
signature   *witness*

. . . .
name and title   *name and title*

CONTRACTOR

. . . .
name

. . . .

. . . .
signature

. . . .
name and title

. . . .
signature   *witness*

. . . .
name and title   *name and title*

N.B. Where legal jurisdiction, local practice, or Owner or Contractor requirement calls for proof of authority to execute this document, proof of such authority in the form of a certified copy of a resolution naming the person or persons in question as authorized to sign the Agreement for and on behalf of the corporation or partnership, parties to this Agreement, should be attached.

DEFINITIONS

The following Definitions shall apply to all Contract Documents.

1. **The Contract**

   The Contract is the undertaking by the parties to perform their respective duties, responsibilities and obligations as prescribed in the Contract Documents and represents the entire agreement between the parties.

2. **Contract Documents**

   The Contract Documents consist of the executed Agreement between the Owner and Contractor, the Definitions, the General Conditions of the Contract, Supplementary Conditions, specifications, drawings and such other documents as are listed in Article A-2 — CONTRACT DOCUMENTS including amendments thereto incorporated before the execution of the Contract and subsequent amendments thereto made pursuant to the provisions of the Contract and agreed upon between the parties.

3. **Owner**

   The Owner is the person, firm or corporation identified as such in the Agreement and is referred to throughout the Contract Documents as if singular in number and masculine in gender. The term Owner means the Owner or his authorized agent or representative as designated to the Contractor in writing but does not include the Consultant.

4. **Consultant**

   The Consultant is the person, firm or corporation identified as such in the Agreement, and is an Architect or Engineer licensed to practice in the province or territory of the Place of the Work, and is referred to throughout the Contract Documents as if singular in number and masculine in gender.

5. **Contractor**

   The Contractor is the person, firm or corporation identified as such in the Agreement and is referred to throughout the Contract Documents as if singular in number and masculine in gender. The term Contractor means the Contractor or his authorized representative as designated to the Owner in writing.

6. **Subcontractor**

   A Subcontractor is a person, firm or corporation having a direct contract with the Contractor to perform a part or parts of the Work, or to supply products worked to a special design according to the Contract Documents, but does not include one who merely supplies products not so worked. The term Subcontractor is referred to throughout the Contract Documents as if singular in number and masculine in gender.

7. **The Project**

   The Project means the total construction contemplated of which the Work may be the whole or a part.

8. **The Work**

   The Work means the total construction and related services required by the Contract Documents.

9. **Products**

   Products means material, machinery, equipment and fixtures forming the Work but does not include machinery and equipment used for preparation, fabrication, conveying and erection of the Work and normally referred to as construction machinery and equipment.

10. **Other Contractor**

    Other Contractor means a person, firm or corporation employed by or having a separate contract directly or indirectly with the Owner for work other than that required by the Contract Documents.

11. **Place of the Work**

    The Place of the Work is the designated site or location of the Project of which the Work may be the whole or a part.

12. **Time**

    (a) The Contract Time is the time stipulated in the Contract Documents for Substantial Performance of the Work.

    (b) The date of Substantial Performance of the Work is the date certified as such by the Consultant.

    (c) Day means the calendar day.

    (d) Working day means days other than Saturdays, Sundays and holidays which are observed by the construction industry in the area of the Place of the Work.

13. **Substantial Performance of the Work**

Substantial Performance of the Work is as defined in the lien legislation applicable to the Place of the Work. If such legislation is not in force or does not contain such definition, Substantial Performance of the Work shall have been reached when the Work is ready for use or is being used for the purpose intended and is so certified by the Consultant.

14. **Total Performance of the Work**

Total Performance of the Work means when the entire Work, except those items arising from the provisions of GC 24 — WARRANTY, has been performed to the requirements of the Contract Documents and is so certified by the Consultant.

15. **Changes in the Work**

Changes in the Work means additions, deletions, or other revisions to the Work within the general scope of the Contract.

THE GENERAL CONDITIONS OF THE COST PLUS CONTRACT
(Hereinafter referred to as the General Conditions.)

GC 1   DOCUMENTS

1.1   The Contract Documents shall be signed in duplicate by the Owner and the Contractor.

1.2   The Contract Documents are complementary, and what is required by any one shall be as binding as if required by all.

1.3   The intent of the Contract Documents is to include the labour, products and services necessary for the performance of the Work in accordance with these documents. It is not intended, however, that the Contractor shall supply products or perform work not consistent with, covered by or properly inferable from the Contract Documents.

1.4   Words and abbreviations which have well-known technical or trade meanings are used in the Contract Documents in accordance with such recognized meanings.

1.5   References to the masculine or the singular shall be considered to include the feminine and the plural as the context requires.

1.6   Unless otherwise stated in the event of conflicts between Contract Documents the following shall apply:

(a)   figured dimensions shown on a drawing shall govern even though they may differ from dimensions scaled on the same drawing,

(b)   drawings of larger scale shall govern over those of smaller scale of the same date,

(c)   material and finishing schedules shall govern over drawings,

(d)   specifications shall govern over drawings and material and finishing schedules,

(e)   the General Conditions shall govern over specifications,

(f)   Supplementary Conditions shall govern over the General Conditions, and

(g)   the executed Agreement between the Owner and Contractor shall govern over all documents.

Notwithstanding the foregoing, documents of later date shall always govern.

1.7   The Contractor shall be provided without charge with as many copies of the Contract Documents or parts thereof as are necessary for the performance of the Work.

1.8   The Contractor shall keep one copy of current Contract Documents and shop drawings at the Place of the Work, in good order and available to the Consultant and his representatives. This requirement shall not be considered to include the executed set of Contract Documents.

1.9   Drawings, specifications, models and copies thereof furnished by the Consultant are and shall remain his property with the exception of the signed contract sets belonging to each party to this Contract. Such documents and models are to be used only with respect to the Work and are not to be used on other work. Such documents and models are not to be copied or revised in any manner without the written authorization of the Consultant.

1.10   Models furnished by the Contractor at the Owner's expense are the property of the Owner.

GC 2   ADDITIONAL INSTRUCTIONS

2.1   During the progress of the Work the Consultant will furnish to the Contractor such additional instructions to supplement the Contract Documents as may be necessary for the performance of the Work. Such instructions shall be consistent with the intent of the Contract Documents.

2.2   Additional instructions may be in the form of specifications, drawings, samples, models or other written instructions.

2.3   Additional instructions will be issued by the Consultant with reasonable promptness and in accordance with a schedule agreed upon for such instructions.

GC 3 CONSULTANT

3.1 The Consultant will provide administration of the Contract as described in the Contract Documents during construction and until completion of any correction of defects under the provisions of GC 24 — WARRANTY, paragraph 24.2 or until the issuance of the certificate of Total Performance of the Work, whichever is later. The Owner's instructions to the Contractor shall be forwarded through the Consultant.

3.2 The Consultant will have authority to act on behalf of the Owner only to the extent provided in the Contract Documents, unless otherwise modified by written agreement in accordance with paragraph 3.13.

3.3 The Consultant will not be responsible for and will not have control or charge of construction means, methods, techniques, sequences or procedures, or for safety precautions and programs required for the Work in accordance with the applicable construction safety legislation, other regulations or general construction practice. The Consultant will not be responsible for or have control or charge over the acts or omissions of the Contractor, his Subcontractors or their agents, employees or other persons performing any of the Work.

3.4 The Consultant will visit the site at intervals appropriate to the progress of construction to familiarize himself with the progress and quality of the Work and to determine in general if the Work is proceeding in accordance with the Contract Documents. However, the Consultant will not make exhaustive or continuous on-site inspections to check the quality or quantity of the Work.

3.5 Based on the Consultant's observations and his evaluation of the Contractor's applications for payment, the Consultant will determine the amounts owing to the Contractor under the Contract and will issue certificates for payment in such amounts, as provided in Article A-4 PAYMENT and GC 14 — CERTIFICATES AND PAYMENTS.

3.6 The Consultant will be, in the first instance, the interpreter of the requirements of the Contract Documents and the judge of the performance thereunder by both parties to the Contract. Interpretations and decisions of the Consultant shall be consistent with the intent of the Contract Documents and in making his decisions he will not show partiality to either party.

3.7 Claims, disputes and other matters in question relating to the performance of the Work or the interpretation of the Contract Documents shall be referred initially to the Consultant in writing for decision which he will give in writing within a reasonable time.

3.8 The Consultant will have authority to reject work which in his opinion does not conform to the requirements of the Contract Documents. Whenever he considers it necessary or advisable he will have authority to require special inspection or testing of work whether or not such work be then fabricated, installed or completed. However, neither the Consultant's authority to act nor any decision made by him either to exercise or not to exercise such authority shall give rise to any duty or responsibility of the Consultant to the Contractor, his Subcontractors, or their agents, employees or other persons performing any of the Work.

3.9 The Consultant will review and take appropriate action upon the Contractor's submittals such as shop drawings, product data, and samples, in accordance with the requirements of the Contract Documents.

3.10 The Consultant will prepare change orders in accordance with the requirements of GC 11 — CHANGES IN THE WORK.

3.11 The Consultant will conduct inspections to determine the dates of Substantial Performance of the Work and Total Performance of the Work in accordance with the requirements of GC 14 — CERTIFICATES AND PAYMENTS. He will receive and review written warranties and related documents required by the Contract and provided by the Contractor and will forward such warranties and documents to the Owner for his acceptance.

3.12 If the Owner and the Consultant agree the Consultant will provide at the site one or more project representatives to assist the Consultant in carrying out his responsibilities. The duties, responsibilities and limitations of authority of such project representatives shall be as set forth in writing to the Contractor.

3.13 The duties, responsibilities and limitations of authority of the Consultant as set forth in the Contract Documents will not be modified or extended without the written consent of the Owner, the Contractor and the Consultant.

3.14 In the event of the termination of the employment of the Consultant, the Owner shall immediately reappoint the Consultant or appoint another Consultant to whom the Contractor makes no reasonable objection and whose status under the Contract shall be that of the former Consultant.

3.15 Nothing contained in the Contract Documents shall create any contractual relationship between the Consultant and the Contractor, his Subcontractors, his suppliers, or their agents, employees or other persons performing any of the Work.

GC 4 DELAYS

4.1 If the Contractor is delayed in the performance of the Work by an act or omission of the Owner, Consultant, Other Contractor, or anyone employed or engaged by them directly or indirectly, contrary to the provisions of the Contract Documents, then the Contract Time shall be extended for such reasonable time as the Consultant may decide in consultation with the Contractor and the Contract Fee may be adjusted by a reasonable amount.

4.2 If the Contractor is delayed in the performance of the Work by a stop work order issued by a court or other public authority and providing that such order was not issued as the result of an act or fault of the Contractor or anyone employed or engaged by him directly or indirectly, then the Contract Time shall be extended for such reasonable time as the Consultant may decide in consultation with the Contractor and the Contract Fee may be adjusted by a reasonable amount.

4.3 If the Contractor is delayed in the performance of the Work by labour disputes, strikes, lock-outs (including lock-outs decreed or recommended for its members by a recognized contractors' association, of which the Contractor is a member or to which the Contractor is otherwise bound), fire, unusual delay by common carriers or unavoidable casualties or, without limit to any of the foregoing, by a cause beyond the Contractor's control, then the Contract Time shall be extended for such reasonable time as the Consultant may decide in consultation with the Contractor, but in no case shall the extension of time be less than the time lost as the result of the event causing the delay, unless such shorter extension be agreed to by the Contractor.

4.4 No extension shall be made for delay unless written notice of claim is given to the Consultant not later than fourteen (14) days after the commencement of delay, providing however, that in the case of a continuing cause of delay only one notice of claim shall be necessary.

4.5 If no schedule is made under GC 2 — ADDITIONAL INSTRUCTIONS, or paragraph 25.6 of GC 25 — CONTRACTOR'S RESPONSIBILITIES AND CONTROL OF THE WORK, no claim for delay shall be allowed because of failure to furnish instructions until fourteen (14) days after demand for such instructions has been made and not then unless such claim is reasonable.

4.6 The Consultant will not, except by written notice to the Contractor, stop or delay the Work pending instructions or proposed changes in the Work.

GC 5 OWNER'S RIGHT TO PERFORM WORK OR STOP THE WORK OR TERMINATE CONTRACT

5.1 If the Contractor should be adjudged bankrupt, or makes a general assignment for the benefit of creditors because of his insolvency or if a receiver is appointed because of his insolvency, the Owner may, without prejudice to any other right or remedy he may have, by giving the Contractor or receiver or trustee in bankruptcy written notice, terminate the Contract.

5.2 If the Contractor should neglect to prosecute the Work properly or otherwise fails to comply with the requirements of the Contract to a substantial degree and if the Consultant has given a written statement to the Owner and Contractor that sufficient cause exists, the Owner may notify the Contractor in writing that he is in default of his contractual obligations and instruct him to correct the default in the five (5) working days immediately following the receipt of such notice.

5.3 If the correction of the default cannot be completed in the five (5) working days specified, the Contractor shall be in compliance with the Owner's instructions if he:

(a) commences the correction of the default within the specified time, and

(b) provides the Owner with an acceptable schedule for such correction, and

(c) completes the correction in accordance with such schedule.

5.4 If the Contractor fails to correct the default in the time specified or subsequently agreed upon, the Owner, without prejudice to any other right or remedy he may have, may:

(a) correct such default and deduct the cost thereof from any payment then or thereafter due the Contractor provided the Consultant has certified such cost to the Owner and the Contractor, or

(b) terminate the Contractor's right to continue with the Work in whole or in part or terminate the Contract.

5.5 If the Owner terminates the Contractor's right to continue with the Work under the conditions set out in this General Condition, he shall:

(a) be entitled to take possession of the premises and products and utilize the construction machinery and equipment the whole subject to the rights of third parties, and finish the Work by whatever method he may consider expedient, and

(b) pay the Contractor upon the Consultant's certificate and in accordance with GC 14 — CERTIFICATES AND PAYMENTS for the costs properly incurred by the Contractor to that time plus the proportionate amount of the fee as provided in Article A-3 CONTRACT FEE, and

(c) pay to the Contractor fair compensation, either by purchase or rental, at the option of the Owner, for any construction machinery and equipment retained for use on the Work, and

(d) assume and become liable for all obligations, commitments and unliquidated claims as certified by the Consultant that the Contractor may have theretofore, in good faith, undertaken or incurred in connection with the said Work, other than such as are properly payable by the Contractor because of neglect or default.

The Contractor shall, as a condition of receiving the payments, execute and deliver such papers and take such action, including the legal assignment in his contractual rights, as the Owner may require for the purpose of fully vesting in himself the rights and benefits of the Contractor under the obligations or commitments to be assumed by the Owner.

5.6   If a performance bond has been provided by the Contractor the provisions of this General Condition shall be exercised in accordance with the conditions of such performance bond.

5.7   The Contractor's obligation under the Contract as to quality, correction and warranty of the work performed by him up to the time of termination shall continue in force after such termination.

GC 6   CONTRACTOR'S RIGHT TO STOP THE WORK OR TERMINATE CONTRACT

6.1   If the Owner should be adjudged bankrupt or makes a general assignment for the benefit of creditors because of his insolvency or if a receiver is appointed because of his insolvency, the Contractor may, without prejudice to any other right or remedy he may have, by giving the Owner or receiver or trustee in bankruptcy written notice, terminate the Contract.

6.2   If the Work should be stopped or otherwise delayed for a period of thirty (30) days or more under an order of a court or other public authority and providing that such order was not issued as the result of an act or fault of the Contractor or of anyone directly or indirectly employed or engaged by him, the Contractor may, without prejudice to any other right or remedy he may have, by giving the Owner written notice, terminate the Contract.

6.3   The Contractor may notify the Owner in writing, with a copy to the Consultant, that the Owner is in default of his contractual obligations if:

(a) the Consultant fails to issue a certificate in accordance with the provisions of GC 14 — CERTIFICATES AND PAYMENTS, or

(b) the Owner fails to pay the Contractor when due the amounts certified by the Consultant or awarded by arbitration or court, or

(c) the Owner violates the requirements of the Contract to a substantial degree and the Consultant confirms by written statement to the Contractor that sufficient cause exists.

The Contractor's written notice to the Owner shall advise that if the default is not corrected in the five (5) working days immediately following the receipt of the written notice the Contractor may, without prejudice to any other right or remedy he may have, stop the Work or terminate the Contract.

6.4   If the Contractor terminates the Contract under the conditions set out above, he shall be entitled to be paid for all work performed together with a percentage fee or a proportionate part of the fixed fee as is applicable and for loss sustained upon products and construction machinery and equipment and such other damages as the Contractor may have sustained as a result of the termination of the Contract.

GC 7   DISPUTES

7.1   Differences between the parties to the Contract as to the interpretation, application or administration of this Contract or any failure to agree where agreement between the parties is called for, herein collectively called disputes, which are not resolved in the first instance by decision of the Consultant pursuant to the provisions of GC 3 — CONSULTANT, paragraphs 3.6 and 3.7, shall be settled in accordance with the requirements of this General Condition.

7.2   The claimant shall give written notice of such dispute to the other party no later than thirty (30) days after the receipt of the Consultant's decision given under GC 3 — CONSULTANT, paragraph 3.7. Such notice shall set forth particulars of the matters in dispute, the probable extent and value of the damage and the relevant provisions of the Contract Documents. The other party shall reply to such notice no later than fourteen (14) days after he receives or is considered to have received it, setting out in such reply his grounds and other relevant provisions of the Contract Documents.

7.3 If the matter in dispute is not resolved promptly the Consultant will give such instructions as in his opinion are necessary for the proper performance of the Work and to prevent delays pending settlement of the dispute. The parties shall act immediately according to such instructions, it being understood that by so doing neither party will jeopardize any claim he may have. The Owner shall pay the Contractor all costs incurred in carrying out such instructions, which costs are to be identified separately as relating to such disputed claim. If it is subsequently determined that such instructions were in accordance with the requirements of the Contract Documents, the Owner shall recover such amounts from the Contractor through a specific amendment to the current certificate for payment as described in GC 14 — CERTIFICATES AND PAYMENTS.

7.4 It is agreed that no act by either party shall be construed as a renunciation or waiver of any of his rights or recourses, provided he has given the notices in accordance with paragraph 7.2 and has carried out the instructions as provided in paragraph 7.3.

7.5 If the parties have agreed to submit disputes to arbitration pursuant to a Supplementary Condition to the Contract, or by subsequent agreement, then the dispute shall be submitted to arbitration in accordance with the provisions of the arbitration legislation of the Place of the Work.

7.6 If no provision or agreement is made for arbitration then either party may submit the dispute to such judicial tribunal as the circumstances may require.

7.7 In recognition of the obligation by the Contractor to perform the disputed work and by the Owner to pay for the work as part of the Cost of the Work, as provided in paragraphs 7.3 and 7.4, it is agreed that settlement of dispute proceedings may be commenced immediately following the dispute in accordance with the aforegoing settlement of dispute procedures.

GC 8 ASSIGNMENT

8.1 Neither party to the Contract shall assign the Contract or a portion thereof without the written consent of the other, which consent shall not be unreasonably withheld.

GC 9 OTHER CONTRACTORS

9.1 The Owner reserves the right to let separate contracts in connection with the Project of which the Work is a part, or do certain work by his own forces.

9.2 When separate contracts are awarded for different parts of the Project, or work is performed by the Owner's own forces, the Owner shall:

(a) provide for the co-ordination of the work of his own forces and of each separate contract with the Work of this Contract, and

(b) ensure that insurance coverage is provided to the same requirements as are called for in GC 20 — INSURANCE. Such insurance shall be co-ordinated with the insurance coverage of this Contractor as it affects the Work of this Contract.

9.3 The Contractor shall co-ordinate the Work of this Contract with the work of Other Contractors and connect as specified or shown in the Contract Documents. If there is a change in the scope of the work required for the planning and performance of this co-ordination and connection, the changes shall be authorized in accordance with GC 11 — CHANGES IN THE WORK, and the value of the changes shall be determined in accordance with GC 12 — VALUATION AND CERTIFICATION OF CHANGES IN THE WORK.

9.4 The Contractor shall report to the Consultant any apparent deficiencies in Other Contractors' work which would affect the Work of this Contract immediately they come to his attention and shall confirm such report in writing. Failure by the Contractor to so report shall invalidate any claims against the Owner by reason of the deficiencies of Other Contractors' work except as to those of which he was not reasonably aware.

9.5 The Owner shall take all reasonable precautions to avoid labour disputes or other disputes on the Project arising from the work of Other Contractors.

GC 10 SUBCONTRACTORS

10.1 The Contractor agrees to preserve and protect the rights of the parties under the Contract with respect to work to be performed under subcontract and to:

(a) enter into contracts or written agreements with his Subcontractors to require them to perform their work in accordance with and subject to the terms and conditions of the Contract Documents, and

(b) be as fully responsible to the Owner for acts and omissions of his Subcontractors and of persons directly or indirectly employed by them as for acts and omissions of persons directly employed by him.

The Contractor therefore agrees that he will incorporate the terms and conditions of the Contract Documents including those specified in paragraph 24.4 of GC 24 — WARRANTY, into all subcontract agreements he enters into with his Subcontractors.

259

10.2	The Contractor shall, before awarding subcontracts, submit to the Owner all bids received for the various parts of the Work to be subcontracted and obtain the Owner's approval of the Subcontractors selected.
10.3	To the extent and for the amounts agreed upon by the Owner the Contractor will request performance bonds from the Subcontractors.
10.4	The Contractor shall not be required to employ as a Subcontractor a person or firm to whom he may reasonably object.
10.5	The Consultant may, upon reasonable request and at his discretion, provide to a Subcontractor information as to the percentage or quantity of the Subcontractor's work which has been certified for payment.
10.6	Nothing contained in the Contract Documents shall create a contractual relationship between a Subcontractor and the Owner.

GC 11 CHANGES IN THE WORK

11.1	The Owner, through the Consultant, without invalidating the Contract, may make changes in the Work by altering, adding to, or deducting from the Work with the Contract Time being adjusted accordingly by written order.
11.2	No changes in the Work shall be proceeded with without a written order signed by the Owner.
11.3	Any changes in Contract Fee required as the result of Changes in the Work, shall be made in accordance with the provisions of Article A-3 CONTRACT FEE.

GC 12 VALUATION AND CERTIFICATION OF CHANGES IN THE WORK

| 12.1 | The value of a change shall be determined in one or more of the following methods: |

(a) by estimate and acceptance in a lump sum;

(b) by unit prices set out in the Contract or subsequently agreed upon;

(c) by cost and a fixed or percentage fee.

12.2	When a change in the Work is proposed or required the Contractor shall present to the Consultant for approval his claim for a change in the Contract Fee and change in Contract Time with appropriate documentation in a form acceptable to the Consultant. The Consultant shall satisfy himself as to the correctness of such claim and, when approved by the Owner, a change order shall be issued to the Contractor amending the Contract Fee and Contract Time as appropriate. The value of work performed in the change shall be included for payment with the regular certificates for payment.
12.3	In the case of changes in the work to be paid for under methods (b) and (c) of paragraph 12.1, the form of presentation of costs and methods of measurement shall be agreed to by the Consultant and Contractor before proceeding with the change. The Contractor shall keep accurate records, as agreed upon, of quantities or costs and present an account of the cost of the change in the Work, together with vouchers where applicable.
12.4	If the method of valuation, measurement, change in Contract Fee and change in Contract Time cannot be promptly agreed upon and the change is required to be proceeded with then the Consultant in the first instance will determine the method of valuation, measurement, the change in Contract Fee and Contract Time subject to final determination in the manner set out in GC 7 — DISPUTES. In this case the Consultant will, with the consent of the Owner, issue a written authorization for the change setting out the method of valuation and if by lump sum his valuation of the change in Contract Fee and Contract Time.
12.5	In the case of a dispute in the valuation of a change authorized in the Work and pending final determination of such value, the Consultant will certify the value of work performed in accordance with his own evaluation of the change and include the amount with the regular certificates for payment. The Contractor shall keep accurate records of quantities and cost of such work.
12.6	It is intended in all matters referred to above that both the Consultant and Contractor shall act promptly.

GC 13 APPLICATIONS FOR PAYMENT

13.1 Applications for payment on account as provided for in Article A-4 PAYMENT may be made monthly as the Work progresses.

13.2 Applications for payment shall be dated the last day of the agreed monthly payment period and the amount applied for shall be the cost of the work performed and products delivered to the Place of the Work or other locations designated by the Owner, during the current month plus the amount of the fee earned in accordance with the provisions of Article A-3 CONTRACT FEE.

13.3 The application for payment shall include a statement showing payroll costs, accounts payable for products delivered to the Place of the Work or other locations designated by the Owner and accounts for work performed by Subcontractors for which payment is due, and all other items of cost as defined in Article A-9 COST OF THE WORK.

13.4 When submitting the second and succeeding applications for payment, the Contractor shall furnish receipted vouchers or other satisfactory evidence of payment for all items included in the preceding applications. If the Owner has reasonable grounds for believing that any amount included in preceding applications has not been paid he may withhold payment in respect of such amount from the current application until satisfactory evidence of payment is given by the Contractor.

13.5 Applications for release of holdback monies following Substantial Performance of the Work and the application for final payment shall be made at the time and in the manner set forth in GC 14 — CERTIFICATES AND PAYMENTS.

GC 14 CERTIFICATES AND PAYMENTS

14.1 The Consultant will, no later than ten (10) days after the receipt of an application for payment from the Contractor submitted in accordance with GC 13 — APPLICATIONS FOR PAYMENT, issue a certificate for payment in the amount applied for or in such other amount as he determines to be properly due. If the Consultant amends the application, he will promptly notify the Contractor in writing giving his reasons for the amendment.

14.2 The Owner shall make payment to the Contractor on account in accordance with the provisions of Article A-4 PAYMENT no later than five (5) days after the issuance of a certificate for payment by the Consultant.

14.3 The Consultant will, no later than ten (10) days after the receipt of an application from the Contractor for a certificate of Substantial Performance of the Work, make an inspection and assessment of the Work to verify the validity of the application. The Consultant will, no later than seven (7) days after his inspection, notify the Contractor of his approval or the reasons for his disapproval of the application. When the Consultant finds that Substantial Performance of the Work has been reached he will issue such a certificate. The date of Substantial Performance of the Work shall be as stated in this certificate. Immediately following the issuance of the certificate of Substantial Performance of the Work, the Contractor, in consultation with the Consultant, will establish a reasonable date for the Total Performance of the Work.

14.4 Immediately following the issuance of the certificate of Substantial Performance of the Work the Consultant will issue a certificate for payment of holdback monies. The holdback monies authorized by this certificate shall become due and payable on the day following the expiration of the statutory limitation period stipulated in the lien legislation applicable to the Place of the Work or where such legislation does not exist or apply in accordance with such other legislation, industry practice or such other provisions which may be agreed to between the parties, providing that the Owner may retain out of such holdback monies any sums required by law to satisfy any liens against the Work or other monetary claims against the Contractor and enforceable against the Owner and that the Contractor has submitted to the Owner a sworn statement that all accounts for labour, subcontracts, products, construction machinery and equipment and other indebtedness which may have been incurred by the Contractor in the Substantial Performance of the Work and for which the Owner might in any way be held responsible have been paid in full except holdback monies properly retained.

14.5 Where legislation permits and where, upon application by the Contractor, the Consultant has certified that the work of a Subcontractor has been totally performed to his satisfaction prior to the Substantial Performance of the Work, the Owner shall pay the Contractor the holdback retained for such Subcontractor on the day following the expiration of the statutory limitation period for such Subcontractor stipulated in the lien legislation applicable to the Place of the Work.

14.6 Notwithstanding the provisions of paragraph 14.5 and notwithstanding the wording of such certificates the Contractor shall ensure that such work is protected pending the Total Performance of the Work and be responsible for the correction of defects in it regardless of whether or not they were apparent when such certificates were issued.

261

14.7   The Consultant will, no later than ten (10) days after the receipt of an application from the Contractor for payment upon Total Performance of the Work, make an inspection and assessment of the Work to verify the validity of the application. The Consultant will, no later than seven (7) days after his inspection, notify the Contractor of his approval or the reasons for his disapproval of the application. When the Consultant finds that Total Performance of the Work has been reached he will issue a certificate of Total Performance of the Work and certify for payment the remaining monies due to the Contractor under the Contract less holdback monies which are required to be retained. The date of Total Performance of the Work shall be as stated in this certificate. Subject to the provisions of GC 18 — WORKERS' COMPENSATION INSURANCE, paragraph 18.1, the Owner shall, no later than five (5) days after the issuance of such certificate, make payment to the Contractor in accordance with the provisions of Article A-4 PAYMENT.

14.8   The release of the remaining holdback monies shall become due and payable on the day following the expiration of the statutory limitation period stipulated in the lien legislation applicable to the Place of the Work, or where such legislation does not exist or apply in accordance with such other legislation, industry practice or such other provisions which may be agreed to between the parties, providing that the Owner may retain out of such holdback monies any sums required by law to satisfy any liens against the Work or other monetary claims against the Contractor and enforceable against the Owner and that the Contractor has submitted to the Owner a sworn statement that all accounts for labour, subcontracts, products, construction machinery and equipment and other indebtedness which may have been incurred by the Contractor in the Total Performance of the Work and for which the Owner might in any way be held responsible have been paid in full except holdback monies properly retained.

14.9   If because of climatic or other conditions reasonably beyond the control of the Contractor there are items of work that cannot be performed, payment in full for work which has been performed as certified by the Consultant shall not be withheld or delayed by the Owner on account thereof, but the Owner may withhold until the remaining work is finished only such monies as the Consultant determines are sufficient and reasonable to cover the cost of performing such remaining work and to adequately protect the Owner from claims.

14.10   No payment made by the Owner under this Contract or partial or entire use or occupancy of the Work by the Owner shall constitute an acceptance of work or products which are not in accordance with the requirements of the Contract Documents.

14.11   All certificates issued by the Consultant shall be to the best of his knowledge, information and belief. By issuing any certificate the Consultant does not guarantee the correctness or completeness of the Work.

14.12   As of the date of Total Performance of the Work, as set out in the certificate of Total Performance of the Work, the Owner expressly waives and releases the Contractor from all claims against the Contractor including without limitation those that might arise from the negligence or breach of contract by the Contractor except one or more of the following:

(a) those made in writing prior to the date of Total Performance of the Work and still unsettled;

(b) those arising from the provisions of GC 19 — INDEMNIFICATION or GC 24 — WARRANTY;

In the Common Law provinces GC 14.12(c) shall read as follows:

(c) those made in writing within a period of six (6) years from the date of Substantial Performance of the Work, as set out in the certificate of Substantial Performance of the Work, or within such shorter period as may be prescribed by any limitation statute of the province or territory of the Place of the Work and arising from any liability of the Contractor for damages resulting from his performance of the Contract with respect to substantial defects or deficiencies in the Work for which the Contractor is proven responsible.

As used herein "substantial defects or deficiencies" means those defects or deficiencies in the Work which affect the Work to such an extent or in such a manner that a significant part or the whole of the Work is unfit for the purpose intended by the Contract Documents.

In the Province of Quebec GC 14.12(c) shall read as follows:

(c) those arising under the provisions of Article 1688 of the Civil Code.

14.13   As of the date of Total Performance of the Work, as set out in the certificate of Total Performance of the Work, the Contractor expressly waives and releases the Owner from all claims against the Owner including without limitation those that might arise from the negligence or breach of contract by the Owner except those made in writing prior to the Contractor's application for payment upon Total Performance of the Work and still unsettled.

14.14   Notwithstanding GC 1 — DOCUMENTS, paragraph 1.6, in the event of conflict between the provisions of this General Condition and Article A-5 RIGHTS AND REMEDIES, paragraph (a), or GC 22 — DAMAGES AND MUTUAL RESPONSIBILITY, the provisions of this General Condition shall govern.

GC 15 TAXES AND DUTIES

15.1 Unless otherwise stated in Supplementary Conditions the Contractor shall pay the government sales taxes, customs duties and excise taxes with respect to the Contract.

15.2 Where an exemption or recovery of government sales taxes, customs duties or excise taxes is applicable to the Contract, the procedure shall be as established in the Supplementary Conditions.

GC 16 LAWS, NOTICES, PERMITS AND FEES

16.1 The laws of the Place of the Work shall govern the Work.

16.2 The Contractor shall obtain the permits, licences and certificates and pay the fees required for the performance of the Work which are in force at the date of the closing of bids, but this shall not include the obtaining of permanent easements or rights of servitude.

16.3 The Contractor shall give the required notices and comply with the laws, ordinances, rules, regulations, codes and orders of the authorities having jurisdiction which are or become in force during the performance of the Work and which relate to the Work, to the preservation of the public health, and to construction safety.

16.4 The Contractor shall not be responsible for verifying that the Contract Documents are in compliance with the applicable laws, ordinances, rules, regulations and codes relating to the Work. If the Contract Documents are at variance therewith, or changes which require modification to the Contract Documents are made to the laws, ordinances, rules, regulations and codes by the authorities having jurisdiction subsequent to the date of bid closing, the Contractor shall notify the Consultant in writing requesting direction immediately such variance or change becomes known to him. The Consultant will make the changes required to the Contract Documents in accordance with GC 11 — CHANGES IN THE WORK, and the value of the changes shall be determined in accordance with GC 12 — VALUATION AND CERTIFICATION OF CHANGES IN THE WORK.

16.5 If the Contractor fails to notify the Consultant in writing and obtain his direction as required in paragraph 16.4 and performs work knowing it to be contrary to any laws, ordinances, rules, regulations, codes and orders of the authorities having jurisdiction, the Contractor shall be responsible for and shall correct the violations thereof and shall bear the costs, expense and damages attributable to his failure to comply with the provisions of such laws, ordinances, rules, regulations, codes and orders.

GC 17 PATENT FEES

17.1 The Contractor shall pay the royalties and patent licence fees required for the performance of the Contract. He shall hold the Owner harmless from and against claims, demands, losses, costs, damages, actions, suits, or proceedings arising out of the Contractor's performance of the Contract which are attributable to an infringement or an alleged infringement of a patent of invention by the Contractor or anyone for whose acts he may be liable.

17.2 The Owner shall hold the Contractor harmless against claims, demands, losses, costs, damages, actions, suits, or proceedings arising out of the Contractor's performance of the Contract which are attributable to an infringement or an alleged infringement of a patent of invention in executing anything for the purpose of the Contract, the model, plan or design of which was supplied to the Contractor as part of the Contract Documents.

GC 18 WORKERS' COMPENSATION INSURANCE

18.1 Prior to commencing the Work and prior to receiving payment on Substantial and Total Performance of the Work, the Contractor shall provide evidence of compliance with the requirements of the province or territory of the Place of the Work with respect to workers' compensation insurance including payments due thereunder.

18.2 At any time during the term of the Contract, when requested by the Owner, the Contractor shall provide such evidence of compliance by himself and his Subcontractors.

GC 19 INDEMNIFICATION

19.1 The Contractor shall indemnify and hold harmless the Owner and the Consultant, their agents and employees from and against claims, demands, losses, costs, damages, actions, suits or proceedings by third parties that arise out of, or are attributable to, the Contractor's performance of the Contract (hereinafter called "claims"), provided such claims are:

(a) attributable to bodily injury, sickness, disease, or death, or to injury to or destruction of tangible property, and

(b) caused by negligent acts or omissions of the Contractor or anyone for whose acts he may be liable, and

(c) made in writing within a period of six (6) years from the date of Substantial Performance of the Work as set out in the certificate of Substantial Performance of the Work, or within such shorter period as may be prescribed by any limitation statute of the province or territory of the Place of the Work.

The Owner expressly waives the right to indemnity for claims other than those stated above.

19.2 The obligation of the Contractor to indemnify hereunder shall be limited to one million dollars per occurrence from the commencement of the Work until Substantial Performance of the Work and thereafter to an aggregate limit of one million dollars.

19.3 The Owner shall indemnify and hold harmless the Contractor, his agents and employees from and against claims, demands, losses, costs, damages, actions, suits, or proceedings arising out of the Contractor's performance of the Contract which are attributable to a lack of or defect in title or an alleged lack of or defect in title to the Place of the Work.

19.4 Notwithstanding GC 1 — DOCUMENTS, paragraph 1.6, in the event of conflict between the provisions of this General Condition and Article A-5 RIGHTS AND REMEDIES, paragraph (a), or GC 22 — DAMAGES AND MUTUAL RESPONSIBILITY, the provisions of this General Condition shall govern.

GC 20 INSURANCE

20.1 Without restricting the generality of GC 19 — INDEMNIFICATION, the Contractor shall provide, maintain and pay for the insurance coverages listed in this General Condition unless otherwise stipulated:

(a) **General Liability Insurance:**

General liability insurance shall be in the joint names of the Contractor, the Owner, and the Consultant with limits of not less than one million dollars inclusive per occurrence for bodily injury, death, and damage to property including loss of use thereof, with a property damage deductible of five hundred dollars. The form of this insurance shall be the latest edition of CCDC Form 101 and shall be maintained continuously from commencement of the Work until twelve (12) months following the date of Substantial Performance of the Work, as set out in the certificate of Substantial Performance of the Work, or until the certificate of Total Performance of the Work is issued, whichever is the later, and with respect to completed operations coverage for a period of not less than twenty-four (24) months from the date of Total Performance of the Work, as set out in the certificate of Total Performance of the Work, and thereafter to be maintained for a further period of four (4) years. Should the Contractor decide not to employ Subcontractors for operations requiring the use of explosives for blasting, or pile driving or caisson work, or removal or weakening of support of property, building or land; CCDC Form 101 as required shall include Endorsement CCDC Form 101-2.

(b) **Automobile Liability Insurance:**

Automobile liability insurance in respect of licensed vehicles shall have limits of not less than one million dollars inclusive per occurrence for bodily injury, death, and damage to property, in the following forms endorsed to provide the Owner with not less than fifteen (15) days written notice in advance of cancellation, change or amendment restricting coverage:

(1) Standard non-owned automobile policy including standard contractual liability endorsement.

(2) Standard owner's form automobile policy providing third party liability and accident benefits insurance and covering licensed vehicles owned or operated by or on behalf of the Contractor.

(c) **Aircraft and Watercraft Liability Insurance:**

Aircraft and watercraft liability insurance with respect to owned or non-owned aircraft and watercraft if used directly or indirectly in the performance of the Work, including use of additional premises, shall be subject to limits of not less than one million dollars inclusive per occurrence for bodily injury, death, and damage to property including loss of use thereof and limits of not less than one million dollars for aircraft passenger hazard. Such insurance shall be in a form acceptable to the Owner. The policies shall be endorsed to provide the Owner with not less than fifteen (15) days written notice in advance of cancellation, change or amendment restricting coverage.

264

(d) **Property and Boiler Insurance:**

(1) All risks property insurance shall be in the joint names of the Contractor, the Owner and the Consultant, insuring a provisional amount that is not less than the full value of the Work at risk from time to time and the full value, as stated in the Supplementary Conditions, of products that are specified to be provided by the Owner for incorporation into the Work, with a deductible not exceeding one percent of the amount insured at the site of the Work. The form of this insurance shall be the latest edition of CCDC Form 201 and shall be maintained continuously until ten (10) days after the date of Total Performance of the Work, as set out in the certificate of Total Performance of the Work.

(2) Boiler insurance insuring the interests of the Contractor, the Owner and the Consultant for not less than the replacement value of boilers and pressure vessels forming part of the Work. The form of this insurance shall be the latest edition of CCDC Form 301 and shall be maintained continuously from commencement of use or operation of the property insured and until ten (10) days after the date of Total Performance of the Work, as set out in the certificate of Total Performance of the Work.

(3) Should the Owner wish to use or occupy part or all of the Work he shall give thirty (30) days written notice to the Contractor of the intended purpose and extent of such use or occupancy. Prior to such use or occupancy the Contractor shall notify the Owner in writing of the additional premium cost, if any, to maintain property and boiler insurance, which shall be at the Owner's expense. If because of such use or occupancy the Contractor is unable to provide coverage, the Owner upon written notice from the Contractor and prior to such use or occupancy shall provide, maintain and pay for property and boiler insurance insuring the full value of the Work, as in subparagraphs (1) and (2), in CCDC Forms 201 and 301, including coverage for such use or occupancy and shall provide the Contractor with proof of such insurance. The Contractor shall refund to the Owner the unearned premiums applicable to the Contractor's policies upon termination of coverage.

(4) The policies shall provide that, in the event of a loss or damage, payment shall be made to the Owner and the Contractor as their respective interests may appear. The Contractor shall act on behalf of the Owner and himself for the purpose of adjusting the amount of such loss or damage payment with the Insurers. When the extent of the loss or damage is determined the Contractor shall proceed to restore the Work. Loss or damage shall not affect the rights and obligations of either party under the Contract except that the Contractor shall be entitled to such reasonable extension of Contract Time relative to the extent of the loss or damage as the Consultant may decide in consultation with the Contractor.

(5) Payment for loss or damage:
The Contractor shall be entitled to receive from the Owner, in addition to the amount due under the Contract, the amount at which the Owner's interest in restoration of the Work has been appraised, such amount to be paid as the restoration of the Work proceeds and in accordance with the requirements of GC 13 — APPLICATIONS FOR PAYMENT and GC 14 — CERTIFICATES AND PAYMENTS. In addition the Contractor shall be entitled to receive from the payments made by the Insurer the amount of the Contractor's interest in the restoration of the Work.

(e) **Contractors' Equipment Insurance:**

All risks contractors' equipment insurance covering construction machinery and equipment used by the Contractor for the performance of the Work, including boiler insurance on temporary boilers and pressure vessels, shall be in a form acceptable to the Owner and shall not allow subrogation claims by the Insurer against the Owner. The policies shall be endorsed to provide the Owner with not less than fifteen (15) days written notice in advance of cancellation, change or amendment restricting coverage. Subject to satisfactory proof of financial capability by the Contractor for self-insurance of his equipment, the Owner agrees to waive the equipment insurance requirement.

20.2 Unless specified otherwise the duration of each insurance policy shall be from the date of commencement of the Work until the date of Total Performance of the Work, as set out in the certificate of Total Performance of the Work.

20.3 The Contractor shall provide the Owner with proof of insurance prior to commencement of the Work and shall promptly provide the Owner with a certified true copy of each insurance policy.

20.4 If the Contractor fails to provide or maintain insurance as required in this General Condition or elsewhere in the Contract Documents, then the Owner shall have the right to provide and maintain such insurance and give evidence thereof to the Contractor and the Consultant.

GC 21 PROTECTION OF WORK AND PROPERTY

21.1 The Contractor shall protect the Work and the Owner's property and property adjacent to the Place of the Work from damage and shall be responsible for damage which may arise as the result of his operations under the Contract except damage which occurs as the result of:

(a) errors in the Contract Documents;

(b) acts or omissions by the Owner, the Consultant, Other Contractors, their agents and employees.

21.2 Should the Contractor in the performance of this Contract damage the Work, the Owner's property or property adjacent to the Place of the Work, the Contractor shall be responsible for the making good of such damage at his expense.

21.3 Should damage occur to the Work or Owner's property for which the Contractor is not responsible as provided in paragraph 21.1 he shall make good such damage to the Work and if the Owner so directs to the Owner's property and the Contract Fee and Contract Time shall be adjusted in accordance with GC 11 — CHANGES IN THE WORK, and the value of the changes shall be determined in accordance with GC 12 — VALUATION AND CERTIFICATION OF CHANGES IN THE WORK.

GC 22 DAMAGES AND MUTUAL RESPONSIBILITY

22.1 If either party to this Contract should suffer damage in any manner because of any wrongful act or neglect of the other party or of anyone for whom he is responsible in law, then he shall be reimbursed by the other party for such damage. The party reimbursing the other party shall be subrogated to the rights of the other party in respect of such wrongful act or neglect if it be that of a third party.

22.2 Claims under this General Condition shall be made in writing to the party liable within reasonable time after the first observance of such damage and may be adjusted by agreement or in the manner set out in GC 7 — DISPUTES.

22.3 If the Contractor has caused damage to an Other Contractor on the Work, the Contractor agrees upon due notice to settle with such Other Contractor by agreement or arbitration, if he will so settle. If such Other Contractor sues the Owner on account of damage alleged to have been so sustained, the Owner shall notify the Contractor and may require the Contractor to defend the action at the Contractor's expense. If a final order or judgment against the Owner arises therefrom the Contractor shall pay or satisfy it and pay the costs incurred by the Owner.

22.4 If the Contractor becomes liable to pay or satisfy a final order, judgment or award against the Owner then the Contractor, upon undertaking to indemnify the Owner against any and all liability for costs, shall have the right to appeal in the name of the Owner such final order or judgment to any and all courts of competent jurisdiction.

GC 23 BONDS

23.1 The Contractor shall promptly provide to the Owner the surety bonds called for in the Contract Documents.

23.2 Such bonds shall be issued by a duly licensed surety company authorized to transact a business of suretyship in the province or territory of the Place of the Work and shall be maintained in good standing until the fulfillment of the Contract. The form of these bonds shall be the latest editions of CCDC Form 221 and 222.

GC 24 WARRANTY

24.1 The Contractor shall be responsible for the proper performance of the Work only to the extent that the design and specifications permit such performance.

24.2 Subject to paragraph 24.1, and in conformity with Article A-9 COST OF THE WORK, the Contractor shall promptly correct defects or deficiencies in the Work which appear prior to and during the period of one year from the date of Substantial Performance of the Work, as set out in the certificate of Substantial Performance of the Work, or such longer periods as may be specified for certain products or work.

24.3 During the period provided in GC 3 — CONSULTANT, paragraph 3.1, the Owner through the Consultant shall promptly give the Contractor written notice of observed defects and deficiencies.

24.4 The Contractor shall enforce the warranty obligations of his stipulated price subcontracts which shall include the following provisions:

(a) The Subcontractor agrees to correct promptly at his own expense defects or deficiencies in the Subcontract work which appear prior to and during the period of one year from the date of Substantial Performance of the Work, as set out in the certificate of Substantial Performance of the Work, or such longer periods as may be specified for certain products or work.

(b) The Subcontractor agrees to correct or pay for damage resulting from corrections made under the requirements of clause (a) above.

24.5 The Contractor shall also enforce the warranty obligations of his manufacturers and suppliers.

GC 25 CONTRACTOR'S RESPONSIBILITIES AND CONTROL OF THE WORK

25.1 The Contractor shall have complete control of the Work and shall effectively direct and supervise the Work so as to ensure conformance with the Contract Documents. He shall be solely responsible for construction means, methods, techniques, sequences and procedures and for co-ordinating the various parts of the Work under the Contract.

25.2 The Contractor shall be solely responsible for construction safety at the Place of the Work and for compliance with the rules, regulations and practices required by the applicable construction safety legislation.

25.3 The Contractor shall have the sole responsibility for the design, erection, operation, maintenance and removal of temporary structural and other temporary facilities and the design and execution of construction methods required in their use. The Contractor shall engage registered professional engineering personnel skilled in the appropriate disciplines to perform these functions where required by law or by the Contract Documents and in all cases where such temporary facilities and their method of construction are of such a nature that professional engineering skill is required to produce safe and satisfactory results.

25.4 Notwithstanding the provisions of paragraphs 25.1 and 25.3, or provisions to the contrary elsewhere in the Contract Documents where such Contract Documents include designs for temporary structural and other temporary facilities or specify a method of construction in whole or in part, such facilities and methods shall be considered to be part of the design of the Work and the Contractor shall not be held responsible for that part of the design or the specified method of construction. The Contractor shall, however, be responsible for the execution of such design or specified method of construction in the same manner that he is responsible for the execution of the Work.

25.5 The Contractor shall review the Contract Documents and shall promptly report to the Consultant any error, inconsistency or omission he may discover. Such review by the Contractor shall be to the best of his knowledge, information and belief and in making such review the Contractor does not assume any responsibility to the Owner or the Consultant for the accuracy of the review. The Contractor shall not be liable for damage or costs resulting from such errors, inconsistencies or omissions in the Contract Documents which he did not discover. If the Contractor does discover any error, inconsistency or omission in the Contract Documents he shall not proceed with the work affected until he has received corrected or missing information from the Consultant.

25.6 The Contractor shall prepare and update as required a construction schedule indicating the timing of the major activities of the Work. The schedule shall be designed to ensure conformance with the required Contract Time. The schedule shall be submitted to the Owner and the Consultant for their information within a reasonable time from the date of Contract award. The Contractor shall monitor the progress of the Work relative to the schedule and advise the Consultant of any revisions required as the result of delays as provided in GC 4 — DELAYS, indicating the results expected from the resultant change in schedule.

GC 26 SUPERINTENDENCE

26.1 The Contractor shall employ a competent supervisor and necessary assistants who shall be in attendance at the Place of the Work while work is being performed.

26.2 The supervisor shall be satisfactory to the Consultant and shall not be changed except for good reason and only then after consultation with the Consultant.

26.3 The supervisor shall represent the Contractor at the Place of the Work and instructions given to him by the Consultant shall be held to have been given to the Contractor. Important instructions shall be confirmed to the Contractor in writing; other instructions shall be so confirmed if requested.

GC 27 LABOUR AND PRODUCTS

27.1 Products provided shall be new unless otherwise specified in the Contract Documents. Products which are not specified shall be of a quality best suited to the purpose required and their use subject to the approval of the Consultant.

27.2 The Contractor shall maintain good order and discipline among his employees engaged on the Work and shall not employ on the Work anyone not skilled in the task assigned to him.

GC 28 SUBSURFACE CONDITIONS

28.1 The Contractor shall promptly notify the Consultant in writing if in his opinion the subsurface conditions at the Place of the Work differ significantly from those indicated in the Contract Documents, or a reasonable assumption of probable conditions based thereon.

28.2 After prompt investigation, should the Consultant determine that conditions do differ significantly, he will issue appropriate instructions for changes in the Work in accordance with GC 11 — CHANGES IN THE WORK, and the value of the changes shall be determined in accordance with GC 12 — VALUATION AND CERTIFICATION OF CHANGES IN THE WORK.

GC 29 USE OF THE WORK

29.1 The Contractor shall confine his apparatus, the storage of products, and the operations of his employees to limits indicated by laws, ordinances, permits or the Contract Documents and shall not unreasonably encumber the premises with his products.

29.2 The Contractor shall not load or permit to be loaded any part of the Work with a weight or force that will endanger the safety of the Work.

GC 30 CLEANUP AND FINAL CLEANING OF THE WORK

30.1 The Contractor shall maintain the Work in a tidy condition and free from the accumulation of waste products and debris, other than that caused by the Owner, Other Contractors or their employees.

30.2 Upon attaining Substantial Performance of the Work, the Contractor shall remove his surplus products, tools, construction machinery and equipment not required for the performance of the remaining work. He shall also remove waste products and debris other than that caused by the Owner, Other Contractors or their employees, and leave the Work clean and suitable for occupancy by the Owner unless otherwise specified.

30.3 Total Performance of the Work shall not be attained until the Contractor has removed his surplus products, tools, construction machinery and equipment. He shall also have removed waste products and debris, other than that caused by the Owner, Other Contractors or their employees.

GC 31 CUTTING AND REMEDIAL WORK

31.1 The Contractor shall do the cutting and remedial work required to make the several parts of the Work come together properly.

31.2 The Contractor shall co-ordinate the Work to ensure that this requirement is kept to a minimum.

31.3 Cutting and remedial work shall be performed by specialists familiar with the materials affected and shall be performed in a manner to neither damage nor endanger the Work.

GC 32 INSPECTION OF THE WORK

32.1 The Owner and the Consultant or their authorized agents or representatives shall at all times have access to the Work. If parts of the Work are in preparation at locations other than the Place of the Work, the Owner and the Consultant or their authorized agents or representatives shall be given access to such work whenever it is in progress.

32.2 If work is designated for special tests, inspections or approvals in the Contract Documents, or by the Consultant's instructions, or the laws or ordinances of the Place of the Work, the Contractor shall give the Consultant timely notice requesting inspection. Inspection by the Consultant shall be made promptly. The Contractor shall arrange for inspections by other authorities and shall give the Consultant timely notice of the date and time.

32.3 If the Contractor covers or permits to be covered work that has been designated for special tests, inspections or approvals before such special tests, inspections or approvals are made, given or completed, he shall, if so directed, uncover such work, have the inspections or tests satisfactorily completed and make good such work at his own expense.

32.4 The Consultant may order any part or parts of the Work to be specially examined should he believe that such work is not in accordance with the requirements of the Contract Documents. If, upon examination such work be found not in accordance with the requirements of the Contract Documents, the Contractor shall correct such work and pay the cost of examination and correction. If such work be found in accordance with the requirements of the Contract Documents, the Owner shall pay the cost of examination and replacement.

32.5 The Contractor shall furnish promptly to the Consultant two (2) copies of certificates and inspection reports relating to the Work.

GC 33 REJECTED WORK

33.1 Defective work, whether the result of poor workmanship, use of defective products, or damage through carelessness or other act or omission of the Contractor and whether incorporated in the Work or not, which has been rejected by the Consultant as failing to conform to the Contract Documents shall be removed promptly from the Place of the Work by the Contractor and replaced or re-executed promptly in accordance with the Contract Documents at the Contractor's expense, where such defective work:

(a) was performed prior to Substantial Performance of the Work and has been rejected by the Consultant on or before the ninetieth (90th) day following Substantial Performance of the Work; or

(b) was performed after Substantial Performance of the Work and has been rejected by the Consultant on or before a date of one year following Substantial Performance of the Work or on or before Total Performance of the Work, whichever is the shorter period.

33.2 Other Contractors' work destroyed or damaged by such removals or replacements shall be made good promptly at the Contractor's expense.

33.3 If in the opinion of the Consultant it is not expedient to correct such defective work or work not performed in accordance with the Contract Documents, the Owner may deduct from the monies otherwise due to the Contractor the difference in value between the work as performed and that called for by the Contract Documents, the amount of which will be determined in the first instance by the Consultant.

GC 34 SHOP DRAWINGS

34.1 The term "shop drawings" means drawings, diagrams, illustrations, schedules, performance charts, brochures and other data which are to be provided by the Contractor to illustrate details of a portion of the Work.

34.2 The Contractor shall arrange for the preparation of clearly identified shop drawings as called for by the Contract Documents or as the Consultant may reasonably request.

34.3 Prior to submission to the Consultant the Contractor shall review all shop drawings. By this review the Contractor represents that he has determined and verified all field measurements, field construction criteria, materials, catalogue numbers and similar data or will do so and that he has checked and co-ordinated each shop drawing with the requirements of the Work and of the Contract Documents. The Contractor's review of each shop drawing shall be indicated by stamp, date, and signature of a responsible person.

34.4 The Contractor shall submit shop drawings to the Consultant for his review with reasonable promptness and in orderly sequence so as to cause no delay in the Work or in the work of Other Contractors. If either the Contractor or the Consultant so requests they shall jointly prepare a schedule fixing the dates for submission and return of shop drawings. Shop drawings shall be submitted in the form of reproducible transparencies or prints as the Consultant may direct. At the time of submission the Contractor shall specifically draw the attention of the Consultant in writing to any deviations in the shop drawings from the requirements of the Contract Documents.

34.5 The Consultant will review and return shop drawings in accordance with any schedule agreed upon, or otherwise with reasonable promptness so as to cause no delay. The Consultant's review will be for conformity to the design concept and for general arrangement only and such review shall not relieve the Contractor of responsibility for errors or omissions in the shop drawings or of responsibility for meeting all requirements of the Contract Documents unless a deviation on the shop drawings has been approved in writing by the Consultant.

34.6 The Contractor shall make any changes in shop drawings which the Consultant may require consistent with the Contract Documents and resubmit unless otherwise directed by the Consultant. When resubmitting, the Contractor shall notify the Consultant in writing of any revisions other than those requested by the Consultant.

APPENDIX G

CCDC 220—1979

Bid Bond

Provided by the Canadian Construction Association, whose permission to reproduce this document is gratefully acknowledged. Copies of this document are available from the Secretary, Canadian Construction Document Committee, 85 Albert Street, Ottawa, Ontario, Canada K1P 6A4.

BID BOND

No.. $...

KNOW ALL MEN BY THESE PRESENTS THAT..

.... as Principal

hereinafter called the Principal, and..

a corporation created and existing under the laws of..

and duly authorized to transact the business of Suretyship in...

as Surety, hereinafter called the Surety, are held and firmly bound unto......................................

.... as Obligee

hereinafter called the Obligee, in the amount of...

.... Dollars ($...)
lawful money of Canada, for the payment of which sum, well and truly to be made, the Principal and the Surety bind themselves, their heirs, executors, administrators, successors and assigns, jointly and severally, firmly by these presents.

WHEREAS, the Principal has submitted a written tender to the Obligee, dated the................................

day of....................19.........for..

....

....

....

NOW, THEREFORE, THE CONDITION OF THIS OBLIGATION is such that if the aforesaid Principal shall have the tender accepted within sixty (60) days from the closing date of tender and the said Principal will, within the time required, enter into a formal contract and give the specified security to secure the performance of the terms and conditions of the Contract, then his obligation shall be null and void; otherwise the Principal and the Surety will pay unto the Obligee the difference in money between the amount of the bid of the said Principal and the amount for which the Obligee legally contracts with another party to perform the work if the latter amount be in excess of the former.

The Principal and the Surety shall not be liable for a greater sum than the specified penalty of this Bond.

Any suit under this Bond must be instituted before the expiration of six months from the date of this Bond.

IN WITNESS WHEREOF, the Principal and the Surety have Signed and Sealed this Bond this.....................................

.... day of ....19.........

SIGNED and SEALED
In the presence of

        (
        (
        (
        (...(Seal)
                                    Principal
        (
        (
        (
        (...(Seal)
                                    Surety

APPENDIX H

CCDC 221—1979

Performance Bond

Provided by the Canadian Construction Association, whose permission to reproduce this document is gratefully acknowledged. Copies of this document are available from the Secretary, Canadian Construction Document Committee, 85 Albert Street, Ottawa, Ontario, Canada K1P 6A4.

PERFORMANCE BOND

No. . . . . $ . . . .

KNOW ALL MEN BY THESE PRESENTS THAT . . . .

. . . . as Principal,

hereinafter called the Principal, and . . . .

a corporation created and existing under the laws of . . . .

and duly authorized to transact the business of Suretyship in . . . .

as Surety, hereinafter called the Surety, are held and firmly bound unto . . . .

. . . . as Obligee,

hereinafter called the Obligee, in the amount of . . . .

. . . . Dollars ($ . . . .)

lawful money of Canada, for the payment of which sum, well and truly to be made, the Principal and the Surety bind themselves, their heirs,
executors, administrators, successors and assigns, jointly and severally, firmly by these presents.

WHEREAS, the Principal has entered into a written contract with the Obligee, dated the . . . .

day of . . . . 19 . . . . for . . . .

. . . .

. . . .

. . . .

in accordance with the Contract Documents submitted therefor which are by reference made part hereof and are hereinafter referred to as the
Contract.

NOW, THEREFORE, THE CONDITION OF THIS OBLIGATION is such that if the Principal shall promptly and faithfully perform the Contract then
this obligation shall be null and void; otherwise it shall remain in full force and effect.

Whenever the Principal shall be, and declared by the Obligee to be, in default under the Contract, the Obligee having performed the Obligee's
obligations thereunder, the Surety may promptly remedy the default, or shall promptly

(1) complete the Contract in accordance with its terms and conditions or

(2) obtain a bid or bids for submission to the Obligee for completing the Contract in accordance with its terms and conditions, and upon determination by the Obligee and the Surety of the lowest responsible bidder, arrange for a contract between such bidder and the Obligee and
make available as work progresses (even though there should be a default, or a succession of defaults, under the contract or contracts of
completion, arranged under this paragraph) sufficient funds to pay the cost of completion less the balance of the Contract price; but not
exceeding, including other costs and damages for which the Surety may be liable hereunder, the amount set forth in the first paragraph
hereof. The term "balance of the Contract price", as used in this paragraph, shall mean the total amount payable by the Obligee to the Principal under the Contract, less the amount properly paid by the Obligee to the Principal.

Any suit under this Bond must be instituted before the expiration of two (2) years from the date on which final payment under the Contract falls
due.

The Surety shall not be liable for a greater sum than the specified penalty of this Bond.

No right of action shall accrue on this Bond, to or for the use of, any person or corporation other than the Obligee named herein, or the heirs,
executors, administrators or successors of the Obligee.

IN WITNESS WHEREOF, the Principal and the Surety have Signed and Sealed this Bond this . . . .

day of . . . . 19 . . . .

SIGNED and SEALED
In the presence of
                          (
                          (
                          (
                          (. . . . (Seal)

                                                             Principal

                          (
                          (
                          (
                          (. . . . (Seal)

                                                              Surety

APPENDIX I

CCDC 222—1979

Labour and Material
Payment Bond

Provided by the Canadian Construction Association, whose permission to
reproduce this document is gratefully acknowledged. Copies of this
document are available from the Secretary, Canadian Construction
Document Committee, 85 Albert Street,
Ottawa, Ontario, Canada K1P 6A4.

LABOUR AND MATERIAL PAYMENT BOND
(TRUSTEE FORM)

No.. $...

Note: This Bond is issued simultaneously with another Bond in favour of the Obligee conditioned for the full and faithful performance of the Contract.

KNOW ALL MEN BY THESE PRESENTS THAT ....

.... as Principal

hereinafter called the Principal, and ....

a corporation created and existing under the laws of ....

and duly authorized to transact the business of Suretyship in ....

as Surety, hereinafter called the Surety are, subject to the conditions hereinafter contained, held and firmly bound unto ....

.... as Trustee

hereinafter called the Obligee, for the use and benefit of the Claimants, their and each of their heirs, executors, administrators, successors and

assigns, in the amount of ....

.... Dollars ($ ....)
of lawful money of Canada for the payment of which sum well and truly to be made the Principal and the Surety bind themselves, their heirs, executors, administrators, successors and assigns, jointly and severally, firmly by these presents.

WHEREAS, the Principal has entered into a written contract with the Obligee, dated the ....

day of .... 19......... for ....

....

....

....

which Contract Documents are by reference made a part hereof, and are hereinafter referred to as the Contract.

NOW, THEREFORE, THE CONDITION OF THIS OBLIGATION is such that, if the Principal shall make payment to all Claimants for all labour and material used or reasonably required for use in the performance of the Contract, then this obligation shall be null and void; otherwise it shall remain in full force and effect, subject, however, to the following conditions:

1. A Claimant for the purpose of this Bond is defined as one having a direct contract with the Principal for labour, material, or both, used or reasonably required for use in the performance of the Contract, labour and material being construed to include that part of water, gas, power, light, heat, oil, gasoline, telephone service or rental equipment directly applicable to the Contract provided that a person, firm or corporation who rents equipment to the Principal to be used in the performance of the Contract under a contract which provides that all or any part of the rent is to be applied towards the purchase price thereof, shall only be a Claimant to the extent of the prevailing industrial rental value of such equipment for the period during which the equipment was used in the performance of the Contract. The prevailing industrial rental value of equipment shall be determined, insofar as it is practical to do so, in accordance with and in the manner provided for in the latest revised edition of the publication of the Canadian Construction Association titled "Rental Rates on Construction Equipment" published prior to the period during which the equipment was used in the performance of the Contract.

2. The Principal and the Surety, hereby jointly and severally agree with the Obligee, as Trustee, that every Claimant who has not been paid as provided for under the terms of his contract with the Principal, before the expiration of a period of ninety (90) days after the date on which the last of such Claimant's work or labour was done or performed or materials were furnished by such Claimant, may as a beneficiary of the trust herein provided for, sue on this Bond, prosecute the suit to final judgment for such sum or sums as may be justly due to such Claimant under the terms of his contract with the Principal and have execution thereon. Provided that the Obligee is not obliged to do or take any act, action or proceeding against the Surety on behalf of the Claimants, or any of them, to enforce the provisions of this Bond. If any act, action or proceeding is taken either in the name of the Obligee or by joining the Obligee as a party to such proceeding, then such act, action or proceeding, shall be taken on the understanding and basis that the Claimants or any of them, who take such act, action or proceeding shall indemnify and save harmless the Obligee against all costs, charges and expenses or liabilities incurred thereon and any loss or damage resulting to the Obligee by reason thereof. Provided still further that, subject to the foregoing terms and conditions, the Claimants, or any of them, may use the name of the Obligee to sue on and enforce the provisions of this Bond.

3. No suit or action shall be commenced hereunder by any Claimant:

    (a) unless such Claimant shall have given written notice within the time limits hereinafter set forth to each of the Principal, the Surety and the Obligee, stating with substantial accuracy the amount claimed. Such notice shall be served by mailing the same by registered mail to the Principal, the Surety and the Obligee, at any place where an office is regularly maintained for the transaction of business by such persons or served in any manner in which legal process may be served in the Province or other part of Canada in which the subject matter of the Contract is located. Such notice shall be given

        (1) in respect of any claim for the amount or any portion thereof, required to be held back from the Claimant by the Principal, under either the terms of the Claimant's contract with the Principal, or under the Mechanics' Liens Legislation applicable to the Claimant's contract with the Principal, whichever is the greater, within one hundred and twenty (120) days after such Claimant should have been paid in full under the Claimant's contract with the Principal;

        (2) in respect of any claim other than for the holdback, or portion thereof, referred to above, within one hundred and twenty (120) days after the date upon which such Claimant did, or performed, the last of the work or labour or furnished the last of the materials for which such claim is made under the Claimant's contract with the Principal;

    (b) after the expiration of one (1) year following the date on which the Principal ceased work on the Contract, including work performed under the guarantees provided in the Contract;

    (c) other than in a Court of competent jurisdiction in the Province or District of Canada in which the subject matter of the Contract, or any part thereof, is situated and not elsewhere, and the parties hereto agree to submit to the jurisdiction of such Court.

4. The Surety agrees not to take advantage of Article 1959 of the Civil Code of the Province of Quebec in the event that, by an act or an omission of a Claimant, the Surety can no longer be subrogated in the rights, hypothecs and privilges of Said Claimant.

5. Any material change in the contract between the Principal and the Obligee shall not prejudice the rights or interest of any Claimant under this Bond, who is not instrumental in bringing about or has not caused such change.

6. The amount of this Bond shall be reduced by, and to the extent of any payment or payments made in good faith, and in accordance with the provisions hereof, inclusive of the payment by the Surety of Mechanics' Liens which may be filed of record against the subject matter of the Contract, whether or not claim for the amount of such lien be presented under and against this Bond.

7. The Surety shall not be liable for a greater sum than the specified penalty of this Bond.

IN WITNESS WHEREOF, the Principal and the Surety have Signed and Sealed this Bond this . . . .

day of . . . . 19 . . . .

SIGNED and SEALED
In the presence of

    (
    (
    (
    (. . . . (Seal)
                                        Principal
    (
    (
    (
    (. . . . (Seal)
                                        Surety

Glossary

acceleration a claim by a contractor who has experienced an excusable delay and who has been instructed to meet the contractual completion date.

acceleration, constructive an acceleration claim for which the owner refuses to acknowledge that an excusable delay has occurred.

ADR alternative dispute resolution; commonly refers to arbitration and mediation.

agency the legal mechanism that allows one party (the agent) to bind a second party (the principal) to a contract with a third party.

agency shop an agreement between an employer and a union that provides that all employees must pay union dues whether or not they become members of the union.

all-risk a form of property insurance that covers all perils except those specifically excepted; also referred to as builder's risk insurance

anti-trust illegal acts to restrict competition; usually involves two or more parties to fix prices.

arbitration use of an impartial third party chosen by the parties to a dispute to resolve the dispute, usually by making a binding award.

bid bond a bond that guarantees the bidder's obligation to enter into a contract if requested to do so by the owner (or other obligee of the bond).

bid depository an organization used by owners, contractors, and suppliers that is designed to facilitate bidding according to specific rules.

bidding process a method of contract formation commonly used in the construction industry that involves the submission of prices or proposals by contractors, which are then evaluated by the owner.

bid shopping the practice (widely considered unethical) of using one bid price to obtain a lower price from a competitor of the party who submitted the bid.

bond a suretyship agreement by which one party (the surety) guarantees performance of an obligation owed by another party (the principal).

breach of duty failure by a party to satisfy a duty or obligation that is owed either by contract, by statute, or at common law.

builders' risk see *all-risk*.

burden of proof the legal test for proving a case; for criminal matters, the burden of proof is "beyond a reasonable doubt," and for civil disputes the test varies but is in substance "on a balance of probabilities."

CGL policy comprehensive general liability (or commercial general liability) insurance policy.

change order a contract amendment that adds, deletes, or modifies the contractor's obligations under the contract; a price adjustment may or may not be associated with each change; changes that increase the total price are called extras.

claims-made policy an insurance policy that covers claims that are made while the policy is in force.

closed shop an agreement between a union and an employer that provides that union membership is a prerequisite to hiring.

collective agreement an agreement between an employer and a union that sets the terms of employment for the employees represented by that union.

common law the body of case law, or judge-made law, that serves as precedent for future decisions of courts and defines rights, obligations, and liabilities of parties.

consequential damages indirect loss or damage suffered by a party as a result of a breach of contract, such as loss of business.

consideration something of value given or promised by each party to a contract in order to make it enforceable.

constructive changes an extra or change that is ordered by the owner without an acknowledgment that it is outside the original contract scope.

contract a voluntary, binding agreement between two or more parties.

cost plus a form of contract under which the owner compensates the contractor for all costs incurred in performing the contract, plus a fee; costs are defined in the contract.

counterclaim a claim made by a defendant against the plaintiff.

critical path method (CPM) a method of project scheduling that uses a network logic diagram to determine the timing and sequence of events.

custom and usage normal industry practice.

damages a money award claimed or ordered in a lawsuit to compensate for losses suffered.

delay, compensable a delay to project completion that entitles the contractor to additional time and compensation.

delay, excusable a delay to project completion that entitles the contractor to an extension of time.

deposition pretrial cross-examination of a witness under oath.

design/build a contract under which one party, usually the contractor, assumes the obligation to design and build the project; in some countries, also referred to as a turnkey contract.

discovery pretrial disclosure of evidence through deposition, production of documents, site inspection, interrogatories, and other methods.

duress extreme pressure that eliminates the element of voluntariness during the process of contract formation.

Eichleay formula a mathematical formula for calculating home office overhead for the purpose of determining delay claim damages.

estoppel a rule of law that prevents a party from enforcing its legal rights because that party has done or said something that causes another party to reasonably rely, to its detriment, on that act or statement.

extras see *change order.*

fiduciary relationship a relationship imposed at law on parties who are in a position of trust and confidence.

firm bid rule a rule that makes a bid irrevocable until the owner has had a reasonable opportunity to evaluate it.

fixed price a form of contract that stipulates the contractor's total compensation; also referred to as a stipulated price contract.

float the amount of time, as shown on a CPM schedule, that an event can be delayed without delaying completion of the project.

force majeure acts or events that are beyond the control of either party to the contract; sometimes referred to as acts of God.

frustration an event, not anticipated by the parties to a contract at the time of its formation, that makes performance of the contract purposeless.

grievance a complaint by one of the parties to a collective agreement that the other party has committed a breach.

guaranteed maximum a hybrid form of contract that contains elements of both fixed price and cost plus contracts.

impartiality lack of bias, interest, or prejudice.

implied agency a rule of law that creates an agency relationship based on representations by the principal to a third party.

impossibility an event, not anticipated by the parties to a contract at the time of its formation, that makes performance of the contract impossible.

indemnity a requirement or agreement by one party to secure another party against loss; the type of loss is specified in the indemnity agreement or clause.

injunction an equitable remedy ordered by a court that restrains or prohibits (that is, enjoins) a party from doing a particular act.

interrogatories a form of discovery that allows one party to a lawsuit to compel another party to the lawsuit to answer a series of written questions.

joint and several liability a method of assigning liability whereby each of the defendants or creditors is individually liable for the full amount of a debt or claim.

jurisdictional dispute a dispute between craft unions over which union's members have the right to perform work.

L & M bond labor and material payment bond; a bond that guarantees that the principal (usually the contractor) will pay all parties working for it on a project.

latent defect a hidden defect that could not be discovered by reasonable inspection.

lien a charge or encumbrance against property; mechanics' liens are creatures of statute.

lien, holdback funds that are held back from a contractor, in accordance with the applicable lien statute, to secure payment for liens that may be filed.

limitation period a statutory or contractual time limit for taking a step in a legal proceeding, such as commencing a lawsuit or filing a lien.

liquidated damages a genuine estimate of damages, made prior to formation of a contract, that a party would be expected to suffer as a result of a breach and included in the contract as a statement of damages.

material nondisclosure failure by an insured party to disclose all relevant information when purchasing an insurance policy.

measured mile approach a method used to quantify loss of productivity for delay claims involving a comparison of productivity between portions of the project that were unaffected by delay with delayed segments.

mediation use of an impartial third party chosen by the parties to the dispute to assist in the negotiation process.

mitigation the legal obligation of anyone who has suffered a loss to take reasonable steps to reduce or minimize the loss.

negligence failure to use the level of care and prudence (or skill in the case of a professional or tradesperson) that a reasonably careful (or skilled) person would be expected to use in similar circumstances.

occurrence policy an insurance policy that covers losses for which the insured peril occurred while the policy was in force, without respect to whether the policy continued in force to the date of claim.

offer and acceptance the necessary elements for contract formation.

open shop union membership is not required as a condition of employment.

option contract a contract, for consideration, that gives one party the right to purchase property or accept an offer for a specified period.

payment bond a bond under which the surety guarantees payment by the principal.

performance bond a bond that under which the surety guarantees performance of contractual obligations by the principal.

performance specification a contract specification that defines the contractor's obligations in terms of system performance.

pleadings written documents, filed in court, that set out the parties' claims and defenses.

privity (contractual) relationship between two or more contracting parties.

quantum meruit an equitable doctrine of law that provides that, in the absence of contractual provisions governing the work in question, a party who has requested and benefited from performance of work is required to pay for the fair value of that work, including a reasonable amount for overhead and profits.

quasi-contract legal obligations imposed by law, in the absence of a contract, where one party has been unjustly enriched at the expense of another.

remoteness a legal doctrine that prevents liability from attaching if the consequences of a breach were not reasonably foreseeable.

repudiation refusal by one party to a contract to perform or honor his or her obligations.

sore thumb rule when a material mistake in a bid is obvious, so that it "sticks out like a sore thumb," the bid cannot be accepted; the mistake may be obvious by virtue of the difference in bid price between the bid in question and the other bids submitted.

specific performance an equitable legal remedy available when damages would be inadequate; specific performance requires the party to perform the contract rather than pay damages.

statute law legislation passed by the legislative branch of federal or state (or provincial) government.

stipulated price contract see *fixed price*.

subrogation the right of one party to exercise the legal rights of another against a third party.

suretyship (contract) a written contract whereby one party (the surety) guarantees the obligations of another (the principal) to a third party (the obligee); see *bond*.

target price see *guaranteed maximum*.

total cost approach a method used to quantify delay claims, involving calculation of the difference between the estimated total cost and actual total cost of performance.

trust an equitable doctrine that allows or requires one party (the trustee) to hold property for the benefit of another (the beneficiary).

unconscionability circumstances that cause an extreme inequality of bargaining power, at the time of contract formation, such that an oppressive and unfair agreement is entered into.

unit price a form of contract under which the owner compensates the contractor on the basis of a stipulated amount for each unit or quantity of work performed.

unjust enrichment an equitable doctrine designed to prevent one party from unjustly benefiting at the expense of another.

vicarious liability liability that attaches to a person or corporation indirectly, as the result of the liability of another for whom he or she is responsible.

Index

Acceleration, 112, 116, 118
Acceleration, constructive, 112
ADR, 150
Agency, 4, 25–26, 28–31, 127, 135
Agency shop, 139–40
All-risk, 77, 84–85
Antitrust, 134–37
Arbitrators, arbitration, 130, 142–43, 145,
    150–53

Bidding, 5, 12, 17, 44, 65–73
    bid bond, 17, 65–66, 70–71, 89, 90–93,
      97
    bid depository, 72–73
    bid rigging, 134
    bid shopping, 65, 67, 69–70, 72
    firm bid rule, 70
Breach of duty, 48–53
Burden of proof, 125

CGL policy, 76–77
Changes (extras), 18, 28, 30, 35–39, 95, 129
Claims-made policy, 76, 80–81
Closed shop, 135–39
Common law, 3, 31, 48, 58–59, 62, 72, 91,
    95, 143
Common site picketing, 140–41
Confidentiality, 124, 127–28
Consequential damages, 20, 64, 119
Construction manager, 27
Constructive changes, 23
Contingency, 10, 36
Contingency fees, 126
Contracts, 4, 7–23
    abandonment of contract, 15–16, 22, 39
    anticipatory breach, 22
    breach of, 1, 2, 4, 8, 19–22, 38, 41, 44, 47,
      64, 69, 73
    capacity to, 8

Contracts, *continued*
  consideration, 4, 13–16, 35, 70–71, 75,
    92, 109
  frustration, 8, 19, 21
  fundamental breach, 21–22, 64
  implied contract (implied terms), 7, 10,
    45, 58–59, 92, 114, 143
  impossibility, 19, 21, 25, 58
  mistake, 8, 17, 65, 70, 92
  option contract, 13, 72
  offer and acceptance, 4, 12–13, 66, 75
  oral contracts, 4, 12, 39
  privity, 7, 25, 27, 28, 43, 46, 54, 100
  repudiation, 22
  revocation, 12–13, 14, 68, 70, 92
  unconscionability, 18–19
  corporate veil, 78
Cost plus, 4, 9–10, 23, 39
Counterclaim, 61, 84, 147–48
Craft unions, 138–39
Critical path, 37, 112–13, 119
Custom and usage, 3, 12, 44, 65, 92

Damages, 3, 8, 15, 19–21, 38, 46, 84, 92, 94,
  111, 113, 115–19, 143, 147
Deductible, 77
Delay, 1, 4, 14, 19, 20, 27, 37, 47, 86,
  111–21
  compensable, 111, 114–15
  concurrent, 115
  excusable, 111, 114–15
  no damages for delay, 19, 115–16
  noncompensable, 111, 114–15
  deposition, 149
Design codes, 50–52
Design/build, 26–27
Disclaimers, exclusion clause, 2, 8, 34, 48,
  54–55, 63–64, 85–86, 115–16
Discovery, 148–50
Discrimination, 143
Duress, 18
Duty to defend, 78

Economic loss, 45, 47
Eichleay formula, 117–18
Estimates, 49
Estoppel, 13, 68
Ethics, 5, 52, 69, 123–131
Expert witness, 49, 125

Fiduciary, 29, 124
Fixed price, 4, 8, 10, 23, 39
Float, 112–13
Force majeure, 19, 116

Grievance, 142–43
Guaranteed maximum price, 10

Impact costs, 37
Impartiality, 8, 29, 108, 126, 129–30,
  151–53
Implied agency, 29
Indemnity, 31–34, 75, 78, 91
Injunction, 19, 135, 140, 147
Inspection, 61–62
Insurable interest, 15, 79–80
Insurance, 2, 15, 54, 89–90, 149
Interrogatories, 148
Invitation, 12, 64, 66–68, 91

Joint and several liability, 3, 42, 54
Jurisdictional disputes, 138–39

L & M bond, 96, 108
Latent defect, 45
Liens, 96–97, 99–110
  holdback, 28, 107–8
  priority, 104
  waiver, 109
Limitation periods, 2, 28, 39, 76, 81–82,
  92–93, 96, 101–2
Liquidated damages, 21, 115
Lis pendens, 102
Lockouts, 140–41

Materiality, 17, 70, 82–83, 95
Means and methods, 9, 48, 55, 136
Measured mile approach, 120–21
Mediation, 154
Mitigation, 20, 92

Negligence, 1, 4, 26, 31, 33–34, 36, 41–55,
  64, 76, 78, 80, 81, 85, 113–14, 116, 125,
  147
  causation, 42
  comparative negligence, 26, 32
  duty of care, 41, 42–48, 52, 124
  foreseeability, 20, 36, 42–45, 119
  standard of care, 48–53, 125–26

Negotiation, 153–54
Nondisclosure, 82–83

Occurrence policy, 80–81
Open shop, 139

Partnering, 155
Payment bonds, 96–97
Performance bonds, 93–96, 108
Performance specification, 63
Picketing, 140–41
Pleadings, 146–47
Pre-hire agreements, 136
Presumptions of law, 58–59
Project insurance, 79
Protest, 37–39

Qualified privilege, 47
Quantum meruit, 22–23
Quasicontract, 22–23

Remoteness, 20, 53, 119
Replacement workers, 140
Right-to-work, 139–40
Run-off coverage, 80

Safety, 27, 43–45, 52, 124–25, 143
Seal, 14, 70
Secondary boycotts, 141

Shop drawings, 64
Site conditions, 11, 17–18, 36
Sore thumb rule, 17
Specific performance, 19
Statute law, 3, 99, 143
Statutes of repose, 82
Statutory declarations, 109
Strikes, 140–41
Subrogation, 78–79, 91
Successor company, 141–142
Suretyship, bonds, 70, 89–97

Target price, 10
Termination, 21–22, 128, 143
Third-party beneficiary, 7–8, 27
Third-party claim 147–48, 152–53
Total cost approach, 120–21
Trial, 150
Trust, 96, 105–7, 128
Turnkey contract, 4

Unfair labor practice, 137–38
Union shop, 139
Unit price, 10–11
Unjust enrichment, 69, 71, 100

Vicarious liability, 32
Void, voidable contracts, 16–19